AF361469

Aspects of Cognitive Ethnolinguistics

Advances in Cognitive Linguistics

Edited by: Benjamin K. Bergen, University of Hawaii, Manoa, Vyvyan Evans, University of Sussex, and Jörg Zinken, University of Portsmouth

Cognitive Linguistics is an approach to the scientific study of language that endeavours to explain facts about language in terms of known properties and mechanisms of other dimensions of the human mind/brain. While earlier cognitive approaches to language were based on philosophical thinking about the mind, recent work places special importance on securing convergent evidence from a broad empirical basis, e.g. using samples of unrelated languages and employing methods from cognitive sciences such as (Neuro-) Psychology and Computer Science.

Advances in Cognitive Linguistics provides a central outlet for the best new work by both established and younger scholars in this rapidly moving field. The series welcomes theoretical and empirical work on language and cognition. The series publishes work that promotes innovative approaches to Cognitive Linguistics in the form of works of reference, scholarly monographs and coherent edited collections.

CONSULTANT BOARD

Jerzy Bartmiński, Marie Curie Sklodowska University, Poland
Melissa Bowerman, MPI for Psycholinguistics, Nijmegen, Netherlands
Wallace Chafe, University of California at Santa Barbara, USA
Paul Chilton, University of East Anglia, UK
Gilles Fauconnier, University of California, San Diego, USA
George Lakoff, University of California, Berkeley, USA
Ronald Langacker, University of California, San Diego, USA
Günter Radden, University of Hamburg, Germany
Chris Sinha, University of Portsmouth, UK
Kazuko Shinohara, Tokyo University of Agriculture and Technology, Japan

Published:
The Cognitive Linguistics Reader
Edited by Vyvyan Evans, Benjamin K. Bergen and Jörg Zinken

Forthcoming:
Language, Cognition and Space: The State of the Art and New Directions
Edited by Vyvyan Evans and Paul Chilton

Language and Representation: A Socio-Naturalistic Approach to Human Development (second edition)
Chris Sinha

Aspects of Cognitive Ethnolinguistics

Jerzy Bartmiński

Edited by

Jörg Zinken

Published by

Equinox Publishing Ltd

UK: Unit 6, The Village, 101 Amies St, London, SW11 2JW
USA: DBBC, 28 Main Street, Oakville, CT 06779

www.equinoxpub.com

Aspects of Cognitive Ethnolinguistics
First published 2009

British Library Cataloguing-in-Publication Data
A catalogue record for this book is available from the British Library.

ISBN-13   9781845533427   (hardback)

Library of Congress Cataloging-in-Publication Data

Bartminski, Jerzy.
  Aspects of cognitive ethnolinguistics / Jerzy Bartminski ; edited by Jörg Zinken.
       p. cm. -- (Advances in cognitive linguistics)
  Includes bibliographical references and index.
  ISBN 978-1-84553-342-7
  1. Anthropological linguistics. 2. Semantics. 3. Cognitive grammar. I. Zinken, Jörg. II. Title.
  P35.B275 2009
  306.44--dc22
                          2008052639

Typeset by Catchline, Milton Keynes (www.catchline.com)

Contents

Acknowledgements

I wish to express my heartfelt gratitude to Dr. Jörg Zinken. Dr. Zinken took the initiative in making the work of Polish ethnolinguists available in English by guiding the publication of this book through all its stages, as well as by suggesting amendments to the original papers in order to make them more accessible for English-language readers. I thank Prof. Andreas Musolff and Prof. Anna Wierzbicka for favourable opinions on my work while the book was being considered for publication. Their comments have helped me shape the volume and bring it into its present form. Special thanks are due to the translator, Adam Głaz, who doubled as a consultant in questions regarding the content of the book and its arrangement. I am indebted to my wife, Stanisława Niebrzegowska-Bartmińska, for her help in selecting the material for publication, as well as for severe but outstandingly accurate critical comments on former drafts of the manuscript. Last but not least, I am grateful to Equinox Publishing for taking the risk of introducing the work of a Polish author into the English-speaking community of scholars.

Original sources of papers

Chapter 2: written especially for the volume; very loosely based on Bartmiński, J. (1986) Czym zajmuje się etnolingwistyka? *Akcent* 4 (26): 16–22.

Chapter 3: written especially for the volume; very loosely based on Bartmiński, J. (2006) Pojęcie językowego obrazu świata. In J. Bartmiński, *Językowe podstawy obrazu świata*. 11–21. Lublin: UMCS.

Chapter 4: Bartmiński, J. (2003) Miejsce wartości w językowym obrazie świata. In J. Bartmiński (ed.) *Język w kręgu wartości*. 59–86. Lublin: UMCS.

Chapter 5: Bartmiński, J. (1985) Stereotyp jako przedmiot lingwistyki. In M. Basaj and D. Rytel (eds) *Z problemów frazeologii polskiej i słowiańskiej III*. 25–53. Wrocław: Zakład Narodowy im. Ossolińskich.

Chapter 6: Bartmiński, J. (1988) Definicja kognitywna jako narzędzie opisu konotacji słowa. In J. Bartmiński (ed.) *Konotacja*. 169–183. Lublin: UMCS.

Chapter 7: Bartmiński, J. (1990) Punkt widzenia, perspektywa, językowy obraz świata. In J. Batrmiński (ed.) *Językowy obraz świata*. 109–127. Lublin: UMCS. [2nd edition 1999, 3rd. ed. 2004]

Chapter 8: Bartmiński, J. and Niebrzegowska, S. (1998) Profile a podmiotowa interpretacja świata. In J. Bartmiński and R. Tokarski (eds) *Profilowanie w języku i w tekście*. 211–224. Lublin: UMCS.

Chapter 9: Bartmiński, J. and Niebrzegowska-Bartmińska, S. (2004) Dynamika kategorii punktu widzenia w języku, tekście i dyskursie. In J. Bartmiński, S. Niebrzegowska-Bartmińska and R. Nycz (eds) *Punkt widzenia w języku i w kulturze*. 321–358. Lublin: UMCS.

Chapter 10: an abbreviated and modified entry for SŁOŃCE (SUN) in *SSSL* ('Dictionary of Folk Symbols and Stereotypes') (1996, vol. 1–1: 119–157), compiled and edited by J. Bartmiński and S. Niebrzegowska.

Chapter 11: Bartmiński, J. (1998) Podstawy lingwistycznych badań nad stereotypem – na przykładzie stereotypu matki. *Język a kultura* 12: 63–83.

Chapter 12: a substantially modified version of Bartmiński, J. (1997) Dom – świat. Opozycja czy wpółdziałanie? In G. Sawicka (ed.) *Dom w języku i kulturze.* 11–22. Szczecin: JotA. [Also published as Bartmiński, J. (2006) *Dom i świat – opozycja i komplementarność.* In J. Bartmiński, *Językowe podstawy obrazu świata.* 167–177. Lublin: UMCS.]

Chapter 13: Bartmiński, J. (1998) Dynamika polskiego pojęcia ojczyzny. *Prace Filologiczne* 43: 53–60.

Chapter 14: Bartmiński, J. (1994) Jak zmienia się stereotyp Niemca w Polsce. *Przegląd Humanistyczny* 5: 81–101.

Chapter 15: Bartmiński, J. (2006) *Prawica – lewica.* Sposoby profilowania pojęć. In. J. Bartmiński, *Językowe podstawy obrazu świata.* 201–207. Lublin: UMCS.

Chapter 16: Bartmiński, J. (2000) Polska 'dola', rosyjska 'sud'ba'. *Etnolingwistyka* 12: 25–37. [Reprinted in Bartmiński, J. (2006) *Językowe podstawy obrazu świata.* 242–251. Lublin: UMCS.]

Chapter 17: Bartmiński, J. (2005) Koncepcja językowego obrazu świata w programie slawistycznych badań porównawczych. *Studia z Filologii Polskiej i Słowiańskiej* 40: 259–280. Warszawa: Instytut Slawistyki PAN. [Reprinted in Bartmiński, J. (2006) *Językowe podstawy obrazu świata.* 229–241. Lublin: UMCS. 2nd edition 2007]

Key to questionnaires

AXL-90 (Axiological lexis). Unpublished results of a questionnaire administered in 1990 to groups of students in Lublin as part of the project 'Axiological lexis in contemporary Polish' (Jerzy Bartmiński, Piotr Brzozowski and Małgorzata Mazurkiewicz-Brzozowska). The questions concerned the features of the 'true' mother (cf. chapter 11) and those of a 'true' German (cf. chapter 14). The latter question ('What in your opinion is the defining feature of a true German?') was answered by 103 students (51 female and 40 male; in some cases the sex was not indicated): 13 from the Medical Academy, 17 from the Agricultural Academy, 8 from the Catholic University of Lublin (Department of Psychology), 21 from the Lublin Polytechnic, 44 from Maria Curie-Skłodowska University (Departments of Polish, Pedagogy, Law, Philosophy and Mathematics).

LSQ-90 (Lublin student questionnaire). Administered in 1990 at the Department of Polish, Maria Curie-Skłodowska University in Lublin, in Jerzy Bartmiński's seminar. It concerned family-related and national stereotypes (cf. chapters 11 and 14, respectively).

SD-93 (Semantic differential questionnaire). The questionnaire 'How do Lublin students perceive their neighbours?', administered in Lublin in 1993 with the use of Osgood's semantic differential method among 100 students, 32 male and 68 female (cf. chapter 14 and Bartmiński 1995).

URB-93 (Jolanta Urban's questionnaire). A four-point questionnaire administered as a part of Jerzy Bartmiński's M.A. seminar at the Department of Polish, UMCS, Lublin. It concerned seven nationalities (the data relating to Germans are discussed in chapter 14 and in Urban 1993) and contained questions about synonyms, collocability of national adjectives, ways of completing the contrastive construction 'X is a German but ...' as well as two other constructions: 'I like the fact that Germans ...' and 'I don't like the fact that Germans ...'.

1   The Ethnolinguistic School of Lublin and Anglo-American cognitive linguistics

Jörg Zinken

Jerzy Bartmiński and his team have developed, over the last 30–40 years, a distinctive cognitive-linguistic approach to the study of language in its cultural context – an approach which I will refer to, in this introduction, as the 'Ethnolinguistic School of Lublin' (Zinken, 2004a). This work is well known in the international Russian-speaking academic discourse of the humanities in Eastern Europe. It is represented by an international journal, *Etnolingwistyka*, which was founded by Bartmiński and has been published annually since 1988. The list of publications of Jerzy Bartmiński alone runs to about 400 entries.[1] However, this work has not until now been available in English. The present book makes some of Bartmiński's key papers accessible to an English-reading audience for the first time. Most chapters are revised versions of the original publications, others have been written specifically for this volume (cf. 'Original sources of papers').

This book appears in a series dedicated to 'Advances in cognitive linguistics'. The 'advance' to which the Ethnolinguistic School of Lublin can contribute concerns the systematic consideration of speakers' socio-cultural situatedness in the linguistic analysis of meaning and understanding. This is an issue that has received considerable attention in cognitive linguistics in recent years (e.g., Frank, Dirven, Ziemke, and Bernárdez, 2008). The substantial convergences between the Ethnolinguistic School of Lublin and Anglo-American cognitive linguistics make me optimistic about the chances of such a contribution. It is the aim of this introductory chapter to outline some of those convergences, and to sketch some of the distinctive characteristics of Bartmiński's cognitive ethnolinguistics.

The work of the Ethnolinguistic School of Lublin has its roots in Bartmiński's research on the folk variety of Polish (Bartmiński, 1973), which combined the dialectological and stylistic description of the phonetics, morphology, vocabulary and syntax of folk poetic texts. From this very beginning, Bartmiński's work has always been grounded in close analyses of a very rich database of ethnolinguistic data, which include everyday conversations, stories, narratives about life and work, and interviews with rural speakers as well as songs, fairy tales, proverbs, and folk poetry. This immersion in a wealth of data is indicative of a passion for the living folk culture in its everyday and artistic dimensions that is the driving force behind linguistic analysis in the Ethnolinguistic School of Lublin. When I first experienced that passion first-hand – in 1999, on a field trip which aimed to find linguistic and folkloristic traces of the bygone multicultural (Jewish-Polish-Ukrainian) life in the contemporary Polish-Ukrainian border region – the ethnolinguistic archive at Lublin contained approximately 1,300 audio and video tapes of data. The development of cognitive-linguistic analytic concepts in this tradition, it seems to me, needs to be understood as much as a response to the necessity of dealing with this amount of rich 'real-world' data, as it needs to be understood as an attempt to give a theoretical account of the relations between language, culture and mind. This orientation towards the description of real-world data is a crucial characteristic of the Ethnolinguistic School of Lublin when compared to Anglo-American cognitive linguistics, which has always been much more focused on theory-development.

The work on the folk variety of language has, over time, developed into an ambitious project: The reconstruction of the 'linguistic worldview' of rural speakers of Polish in the *Dictionary of Folk Symbols and Stereotypes*, which is being published since 1996 (*SSSL*, 1996–1999). Also, in the 1980s, Lublin ethnolinguists developed a second focus of empirical research: the study of terms referring to culturally important (embraced, contested) values (Bartmiński and Mazurkiewicz-Brzozowska, 1993b). This work has spanned terms referring to abstract values (such as *responsibility* and *truth*), human attitudes (such as *equality* or *solidarity*), social life (such as *freedom* or *tolerance*), individual and group behaviour (such as *revolution* or *work*), names for human communities (such as *family* or *nation*), names for political, social, and cultural institutions (such as *church* or *state*), names for persons and objects that are considered cultural values (such as *father* or *bread*), and names for objects that symbolise a value (such as the *cross*). The major project in this area to date has been the comparison of the concept of homeland (fatherland) in twelve European languages (Bartmiński, 1993b). Again, the research on value terms needs to be understood as much as a response to a particular social situation in Poland as it needs to be understood as motivated by a theoretically based conviction about the fundamental importance of values for linguistic meaning (chapter 4). In chapter 2 of the present book, Bartmiński traces the current popularity of ethnolinguistics in Eastern Europe to the socio-cultural experiences of these countries in recent decades, and the phenomenon of communist 'newspeak' in particular. By examining the meaning of value terms as it is entrenched in colloquial language varieties, by analysing its etymological roots and historical changes, contemporary ideological abuses of these terms – and the values they indicate – can be exposed.

These two research areas have been – and continue to be – the main context in which Bartmiński's intuitions and observations about the close links between language and culture have been developed into a coherent and distinctive set of analytic concepts, which is introduced in detail in the first part of the present book (chapters 1–9). Let me introduce some of these concepts in a very small nutshell.

The overall aim of Bartmiński's research is to reconstruct the *linguistic worldview* of an idealised speaking subject: an inhabitant of rural Poland, a student, a child, an average speaker of colloquial Polish, etc. (chapter 3). This 'view' is accessible, reconstructable, via the description of *stereotypes*, understood, following Putnam (1975), as judgements that are primarily descriptive, secondarily evaluative (chapter 5). Stereotypical judgements are captured in the *cognitive definition*, which is intended to be a definition of the concept as it could be given by the envisaged idealised subject (chapter 6). The term *cognitive* here therefore means something like 'as understood by the subject': it is the job of the ethnolinguist to reconstruct the linguistically entrenched interpretation of the world by a subject in terms that are meaningful for that subject (chapter 2). This means that the explication of meaning should take into account the speakers' socio-cultural situatedness. The cognitive definition aims to reconstruct the *point of view* and *perspective* of the envisaged subject (chapter 7), by examining the main *facets*, or *aspects*, through which the object is conceptualised, resulting in a subject-bound conceptual *profile* (chapter 8).

Even this very cursory glance at some of the basic concepts of the Ethnolinguistic School of Lublin should show that there are considerable convergences between this work and certain traditions within Anglo-American cognitive linguistics, in particular work on lexical semantics and conceptualisation. These convergences are based in a shared holistic approach to meaning, the attempt to characterise meaning against a broader experiential background. However, since the Ethnolinguistic School of Lublin has developed independently of Anglo-American cognitive linguistics, and in the context of folkloristic, dialectological and ethnographic work, it is not surprising that the stress is sometimes placed differently.

The concept of profiling is a case in point. Bartmiński introduced this term in a first report on the planned *Dictionary of Folk Symbols and Stereotypes* (*SSSL*) in 1980 (Bartmiński, 1980), and developed it in several later publications. The concept of profiling in Bartmiński's work is a key element in what could be called a 'tamed holism': on the one hand, Bartmiński would agree with Anglo-American cognitive linguists that a description of meaning that appropriately captures speakers' knowledge cannot be restricted to 'necessary and sufficient' features. On the other hand, he stresses that some stereotypical judgements about an object are clearly more important than others from a particular *point of view* (this argument is made explicitly in chapter 11, in a critical discussion of Lakoff's (1987) analysis of the concept *mother*). Overall, Bartmiński's holism remains in friendly contact and discussion with (European) structuralism and schools of thought that have grown out of this tradition, such as the semiotics of Ivanov and Toporov (1965), the ethnolinguistics of Tolstoy (1997), the lexicography of Apresyan (1995), and, most importantly, the cognitive linguistics of Anna Wierzbicka (in particular her 1985 book *Lexicography and Conceptual Analysis*). The concept of profiling aids in a description that reconstructs not just the linguistically entrenched stereotypical judgements about an object, but also their order when the object is seen from a particular *perspective*, understood as a metaphor for the social situatedness of the subject.

Therefore, while the concept of profiling in the work of Bartmiński is close to what Langacker (1987) calls profiling, the focus is clearly placed differently. While Langacker aims to describe a universally operative semantic process, Bartmiński intends to reconstruct a particular socio-cultural situatedness. A profile is a particular con-figuration of linguistically entrenched judgements, a configuration that is typical for a particular speaking subject. This subject is (usually) not an individual person, but an idealised subject: a member of a particular socio-cultural group. The reconstruction of sociocultural situatedness with the help of conceptual profiles is nicely illustrated in Bartmiński's analysis of changes in the stereotype of Germans in Poland (chapter 14). There is a large number of stereotypical judgements about Germans that are entrenched in Polish lexemes, idioms, and 'topoi' (chapter 5 develops the different levels of formal entrenchment of stereotypes). These judgements have a social history, and can therefore be used to reconstruct different profiles of 'a German' that were salient throughout the history of Polish-German contacts: the German *as the prototypical foreigner* (construed from a *cultural* point of view), the German *as the invading enemy* (construed from an *ideological* point of view), the German *as a well-off Western European* (construed from a *civilisational* point of view) etc. Different profiles of the stereotypical judgements that make up the language's 'experiential base' are "at the disposal of the speaker as his or her cultural endowment" (p. 24), and while the perception of Germans as well-off Western Europeans might currently be the 'default' in most situations, the other profiles are also available: entrenched in cultural artefacts, e.g., post-war films, kept alive by particular political groups etc.

The differentiation of conceptual profiles is an important tool for anthropological-linguistic studies: it brings out the *intra-linguistic* cultural diversity that can be at least as striking as cross-linguistic cultural diversity. Different linguistic 'worldviews' can exist within a community of people speaking the same language. This important point is exemplified most clearly in the contrastive analysis of the Polish concepts *los* and *dola*. Both of these can be described with the English word *fate*, but they provide very different 'perspectives' onto the human situation: Bartmiński, following Wierzbicka, traces *los* to the Enlightenment period, which promoted a belief in the possibilities of the individual to determine their 'fate'. *Dola*, on the other hand, is traced to the perspective of the 'simple' peasant, who experiences the determining nature of 'fate' for the individual's life. Importantly, this intra-linguistic cross-cultural approach cautions against premature conclusions about the 'mythical national character' (p.211) of the speakers of a language, an argument that is made in a critical discussion of Wierzbicka's juxtaposition of Pol. *los* with Russ. *sud'ba* (see chapter 16).

The 'cultural' orientation of the Ethnolinguistic School of Lublin has ramifications for the understanding of some important cognitive linguistic concepts. One of these is the concept of experience, or the 'experiential frame' within which profiles operate (chapter 8). In Bartmiński's work, it is not only an individual's 'first hand' experience that enters their experiential frame, but also experience entrenched in 'social memory', i.e. in stereotypical judgements. Put differently, verbal encounters and verbally mediated learning are themselves important experiences that provide resources for conceptualisation. Furthermore, experiencing always happens in an already culturally meaningful world. The individual always experiences a culturally meaningful environment – an environment in which salient objects can be intangible (the telling of a narrative) or 'concrete' (moving around in one's home). In the case of Pol. *dom* (house/home) (chapter 12), Bartmiński distinguishes three aspects, or dimensions, in which this object is understood: a spatial dimension (the building), a social dimension (a community), and a functional dimension (an institution: the family). He goes on to emphasise that '[t]hese are by no means separate dimensions; on the contrary, they make up a conceptual whole with different aspects' (p.150). The contention that the 'spatial' aspect of 'concrete' objects, such as houses, should not be treated as conceptually separate from, or even basic to, 'communal' aspects of those objects can serve as a reminder of the fact that 'purely spatial' concepts are a modern invention, that the separation of an abstract dimension of 'space' from the world of experienced places is a relatively recent development (Urry, 2000).

This characterisation of the experience of the 'spatial' world as always already socio-culturally meaningful seems perfectly in line with some early definitions of experience in Anglo-American cognitive linguistics, which emphasised the cultural nature of all experience (Lakoff, 1987; Lakoff and Johnson, 1980). It therefore seems that the work of Bartmiński, which specifically focuses on this cultural dimension, might usefully complement work in Anglo-American cognitive linguistics, and enrich our thinking about the nature of 'experience' as a background for linguistic meaning.

A final caveat: fruitful exchange between academic traditions is not easy. Relatively superficial differences can sometimes block the path to an understanding, and enrichment, of what is shared. This seems to be notoriously so when the encounter occurs between an 'Anglo-American' and a 'Continental' tradition (Kuhn, 1979). Nevertheless, I think that it will become evident to the reader of this book that cognitive linguistics and the Ethnolinguistic School of Lublin have a lot in common, and I hope that the reader will find an engagement with the work of Jerzy Bartmiński both enjoyable and intellectually stimulating.

Notes

1   See also Bartmiński (2004b).

2 What is cognitive ethnolinguistics?

1 The revival of ethnolinguistics

Ethnolinguistics emerged and grew to its mature form in America, though it is rooted in European, especially German scholarship. This stage in its development is relatively well known and has even received encyclopedic treatment (cf. e.g. *EJO*, 1999; *WE PWN*, 2000–2006, vol. 8; Gudavičius, 2000; Yudin, 1998; Senft, 1998). The last decades of the twentieth century saw a 'rebirth' of ethnolinguistics in Eastern and Central Europe (Tolstoy, 1995): the Sapir-Whorf hypothesis received renewed attention, research on language as a cultural phenomenon gained momentum. This was accompanied by a wave of criticism of structuralist thinking, which isolates language from its psychological, social and cultural context. This trend also had social and political aspects. Citizens of communist (now post-communist) countries actually experienced the influence of language on their worldview, feelings and behaviour; they knew what linguistic intimidation really was. There was one dominant ideology and one type of public idiom; whole societies experienced the painful incommensurability of the prevalent communist newspeak with reality. This resulted, on the one hand, in social resistance to the imposition of what was perceived as 'linguistic hypocrisy', and on the other hand in profound reflection on the social and cultural aspects of language. Jerzy Bralczyk, Anna Wierzbicka, Michał Głowiński, Jolanta Rokoszowa, Mirosława Marody and others researched the parlance of the communist propaganda, in which language, in an outdated pseudo-magical manner, took priority over the real world. On the theoretical plane, emphasis was placed on the problem of linguistic worldview, a picture of the world suggested or imposed (on those not used to reflective thinking) by language.

It was not by accident that two very similar publications on the subject appeared almost simultaneously in Russia (Serebrennikov, Kubryakova, Postovalova et al., 1988) and Poland (Bartmiński, 1990a[1]), which inquired into the influence of language on the perception and evaluation of reality. In the introduction to the latter publication I write with some reserve:

> To liberate oneself from the 'bondage of words', to overcome illusion and false evaluation imposed by language, to arrive at the 'naked' truth about the world is perhaps not possible, for it is in the nature of language to simplify, interpret and evaluate. We are too deeply immersed in language to be able to really go beyond it. However, linguists must not evade the challenge of recognising this dependence, of determining the nature and depth of our linguistic entanglement. (Bartmiński, 1990a: 8)

Several other research projects were launched in the 1980s with the intention of reconsidering the problems of the social functions of language and its relation to people and reality; of investigating the diversity of style and genre in public discourse; and of uncovering the linguistic basis of the worldview entertained by a society or of the systems of values either truly professed or merely declared in that society. After the collapse of the Soviet Union and the Eastern Block, when aspirations to independence began to materialise in several previously dominated nations, one saw a renewed interest in the role of language in the creation, expression and preservation of national and group identity, also in the local or regional sense.

One of these projects, or better, an enterprise, is the subject of this book: Cognitive Ethnolinguistics. It is associated with work on a dictionary of folk symbols and stereotypes (*SSSL*, 1996–1999) and with the journal *Etnolingwistyka* ('Ethnolinguistics'), published by the Maria Curie-Skłodowska University Press in Lublin, Poland.

2 Problems with terminology

This field of linguistics has received various names. Apart from *ethnolinguistics*, there are analytical and less ambiguous terms: *cultural linguistics* (Anusiewicz, 1995), *linguoculturology, anthropological linguistics, anthropological-cultural linguistics*, or *linguistic anthropology*. They are all close to one another; indeed, *anthropological linguistics* or *anthropological-cultural semantics* are often treated as synonymous with *ethnolinguistics*. I prefer the latter term for several reasons.

First, it has a long tradition. It appeared in English in reference to research on Native American languages and has a wide international circulation, cf. French *ethnolinguistique*, German *Ethnolinguistik*, Russian *etnolingvistika*, Slovak *etnolingvistik*, Lithuanian *etnolingvistik* etc.

Second, the Greek element *ethno-* is semantically very capacious and allows for both a wide and a narrow understanding. It embraces the notions of a nation, society, social group, a people or tribe, so that one can apply it to various orientations within the field. In Western circles, the component *ethno-* may have negative connotations, being associated with nationalist or even racist ideology. My understanding of it is very different. I take the meaning of *ethno-* to be 'connected with a people, nation, society or social group (*ethnogenesis, ethnopsychology*)' (*SWO*, 1980: 202).

Third, it directly relates language to its collective subject, a community of speakers, and indirectly to what binds that community, i.e. culture.

All these terms contain the same basic idea: the study of language must also take into account the speech community and its culture. With some simplification, the semantic components of the terms in question can be represented in the following way:

> *cultural linguistics* and *linguoculturology* = language + culture
> *anthropological linguistics, anthropology of language* = language + speakers
> *anthropological-cultural linguistics* = language + speakers + culture
> *ethnolinguistics* = speakers (community of speakers) + language

The hierarchies and configurations of the components 'language', 'speakers (people)' and 'culture' are different, so the terms profile the same conceptual content in different ways. The term *ethnolinguistics* highlights above all the connection of language with the community of speakers who use it, and secondarily (by implication) with the culture of that community. *Anthropological linguistics*, on the other hand, stresses the relationship between language and culture, with the subject being implied rather than explicit. Given the choice, I opt for *ethnolinguistics* because it foregrounds the speaker, the human subject and the community, and only secondarily relates those to culture.

Last but not least, *ethnolinguistics* is concise and synthetic; it also gives rise to neat and useful derivatives (*ethnolinguistic, ethnolinguist*) more readily than the other terms.

The term *ethnolinguistics* may easily function in the network of other terms, those used for well-established scholarly endeavours in the humanities. Specifically, it can be placed along the axis between the traditional *ethnology*, which deals with peoples (and which, incidentally, is undergoing a crisis in Europe due to the decline of the traditional conception of a people),[2] and the modern *ethnoscience*, concerned with a reconstruction of the subject from the point of view of a representative of a given culture.

One more general comment is in order. The 'inner form' of the term *ethnolinguistics* allows or even favours the subjective interpretation of the component *ethno-*. That subjective understanding puts it together with other terms, such as *ethnoscience, ethnobotany* 'science of the folk knowledge of plants', *ethnophilosophy, ethnohistory/folk history* 'science of the social perception of history', *medical ethnoscience* 'science of beliefs and practices connected with health and methods of treatment'. Other terms include *ethnopoetics, ethnosemantics* (*IEL*, 1992), *ethnosyntax*,[3] with a few more possibilities opening up with the ethnolinguistic paradigm, such as *ethnophraseology*.

The basic understanding of ethnolinguistics finds support in *ethnomethodology*, which focuses on the 'subjective reconstruction' of folk understanding of phenomena. It renders ethnolinguistics similar to cognitive anthropology, as well as justifying the use of the term *cognitive ethnolinguistics* in the title of this book.[4]

3   The dilemmas of Slavic ethnolinguistics

Contemporary views of Slavic linguists on the scope of ethnolinguistics have been mainly shaped by the Moscow school of Nikita I. Tolstoy's (1995). Tolstoy defined ethnolinguistics narrowly, as a branch of linguistics dealing with language in its relation to culture, or broadly, as a complex discipline whose focus is the whole 'content plane' of culture, folk psychology and mythology, understood independently of the means and methods of their formal representation (a word, thing, custom, belief, etc.) (cf. Tolstaya, 2006). Thus arose ethnolinguistics' first dilemma: should it be a branch of linguistics or an interdisciplinary field?

The extensive research of the Moscow group, which dealt with Slavic spiritual values, was based on the broad understanding and went beyond the verbal code into the realm of behaviour (the actional code) and beliefs (the mental code), as well as into 'all kinds, genres and forms of folk culture' (Tolstaya, 2006). The problem of the focus and data for ethnolinguistic analysis has been solved in a similar manner in *SSSL*. The dictionary is also based on three categories of data: linguistic (dialectological), folkloristic and ethnographic, with the intention to integrate them all on the semantic level.

Does this encroachment of the research scope of ethnolinguistics into culture, in both the Moscow and the Lublin tradition, entail an extension of ethnolinguistics beyond linguistics proper and onto the interdisciplinary platform? I think not. If we accept that culture is 'a set of norms and beliefs, which exist in people's minds and pertain to the recommended courses of action and proper judgements' (Kłoskowska, 1991: 23, following the ideas of American anthropology[5]), i.e. if the most important aspect of culture is the sphere of consciousness and a plan of action, we can conclude that culture exists in language and constitutes its inalienable component. The debate on what has a linguistic and what an extra-linguistic nature called into question structuralist formalism and the conception of an autonomous language code, as well as providing arguments for the linguistic relevance of extra-linguistic knowledge (Putnam, 1975; Muszyński, 1988) and the socio-cultural context. Such an integrational approach is characteristic of the now influential communication-oriented linguistics (Harris, 1990). Therefore, one is justified in claiming that although ethnolinguistics deals with extra-linguistic matters such as stereotypes and beliefs (cf. chapter 5 for a discussion of stereotypes), that although it treats speaking as action and combines it with somatic gestures and all kinds of behavioural signs on the functional plane, it nevertheless remains a branch of linguistics. Non-verbal signs are not 'extra-linguistic' but 'ad-linguistic': they co-create the context of linguistic texts.

The second dilemma concerns an important choice, still pending, between 'micro-' and 'macro-ethnolinguistics'. The former option prefers research on small ethnic communities and their oral 'micro-languages', i.e. rural folk dialects in connection with the specific folk culture. The broader option tends to focus on national languages, also those of an international application, such as English or Russian. The choice between the two is especially important in the Polish context, where, in contrast to the eastern Slavic area, the boundary between rural dialects and the national standard is particularly well protected by the elites of the intelligentsia. The study of folklore does not have a very good press in Poland, and neither does ethnographic and dialectological research, which was once popular but is now being marginalised. However, although one may understand why prescriptive linguists and language purists may be unsympathetic towards folk, rural dialects, the disregard of research on folk data on the part of semanticists (Ryszard Tokarski, Janusz Anusiewicz, Renata Grzegorczykowa, Katarzyna Kłosińska), sometimes seems like 'demophobia'.

The causes of and reasons for excluding folklore from descriptions of national languages and cultures merit a separate study. I will only say here that ethnolinguistics can overcome this isolation because *ethno-* can have a narrower or a broader meaning, from 'social group' or 'people' to 'nation' or even 'community'. Ethnocentrism is a feature of every natural language, including the 'big' ones, even if larger communities usually assume that their languages have a universal nature.[6] In fact, the lexis and semantics of both regional micro-languages and standard varieties is subject to the same historical and cultural influences and can be described with the use of the same concepts and methods. This kind of elastic approach to the scope of research was accepted by Tolstoy (1990) in his suggestion of a hierarchical arrangement of language variants (the literary variant, colloquial speech, dialects, jargons) and an analogical hierarchical arrangement of cultures (the elite, mass, folk, and traditional-professional culture). Each of the linguo-cultural pairs, i.e. the literary variant plus elite culture, colloquial speech plus mass culture, rural dialects plus folk culture, jargons plus a particular professional environment, can be described with the same set of features.

Different linguistic and cultural spheres of the application of ethnolinguistics – local, regional, super-regional, national – are concentrically organised and the choice of one is in fact dictated by independent, practical factors. In the past, ethnolinguists have mostly been interested in micro-languages and micro-cultures, in rural folk dialects and folk culture. This, however, need not be so in the future and a certain change can already be observed.

The third dilemma, so far unresolved, has far-reaching methodological implications. The definition of ethnolinguistics as 'a branch of linguistics that deals with the language-culture relationship' (the 1969 supplement to *SJPDor*, 1962) can mean research on the place of language in culture or vice versa. In fact, the two conceptions of ethnolinguistics do exist side by side: one is concerned with external, social aspects of language, the other with its internal characteristics, with a pairing of cultural content and linguistic forms, with grammar, lexis and their usage. The former investigates the status, prestige and power of language in culture, its contact with other languages, bilingualism, languages of national minorities and social groups (cf. Crystal, 1997; Zieniukowa, 1998; Ziółkowski, 1987). In this context ethnolinguistics is treated as a subfield of sociolinguistics (Helbig, 1986: 239) or ecolinguistics (Haugen, 1972). In the latter understanding, ethnolinguistics deals with manifestations of culture in language. It investigates linguistic structure in relation to the history and culture of specific communities, especially with the mentality of the group, its behaviours and value system. It attempts to discover the traces of culture in the very fabric of language, in word meanings, phraseology, word formation, syntax and text structure. It strives to reconstruct the worldview entrenched in language as it is projected by the experiencing and speaking subject, *homo loquens* (cf. the entry *Etnolingwistyka* in *WE PWN*, 2000–2006, vol. 8: 380–381). This is the conception I embrace.

Finally, let me mention the fact that ethnolinguistic research embraces both the oftentimes archaic linguistic past, e.g. Proto-Slavic and Proto-Indo-European, and the linguistic present. Thus, Russian ethnolinguistics is predominantly historically-oriented, while Polish ethnolinguistics is more concerned with the present. However, the diachrony-synchrony distinction is not so important now as it was in structuralism and sometimes not even overtly recognised: panchronic accounts are frequent and the past-vs.-present question is resolved through the conception of 'the heritage of the past in the present'. A particularly apt formula, *zhivaya starina* 'living ancestry', is used by Russian scholars who publish the results of their research in a journal with the same title.

4   Ethnolinguistic research in Lublin

Against the Slavic background, Lublin ethnolinguistics (cf. Bartmiński, 1986) must be considered a subfield of linguistics for a few reasons. First, it is based above all on linguistic data, although it also pays much attention to the social and cultural context, the 'ad-linguistic' data, relevant to the process of linguistic communication. Second, it starts with descriptions of small communities, regional folk dialects, but by definition it also transcends the boundaries of folklore onto the national variety of Polish (its literary and colloquial varieties, elite and mass culture) and even into the inter-ethnic, trans-cultural sphere. Third, it poses questions about the manifestations of culture in language, not about the position and role of language in culture. Finally, it focuses on the contemporary status quo, which it treats as a stage in the historical process of the development of the language. When it addresses the relationship between language and the mentality of the people who speak it, it draws near and even converges with cognitive linguistics. Hence, it has for some time now been called 'cognitive', which distinguishes it from the otherwise related dialectological and etymological Moscow ethnolinguistics.

4.1   Language and culture

It is only natural that ethnolinguistics so understood deals with the general but nevertheless fundamental problems of language and culture, the function(s) of language and its internal differentiation into variants and styles, the lexis as a classifier of social experience and semantic categories with their formal exponents. It also deals with the more rarely investigated problems of text as the basic unit of linguistic communication or with the important and complex issue of judgements, norms and evaluations present in and conveyed through language. The ultimate aim has always been to arrive at the speaking subject, *homo loquens*, his perception and conceptualisation of the world, mentality and value system.

What are the concrete solutions and achievements in the face of these questions? To what extent do the answers proposed and concepts used constitute a coherent set? Are these concepts operative, i.e. are they useful in analysing linguistic material? Some of these questions have been answered by external observers[7] and in this brief presentation I will only point to a few basic issues.

A crucial element in the definition of ethnolinguistics is the language-culture relationship. However, it escapes simple interpretation; it is even paradoxical in the sense that although both disciplines are largely autonomous, they are in some respects similar and interdependent.

The deep-seated similarity between language and culture results from the fact that both are transmitted in a specific environment, rather than being inherited biologically. They are universal, semiotic and highly organised, i.e. they are systems. With respect to their internal organisation, they even exhibit 'structural isomorphism' (Tolstoy, 1990), so that they can be investigated with similar methods and described in the same conceptual terms: a system and its realisations, a model and its variants, paradigmatic and syntagmatic relations, oppositions and equivalence, text, genre convention, style. The relationship between them is not that of subordination because language may be treated as an aspect or repository of culture, something that embraces, expresses and gives breath to culture.

As an aspect of culture, language is a semiotic system, together with literature, art, religion, custom and myth. At the same time, it is *primus inter pares*: Lévi-Strauss (in Charbonnier, 1961) claims it is 'the most perfect of all cultural systems'. Alternatively, language conditions culture, for without it one cannot participate in culture or in social life, even in their crudest forms. Sapir says that the 'essential perfection [of language] is a prerequisite to the development of culture' (1957: 1).

4.2 The speaking subject

As if this were not complicated enough, I contend that this is a tripartite, rather than a binary relationship: the third inalienable element is the human subject, the experiencing and acting individual, a person, but also a community, a collective subject, an ethnos. But humans, as individuals and as communities, also represent and cherish values. Values are always linked to a subject, they are values 'for someone' (Puzynina, 1992: 23). A community arises on the foundation of specific practical, cultural and moral values, the so called 'entrusted values'.[8] For example, the entrusted values for Poles and many other European nations are freedom and sovereignty, peace and well-being, democracy and solidarity. Values bridge language and culture. They lie at the core of culture; they constitute the very foundation of language and the basic component of all speech (Głowiński, 1986). The most radical formulation of this conception in Poland is the work of Tomasz P. Krzeszowski (1994, 1997, 1999), in whose view the axiological parameter of language is omnipresent (see chapter 4 below).

In order to fully address the language-culture-subject relationship one must consider how subjectivity or 'subjectness' is realised in language (cf. Bartmiński and Pajdzińska, 2008). Subjectivity has traditionally been linked with speaking, with the production of texts by the speaker, not with the language system, apparently devoid of that feature. This approach is now seen as inadequate. First, the contrast between system and text becomes insufficient in the light of the psychological, social and cultural aspects of linguistic communication. Second, reflection on the functions of language and its role in discovering the nature of human being has led to the identification of subjectivism beyond the realm of the traditionally understood individual and textual expressivity.

Anthropological research has been enriched in interesting ways by those linguistic theories which supplement Saussure's opposition between a system and its textual realisation by the notions of social norms, i.e. conventionalised applications of systemic rules in communicative acts (Hjelmslev, 1943; Coşeriu, 1975: 85ff). In other words, linguistic competence is not merely grammatical, but also communicative and cultural competence. The conception of the social norm is important inasmuch as it allows recognition of different degrees of subjectivity in language units.

For example, the tripartite model of system-norm-usage in lexical semantics allows one to include, in the reconstructed word meanings, not only the core features or strong connotations but also the weak or peripheral ones, present in the social semantic norm. Thus, *mother* or *father* is described not only as a person of a specific sex who 'has a child', but also who 'loves', 'forgives', 'nourishes' and 'raises' the children (mother) or 'is strict', 'demanding' and 'punishes for disobedience' (father). Or take *water*: it is not merely a 'colourless liquid', but also something that 'quenches thirst'.[9]

Both general reflection on the role of language in comprehending the world and specific lexical semantic analyses (of the words for 'home', 'mother', 'sun', 'earth', 'water') reveal the anthropocentric nature of language and various manifestations of its subjectivity (cf. the work of Apresjan, Wierzbicka, Tabakowska, Grzegorczykowa, Pajdzińska and others). Subjectivity also permeates the signs whose function is 'representative' (Bühler's (1934) *Darstellungsfunktion*), for this function is by no means an 'impersonal' pairing of language forms with the external world. Behind the semantic content of a linguistic sign there is always the speaking subject, responsible for the construal of the object.

The representative function of language is now interpreted in two ways: as the cognitive, ideational function and as the communicative (interpersonal) function.[10] The distinction allows for a better description of certain interdependencies between a text and its meaning. The cognitive function evokes the conception of linguistic worldview; the communicative function leads to text. Linguistic worldview and text are deeply interconnected. Let me elaborate.

4.3 Text, style and genre

The cognitive function of linguistic signs, that of representing, symbolically, extralinguistic objects and phenomena, is present both when the objects belong to the real world and when they are 'intentional entities', images of culture which constitute the 'second reality' (Fleischer's (2002: 314ff.) elaboration on the work of Popper, 1979). Thus, not only a *pióro* 'feather' is an object, but an *upiór* 'vampire' is as well (the two words are etymologically related: one of the features of *upiór* 'vampire' is that it is covered with *pióra* 'feathers'), not only *woda* 'water' but also *topielec* 'spirit of a drowned person', not only *bocian* 'stork' but also *bocianówka* 'magic water which causes pregnancy' etc. The cognitive function, in this understanding, constitutes the basis of the linguistic worldview conception, a subject-oriented interpretation of reality (more on this in chapter 3).

The communicative function realised in dialogue points to the basic unit of communication, i.e. text. The recognition of the importance of text in linguistic research has been anything but unproblematic. However, it is now accepted with little resistance that text (not a word or sentence) is the basic unit of communication and must, accordingly, be the first and fundamental object of linguistic description. Smaller units, such as sentences, words, morphemes or phonemes, are isolated from text, which is a larger, integrated whole (cf. Humboldt, 1836 and Malinowski, 1965 [1935]). Linguistic descriptions which do not go beyond the level of a sentence omit to address a host of vital problems.[11] Text is qualitatively different from sentences in that it is directly connected with the subject and has an intentional communicative orientation, which may be called a stylistic-generic characterisation.[12]

With this observation we move on to the level of social linguistic forms, the notions of style and speech genre. What is hidden behind these notions? Why is it the case that the diversity of language varieties and stylistic variants, as well as the richness of speech genres, may be treated as a measure of cultural development?

If one assumes that 'style presupposes the presence of authoritative points of view and authoritative, stabilised ideological value judgments' (Bakhtin, 1984: 192), the emergence of a new style indicates an adoption of a new point of view, together with its judgements and valuation. We may develop Bakhtin's idea and say that at stake are certain 'view-of-the-world' qualities, linked with viewpoint and perspective (cf. chapters 7 and 9); these are: the worldview projected in a given style, the ontological status of that worldview, the rationality and communicative intentions it assumes. These are fundamental, constitutive qualities of style, which reside in its 'deep' layer as its 'values'.[13] The problems of formal exponents of style (found on all levels of language: phonetic, morphological, lexical, syntactic and textual), the principles which organise the exponents and render the style recognisable in communication, are second in line.

Language styles in this anthropological, rather than purely pragmatic, understanding are not equivalent in their application or the repertoire of means at their disposal. At the centre of the stylistic system of language is the colloquial style, the most frequently used and the richest in expressive means. Others, such as the artistic, official, scientific style, are its stylistic 'derivatives' (Bartmiński, 1991d).

We now come to the problem of colloquialness. What is colloquialness as a linguistic category? Do not lexicographic definitions, which underscore its unofficial, stereotypical, unscientific (*ISJP*, 2000) or emotional nature, relegate it to the margins of language? Do they not deprive it of its high rank of universality and general comprehensibility, the rank it deserves and actually receives in cultural practice? In contrast to these suggestions, I assume that colloquialness, together with the accompanying and genetically related orality, is the central stylistic category. The colloquial style, a verbalisation of a particular experience of the world, is based on naive realism and commonsense rationality. It is a linguistic correlate of what van Dijk (1998) calls the 'cultural common ground', on which specialised ideological discourses are based and to which they relate.

An anthropological understanding of style allows one to attribute people's attitudes, collectively framed in social norms, to specific styles. Colloquial style goes with an anthropocentric and practical attitude; religious style with a theocentric, cultic attitude; artistic style with a contemplative attitude; scientific style with an epistemological attitude concerned with objective reality; official style with a directive attitude; the language of magic and propaganda with a situationally-causal attitude (cf. Bartmiński, 2001b).

Style is inextricably connected with speech genres (Bakhtin, 1986), which also belong to the level of social convention and testify to the internal richness of the culture. Genre marking is characteristic of every utterance, even the most idiosyncractic, because it always realises a pattern used by both the speaker and the hearer as an orientation frame. The repertoire of genres is open and changes throughout history. Even the oldest and the most universal ones, such as the myth, fable, proverb or ritual song, which maintain their position and their poetics, are subject to modification under the influence of new forms: manifestos, novels, aphorisms, pop songs, sophisticated poetic forms etc. Generic differentiation basically takes place within styles (although, e.g., the letter is an interstylistic genre) and the traditional canonical forms are accompanied by multiplying genre varieties. The colloquial style includes not only conversation on sundry topics, arguments or quarrels, but also jokes, toasts and mobile text messages; in the literary style many prosaic and rhymed varieties have emerged and gained popularity since the times of the tragedy, epos or novel (e.g. the limerick); in the official style we have not only regulations or applications but also instructions, CV and tax form; the scientific style includes not only the treatise, lecture or review, but also the abstract and poster, etc. Writers may also mix genres and create 'polyphonic' texts. An interesting research endeavour for ethnolinguistics is to identify the genres characteristic to a given national, regional or local culture: the Jewish psalm, German saga, Russian *bylina* and *skaz*, Polish *gawęda* 'a short story of free structure', *szczodrak* 'ritualistic New Year wishes', *kawał* 'joke', etc.

The genre patterns of texts depend above all on the speakers' intentions in various communicative situations (cf. Wierzbicka, 1983, 1991, chapter 5). However, a description of a genre, especially produced from the point of view of an external observer (a reader or commentator) must not disregard formal features of text, situational factors, typical roles of the sender and receiver, or sometimes the text's subject matter. I believe that a description of a speech genre should be multiaspectual, should combine the semantic aspect with the communicative and formal perspectives. This is to ensure that a given text is not deprived of its processual character or its connections with the communicative dimension but, indeed, that the structural characteristics of text as a product of a speech event are taken into account.[14] Thus, the definition of *toast* would not only take into account the speaker's intentions (wishes for and praise of the celebration's participant) but also the form (a short text) and circumstances (at a celebration, before drinking alcohol, a public performance).[15]

The multiaspectual understanding of a genre is grounded in the semantics and valence of verbs referring to the very act of speaking, i.e. the verbs from which genre names are derived. Consider Table 2.1.

Table 2.1 Verbal elements and genre names derived from them

I	II
Witam serdecznie! 'Welcome!' (lit. 'I welcome you warmly')	*serdeczne powitanie* 'a warm welcome'
Żegnam gości! lit. 'I say good-bye to the guests'	*pożegnanie gości* 'a good-bye to the guests'
Odpowiadam krótko 'I answer briefly'	*krótka odpowiedź* 'a brief answer'
Proszę usilnie o spotkanie lit. 'I earnestly request to see you'	*usilna prośba o spotkanie* 'an earnest request for an appointment'
Zapraszam na ślub 'I invite you to the wedding'	*zaproszenie na ślub* 'wedding invitation'
Pozdrawiam serdecznie lit. 'I greet (sb) warmly'	*serdecznie pozdrowienia* 'warm greetings'

The first column contains verbs referring to actions, the second column contains nouns referring either to actions or to the 'products' of those actions. The same event (speaking) is profiled differently through the use of grammar: a verb with its obligatory marking of tense and person underscores the very act, the doer (the subject, in Polish usually coded in the form of the verb) and the manner (briefly, earnestly, warmly), while an abstract noun (without tense and person marking) highlights only one aspect of the event complex, i.e. the result of the action and its features (brief, earnest, warm). (Profiling is discussed in chapter 8.)

Speech genre and, especially, language style are constructs of a high level of generality. The entities directly accessible to analysis are texts, i.e. holistically organised units with a theme, sender and receiver, as well as a specific communicative context. Linguists approach texts in two ways: compositionally and holistically (cf. Busse, 1992).

In the compositional approach, texts are treated as constructions in which one may observe smaller units, sentences and words, with their context, syntagmatic connections (sequences) and paradigmatic relations (substitutions, oppositions, equivalences). In this approach, text is a communicative manifestation, *in praesentia*, of a system – indeed, it is contrasted with the system, *in potentia*, as a set of grammatical rules.

The holistic approach, closer to the entholinguistic spirit and supported by the authority of Humboldt (1836),[16] Malinowski (1965 [1935])[17] and Bakhtin (1986), assumes that text in itself is a highly organised linguistic and communicative whole with its own principles, grammar, semantics and rules of interpretation. The rules constitute a subcomponent of systemic rules and texts assume a status comparable to that of units at the syntactic and lexical levels.

From the ethnolinguistic point of view, the second approach is particularly important. Two ideas professed by students of oral tradition are especially noteworthy.

The first of these concerns the specificity of what we will call 'stereotyped texts'. Out of the richness of speech, dominated by idiosyncratic utterances constructed anew in each instance of occurrence, it is always possible to extract a group of texts reproduced many times and in effect socially established, with the status of linguistic 'plates' or 'matrices' (the conception was first presented by Permyakov, 1970). These stereotyped texts are used as holistic, socially recognised units; they make up repertoires of the collective memory and can be systematised and organised into *sui generis* 'lexicons'.[18] They preserve collective knowledge and document group mentality.

Secondly, there is the conception of the primacy and naturalness of texts of folklore. In synchronic coding and decoding, when the transfer of the message cannot be stopped or reversed and when the aural reception must keep pace with speech, oral stereotyped texts exhibit maximal naturalness and engage the fundamental mechanisms of perception and memory. Their structure and semantics is the most functional from the point of view of human neurophysiology and psychology. Hence the patterns of text construction are clear and unambiguous (Niebrzegowska-Bartmińska, 2007).[19]

4.4 Lexis

A privileged position in ethnolinguistic research is occupied by lexis, which is viewed as a classifier of social experience. It provides access to the conceptual sphere, to the realm of ideas and images important in a given culture. Of interest is the organisation of whole lexico-semantic fields (colour, measurement and kinship terms, emotion and value terms), the axiological and semiotic oppositions within it (good/bad, close/distant, us/them etc.) and the semantic content of individual lexical items, especially the cultural keywords or 'collective symbols'. The methods of linguistic semantics allow one to penetrate the richness of lexical meanings, inquire into the worldview and the system of judgements and values inherent in the lexemes. Through lexical meanings, language is deeply entrenched in culture. As an instrument of the investigation of those meanings I propose the cognitive definition (chapter 6).

Results of systematic research on lexis in its cultural aspect are published in ethnolinguistic dictionaries. *SSSL* presents findings of rather extensive inquiries into the linguo-cultural pictures of the universe, plants, animals and people (cf. the analyses of the sun, mother, house/home, homeland, left wing-right wing and Germans in this volume). In the Moscow dictionary *Slavyanske drevnosti* (*SD*, 1995–2004) one finds such symbols of Slavic spiritual culture as God, angel, hell, goddess, witch or evil spirits; cultural pictures of trees, animals, illnesses and customs, as well as the oppositions of human vs. animal, up vs. down or left vs. right.

4.5 Categories

Grammatical categories became important in the research programme of ethnolinguistics once they were put in the spotlight of contemporary semantics (Langacker, 1987; Wierzbicka, 1988; Taylor, 1989 (3rd ed. 2004); Grzegorczykowa and Szymanek, 2001 (1st ed. 1993)).

The ethnolinguistic approach to language endorses the treatment of all category types as linguistic categories, as well as (or indeed, above all) the superordinate status of conceptual, semantic categories. The term 'linguistic categories' embraces grammatical categories (syntactic, such as subject, predicate or object, and morphological, i.e. word-formational[20] and inflectional, such as number and case), lexical categories (names of activities, tools, places), phonological and semantic or conceptual categories, which are the highest in the hierarchy (actions, processes and states; people, animals, objects; quantity, time, space, etc.). It is the latter category type that I take as the most important for the understanding of language and its functioning.

Conceptual categories may be expressed in various ways: lexically, grammatically or phonetically. From the semantic perspective one can observe an isofunctionality of word-formational, inflectional, lexical and syntactic categories: none is autonomous, all function as exponents of the same semantic content. Let us take the conceptual category of PERSON in Polish. It is strongly coded as an inflectional category in verb conjugations: (*ja*) *mówię* 'I say', (*ty*) *mówisz* 'you say', (*on/ona/ono*) *mówi* 'he/she/it says' (in plural: (*my*) *mówimy* 'we say', (*wy mówicie*) 'you say', (*oni/one*) *mówią* 'they say'). The differences in verb forms show that the major distinction is drawn between the first and second persons on the one hand and the third person on the other. The situation is peculiar because clear inflectional distinctions between three persons are only present in the indicative mood, while in the imperative mood only the 1st and 2nd persons are distinguished in this way: 1st person *jedźmy* 'let's go!' vs. 2nd person *jedź* 'go!'. For the 3rd person only weak, analytic forms are possible: *niech jedzie* 'let him go, may he go'; similarly in the 1st person singular: *niech skonam* (*jeśli kłamię*) 'may I die (if I lie)'. Some verbs, in turn, can only be used in the 3rd person: *zdaje się* 'it seems', *mdli mnie* 'I feel queasy', lit. 'it makes queasy me', *świta* 'the day is dawning', *ściemnia się* 'it's getting dark'.

This diversity is confirmed at the lexical level in a number of ways. First, it can be seen in the system of pronouns: *ja* 'I', *ty* 'you', *on/ona/ono* 'he/she/it' – again, the first two pronouns have a different rank than those for the third person.[21] The speaker and the hearer form the basic dialogic relationship, without which language cannot exist. The third person (or a third person) is not a partner in the communicative event but an object. In addition, note that both in Polish and English the first and second person pronouns are not differentiated for gender, whereas the third one is: *on* 'he', *ona* 'she', *ono* 'it'.

The conceptual category of PERSON is also coded lexically through a series of names referring to people (the feature 'person' may in those names be foregrounded or backgrounded). These include general terms (for 'man', 'woman', 'child'), kinship terms (for 'father', 'mother', 'brother') and an extensive category of anthroponyms, such as first names, surnames, nicknames, pseudonyms and suchlike. At the interface of lexis and grammar one finds names of people derived by suffixation from their occupations, professions, characteristic features, family relationships, places of origin etc. One may talk here about word-formational exponents of the category of PERSON, e.g. the words referring to doers of actions (*piekarz* 'baker', *wykładowca* 'lecturer'), to people with specific characteristics (*siłacz* 'strongman', *mędrzec* 'sage, wise man'), to dwellers of cities (*warszawiak* 'Warsaw dweller') or kinship terms (*Zarębina* 'Zaręba's wife'). The category also functions at the level of syntax, as some verbs connote a personal subject. These include the verbs of speaking, cognition and emotion, such as the counterparts of the English *speak, know, think, presume, love, hate, suspect, praise* etc.

In a similar manner one can describe other conceptual categories, realised by various formal and linguistic exponents (cf. Adamowski, 1999 on space and Nowosad-Bakalarczyk, 2006 on gender).

Finally, categories are relative because different languages categorise the world in different ways. Categorisation is a portion of a larger process of conceptualising reality, creating its linguistic and mental representation, specific to individual ethnic languages and internal variants of each language (more on the subject in chapter 3).

5 A synopsis: basic concepts of cognitive ethnolinguistics

Let me briefly recapitulate by listing the key notions of the cognitive entholinguistic enterprise. The apparatus of cognitive ethnolinguistics consists of a few concepts:

    i)   the linguistic worldview;
    ii)   the values underlying that worldview;
    iii) stereotype as a component of the linguistic worldview;
    iv) the cognitive definition as a method of describing stereotypes;
    v)   viewpoint and perspective;
    vi) profiling;
    vii) the conceptualising and profiling subject.

These notions are interlinked with one another and together constitute what I hope is a coherent conception. Since 1981, they have been subjected to discussion at a series of conferences called 'Language and Culture'.[22] I devote a chapter of this book to most of these concepts and the arrangement of the chapters is not arbitrary: it is aimed to show the mutual relationships between these notions (the conception of the subject, not discussed in a chapter of its own, is dealt with in many places, notably in the discussion of viewpoint and valuation).

First (in chapter 3) I discuss the linguistic worldview conception, based on the cognitive function of the sign. It invokes the cultural aspects of language and its relation to the speakers' mentality. The conception, apart from the cognitive definition and subject-related profiling, has become a key idea of Lublin ethnolinguistics. Moreover, it is used by scholars who do not consider themselves ethnolinguists; some even consider it to be 'the central idea of cognitive linguistics', which 'has opened new vistas to comparative semantic research' (Grzegorczykowa, 2001: 162).

Because the linguistic worldview conception is strictly semantic and unites all levels of language, it has become a tool for the holistic and integrated description of language, without a split into unrelated fields, such as lexicology and grammar, text linguistics and pragmatics, syntax and morphology. Each of these fields is very detailed and precise in its findings but becomes largely autonomous in the process. The linguistic worldview approach facilitates their integration, in accordance with the colloquial understanding of language as a coherent collection of means used together in communication.

All the other notions relate to the linguistic worldview conception in a more or less direct manner. What are those relationships? First, linguistic worldviews are constructed on the basis of values assumed by speakers (chapter 4). Second, they comprise stereotyped elements (chapter 5). Third, stereotypes and their internal structure can be described in terms of the cognitive definition (chapter 6). Fourth, linguistic worldviews depend on the speaking subject's viewpoint and perspective (chapter 7). Next, linguistic worldviews function in discourse in the form of variants called 'profiles' (chapters 8 and 9). Finally, it is the speaking subject who profiles a worldview on the basis of his or her values and intentions (mainly chapters 4 and 9).

Notes

1 Second edition 1999; third 2004.

2 The 19th century tradition understands other terms in a similar manner: *ethnography* 'science of a people or peoples', *ethnomusicology* 'musicology concerned with folk music', *ethnoarcheology* 'ethnographic archeology', *ethnopsychology* or *ethnosociology*. In this context, *ethnolinguistics* can be understood as the linguistics of the languages of ethnic communities.

3 Wierzbicka (1988: 169) writes: '[E]very language embodies in its very structure a certain world-view, a certain philosophy. […] [T]he syntactic constructions of a language embody and codify certain language-specific meanings and ways of thinking'.

4 The term *cognitive ethnolinguistics* was probably used for the first time by Jörg Zinken (2004a), followed by Lidia Nepop-Ajdaczyć (2007). That the Lublin ethnolinguistic research is close to or even convergent with the cognitive linguistic enterprise as initiated in America was first pointed out by Kardela (1990) and later by e.g. Tabakowska (2004a).

5 According to Ward H. Goodenough (1964), culture is what exists in people's minds and hearts, what one should know and what one should believe in order to be a member of a given community.

6 For a discussion of this issue in connection with English cf. Wierzbicka (2006).

7 Tolstaya, 1993; Tabakowska, 2004a; Zinken, 2004b; Plas, 2006.

8 Following Władysław Stróżewski (1981: 294), I take 'entrusted values' to be those values in the name of which a given community acts in order to achieve its aims, as well as building and maintaining its identity.

9 Putnam included in his definitions only the weaker connotations (of e.g. water) as stereotypical features. If, however, one views stereotypes as containing core, categorial features (as these, too, play a role in subjective choices), distinguishing separate spheres of meaning seems unnecessary.

10 Cf. Halliday's (2004) distinction between the ideational and interpersonal levels.

11 The lack of attention to the level of text as a level with its own rules, different from the sentential level, is characteristic of the work of structuralists (e.g. Roman Jakobson).

12 In van Dijk's (1972: 148) model of text derivation, the characterisation is treated as a rule assuming the obligatoriness of the text qualifier, which is brought into being by modal and performative categories, such as statement, question, order etc.

13 I use the term *value* as *valeur*, in the sense proposed by the French linguistic tradition; cf. *SemD* (1979). In my work on the derivation of style I mention the following values: ontological assumptions, the rationality of the speaker, subjective viewpoint, viewpoint-derived worldview, general communicative intentions.

14 A multidimensional description of Polish was first proposed a long time ago by Stefania Skwarczyńska (1965).

15 The definition of *toast* in *USJP* (2003) reads: 'a short speech usually given at a reception or banquet in order to praise and honour someone, followed by having an alcoholic drink'. Wierzbicka defines it in the following way:

I say: I want something good to happen to X

I imagine that if we say this when we drink this alcohol, this will happen

I say this because I want to say that we have good feelings towards X

(Wierzbicka, 1983: 133)

16 Humboldt views grammar not as putting words together to produce speech but as breaking speech up into words. It is speech, not words, that is primary.

17 In *Coral Gardens*, Malinowski writes: 'I think that it is very profitable in linguistics to widen the concept of context so that it embraces not only spoken words, but facial expression, gesture, bodily activities, the whole group of people present during an exchange of utterances and the part of the environment in which these people are engaged' (Malinowski, 1965 [1935]: 22).

18 Stereotyped texts are never petrified; on the contrary, they are subjected to situational adaptation. In folklore, experts say, there are no canonical texts. Texts of folklore function as variants; the degree of a text's variation is the measure of its entrenchment in folklore (Gusev, 1967).

19 For example, two basic principles of thematic sequence in text, the chain model (the principle of concatenation) and the series model (with the superordinate theme), described by Daneš (1974) as 'thematization of rheme' and 'rhematization of theme', are very clearly realised in folk songs. In prose, plot schemas have been identified and their description in Russian fables by Propp (1928) is regarded as the first 'grammar of text'.

20 I.e. groups of words with a similar structure and structural meaning, e.g. *kierownik* 'head of institution' and *kierowca* 'driver' – a person who heads or directs something.

21 The pronouns I and YOU belong to Wierzbicka's list of semantic primes. The author says: 'There are no languages in the world which would be 'free' of words for I and YOU (in the sense THOU)' (Wierzbicka, 1996: 36).

22 Proceedings of these conferences have been published in two book series (in Lublin and Wrocław, Poland), and to some extent in the journal *Etnolingwistyka* – altogether 65 volumes.

3 Linguistic worldview and how to reconstruct it

1 A little history

Almost a century ago, a linguist and a logician independently formulated very similar opinions on the role of language in the process of learning things about the world. Edward Sapir wrote:

> Language is heuristic […] in the […] sense that it forms for us certain modes of observation and interpretation. This means of course that as our scientific experience grows we must learn to fight the implications of language. (Sapir, 1957: 7; from the essay *Language* first published in 1933 in *The Encyclopedia of the Social Sciences*, New York, vol. IX, pp. 155–169)

Kazimierz Ajdukiewicz, a Polish logician, stated:

> Not only some but in fact all judgements which we accept and which make up our world view, depend on the conceptual apparatus we use to portray our experience, rather than on the experience itself. The choice of this or that apparatus will change the picture. (Ajdukiewicz, 1934/1985: 175)

Today, it makes little difference that one statement pertains to language while the other to thinking because one of 'the most significant achievements of the cognitive linguistics enterprise' is 'an integrated view of language and thought' (Evans, Bergen and Zinken, 2007: 29–30). The conception which unites language and thinking, what is linguistic and what is mental, as well as providing the basis for their methodical analysis, is the linguistic worldview conception.

This conception derives from the American ethnolinguists Eward Sapir and Benjamin Lee Whorf, but is also related to German ethnolinguistic thought (cf. Wilhelm von Humboldt's (1836) *Weltansicht* and the work of his continuator Leo Weisgerber) or French and Italian Enlightenment (Anusiewicz, 1990). According to Philip Bock (2003), its roots lie in Aristotle's idea of *topoi* (*loci communes*), i.e. generally known and acceptable judgements which define what is and is not possible, which establish common points of reference in the process of deduction and argumentation, which underlie logical syllogisms and aid speakers in their task of convincing listeners (Aristotle, *Poetics*, II, 21–22). Since the 1970s the worldview conception has been developing intensively in Slavic countries, especially in Poland and Russia, but recently also in Belarus, Ukraine and the Czech Republic (Bartmiński, 2004a; Yudin, 2004b).

In Poland, the conception was introduced to a wider audience by Walery Pisarek (1999). Bartmiński (1980), an 'ethnolinguistic manifesto' of sorts, initiated research on the view of the world entrenched in Polish folklore and rural folk variants of the Polish language. In 1986, the Lublin ethnolinguistic team published a collection of analyses in the journal *Akcent* (no. 26), preceded by my essay 'What do ethnolinguists do?' In the same year Ryszard Tokarski and I published an article on linguistic worldview and textual coherence (Bartmiński and Tokarski, 1986), while Jolanta Maćkiewicz (1988) published her study of how we see the world through language.

A significant influence on the development of the conception took place during a conference I organised in Puławy, Poland, in 1987 (the proceedings are published as Bartmiński, 1990, subsequent editions in 1999 and 2004).[1] In the preface to the first issue of the journal *Etnolingwistyka*, published in 1988, I proposed that the linguistic worldview conception, the 'naive' picture at the very basis of language, be treated as the key object of ethnolinguistic research. Subsequent issues of the journal, as well as the series *Język a kultura* ('Language and Culture') and various other publications contain many studies devoted to the conception. The linguistic worldview conception has been verified, operationalised and above all applied to portions of worldview in many publications in book form.

Lublin ethnolinguistic research is linked to the work of Anna Wierzbicka, who has proposed a method of intercultural research based on the Natural Semantic Metalanguage (NSM). In a series of books and articles she reconstructs the meanings of keywords in several cultures, e.g. *homeland, freedom, friendship, humility, courage, soul,* and their counterparts (always partial equivalents, at best) in other languages and cultures. She has shown the profound relationship between the language, history and culture of specific national communities. Similar comparative work is being carried out in Warsaw by Jadwiga Puzynina, Renata Grzegorczykowa, Zofia Zaron, Krystyna Waszakowa and their students. A systematic description of the linguo-cultural worldview of the folk variety of Polish (one of the two basic varieties of the language) is a dictionary of folk symbols and stereotypes (*SSSL*, 1996–1999).[2] Folk tradition constitutes the historical basis of national tradition and is still a living component of the latter. A few collected volumes (Bartmiński and Mazurkiewicz-Brzozowska, 1993b; Bartmiński, 1993b, 2003, 2006a) make up a series of methodologically similar studies of Polish axiological lexis, based on questionnaires and contemporary standard Polish texts.

2   What is linguistic worldview?

Linguistic worldview is a language-entrenched interpretation of reality, which can be expressed in the form of judgements about the world, people, things or events. It is an interpretation, not a reflection; it is a portrait without claims to fidelity, not a photograph of real objects. The interpretation is a result of subjective perception and conceptualisation of reality performed by the speakers of a given language; thus, it is clearly subjective and anthropocentric but also intersubjective (social). It unites people in a given social environment, creates a community of thoughts, feelings and values. It influences (to what extent is a matter for discussion) the perception and understanding of the social situation by a member of the community.

The definition of linguistic worldview is not fully agreed on but it oscillates between a 'picture of the world reflected in a given national language' (Pisarek, 1999: 168), a 'conceptual structure fossilised in the system of a given language' (Grzegorczykowa, 1990: 43) and a 'set of regularities' in grammatical and lexical structures, manifesting various ways of perceiving the world (Tokarski, 1998: 10). My own definition of linguistic worldview as a 'set of judgements' reveals its epistemological (interpretive) nature, does not limit it to what is 'fossilised' or closed as a 'structure', makes room for the dynamic, open nature of the worldview, and does not favour the abstract 'regularity' in grammar and vocabulary. How the conception of linguistic worldview is operationalised, how it functions in texts and how it is profiled in discourse is the subject of exemplary studies (of the sun, home, homeland etc.) in later chapters of this book.

First of all, linguistic worldview is an aspect of national language, used by an average speaker of a natural language: the worldview reflects the speaker's needs, aspirations and mentality. The worldview is 'naive' in the sense of Apresyan, i.e. constructed by a human being, relative to human measure, anthropocentric, but also adapted to social needs and ethnocentric mentality (Aprean, 1994). This is the conception of linguistic worldview one finds in the basic, most common variant of national language, namely the colloquial variant (or style), whereas in the scientific style the worldview is subjected to strong differentiation with regard to a given discipline and its state of the art. It is also differentiated in other styles derived from colloquial style: official, journalistic or the most individualised and creative literary style.

In the colloquial, folk or naive view of humans and their world, the sun still *rises* and *sets* (five centuries after Copernicus!), stars *twinkle*, the road *goes* form one place to another, water is *healthy* or not, plants are *good* and *useful* (corn, herbs) or not (weeds), things are *cold*, *heavy* or *tall* in relation to an average person, etc. The worldview is based on sensory stimuli, concrete and practical: it suffices for the purpose of everyday communication. It is at the disposal of the speaker as his or her cultural endowment: as all linguistic constructs, it may be subjected to individual modulation (cf. chapters 8 and 9 below).

The linguistic worldview conception corresponds well with the cognitive and communicative revolution in contemporary linguistics, which emphasises the symbolic (cognitive) and communicative (interpersonal) functions of language. This conception has a strictly semantic nature; it links all layers of language, though they do not reveal the picture to the same degree. It could thus become an instrument for a holistic description of language and make it possible to overcome the disintegration of linguistic research into separate disciplines, which conflicts with the everyday conception of language as a collection of means used jointly in the process of communication. The work of Lublin ethnolinguists, especially *SSSL* 1996–1999, restores this everyday conception and reunites the various 'levels' or 'subsystems' of language, which even in the not so distant past were treated as isolated.

For all these reasons, I think that while investigating the linguistic picture of house/ home (Pol. *dom*), mother (*matka*) or German (*Niemiec*), one has the right to take into account:

- the nomination and onomasiological basis revealed through structural and etymological analysis (*dom* 'house/home' from the process of building,[3] *Niemiec* 'German' from *niemy* 'mute', *matka/mama* from a child's first words, based on the syllable *ma-*);
- the meanings included in dictionaries (*dom* 'building' but also 'family', 'dynasty', 'household'; *matka* 'the woman who has given birth' but also 'the most important player in a sports team', 'the Mother Superior in a religious order' – with some meanings being derived from others);
- word-formational derivatives which take over and bring out hidden connotations of the base term (*domowy* 'loose', 'casual'; *matkować komuś* 'to mother someone');
- metaphorical extensions (*czuć się jak w domu* 'to feel at home'; *statek-matka* 'mother-ship');
- phraseological units and proverbs (*nie mieć wszystkich w domu* lit. 'not to have everyone at home', i.e. 'be insane'; *potrzeba matką wynalazków* 'necessity is the mother of invention');
- finally, texts ('When the father dies, the child is a half-orphan, but when the mother dies, the child is fully an orphan'; 'He's a German but a good man'; 'Nothing like the home').

I discuss these issues in a more systematic manner in subsequent chapters; here let me only touch upon certain important problems and indicate the general direction followed by the representatives of ethnolinguistic research in Lublin.

3 Reconstructing linguistic worldview

The first question is a general one: to what extent is linguistic worldview, entrenched in and acquired with language, imposed on the speakers, and to what extent is it merely suggested? In the light of the experience of societies indoctrinated for a number of years, as well as through critical scholarly reflection, one must conclude that the deterministic version of the Sapir-Whorf hypothesis cannot be defended. Wierzbicka writes:

> Neither Sapir nor Whorf (regardless of the rather radical formulation of some of their theses) ever claimed that language determines consciousness. On the contrary, Sapir considered this view naive. Every language has the potential to express all content; there is no experience which could not be reconciled with any language. But there is an important difference between what a given language 'does not make impossible' and what it offers, suggests and facilitates. There is a difference between potential and 'habitual' thinking. (Wierzbicka, 1978: 22)

While accepting that language is the key to the world of thought and culture, as well as a 'guide to social reality' (Sapir), and that the speaker's interpretations of reality may depend on his or her historically determined social and cultural needs, I am also ready to admit that linguistic categorisation is partly dependent on the neurophysiological qualities of the human cognitive apparatus. Biological determinism and relativism constitute two poles between which language is located.

A question arises, then, whether a single national language encodes one or more worldviews. After all, the picture of the world which emerges from research on dialects and folklore is different from that entrenched in standard, general Polish; also, the understanding of basic concepts, such as justice or equality, in the respective discourses of the left and right wing is sometimes radically divergent. The differences between worldviews within a single language are sometimes more profound than those between languages (Chlebda, 2005: 414).

Attempts to explain this status quo must take note of social and stylistic variants, the multitude of speech genres (each with its own intentionality and poetics), and the ideological foundations of utterances – all that can be interpreted in terms of broad systemic rules, in terms of somewhat narrower socially and functionally determined conventions, and in terms of situated, contextual, individual and idiosyncratic usage (Hjelmslev, Coşeriu).

The question of the strength with which linguistic worldview is imposed on the speakers, and of the internal diversity of any tongue, is connected with how anthropo-logical and cultural categories are manifested in language. The question can be asked in a technical manner from the point of view of the linguist: what linguistic facts can constitute the basis of the description of linguistic worldview and to what extent are they unambiguous? If such reconstruction is to be a set of judgements about the world, what 'linguistic evidence' can be adduced to support the selection of some judgements as constitutive of the worldview at the expense of others? What is the evidential strength of specific data?

3.1 Lexis

The most obvious, unquestionable basis for investigating linguistic worldview has so far been the lexis. Sapir emphasised the difference between grammar and lexis in their relation to culture: although 'there is no general correlation between cultural type and linguistic structure', the matter looks differently 'when we pass from general form to the detailed content of a language. Vocabulary is a very sensitive index of the culture of a people' (Sapir, 1957: 34, 36). In this context, the first and fundamental question is the very range of lexis (words and concepts); lexis as an 'inventory of culture', living and dynamic, continually enriched with new items, a kind of seismograph registering changes in the society, civilization and culture.

Research on the new vocabulary in Polish (Smółkowa, 2001) has shown that two fac-tors are crucial in this respect: (1) the objective necessity to give names to new inventions (computer, TV clip), discoveries (bacteria, genome, neutrino), institutions and situations (monitoring, decommunisation, robotisation), and (2) a subjective desire to express one's attitudes to reality, frequently novel attitudes (callousness, Catholic-left, Eurocentrism, globalisation, antiglobalism etc.). New social phenomena and relationships are named with new expressions, such as *prawa człowieka* 'human rights', *społeczeństwo obywatelskie* 'civil society', *proces pokojowy* 'peace process', or *małe ojczyzny* 'little homelands', and sometimes borrowed, such as *monitoring, mobbing*, or *PR*.

The next issue is that of lexical meaning. I understand the meaning of a word in the integral sense, comprising both the core with the superordinate hyperonymous category (e.g. *donkey* – animal) and a number of characteristics attributed to the object on the basis of 'encyclopedic' information about it (a donkey is 'a domesticated animal, pack or draught', 'grey', 'with long ears', 'with a thin tail', 'half as tall as a person', 'with a big head', 'similar to a horse'). The meaning also includes several clearly subjective features, traditionally called 'lexical connotations' and excluded from linguistic description (a donkey is 'stubborn, stupid', hence Pol. *osioł* also means 'a stupid, stubborn person').[4] The whole recognisable semantic richness of a word, with its lexical, encyclopedic and cultural connotations, can be described by means of the cognitive definition (chapter 6).

Next, comparative research on values and value terms has shown that the semantic content and ranges of words change over time under the influence of new social and cultural conditions – in contemporary Polish this is the case with such words as *równość* 'equality', *praca* 'work', *wolność* 'freedom/liberty', *niepodległość* 'independence', *pokój* 'peace', *szowinizm* 'chauvinism' (cf. Bartmiński, 2006a).

Significant differences, obviously, can also be found *between* languages and cultures; above all in cultural 'keywords' (Wierzbicka, 1997), 'collective symbols' (Fleischer, 1995) or 'leading symbols' (Pisarek, 2002). Particularly noteworthy today are the divergent interpretations, in Eastern and Western Europe, of the concepts of FREEDOM/LIBERTY (Abramowicz and Karolak, 1991; Wierzbicka, 1997), HOMELAND (Bartmiński, 1993b; Wierzbicka 1997), A PEOPLE (Abramowicz and Bartmiński, 1998), but also EQUALITY, DEMOCRACY, NATION, NATIONALISM, PATRIOTISM, COSMOPOLITISM, ECUMENISM and many others. (The problems of understanding and describing meaning are discussed in chapter 6.)

An important aspect of linguistic worldview is the so called 'inner form' of a word (Humboldt's *innere Sprachform, innere Gedankenform*), also mentioned by Jan Rozwadowski (died 1935), a pioneer of the cognitivist approach in Poland. Especially in the case of languages with rich word formation, e.g. the Slavic branch, asking questions about the mechanism of creating names and about their onomasiological foundations allows for accessing the linguistic means of interpretation of a given object or phenomenon. The inner form may be investigated both in reference to living word-formational units, whose structural meanings are transparent, and in reference to dead, lexicalised formations, whose contemporary meanings are removed from their original structural meanings, now opaque and only accessible through etymological analysis.

The first type of formations may be exemplified with the names of customs, such as *andrzejki* 'celebrations of St. Andrew's Day', *mikołajki* 'St. Nicolaus' Day', *walentyki* 'St. Valentine's Day', *wesele* 'wedding' (from *weselić się* 'be joyful'), *pogrzeb/pochówek* 'funeral' (from *grzebać/chować* 'bury'), or of participants in military activities, whose names are ideologically loaded, such as *powstaniec* 'insurgent' (from *powstać* 'rise'), *bojownik* 'fighter, militant' (from *bój* 'fight, battle'), *buntownik* 'rebel' (from *buntować się* 'to rebel'), *żołnierz/żołdak* 'soldier' (from *żołd* 'soldier's pay'), *terrorysta* 'terrorist' etc.

The second type of formations include e.g. the names of Slavic pagan gods (*Perun, Swarog/Swarożyc, Dadźbog, Mokosz, Wołos/Weles, Świętowit, Jaryło*), which, etymologists assume, contain information about the primeval conceptualisation of the sacred by Proto-Slavs (Jakobson, 1966; Ivanov and Toporov, 1965).

The conceptualisations of natural phenomena can also be revealed through an analysis of their names. For example, a rainbow may receive its name from its connection with clouds (e.g. the Polish *tęcza* is related to Russian *tucha* 'cloud'), the rain (German *Regenbogen*, English *rainbow*), an arch-like shape (French *arc-en-ciel*, Lithuanian *vaivorykštė*, English *rainbow*). The Earth's satellite is called *księżyc* in Polish ('a young priest', 'prince', originally 'new moon') or *miesiąc* (from measuring time; the root **mēs-* 'measure' is present in many other languages); in Russian it is called *luna* (from *luna*, Pol. *łuna* 'glow in the sky', cf. *REW*, 1950–1958). The planet Venus is colloquially categorised as a star and termed relative to the time of its appearance: *Gwiazda Poranna* 'The Morning Star'/*Jutrzenka*, from *jutro* 'tomorrow', or *Gwiazda Wieczorna/Wieczornica* 'The Evening Star' (*SSSL*, 1996–1999, vol. 1–1[5]), or the time when it can be seen, cf. Ukrainian *Zirnytsia*, from *zora* 'light, glow', Russian *Dennitsa*, from *den* 'day'. The names of other stars are clearly mythological, e.g. the Pleiades, in Polish folk tradition called *Baby* 'women', *Kwoka* 'broodhen' (with chiks), or *Sito* 'sieve'. The last name is connected with the image of the sky as a dome with holes in it through which the light of heaven can be seen (cf. *SSSL*, 1996–1999, vol. 1–1: 246–249).

Names contain a perspective from which reality is viewed. The Polish *suwerenność* 'sovereignty' is treated as a synonym of *niezależność, niezawisłość* and *niepodległość* 'independence', but each form represents a different viewpoint. *Suwerenność* is an adapted borrowing of the French *souverenité* and is conceptually related to *zwierzchnictwo* 'supremacy': it is a manifestation of the 'top-down' perspective. *Niezależność, niezawisłość* and *niepodległość* manifest a rank-and-file perspective, from the point of view of the party threatened with the loss of self-government and self-sufficiency, with dependence and subordination. A similar internal form can be found in other languages: Russian *nezavisimost'*, Ukrainian *nezalezhnist'*, German *Unabhängigkeit*.

The results of analysing the structural meaning may correspond to the contemporary meaning of a word, but etymological analysis may reveal meanings totally absent or functioning only marginally in the present-day understanding of lexical units. For example, the word *nietoperz* 'bat' in the light of etymological analysis contains the information that the animal was once considered similar to a bird (whose characteristic feature in colloquial understanding are feathers, Polish *pióra*), but not a 'real' bird (*nie* means 'not'). Maybe *nietoperz* is etymologically connected with the folk daemon called *upiór* or *wampierz* (cf. Eng. *vampire*), imagined to be 'a night bird with a long sharp beak which it uses to suck the blood of the victim' (*SEJP* 1927: 594). Perhaps in this way, through the root *per-* 'fly', both terms are genetically related to *ptak* 'bird'.[6]

A more general question is: what is the relationship between the etymological meaning and the contemporary meaning of a word? 'Contemporary' may mean restricted to the core, or more broadly, including the peripheral and marginal components. Maybe there is a relationship between the uncertain, hypothetical etymological meaning and the weak, marginal connotations of a word?

Lublin ethnolinguistics relatively early (Bartmiński, 1984) rejected the conception of meaning as limited to 'necessary and sufficient' features, which in accordance with the requirements of structural semantics excludes the 'non-core' spheres from the definition of the 'proper meaning' as 'lexical' or 'cultural' connotations. The long-disregarded 'connotation' has been programmatically included into descriptions of meanings.

Analyses of the relationship between etymology and connotation on the basis of the standard Polish *praca* and colloquial *robota* (both meaning 'work'), as well as the folk names of stones, have confirmed the view that 'the etymological meaning is usually preserved in the word's connotations' (Mazurkiewicz, 1988: 111). A good illustration of this thesis can also be found in the names of emotions and feelings (Nowakowska-Kempna, 1995). In Polish verbs from this domain one can find associations with somatic behaviour: *kochać* 'love', form Proto-Slavic **kasati* 'touch'; *przerazić* 'scare', from *razić* 'hit'; or *zachwycać* 'delight', from *chwytać* 'grasp'. The same process of metonymic shifts can be found in contemporary Polish, as exemplified by the expressions *zagiąć kogoś* 'ask someone a question they cannot answer' (lit. 'bend someone'), *zgasić kogoś* 'cause someone to lose their aplomb through a critical remark' (lit. 'to put someone out'), *zdołować* 'make someone lose spirit; make them feel depressed' (from *dół* 'ditch'), etc.

Another problem is that of hyperonyms. It is important in defining words to establish the point of departure, i.e. the superordinate category to which a given object is assigned and in terms of which it is characterised. A definition which aims to reflect the conceptualisation of the object *must*, in the case of, say, bluebottle, choose between a 'plant', 'flower' and 'weed', in the case of wheat between a 'plant', 'grass' and 'corn', in the case of the sun between a 'gaseous sphere', a 'heavenly body', a 'star', 'light' etc. Each choice has its consequences, for it determines the perspective of conceptualisation, as well as introducing more or less distinct characteristics. Sometimes the superordinate categorising element determines the content and structure of the definition. If the dictionary definition is to have a linguistic nature, to reflect the understanding of the object by the speaker and to contribute to the reconstruction of linguistic worldview, it must respect the colloquial conceptualisation. First, it must select the hyperonym from the closest taxonomic level, relative to the language user, not the researcher (e.g. wheat is a corn, not a plant – the principle is discussed in Bartmiński, 1991a). Second, it must take note of the point of view of the subject (the sun is light, not a gaseous sphere). The selection of the superordinate category is also related to the accepted system of values: the identification of categories such as weeds and corn derives from the pragmatic outlook onto the plant world typical of a farmer.

As is well-known, the lexicon of a language is not a set of loose signs but is organised into lexical-semantic fields according to specific principles. The reconstruction of linguistic worldview is informed both by semantic fields, with their internal structure, number and value of their lexical exponents, and by the whole extensive network of relations between the elements of a given field. These relations are hypero- and hyponymic, equonymic (i.e. synonymic and antonymic), regular derivational sequences of a word-formational and semantic nature, as well as syntagmatic, describable in terms of Fillmore's conception of semantic roles. I will illustrate this with the entry for *koń* 'horse' from *SSSL*.

The horse in traditional village culture is perceived not so much as an animal, but as a 'domestic animal', an element of the livestock. The closest hyperonyms of *koń* are *inwentarz żywy, żywina, chudoba* 'livestock'. Hyponyms of *koń* are, with regard to sex: *kobyła* 'mare' and *ogier* 'stallion'/*wałach* 'gelding'; with regard to age: *źrebię* 'foal'; with regard to colour: *kasztan* 'chestnut', *bułan/bułanek* 'dun', *siwek* 'grey' etc. Co-hyponyms of *koń* as an element of livestock are other domestic animals: first of all *wół* 'ox' and *krowa* 'cow', *wieprz* 'hog' and *świnia* 'pig', *baran* 'ram' and *owca* 'sheep', then *pies* 'dog' and *suka* 'bitch'; also the so called *żywioła*, i.e. the poultry tended by women and recognised as a separate category in some dialects: *kogut* 'cock' and *kura* 'hen', *kaczor* 'drake' and *kaczka* 'duck', *gęsior* 'gander' and *gęś* 'goose'.

The horse is perceived in certain typical collections: with a saddle, reins and bridle (a saddle-horse), with a cart and a plough (a draught-horse) or with a man who rides it (a cavalryman, a soldier). With regard to its strength the horse is similar to the bull, lion and bear; the sun is also compared to the horse. Cultural equivalents of the horse are the motor-bike and the car. The horse is conventionally contrasted with the gentle ox, stupid donkey, slow slug, wild and stupid wolf, small and limp frog and the useless mouse.

The word *koń* enters into regular semantic derivations, is subjected to the process of metaphorisation: a grown-up man is called *stary koń* 'old horse', a sexually active man is called *ogier* 'stallion', if someone laughs too loudly, the person *rży* 'neighs', someone who has died *wyciągnął kopyta* 'stretched his/her hoofs', a horse may be sorry for its owner (in a soldier's song) or may laugh (*koń by się uśmiał*, lit. 'a horse would laugh', used when a joke fell flat).

The lexeme also participates in word-formational derivational sequences: *koński* 'of a horse; like a horse; equine' but also in the qualitative sense in *końska dawka leków* 'big, powerful dose of medication', *koński ząb* 'a type of maize with long seeds which have a hollow at the top'; *koński ogon* 'pony tail'.

The entry for *koń* in *SSSL* contains collocations, in the form of defining statements, which answer the following questions:

- what is a horse like? the characteristics: strong, bay, grey;
- what is a horse built like? it has a mane and a tail, hoofs, the head, four legs;
- how is the horse quantified? in what numbers does it occur? a pair, a herd of horses;
- what does the horse do? the behaviour: eats hay, snorts, neighs, kicks about;

- what is done to the horse? what is it the object of? they buy it, saddle it, harness it to the plough;
- what is the horse used for? for horseback rides, pulling carts, ploughing;
- where does the horse stay? the location: the stables.

This kind of collection of trivial bits of information about an object, accompanied by the establishment of the place of the object's name in the lexical system of the language, gives an extensive characteristic of the subject, involves it into an extensive network of relationships, reconstructs its socially entrenched linguo-cultural picture, i.e. its stereotype. This idea of the importance of the whole extensive network of conceptual links is also present in American cognitive semantics, especially in the work of George Lakoff.

In the dictionary of symbols and stereotypes (*SSSL*), which is a record of a traditional linguistic worldview, all entries are explicated in more or less that way. Depending on the specific nature of individual entries, various semantic subcategories are distinguished, such as collections of objects, the structure (the components of the object), attributes, quantification, actions (the object as the agent, sensor, stator, processor), the origin, the object as the source or stimulus of people's sensations, the theme of activity, the addressee of utterances, the object as a tool or instrument, the place and time of its occurrence, its similarities to other objects etc.

A similar model was proposed by Russian scholars compiling a Slavic ethnolinguistic dictionary (Tolstye [Svetlana Tolstaya and Nikita Tolstoy], 1984) and researching the language of folklore (Nikitina, 1992). Then semantic subcategories containing similar ideas began to be referred to as *facets*.

3.2 Phraseological units, collocations, metaphors

Researchers of linguistic worldview are especially interested in phraseological units, although many of the latter are idiomatic combinations with opaque motivations (e.g. *wieszać psy na kimś* 'abuse someone', lit. 'hang dogs on someone'). Their conventionality can be seen in cross-linguistic comparisons. For example, referring to someone's speedy escape Poles say *wziąć nogi za pas*, lit. 'take one's legs behind one's belt', Germans say *die Beine in die Hand nehmen*, lit. 'take legs in the hand', the English say *to take to one's heels*, the French say *prendre ses jambes a son cou*, lit. 'take the legs on the neck', and Slovaks say *vziat' nohy naplecia*, lit. 'take the legs on the back' – and it is difficult to draw any far-reaching conclusions from those data. The 'phraseological picture of the world' has certain peculiar characteristics and is usually based on historical, often fossilised knowledge, which can only be accessed through etymological investigations. Closer to contemporary linguistic feeling, more informative for the contemporary interpretation of the world are living collocations.

For example, much can be learned about the colloquial conceptualisation of the category TEKST (English *text*) from the collocability of the word *tekst* with other words. The analysis of collocations (Niebrzegowska–Bartmińska, 2007: 23–31) allows one to reconstruct the colloquial picture, whose features are grouped into facets, pertaining to:

[AUTHOR]	*tekst poety/polityka* 'a poet's/politician's text';
[STYLE]	*tekst urzędowy/poetycki/naukowy* 'an official/poetic/scholarly text';
[GENRE], [SUBJECT MATTER]	*tekst dramatu/pieśni* 'a play's text/song lyrics';
[STRUCTURE]	*tekst podzielony na rozdziały i akapity* 'a text divided into chapters and paragraphs';
[CHARACTERISTICS]	*tekst rozwlekły/krótki* 'a verbose/short text';
[ACTION IN RELATION TO IT]	*redagować/korygować/streszczać tekst* 'edit/correct/summarise a text'; *rozumieć/przyswoić/objaśnić tekst* 'understand/explain a text';
[ADDRESSEE]	*teksty niezrozumiałe dla niewtajemniczonych* 'texts inaccessible to the uninitiated'; *mówić otwartym tekstem* 'speak openly', lit. 'in an open text';
[TIME]	*tekst z okazji imienin* 'a text for someone's birthday';
[PLACE]	*tekst w gazecie/na murze* 'a text in a newspaper/on the wall'.

In Polish, texts are conceptualised metaphorically in a number of ways: as a result of the work of a craftsman, such as a weaver (*snuć opowieść/wątek/nić opowiadania*, lit. 'spin a story/motif/the thread of a story'), a cook (a text may be *pikantny* 'spicy', *smakowity* 'delicious', *niestrawny* 'unpalatable'), a builder (*plan/szkic tekstu* 'a plan/sketch of a text'; *piętra tekstu* 'several storeys of a text'; *budować/klecić tekst* 'to build/botch up a text'); a farmer or gardener (*tekst dojrzewa* 'a text ripens'; *pomysł kiełkuje* 'an idea sprouts'; *tekst jest owocem pracy* 'a text is the fruit of one's work'); an artist or a musician (*rama tekstu* 'the frame of a text'; *drugi plan tekstu* 'the background of a text'; *autor maluje coś w jakichś barwach* 'the author paints something in such and such colours'; *autor porusza czułą strunę* 'the author pulls a sensitive string'). A text may *ranić* 'hurt' and be *ostry* 'sharp' or *cięty* 'biting' – thus it may be conceptualised as an instrument or a weapon. Niebrzegowska-Bartmińska says:

> A survey of all metaphorical models clearly shows that metaphors are selective and concentrate on some characteristics at the expense of others. […] In all models, text is treated as the result of the activity of a given subject. (2007: 31)

Hence, metaphors select features from a rich, multiaspectual characterisation of text and 'profile' the concept (cf. chapter 8).

3.3 Grammar

The most stable, unquestionable basis for the reconstruction of linguistic worldview is grammar, uniform throughout a national language. The categories of person, number, gender, tense, mood or case are relatively easily observable and comparable (on the cross-cultural scale) mechanisms of the conceptualisation of reality. The conceptualisation is forced by the language system, though as all linguistic forms it can be used by the speaker in various ways, also consciously omitted or even contested.

Let me offer an example. In Polish inflectional morphology, in noun declensions, there exist the categories of masculinity and non-masculinity: the endings *-i* and *-owie* in Nom.Pl. occur with nouns referring to persons of male sex (*chłop-i* 'peasants', *pan-owie* 'gentlemen'), while the remaining nouns, i.e. referring to non-male persons and things, occur with a single ending *-y* (*kobiet-y* 'women', *kot-y* 'cats', *stoł-y* 'tables', *problem-y* 'problems'). The distinction also occurs in verbs in the past tense: *stal-i* 'they (male persons) stood' vs. *stał-y* 'they (non-male persons or things) stood'). The greater salience of reference to male persons is treated as a manifestation of the 'virilisation of Polish' (Baudouin de Courteney's expression) and is thought to be a remnant of male dominance in public life. The dominance is a tradition-sanctioned relic, recently contested as a manifestation of linguistic discrimination of women (Szpyra-Kozłowska and Karwatowska, 2005). Are the critics of the language-encoded 'male chauvinism' right? That reasoning is unsupported by data from folk varieties of Polish, in which the masculine gender is not distinguished: the same grammatical forms are used for men, women, animals and things: *chłopy orali/oraly* 'men ploughed', *baby doili/doily* 'women milked (the cows)' (cf. *EJP*, 1999: 324). This, however, has nothing to do with a change in the social position of women, whose status in peasant communities is much lower than that of men.

3.4 Texts

Linguistic research at large, including the reconstruction of linguistic worldview, is primarily based on analyses of texts, i.e. holistic messages with a topic, sender, receiver and a communicative context. Texts contain both systemic features and manifestations of social conventions (stylistic and generic norms), as well as individual features, which result from the creativity of the speaker. Let us begin with what I call 'stereotyped texts' (cf. chapter 2).

The shortest stereotyped texts are proverbs. They express the so called 'folk wisdom', general knowledge passed on to individual receivers by the community for pedagogical purposes. They tend to contain universal quantifiers, such as *every, no, always, never*, as is typical of stereotypes (cf. chapter 5). Proverbs are based on typical events and figures from the represented world, which allows one to use them as linguistic evidence in the reconstruction of the worldview.

The tendency to portray typical events and figures, characteristic of colloquial language, is elevated to the status of a rule also in other genres of folklore. This pertains to legends, which address the question of 'why something is what it is', cosmogonic myths, fables, anecdotes, songs and ritual texts, riddles, puzzles etc. Texts in these categories contain whole repetitive scenarios of behaviour and action, which correlate with the socially accepted roles, with what is expected and what may be breached. The scenarios can be recorded in the form of stereotypical motifs containing judgements about people, objects and events.[7] The motifs constitute ready-made material for reconstructing the linguistic and cultural picture, for compiling cognitive definitions. In this way motifs extracted from various genres of traditional texts are used in *SSSL*; in the same way as mythological messages are used in dictionaries of symbols.[8]

In authored rather than reproduced texts, the element of authorial creation is very strong,[9] so the texts require a special analysis, distinguishing what is communicated as a novelty and asserted from what has been used as a point of departure, the background, a hidden presupposition. The communicative strategy requires that novel information be conveyed (one usually apologises for platitudes). For the researcher of linguistic worldview it is the opposite: attention is paid to what in the utterance is treated as obvious, unquestionable, trivial or banal.

A special role in this context is played by coordinate contrastive clauses, clauses of concession, result or cause, introduced by the conjunctions and adverbs *but*, *so*, *because* or *therefore*: 'John is a father but he does not look after his children' (presupposition: fathers look after their children); 'Mikhail does not like music, though he comes from Ukraine' (presupposition: Ukrainians are music lovers); 'He got himself a dog, so he felt safer immediately' (presupposition: a dog gives its owner the feeling of safety); 'I told him everything frankly because I considered him a friend' (presupposition: a friend can be trusted).

3.5 'Ad-linguistic' data

A full reconstruction of linguistic worldview must also take into account yet another type of data, which I call 'ad-linguistic', composed of the socially entrenched, belief-based knowledge of the world, common to the speaker (sender) and the hearer (receiver). Without reference to this type of knowledge, normal communication or interpretation of utterances is impossible (Muszyński, 1988; Korżyk, 1999). The set of ad-linguistic data, relevant to the process of communication, also includes conventionalised patterns of behaviour. Regardless of the fact that speaking as such is behaviour and action (Austin, 1962), an important clue in interpreting verbal texts is the awareness of obligations, especially those obtaining in a given culture. For example, doubts as to a metaphorical or mythological understanding of sentences such as 'The sun is joyful', 'The stars look upon us', 'The heaven/sky is angry' or 'The earth gives birth' is decided by the knowledge of beliefs relating to the animistically understood nature and to the principles of behaviour with respect to it.[10] Let us take the heavenly bodies. In archaic folk tradition, one must behave towards them in the same way as one would towards living creatures: the earth must not be hit with a stick in spring, when it is pregnant with new life, the sun must not be pointed at, etc. Therefore, the sentences above have, for the members of the community in which they exist, a mythological, rather than a metaphorical, sense. It is the behaviour (obligations or prohibitions) that 'definitely interprets' the meanings of terms in the sense proposed by Charles Peirce.

3.6 Questionnaires

A distinct place in research on linguistic worldview is reserved for questionnaires. Open questions about the meanings of words and characteristics of objects are particularly valuable, but they are more difficult to interpret than 'closed' ones, which contain ready-made answers to choose from. Those are easier for the researcher to handle but pose a danger of creating artifacts.

The examples of home, mother, homeland or a German (discussed in later chapters) show that experimental (questionnaire-based) research gives access to the contemporary linguistic awareness of speakers, allows one to reveal more features attributed to the object, and indicates different degrees of entrenchment of specific features (manifested as different ranks in frequency lists). Systemic data, on the other hand, embrace well-entrenched, historical, sometimes frozen features, which, however, are not numerous. Results of questionnaires may diverge from systemic data but the two may certainly be reconciled. Indeed, they complement each other.

At the stage of statistical breakdown of questionnaire data, an important characteristic of meaning is manifested, namely its openness. For example, features attributed to a typical mother are indicated with different frequencies (from about 35% to a mere handful), which points not only to different degrees of their entrenchment but also to a lack of a clear threshold level below which a given feature is not included in the word's meaning as insignificant in the speakers' awareness. Is it 50%, 40% (Kapiszewski, 1978) or perhaps 20%? In closed questionnaires the percentage is higher; in open ones it is much lower.[11]

Two factors are worth mentioning here. First, rare or idiosyncratic answers may be very interesting from the cognitive perspective, as they may signal new, emerging linguistic tendencies. Second, if the rare answers are collected from large numbers of respondents and analysed collectively, they may indicate changes in the evaluation of the object or show otherwise hardly noticeable shifts in the object's linguistic profiling. This is exactly what we observed in our axiological questionnaires, consisting of a hundred questions each, administered in 1990 and 2000 to two thousand students in Lublin (results in Bartmiński, 2006a).

The fact that the results of questionnaires need not coincide with dictionary definitions or with phraseological analyses must not be taken, in the spirit of Kiklevich (2007), as an indication of flaws in the former. It may suggest that lexicographic definitions are imperfect (it is enough to compare definitions from various dictionaries) and should in fact be verified with respect to the more reliable questionnaire data (cf. Bartmiński, 2007b: 50–52).

4   A final word

The multitude of information available in the reconstruction of linguistic worldview may result in inconsistencies of the final picture. Does that mean, though, that one must narrow down the range of the linguistic material? Are we not dealing with a hidden, as yet unrecognised factor here? If judgements about the object, based on systemic, textual and questionnaire-derived data are incompatible or even contradictory, one should search for the cause of the status quo rather than rejecting the data of one type. At play may be a number of contextual factors, as well as the ambivalent nature of the object itself. Stanisław Jerzy Lec, a Polish aphorist, says: 'Proverbs contradict one another. That's why they are full of wisdom'.

A linguistic worldview is a subjective interpretation of reality, a 'second', cultural reality of sorts, different than the scientific picture of the world. It is relativised to the accepted system of values, viewpoint and perspective of the subject/conceptualiser (cf. chapters 4 and 7).

As a collection of linguistically-entrenched judgements, linguistic worldview can be reconstructed on the basis of three types of data: systemic, conventionalised and textual. Questionnaires obviously provide access to systemic features but also contain a number of individual, idiosyncratic characteristics. Although 'commissioned' and 'solicited', they have the qualities of ordinary texts.

The global linguistic worldview includes stereotypes. These are collective images of people, places and events, containing features treated as 'normal' and typically attributed to those objects and events (cf. chapter 5). The content and cognitive structure of stereotypes can be systematically captured in the cognitive definition (chapter 6). Linguistic worldview is diversified for style and genre, and at the level of discourse it is subjected to profiling depending on the intentions of the speaking subject (chapter 8). Rather than focusing on individual, idiosyncratic usages, it is more important for the reconstruction of linguistic worldview to capture the regularities surfacing in several examples of usage.

Finally, the linguistic worldview conception can play a major role in comparative research, to which issue I devote chapter 17.

Notes

1   The volume contains attempts to define the conception (Renata Grzegorczykowa, Jolanta Maćkiewicz, Jerzy Bartmiński), to describe the role of metaphors and phraseological units in the reconstruction of the worldview (Ryszard Tokarski, Anna Pajdzińska), as well as specific, methodologically close analyses of elements of the Polish linguistic worldview: work (Małgorzata Mazurkiewicz-Brzozowska), river (Ewa Masłowska), island (Jolanta Maćkiewicz), ditch (Jan Adamowski), stars (Stanisława Niebrzegowska). Janusz Anusiewicz surveys the history of the idea in German linguistics and philosophy.

2   The first attempt to describe the ultimate model of the dictionary entry is Bartmiński and Niebrzegowska (1994).

3   Cf. Greek *demo-* 'build' and the English *demiurge* 'builder; artificer'. More detailed information in chapter 12.

4   I argue for the linguistic significance of cultural connotations in Bartmiński (1984).

5   The dictionary also mentions other names: *Świtalna Gwiazda* 'The Sunrise Star', *Zorza Ranna* 'The Morning Light', *Gwiazda Zachodowa* 'The Sunset Star', *Mrocznica* 'The One at Dusk', *Pierwsza Gwiazda* 'The First Star', *Gwiadza Bydlęca/Zwierzęca/Zającowa/Wilcza* 'The Animal/Hare/Wolf Star' – its appearance marked the time when wild animals began to prey or when domestic animals came to the watering place.

6   Such is the view of Brückner (*SEJP*, 1927); Vasmer also thinks it possible (*REW*, 1950–1958); the entries for *netopyr', upyr'*) but Boryś (2005) doubts it.

7   Niebrzegowska-Bartmińska (2007) analyses magic spells, carols and fables in these terms.

8   This pertains above all to stereotyped texts but not necessarily so – also to one-off texts (for also there one may observe how the object functions in collections and oppositions, while semantic connotations are invoked covertly as presuppositions).

9   Although creativity is a distinctive feature of poetic texts, the latter do not lack what is entrenched in the language system (Pajdzińska and Tokarski, 1996).

10   The sentence 'The sun is joyful' is analysed in Niebrzegowska (1986).

11   In open questionnaires the highest indications oscillate around 20%; in Fleischer's half-open questionnaires (Fleischer, 2003) from 20% to 50%.

4   Values as the foundation of linguistic worldview

1   Two conceptions of linguistic axiology

Two conceptions can be identified in publications on values in language, as well as on the range and methods of inquiry into linguistic axiology: I will call them the residual and the holistic conception. According to the former, values are a part of language as a distinct inventory of linguistic facts; according to the latter, they permeate the whole of language. The two views are anchored, respectively, to the structural and cognitive views on language. With some oversimplification, they may be associated in Polish linguistics with the names of Jadwiga Puzynina and Tomasz P. Krzeszowski.

Puzynina (1992, 1997) starts from the assumption that the linguist-axiologist should be concerned with 'how and within what range values are expressed by the units of the language system' (Puzynina, 1989: 185). Specifically, she proposes to address the following:

(1) What is valuation? (2) Who performs the act? (3) What is being valuated? (4) For whom is something a value? (5) Is a given word purely (primarily) evaluative or is it only secondarily evaluative? (6) What category of values does the word concern? (7) Is the word emotionally marked? (8) Is it marked in its intensity? (9) If it is secondarily evaluative, is the evaluative component definitional or connotative? (Puzynina, 1992: 9).

In a sense, values are separate from language. They may be 'expressed at the level of the linguistic code, the level of written text and the level of living speech. […] The means of expressing valuation in the code are the poorest, since they are conventionalised and purely linguistic', while textual means, being aided by the verbal and situational context, are richer (Puzynina, 1992: 61).

Puzynina uses an extended typology of values related to Max Scheler's (1913–1916) work. She regards transcendental and cognitive values as the highest in the hierarchy, while the values of vitality and sensation are the lowest. She grounds her definitions of values and evaluative lexemes (a lie, manipulation, tolerance etc.) on Apresjan's theory of meaning, identifying definitional, 'necessary and sufficient' characteristics plus connotative, usage-based ones. Valuation may be a part of definition, but it more often appears as a 'connotation' accompanying meaning and belongs to the pragmatics rather than the semantics of language signs. Puzynina's analyses of value terms are based on de Saussure's classic distinction between system and usage as well as on the structural and functional conception of meaning. Some of her later work, however, dealing, e.g., with truth, tolerance or friendship (Puzynina, 1997), is inspired by cognitivist views.

Tomasz P. Krzeszowski's 'axiological semantics', based on the work of American cognitive linguists such as George Lakoff and Mark Johnson, assumes a closer connection between language and values. Following Osgood (1980) and Suchecki (1983), Krzeszowski claims that emotions and values determine information processing and conceptual structure (1997: 9) and that 'values constitute an indispensable component of meaning description' understood as a conceptualisation of reality (Krzeszowski, 1999: 18). The most important element in Krzeszowski's theory is the claim that the 'axiological parameter', i.e. the good–bad opposition, is all-important, instilled already in preconceptual image schemas. These schemas are based on the orientational oppositions up-down, front-back, left-right, as well as on a small number of basic oppositions such as part-whole, centre-periphery, source-path-goal etc. In the domain of values Krzeszowski distinguishes two coordinates: horizontal (a scale of positive and negative values) and vertical, hierarchical, based on the experience of reality as a Great Chain of Being, in which God and people are at the 'top', whereas animals, plants and non-organic beings are at 'lower' levels (1997: 64).

Furthermore, Krzeszowski rejects the distinction between denotation and connotation and assumes that 'all properties characterising the 'emotive' or 'connotative' aspects of word meanings must be taken into account in Gestalts which make up the Idealised Cognitive Models relative to which, in turn, words are defined' (Krzeszowski, 1994: 30). Accepting the 'experiential myth', he assumes that somatic, sensorimotor values are basic and that bodily experiences underlie both concrete and abstract concepts. It is that kind of experience, Krzeszowski claims, that via metaphorical extensions gives rise to abstract meanings, including ethical evaluative concepts.

2   Values and language: the range and type of relations

By values I mean that which in the light of language and culture people consider precious. I do not wish to engage here in detailed typologies of values, distinctions between absolute and subjective values or between declared and actually professed ones. What I have in mind are characteristics of things but also things themselves, including concepts, states and situations, attitudes and behaviours, which function as 'guiding ideas' motivating people's actions. Thus, my understanding of values is that of folk philosophy.[1]

I would like to hypothesise here that linguistic worldview is derived from the overtly or covertly assumed system of values. Values are connected with the viewpoint and perspective in seeing the world (cf. chapter 7 for a more detailed explication of these terms). They guide the construction of the image of reality by the experiencer and conceptualiser, i.e. by an individual or a community of speakers; they integrate the tradition-sanctioned worldview of that community. In effect, values constitute the cultural and social identity of the speaker.

Many scholars have pointed out the intrinsic and global connection between natural language and values. Before Krzeszowski, this view was most fully expressed by Michał Głowiński:

> Valuation and axiology is a stable component of language. When I speak, I do not only speak about facts or express my views – I also capture them in evaluative schemas. I need not overtly mention the evaluative aspect but I do evoke it, subconsciously and inadvertently. It is so because the matter which I use to build utterances (words, fixed expressions) is permeated with values or at the very least is not neutral. (Głowiński, 1986: 180)

Contributing to the philosophical discussion on constructing a value-free (*wertfreie*) language, Głowiński concluded that this is impossible (Pawłowski, 1978: 6).

This, however, does not mean that everything in language is axiologically marked in the same way. The question is in what way, to what extent (overtly or covertly), and at which level of linguistic organisation, values are present. Various answers have been given so far.

For example, some approaches have highlighted the differences in the axiological load of different language styles. Valuation, especially of the emotional type, is a significant feature of everyday behaviour and colloquial language, while official, scientific or formal contexts are supposedly value-free. This view is sensible only if valuation is treated in the emotional sense. But what about intellectual valuation? The scientific style, unemotional in its nature, follows its own system of values: cognitive values, linked with the conception of the truth, but also heuristic, praxeological, moral and sometimes aesthetic values (cf. Gajda, 2001). Similarly, the 'dry', impersonal style of official documents, which does not allow for an expressive tone, tends towards precision and is based on such values as justice and social order between citizens or members of an institution (Wojtak, 2001).

I would like to consider what it means that 'language is permeated with values', as there exist all-encompassing and multifarious links between the two.

In the title of her major work (as well as in her other writings), Puzynina (1992) uses the synthetic formula 'the language of values'. This formula is both handy and ambiguous; one is tempted to say: it is handy *because* it is intentionally ambiguous. In my view, the expression refers to at least three different types of relation between language and values, which can be captured in the form of the following formulae: 'language is a *tool* of valuation', 'language is a *source of information* about the values accepted by its speakers', and 'language is a *carrier* (*substrate*) of values'.

First of all, then, language may be treated as a tool for valuation, for it is in language that one can find a rich repertoire of useful evaluative expressions. This kind of relation is studied most frequently. Attention is usually drawn to the fact that valuation is achieved through the use of words but also through grammar, text structure and phonological features. Also, the explicitness of valuation is graded. The distinction between explicit and implicit, overt and covert valuation, is a significant one. I will return to this problem below.

Second, one may ask what language can tell us about values, what information about them can be extracted from language. This approach is based on the assumption that values are somehow 'stored' in language, in the meanings of words (words are usually mentioned first) and in their combinations (collocations and phraseological units), as well as in texts, especially in stereotyped texts, such as proverbs. The final result of this kind of research may be a reconstruction of the *system of values* transmitted via language, at a given stage of its development, in texts of specific styles and genres: colloquial, journalistic, essayistic and political. Values are always *someone's* values, the ultimate reference point being *Homo loquens*, who conceptualises and evaluates reality in text and talk, thus revealing his or her mentality.

Finally, one may investigate language from the point of view of what values are attributed to or realised in it as a substrate, what values are manifested in language as such, predicated about language and its textual manifestations. Language is described as 'clear', 'precise', 'beautiful', 'elegant', 'dignified', 'fluent', or as 'vague', 'ugly', 'mediocre', 'aggressive', 'obscene' etc. This approach is characteristic of linguists who observe the development of national languages, evaluate the efficiency of linguistic communication and codify linguistic norms. For example, Witold Doroszewski views clarity as the most important value, the foundation of the truthfulness and beauty of language; Puzynina attributes importance to its reliability and truthfulness (1997: 123), Andrzej Markowski to adequacy and functionality (*NSPP*, 1999). Poets, such as Juliusz Słowacki, Czesław Miłosz or Stanisław Barańczak, value a language that is flexible but also concise and full of content. For some others, it is beauty (melody, imagery) that is more precious. And so on.

Each of these three conceptions opens up the possibility of a different research programme. In anthropological-cultural research on language, which is mainly concerned with the mentality and cultural formation of a given speech community, language is treated as a source of knowledge about values, judgements, cultural patterns and ideals important for that community.

The most useful information about values comes from their names, which function as 'cultural keywords' (Wierzbicka, 1992, 1997, 2006), 'leading words' (Pisarek, 2002), 'collective symbols' (Fleischer, 1995) or 'leading ideas' in the form of triads of the type 'good–truth–beauty' (Greek philosophy, then Christianity), 'faith–hope–love' (the Bible), 'liberty–equality–fraternity' (the French revolution), 'God–honour–homeland' (Polish national spirit) etc. Such keywords have become the subject of numerous semantic studies based on various analytical methods (Zaron, 1985; Puzynina, 1992, 1993, 1997; Abramowicz and Karolak, 1991; Wierzbicka, 1992, 1997, 2006 and others). Terms of valuation are often used in sociological studies on hierarchies of values in various social groups. An important direction of research is the investigation of changes in the semantics of (anti-)value names such as dignity and honour, tolerance, freedom, liberalism, work, strike, unemployment, career, success, solidarity, justice, competition, society, nation, authority, state, region, regionalism, homeland, patriotism, sovereignty, 'Europeanness' or globalisation.[2]

3   Overt valuation and its criteria: an assumed ideal of a person

Overt means of valuation are relatively well-identified. The basic means of positive and negative linguistic valuation are words, of which many are 'purely evaluative' or 'primarily evaluative' (Puzynina). They are characterised by a global contrast: good–bad, positive–negative. In contemporary Polish, the contrast is asymmetrical in the sense that there are more negative than positive evaluative terms. This phenomenon is not restricted to Polish, although a rise in criticism and self-criticism on the part of Poles in the 1990s, both in journalism and literature, makes them more conspicuous in this respect than their neighbours. Especially noticeable is the negative evaluation of people, verging on abuse (cf. Tokarski, 1990; Grochowski, 1995; Kamińska-Szmaj, 2001; Stomma, 2000).

Valuation above all has an ethical aspect (e.g. honest–dishonest), but its nature can also be social (friendly–unfriendly), epistemological (true–false), hedonistic (pleasant–unpleasant) or aesthetic (beautiful–ugly). Lexical-semantic fields of these categories are built from antonymic pairs of names referring to values and anti-values: good–bad/evil, love–hate, justice–injustice, fidelity–infidelity/betrayal, freedom–captivity, hope–despair, truth–falsehood/lie, pleasure–distress, beauty–ugliness. The fact that these terms necessarily function in oppositions may be treated as the criterion for distinguishing the set of canonical values (although antonymy in language is not only used for valuation) from a broader set of names for 'good things' and 'valuable entities'. A reconstruction of linguistic worldview must address the criteria underlying the evaluative lexicon and the hierarchy of those criteria.

For linguistic axiology, it is interesting to investigate the terms used in reference to 'more' and 'less' important people, especially the terms of abuse used in arguments. Depending on whether communication is private or official, some behaviour is treated as normal while other behaviour is not. On the basis of diction one is able to reconstruct the assumed ideal of a person.

Tokarski (1990) shows that colloquial Polish expressions of the type *zwierzę nie człowiek* '(he is) an animal, not a person', *Azjata* 'an Asian', *heretyk* 'a heretic', *baba nie chłop* '(he is) a woman, not a man', *zniewieścialec* 'an effeminate man' are based on valuation performed from the point of view of, respectively, a human being, a European, a Catholic, a knight and a male. A closer look at the semantics of these expressions reveals that the criteria used by the speaker are moral or social. The underlying folk ethics favours integrity, kindness towards others, resourcefulness, fitness and high intellectual capacities, while it rejects insincerity (*szuja* 'scoundrel'), gain at the expense of others (*oszust* 'cheat', *naciągacz* 'con man', *efekciarz* 'show-off'), stupidity (*jełop* 'blockhead'), and naivety and incapability (*naiwniak* 'gull', *frajer* 'sucker') (cf. also chapter 7).

The language of Polish politics of the 1990s, which readily resorts to terms of abuse of the type *aferzysta* 'swindler', *oszust* 'cheat', *maniak* 'maniac', *aparatczyk* 'apparatchik', *beton partyjny* 'party hardliner', *oszołom* 'fanatic, crank', *kretyn* 'idiot', *krętacz* 'cheater', *nieudacznik* 'loser', *rżnąć głupa* 'to play idiot' etc. (cf. Kamińska-Szmaj 2001), discloses the ideal of an honest, intelligent and sensible person. However, terms of abuse quickly 'desemanticise', lose descriptive content and become monstrously expressive in the negative emotional sense. They become tools for destroying the opponent (cf. Stomma, 2000).

4   Valuation in symbolic contexts. Linguistic stereotypes

There are certain speech genres whose major *raison d'être* is valuation. In mass, popular culture these genres are the dream book and the horoscope. Research on folk interpretations of dreams in Polish has shown that dreams (objects, events and their properties) are evaluated relative to the basic good–bad dichotomy, superimposed on the characteristics stereotypically attributed to the images. Generally speaking, whatever is young, bright, clear, fat, ripe, complete, clothed, raw and made of metal is explained as a sign of health, young age, wealth, good harvest, harmony, visit of welcome guests, happiness and joy; whatever is old, dark, dirty, thin, unripe, fragmented, naked, cooked and made of paper is thought to signify bad things, such as disease, death, old age, poverty, bad harvest, disagreement, an unwelcome guest, unhappiness or sorrow. The most highly cherished values are life, health and joy (Niebrzegowska, 1996b and c).

Axiological interpretations of dreams are a perfect example of covert valuation, hidden in a peripheral sphere of meaning, e.g. in words such as *oko* 'eye', *głowa* 'head', *chleb* 'bread', *miód* 'honey'; *koń* 'horse', *osioł* 'donkey, ass', *świnia* 'pig, swine'; *ojciec* 'father', *matka* 'mother', *dom* 'house/home', *wieś* 'country(side)', *region* 'region'; *bajka* 'fairy tale', *poezja* 'poetry', *gawęda* 'a short story of free structure'; *roszczenia* 'claims', *strajk* 'strike', *kariera* 'career' etc. A good example of the axiological aspect of primarily descriptive terms are denominal adjectives of the type *chłopski* 'peasant', *pański* 'lordly', *mieszczański* 'middle-class, bourgeois'; *psi* 'canine, dog's', *koci* 'feline, cat's', *wilczy* 'lupine, wolf's'; *drewniany* 'wooden', *żelazny* 'iron', *złoty* 'gold; golden' etc., which activate peripheral semantic features present in the stereotypes of, respectively, a peasant, lord, middle-class city dweller, dog, cat, wolf, tree, iron and gold. The purely relational adjectival meaning 'pertaining to a given thing, characteristic of that thing' is usually superimposed by qualitative features, resulting from the stereotypical functioning of a given thing with clearly evaluative elements: *chłopski rozum*, lit. 'peasant's mind' is not so much 'a mind characteristic of peasants' but 'healthy, sober, non-speculative, free from doubt'; *pański gest* 'lordly gesture' is not only one characteristic of a lord or master but one that is magnanimous and generous; *mieszczański* does not only mean 'such as is characteristic of middle-class city dwellers' but 'materialistic, conservative' etc. The valuation may be positive or negative, depending on the context: *wiejskie maniery*, lit. 'countryside manners', are manners judged low by the speaker, while *wiejski serek* 'country cheese', *wiejskie masło* 'country butter' or *wiejska kiełbasa* 'country sausage' are judged positively by contemporary ecologically minded consumers. Collocations such as *drewniany stół* 'wooden table' and *drewniany język* (lit. 'wooden language') or *psi węch* 'dog-like smell' and *psia pogoda* 'lousy weather' (lit. 'dog's weather') are also located on the plus–minus axis in a similar manner. Inspired by the work of Hilary Putnam (1975), who introduced the stereotypical component to word meaning and the concept of stereotype to the inventory of basic concepts of linguistic semantics, dictionary definitions only just begin to take note of taxonomically 'redundant', descriptive and/or evaluative features, traditionally called 'cultural connotations'.

5   The axiology of space

Stereotypical images with a strong axiological load can easily be found in the realm of geographical names (Adamowski, 1999). A new mental map of the world (Chlebda, 2002) is constructed not only along physical and geographical but also axiological axes. Especially the two oppositions fundamental to Polish culture, i.e. Europe–Asia and West–East, clearly receive evaluative markings.

The image of Europe and the relationship between Europe and Poland is highly idealistic and based on social aspirations. The dominating feeling is that of admiration of the Western standard of living, many Poles' dream and desire. Anti-European slogans did not gain social acceptance during the 2000 presidential elections, nor are they widely accepted now, despite the views promoted by 'Euro-skeptics'. The clearest manifestation of the idealistic understanding of Europe (which, incidentally, contrasts with the much less enthusiastic, and sometimes downright critical attitude of e.g. such Czech politicians as Vaclav Havel or Vaclav Klaus) was given as if 'on the behalf' of Poles by the Polish politician Władysław Bartoszewski in his 1995 speech in the German parliament in Bonn:

> The term *Europe* must not be understood in a purely geographical sense…
> [It] acquired a civilizational meaning and became a collective symbol of
> fundamental principles and values. Europe above all means individual freedom
> and human rights, political and economic. It symbolizes a democratic and civic
> order. It stands for a law-respecting state. It means effective economy, based on
> individual entrepreneurship and initiative. Simultaneously, it is a reflection on
> human fate and moral order, deriving from Judeo-Christian tradition. It is also
> the everlasting beauty of culture. (*Gazeta Wyborcza*, no. 101, 1995)

This view of Europe differs from the institutionalised conception entertained in German and the geographical conception typical of Russian public discourse (Zinken, 2002). The West remains for Poles the civilisational and cultural centre, the mainstay of stability, democracy and welfare – as opposed to the East, associated with aggressiveness and poverty (Bartmiński, 2001a, 2007a).

6   Changes in contemporary national stereotypes

Changes in some of the national stereotypes, their cognitive content and evaluation are linked with those in the official political orientation of Poland after 1989. I will limit my comments to a few most conspicuous examples.

In the social system of values, Western-type values of pragmatism and consumerism are on the increase. In the realm of linguistic stereotypes, the stereotype of a German evolves towards a more positive image (cf. chapter 14), that of a Russian towards a more negative one. The stereotype of an American is unchangeably highly positive. What do Poles like and what do they dislike in other nationalities? The dominant feature in the Polish image of a German is the latter's diligence and wealth, although Germans are still seen by the sociable Poles as haughty and conceited. To younger generations of Poles, Germans are rich and educated Europeans, features especially highly evaluated in Poland's new reality. Russians are, in contrast, perceived as slovenly, brutal and aggressive: this is the Polish image of an Asian (Bartmiński, 1995, 1997). Americans are perceived as rich, enterprising, self-confident and easygoing, thus correlating well with the system of values dominant among the younger generation of Poles. The adjectives 'German', 'Russian' and 'American' covertly inherit those positive or negative connotations, even though the connotations may not be formally entrenched.

Comparisons of Polish and German stereotypes of a Pole, Czech and Russian reveal the subjective nature of valuation. Polish students strongly contrast the characteristics of a Czech and Russian, e.g. with respect to the features 'tidy/slovenly', 'rich/poor', 'well-mannered/ill-mannered', which partially results from more general oppositions, extremely significant for the Polish perception of the world in terms of East–West or Asia–Europe. German students, in turn, attribute many common features to all three nationalities as Slavs, representatives of the East. The Polish image of a Czech is more positive than that of a German: Czechs are seen as more Western or European. In contrast, Russians are deemed more Eastern or Asian (in the negative sense) (Bartmiński, 1997).

In questionnaire-based sociological research on stereotypes, a standard element is usually a general question about the acceptance of different nationalities. Such was for example the nature of the 2002 TNS OBOP (Centre for Investigating Public Opinion) questionnaire concerning the Polish image of a Jew, in which the major generalising category was 'antisemitism', i.e. an attitude of rejection (Sułek and Kublik, 2002).

This is a gross oversimplification. It is a shame, for example, that no effort was made to investigate the attitude of acceptance or philosemitism, more and more popular especially among younger Poles. If in research on stereotypes one goes onto a more detailed level and asks about specific features and their valuation, it turns out that the same typical representative of a given group manifests ambivalent valuation: acceptance in some respects and rejection in others. A German, for example, is disliked by Poles in the social sense as someone withdrawn and conceited but admired for aspects of everyday behaviour, such as diligence and punctuality. A Russian is judged negatively for aggressiveness and desire to dominate but positively for liking company, openness and musical talent. The Polish attitude towards Jews is similarly ambivalent: they are seen in a negative light as false and dishonest in trade, but in a positive light for their attachment to religion, their intelligence and entrepreneurship. Ambivalence is also found in the self-stereotypical image of Poles, who evaluate themselves positively as courageous, proud, intelligent, educated and wise but much more critically for their laziness, extravagance or unmethodical conduct (Bartmiński, 1995).

7 Two planes of valuation: speaker vs. participant

The evaluating subject may be situated at different semantic levels of the utterance: interactive and/or object-oriented. The subject may be the speaker or a participant of the event being presented. Let us consider the following cases. 'To owe something to someone' (Pol. *zawdzięczać coś komuś*) means 'to be in a relationship to someone such that someone has done something good for us and we are ready to do something good for them'. The axiological element is prototypically present both at the level of the consciousness of the speaker and the participant of the event (the same as the speaker or not): 'John owes his post to Smith', 'I owe my promotion to him'. The result of an act performed by X and obliging Y to gratitude is viewed by the speaker Z as something valuable for Y and similarly evaluated by Z. This convergent positive evaluation of an event by a participant (Y) and the speaker (Z) is obligatory.[3]

However, valuation from the point of view of the speaker (Z) need not oblige the participant Y, who may not agree with the evaluative judgement of the speaker but be an ingrate instead: 'Children owe their good financial position to their parents but do not appreciate it', 'The athletes voted against their coach, although they owed so much to him'. Even in these sentences, however, the speaker assumes the existence of an objective obligation, independent of the subjective judgement of the participant.

The difference between valuations of the speaker and those of a participant in the event is particularly conspicuous when the two stand in contrast to each other. When someone uses the verbs *schlebiać* 'flatter', *podlizywać się* 'crawl', *przymilać się* 'fawn on somebody', *kadzić* 'butter up somebody' or *wynosić pod niebiosa* 'praise somebody to the skies', the speaker distances him- or herself from the positive valuations, attitudes or behaviours of the participant and views them negatively. A similarly negative, distancing position may be assumed when the participant evaluates someone else negatively; cf. the expressions *oczerniać* 'slander', *szkalować* 'vilify', *obrzucać błotem* 'fling mud at somebody' etc.

The speaker can negatively evaluate the behaviour of a participant when objectively existing values are assumed, valid regardless of the participant's attitude. This understanding of values underlies the concepts of betrayal and fidelity (Bednarek, 1996): 'The politician betrayed public interest for his own private interest', 'The representatives of the company betrayed it'.

8 Values in conceptualisation and profiling

Values steer the process of categorisation. Herbs, corn or weeds are distinguished within the world of plants as sets with a special (instrumental) value for people's lives, since they can be used as medication or food. Similarly, an instrumental, functional and ultimately axiological character is present in the concepts such as 'toy', 'tool', 'vehicle', 'weapon', 'clothing' or 'decoration', whose definitions take into account the purpose for which they have been made (as in Wierzbicka's approach). Human action is steered by values. Values, then, are active in establishing the basis for conceptualisation, which is reflected in the process of defining through the choice of the hyperonymic *genus proximum*. A bluebottle may be treated as a plant, weed or flower, depending on the axiologically motivated point of view (Bartmiński, 1993a). The preliminary stage of categorisation determines the choice of other features defining the object. In this approach values determine the conceptualisation of the object, its image, and so are situated in a way at the meta-linguistic level.

The values accepted by the speaker determine the functioning of base concepts at the level of discourse; their profiling is connected with the style and genre of the utterance, and so ultimately with the speaker's communicative intention. The speaker's communicative intention, in turn, is always connected with his or her values. In chapter 13, devoted to the concept of 'homeland', I show how this is realised in practice.

Clues about values and the relationships between them are also manifested in the order in which words appear in expressions and in whole texts. Jolanta Szpyra (1996) conducted an interesting survey of word combinations of the type *za i przeciw* 'for and against', *tu i tam* 'here and there', *dziś i jutro* 'today and tomorrow', *żyć nie umierać* 'to live rather than die', in which the ordering of the elements is fixed and the first element tends to be more important. A systematic analysis of examples from three languages, Polish, English and Hungarian, has revealed a system of values underlying these expressions. The values are: life (*sprawa życia lub śmierci* 'a matter of life and death', *człowiek i świat* 'man and the world'), masculinity (*mąż i żona* 'husband and wife', *dziad i baba* 'old man (grandfather) and old woman (grandmother)', adulthood (*ojciec i syn* 'father and son'), spatial and temporal proximity (*z kraju i ze świata* 'home and world (news)', *teraz i zawsze* 'now and forever'), being positive or affirmative (*tak czy nie* 'yes or no', *za i przeciw* 'for and against', *blaski i cienie* 'pros and cons') and others. The author sums up her observations in the following way:

> This is a world based on traditional characteristics of European societies, such as their patriarchal nature (with certain elements of gallantry towards women), the dominant position of parents over children or of older people over younger people. In the centre of that world is a human being, its most important component, the source of strength and action, bringing the rest of the world, both animals and inanimate beings, into subjection. (Szpyra, 1996: 70)

The principle of axiological dominance for the first element is with a fair degree of consistency present in folk texts, which as a product of communal creativity reflect more general regularities of texts and worldviews. For example, one of the most popular songs performed at a Polish folk wedding is one in which the young bride bids farewell to her home and family. From the axiological point of view it appears to be important who is addressed and in what order: the father, the mother, the brother, the sister. The sequence reflects the family hierarchy accepted in that society (Niebrzegowska-Bartmińska, 2007: 379).

Another axiologically loaded compositional schema is based on the conception of end-focus. For example, in Polish and Ukrainian folk New-Year wishing songs there is the motif of the beloved one, praised for doing something that the mother, father, brother or sister did not do, but the beloved, being the most important person, is mentioned last in the enumeration (Bartmiński, 1989b; Niebrzegowska-Bartmińska, 2007: 381–382; Dey, 1978). A valuation-based hierarchical arrangement is found in official style (e.g. in welcoming speeches at meetings) and obviously in liturgical texts (the Father, the Son, and the Holy Spirit; Jesus, Mary, Joseph; the apostles and the martyrs), which should perhaps be treated as the prototypical case.

9   Sources of values: only sensual or also cultural?

Let me finally cast some doubt on the idea that values have a somatic basis. In Polish linguistics the somatic conception is most strongly formulated by Krzeszowski, who claims that plus–minus valuation is already present in preconceptual image schemas, on which the whole conceptual system is founded. This 'preconceptual bodily experience underlies material (specific) concepts directly and abstract concepts indirectly, via metaphorical extension. In this way abstract ideas are grounded in and motivated by bodily experience' (Krzeszowski, 1994: 31). Furthermore, values, similarly to other components of meaning, derive from the human experience of reality so that axiology, just like semantics, grows out of the experience of reality (Krzeszowski, 1997: 20). 'Experience' is understood here as 'everyday', 'bodily' experience. The author refers to David Levin's work in psychology, who had noticed that:

> [t]he ethical notions of uprightness and fallenness, together with their psychological correlates, pride and guilt, are existential understandings *grounded* in the child's experiencing of the step-by-step learning which is involved in the ability to stand up (right) and walk forward (into the future) without losing a basic balance, stumbling and falling (Levin, 1985: 241, quoted in Krzeszowski, 1997: 112).

This approach, although convincingly supported, does not take into account two important problems. First, it seems dubious whether the elementary existential experience of a human being could be reduced to mere experience of bodily functions, without regard for the psychological aspect of the mother–child relationship. The relationship leads to bonds of a social and cultural nature. Krzeszowski himself, when studying the source domains of biblical metaphors (or rather, ethical ones) mentions social phenomena of trade and law, rather than somatic ones. When contemporary Russian, German and Polish journalists describe the process of 'Europisation', they use the image of the house/home as the source metaphor (Zinken, 2002), which is a psychosocial as well as a physical, spatial reality (more on this in chapter 12).

Second, not all elementary directional and spatial oppositions, taken by Krzeszowski as basic, can in their axiological functions be derived from somatically based valuation. Although the positive valuation of 'up' and 'front' may well be motivated by the orientation and functioning of the human body, the third important opposition, that of 'left'–'right', does not yield to this simple sensorimotor interpretation. The purely biological basis would rather point to the left side as positive: the side of the heart. It seems that one should accept the views of those authors who see in this opposition a certain socially entrenched cultural convention (Ivanov and Toporov, 1965, Dukova, 1992). A significant percentage of people are born with a propensity to use the left hand, right-handedness being imposed by culture. On a higher plane, valuation of the political left and right in public discourse, not only in Poland (cf. Bartmiński, 1991c), may be a good example of the cultural factor dominating over the somatic one (more in chapter 15).

Notes

1   According to Puzynina, 'values [...] always concern the most generally understood characteristics, states and behaviours of entities, obviously including people. [...] In the language of predicate and argument semantics, valuation in its primary sense is always a higher-order predication, predication with an event-type argument' (Puzynina, 1989: 194). This type of value is situated at a very high level of abstraction. However, Puzynina does not reject the colloquial understanding of values. She writes: 'There is an enormous scale of what people accept as or sense to be values. A value for us is above all the subject of evaluated features or behaviours; therefore we say that God, a person, home, a friend or a car are values. If we treat an object or a person as a value, their parts also become valued (the doorstep, someone's eyes, the car's lights), either because they have their own positive features or because they signal the valuable object, or simply because they are a part of or connected with that object (as in the case of souvenirs). Also people who bring about positively valued states are values or anti-values: a doctor, teacher or priest. Finally, the place and time associated with positive feelings may also become a value: one's home, country, childhood, youth, holidays etc. In this way values radiate onto the world around us' (Puzynina, 1989 JAK: 194–195). I use these observations to build my conception of axiological research in anthropological linguistics, where folk, everyday thinking (and style) are more important than scientific, scholarly or professional thinking (and style).

2   Longitudinal questionnaire-based research on terms of valuation shows that despite political changes, the semantics of value names remain stable (cf Fleischer, 1995; Bartmiński, 2006a).

3   It is also possible to fill the position of the object with an anti-value (*Zawdzięczam mu moją klęskę/bankructwo* 'I owe my failure/bankruptcy to him'). Divergent values are at play and as a result irony arises. The verb *zawdzięczać* may also be said to change its meaning into purely causative, i.e. to undergo 'deaxiologization'. In contemporary Polish the phenomenon is often found in the preposition *dzięki* (*czemuś*) 'thanks to (something)', e.g. in the following sentence, usually deemed ungrammatical: *Dzięki chorobie nie uczestniczył w rajdzie* 'Thanks to his illness he did not participate in the race'. A wider context, though, may cause further reevaluation by attributing a positive value to the consequences of the event spoken of: *Dzięki chorobie nie uczestniczył w rajdzie i uniknął nieszczęśliwego wypadku* 'Thanks to his illness he did not participate in the race and escaped a bad accident'.

5   The stereotype as an object of linguistic description

1   A few questions

The contemporary concept of stereotype is interdisciplinary. Introduced by Walter Lippman in 1922 (cf. Lippmann, 1961 [1922]), developed in sociology and social psychology, it has also been analysed from the point of view of communication (Bartoszyński, 1971), history of literature and culture (cf. Bystroń, 1924; Kot, 1955) or the philosophy of language (Putnam, 1975; Schaff, 1978). It is paradoxical that although scholars have generally been in agreement about the importance of stereotypes for language, they have not devoted too much time and attention to this issue.[1] This restraint or unwillingness may be explained in two ways. First, if research on stereotypes entails the investigation of repeatable, predictable human actions regulated by 'hidden' systems, then research on the structure of language deals with stereotypes by definition. Second, there is a widespread assumption that linguistic semantics should concentrate solely on the system of language and not on additional, 'superfluous' features or meanings. But in fact the issues associated with the concept of stereotype extend beyond the repeatability and functionality of language units and cannot be properly described in terms of structuralist constructs and methods.

I suggest that in order to study stereotypes in a systematic manner, a linguist must answer the following questions:

i)   What is, linguistically speaking, a stereotype? To what extent is it a matter of the system (competence) and to what extent of speech (performance)? How does it relate the norm to usage (in Coşeriu's understanding), how does it provide an interface between the possibilities of the linguistic system and their specific manifestations in the sociologically and culturally determined speech event?

ii)   How do stereotypes relate to content and form?

iii) How do they correspond to such aspects of lexical meaning as 'sense' and 'denotation'?[2]

iv)   What role do they play in the process of communication and, more generally, how do they connect to the functions of speaking and language use as a whole?

v)   In what language varieties and styles are stereotypes especially common and why (the colloquial or formal style, the journalese)? What styles do not admit stereotypes (scientific)?

vi)   What groups of lexis are stereotypes linked with? Are these only names of people or also other names?

vii) What are the linguistic exponents of stereotypes in text, i.e. how can stereotypes be identified and described? If, as assumed in the semantic conception of the stereotype, not all of its components are revealed, what methods can be used to investigate and describe them? What makes them indispensable in linguistic analysis?

viii) What methods can be used to establish the content of stereotypes?

2 Sociological conceptions of the stereotype

Questions about the nature and function of stereotypes have mainly appeared in work on the sociology, psychology and philosophy of language. These questions have been answered in various ways depending on whether stereotypes were understood in the social, psychological or epistemological sense.

In his pioneering book *Public Opinion*, Walter Lippmann (1961 [1922]) views stereotypes as one-sided, fragmentary and schematic 'pictures in the head' which are based on opinions about the given phenomenon. Such schematic images derive from culture and meet certain important psychological needs. Lippmann points out the double function of stereotypes: psychological (the effort of getting to know the world is minimised) and social (one's social position is defended). Let me quote from chapter VI, titled 'Stereotypes':

> We are told about the world before we see it. We imagine most things before we experience them. And those preconceptions, unless education has made us acutely aware, govern deeply the whole process of perception. They mark out certain objects as familiar or strange, emphasising the difference, so that the slightly familiar is seen as very familiar, and the somewhat strange as sharply alien. They are aroused by small signs, which may vary from a true index to a vague analogy. Aroused, they flood fresh vision with older images, and project into the world what has been resurrected in memory. Were there no practical uniformities in the environment, there would be no economy and only error in the human habit of accepting foresight for sight. But there are uniformities sufficiently accurate, and the need of economising attention is so inevitable, that the abandonment of all stereotypes for a wholly innocent approach to experience would impoverish human life. (Lippmann, 1961 [1922]: 90)

For the most part we do not first see, and then define, we define first and then see. (p. 81). Then, in chapter VII, the other, social function of stereotypes is discussed:

> There is another reason, besides economy of effort, why we so often hold to our stereotypes when we might pursue a more disinterested vision. The systems of stereotypes may be the core of our personal tradition, the defenses of our position in society.

> They are an ordered, more or less consistent picture of the world, to which our habits, our tastes, our capacities, our comforts and our hopes have adjusted themselves. They may not be a complete picture of the world, but they are a picture of a possible world to which we are adapted. In that world people and things have their well-known places, and do certain expected things. We feel at home there. We fit in. We are members. We know the way around. There we find the charm of the familiar, the normal, the dependable; its grooves and shapes are where we are accustomed to find them. And though we have abandoned much that might have tempted us before we creased ourselves into that mould, once we are firmly in, it fits us snugly as an old shoe. (p. 95)

Gostkowski (1959) calls this the 'stabilising' function of stereotypes: systems of stereotypes give people the feeling of security and adaptation; their role is not to help know the truth in an intellectual manner but to prolong one's life and make it easier. This is why they are emotionally charged.

Sociologists working on Lippmann's conception narrowed down the research perspective by stressing the relationship between stereotypes and human behaviour, which in effect shapes the image of social reality.

In the 1920s and 1930s a group of sociologists and culture analysts in Poland initiated an inquiry into relations between different ethnic groups in terms of the opposition of US vs. THEM. In his famous study *Megalomanja narodowa* ('National Megalomania') Jan Stanisław Bystroń (1924) describes the tendency within social groups to idealise one's own members, especially at the tribal, national and state level. He points out the universal, in his opinion, mechanism of elevating one's own group above other groups. These include the conviction that 'we are in the centre of the world' (the Chinese, Haitians, Jews), 'we come from the oldest known ancestors' (mythical genealogy), 'we have a glorious history' (idealisation of the past), 'we are better than others' (nationalism), 'God is on our side' etc. Florian Znaniecki (1930) in his conception of the 'humanistic factor' suggests that the dynamic nature of the category of 'alienness' or 'foreignness' is subjective, based on construed and imagistic criteria. Similarly, Józef Obrębski (1936, 1951) uses the notion of stereotypes to interpret the process of group identification, which in his opinion does not consist in naturalistic, geographical or 'encyclopedic' differentiation but, again, has an imagistic nature and functions in individual and collective (social) consciousness. The social function of stereotypes was most fully explicated by Józef Chałasiński in his work on the role of stereotypes in a society in conflict with another society. Let me quote:

> Stereotypes are definitions of people, objects, relations and situations which we continually construct and receive from social tradition. They do not result from logical reasoning but from experience, in which the dominant role is played by instinctive processes. They, nevertheless, make up the most important world of meanings we call social reality. The stereotypes I have in mind are not only the names such as 'a bourgeois', 'a proletarian', 'a member of the intelligentsia', 'a Jew' […] etc. but also less characteristic ones, such as 'a member of the nobility',

'a peasant', 'an official', 'a butcher', 'a professor', 'a parson', 'good manners', 'a person from a good family' etc. The same category includes concepts such as 'socialism', 'clericalism' etc. These are all images, shortcuts to which positive or negative emotional complexes are tied. They never reflect objective reality as it is; indeed, sometimes it is not known what they mean, but they always express an emotional interpretation of reality. They are not purely intellectual images but have a strong emotional colouring and reflect human desires, prejudices, offences and hatred. Social reality is different from biological reality precisely in this way: it is what it is for people, the way people see it, not independently of people. Social reality is not *Ding an sich*, a thing in itself, but an image of our consciousness in which fiction cannot be separated from reality. The father, the mother, the family, the nation: these are all images to which complexes of emotions are tied. What, it might seem, could be more physical than the father? The father is a mere biological fact. Not! It is a cultural category created by humans. For example, the inhabitants of the Trobriand Islands (north-western Melanesia) do not understand the physiological role of the father in the act of conception and do not view him as related to the children (cf. Malinowski's *The Father in Primitive Psychology*, London 1927)! Social reality is thus a world of images with a conventional, changeable content; it is a world of stereotypes and myths. (Chałasiński, 1935: 48–49)

Stereotypic thinking is a variant of mythical thinking, not to be neglected in social relations: 'In antagonistic relations the importance of the myth rises' (Chałasiński, 1935: 49). Chałasiński continues:

Stereotypes are definitions on which the whole social order is founded, in which everyone has their place. Stereotypes define people's roles in collective life. Tradition, being a collection of stereotypes passed on from one generation to another with the whole baggage of emotions they carry, does not only define the place of every human being but makes a person what he or she is. Tradition is social memory and should we lose it one day, we would not know what we are in relation to one another. (Chałasiński, 1935: 50)

Sociologists have also identified various specific functions and configurations of ethnic stereotypes. A new, important aspect was introduced to sociological research on stereotypes by Antonina Kłoskowska, who claims that 'an analysis of the images constructed by children [...] may be important not only in establishing the degree of entrenchment of a stereotype but also in revealing the speakers' system of values' (Kłoskowska, 1969: 78). Having analysed the responses of children and teenagers to the question 'What are Poles like?', the author concludes: 'The images of the Polish nation constructed by fourteen-year-olds include the features of courage, patriotism and hospitality. This triad is part of a commonly known stereotype with a very long historical tradition' (Kłoskowska, 1969: 79).

Some sociological research concerns the relationship between stereotypes and a number of other phenomena, such as prejudice, opinion, belief, superstition etc. Andrzej Kapiszewski proposed how to differentiate them:

> Stereotypes may be verbal manifestations of prejudice [...] or may not have to do with the latter at all. Similarly, prejudice may be manifested either through stereotypes or through other means, without being connected with them in any way. (Kapiszewski, 1978: 32)

3   The views of Adam Schaff

With his book on stereotypes and human action, Adam Schaff (1981) steered the problem into the field of pragmatics, although his starting point was the role of subjective factors in human cognition. These factors, according to Schaff, include the nature of the cognitive apparatus, the way in which the mind perceives and conceives of the world, as well as the so called cultural code, the view of reality imposed by social conditions. The human cognitive apparatus (Schaff refers here to the work of Mead, Bartlett, Gibson, Piaget and Parry) organises experience and acquires knowledge about reality by means of schemas. In the psychological sense, stereotypes are schemas (cf. Schaff, 1981: 25–30). A cultural code influences cognition, among other means, through language, the function of which is viewed in relation to the ideas of von Humboldt and the Sapir-Whorf hypothesis. Schaff writes: 'Stereotypes are *always* verbal because they *always* occur as the content of a word [...] Both the origin and the functioning of stereotypes is strictly connected with linguistic constructs' (Schaff, 1981: 36).

Having surveyed the literature on stereotypes, Schaff concludes that this 'quasi-social agreement' requires a phenomenological description which addresses five issues.

First, most authors emphasise the fact that stereotypes contain a generalised image of reality, given to an individual before and independently of experience. Moreover, this image directs our attention and as a result actually shapes experience. Second, emphasised is the rigidity of stereotypes, their resistance to change and their long-lasting recurrence, sometimes over many generations. Third, the first two points are connected with the proposition that stereotypes contain generalisations of specific observations, which are either contrary to fact or contain only a kernel of truth, unjustly generalised. Fourth, stereotypes involve valuation and an emotional attitude on the part of the person entertaining a stereotype. Finally, stereotypes are said to be connected to units of language, although this view is interpreted in a variety of ways. Some say that the linguistic unit is a word (a name), others that it is a sentence; according to some researchers there is a connection between the stereotype and a word or sentence, according to others the stereotype itself is a linguistic unit etc. (Schaff, 1981: 69–70). All these ideas clearly evoke Lippmann's views.

All in all, Schaff accepts the understanding of stereotype as an 'evaluating (positive or negative) judgment connected with a conviction', entertained by a group, a judgment that is emotional, independent of personal experience, wholly or partially contrary to fact, resistant to change and associated with the name of the relevant group.

Schaff devotes a separate chapter of his book to the functions of stereotypes. The basic one is the social integrative function:

> It is a quasi-religious function, one that cements the group internally, realised spontaneously in the course of language acquisition, later becoming entrenched as a result of the conscious (or sometimes subconscious) desire to integrate with the society or a social group. (Schaff, 1981: 127)

Another function of stereotypes, one that complements the integrative function, is the defensive one. Its role is to keep the mind 'closed' to new, objective information:

> In situations of conflict, when views and attitudes of people (in the sense of readiness for action) do not match reality, and when reality cannot be changed to match the views nor can the views be changed without destroying the subject's ideology, a psychological mechanism comes into play which makes the subject's mind 'information-proof' lest the mind be vexed. (Schaff, 1981: 128–129)

In the realm of specific social practice, Schaff analyses and justifies the 'sociotechnical use of stereotypes for ideological purposes', which for him is but another function of stereotypes. The common denominator of all four functions: the socially integrative, defensive, ideological and political, is that stereotypes 'mask the social reality' (Schaff, 1981: 136).

In the second part of his book, Schaff stresses, in a somewhat one-sided manner, the social functions of stereotypes at the expense of psychological ones, which for Lippmann are fundamental functions which facilitate the process of knowledge acquisition. These psychological functions have often been underscored by psychologists.

Schaff also discusses the relationship between stereotypes and concepts. He draws a clear line between them with regard to their social function, their relation to experience, and their internal structure:

> Concepts, it is assumed, correspond to the requirements of scientific thinking; stereotypes, on the contrary, are resistant to the influence of experience: they are largely independent of experience not only in origin but also in function [...] In concepts, the intellectual component dominates; in stereotypes, it is the emotional component that dominates [...] Stereotypes are relatively stable and resistant to change [...], whereas concepts, especially scientific concepts as exponents of knowledge, undergo modification rather quickly and are open to change [...] Another factor differentiating concepts and stereotypes is their social function: cognitive and epistemological in the case of concepts, defensive and integrative in the case of stereotypes. Stereotypes protect the interests of a group, surfacing as phobias or excessively positive judgments. They integrate individuals into the group by internalising the latter's norms and values. (Schaff, 1981: 113–114)

Another view of these issues can be found in the ideas of Hilary Putnam, discussed below.

4   Uta Quasthoff's approach

A sociotechnical understanding of ethnic stereotype is proposed by Uta Quasthoff, the author of the first extensive work on the subject described in the title as 'linguistic' (1973): *Soziales Vorurteil und Kommunikation. Eine sprachwissenschaftliche Analyse des Stereotyps.* In her view, a stereotype is

> a verbal manifestation of a conviction concerning a social group or individuals in that group. The conviction has the form of a logical judgement attributing or denying specific characteristics of behaviours to a class of people, accompanied by emotional valuation and expressed in a categorical, simplifying and generalising fashion. (Quasthoff, 1973: 28)

Quasthoff's analysis of the function of stereotypes relates back to Austin's and Searle's conceptions of speech acts: the use of stereotypes can be captured in terms of the so called 'verditive acts' comprising valuation and judgement (e.g. *I consider him hard-working*) (Quasthoff, 1973: 210). Stereotype-based use of language in which there is an image of an external enemy ('them', 'those people') integrates the group but also raises a communicative barrier which separates the group from the environment. Such is the effect of stereotypes in the language of propaganda. Against the background of the two coexisting functions one can understand the behaviour of conformists, unsure of their own value: they readily resort to stereotypical thinking in order to obtain acceptance of the group and raise their own position within it. This process is aided by adjusting one's hierarchy of language functions to the expectations of the interlocutor (Hymes, 1968). A person may not approve of stereotypes in their referential function (since they are contrary to fact) but may use them in the phatic function so as to establish and maintain social contacts in the form accepted by a given community. In Germany, references to the terrible Gastarbeiter Turks may replace those to the weather.

However, Quasthoff is not totally happy with the results obtained: she views them as 'temporary'. I would not like to take a definite stand on the issue but the results do seem incomplete, as they capture the functions of stereotype in connection with the use of language in specific speech acts but do not link these functions to the language system, which shapes the social view on and attitude to the world. (Semioticians claim that 'the basic function of every semiotic system is to model the world' and 'the semiotic model of the world may be treated as a template for the behaviour of individuals or communities' (Ivanov, 1977: 97; cf. Vygotsky, 1971). It is, however, unquestionable that Quasthoff's work contributes to the creation of a programme of linguistic research on stereotypes, perhaps not so much due to its analysis of language functions (in this respect the work is not terribly original[3]), but by posing questions about the relationship between stereotype and basic linguistic categories, as well as its manifestations in sentences and texts.

The author devotes a separate chapter to the relationship between stereotypes and the 'competence–performance' dichotomy, starting with linguistic competence in the narrow, grammatical sense and then extending the concept onto phenomena of communicative pragmatics, in accordance with the approach proposed in German linguistics by Dieter Wunderlich (1970). Quasthoff offers a number of interesting observations. Let us consider a few.

Sentences such as

(1)   Rhinelanders are cheerful.

do not pose problems to the hearer – standard linguistic competence is sufficient. The sentence

(2)   My uncle Willy is very Prussian.

assumes (for a proper understanding) a stereotypical judgement: 'Prussians were punctual, meticulous and order-loving people'. One need not share the stereotypical view but cannot negate its existence in the social consciousness of Germans. This meaning of the word *Prussian* has become well-established in the lexicon of the German language. Stereotypical judgments here belong to linguistic competence in the strict sense of the word.

Similarly, the sentence

(3)   He was a Jew towards others.

in the sense 'he was cunning and greedy' refers not to the ethnic meaning of the word *Jew* but to the relevant stereotype. According to Quasthoff (1973), a competent speaker of German easily recognises this usage from context. A parallel case is a sentence like

(4)   He is a Jew but he is very nice.

which contains a quasi-implication 'Jews are generally not nice'. It belongs to the sentence's meaning and is forced by the conjunction *but*.

The following utterance is, according to Quasthoff, somewhat peculiar:

(5)   A friend's husband is very stingy. He's Scottish.

The semantic relationship between the two sentences can only be captured on the basis of the stereotype of stingy Scots. It is only when the stereotype is invoked that one can identify the relationship as an explication. It belongs to the semantic structure of the text. A formally similar utterance

(6)   A friend's husband is very intelligent. He's English.

has a different semantic structure because being intelligent does not belong to the popular stereotype of an Englishman. Linguistic competence, says Quasthoff, is insufficient to distinguish the meanings of utterances (5) and (6): one must refer to the pragmatic or communicative competence, which includes knowledge of the world.

It is unclear why in this analysis stereotypes are sometimes treated as components of linguistic competence in the strict sense of the term (examples (2)–(4), and at other times as components of pragmatic competence and knowledge of the world (*Kenntnis der Welt,* example (5)). In both cases we are dealing with stable phenomena on the semantic plane of language; the form is secondary.[4] In the realm of semantics, the linguist faces an important problem of the boundary between standard world knowledge, which is the basis of language and a component of linguistic (semantic) competence describable as linguistic worldview, and nonstandard, extralinguistic knowledge, extending beyond the linguistic worldview. Despite a rich literature on the subject, the problem remains unsolved because stereotypes may contain elements well or poorly entrenched in language.[5]

A very important aspect of Quasthoff's work is her attempt to classify language structures used for expressing stereotypical judgments. The author reduces the semantic representation of stereotypical judgments to simple predication (a link between a predicate and an argument) or a relationship between elements x and y (R(xy)). She identifies four forms of expressing a stereotype. The basic form is a sentence containing simple predication, such as:

(7) (a)   A German is diligent.

The name used as the subject is seemingly accompanied by the (hidden) universal quantifier ('every'), the same as in the following sentence from scientific discourse:

(7) (b)   Man is a living creature.

However, in the social understanding, one is dealing here with a characteristic transformation of the universal quantifier to another type of modifier, namely 'typical' or 'true'.[6] Should there be non-diligent Germans, those who entertain the stereotype would not treat (7) (a) as false but would only conclude that non-diligent people are not true Germans. (7) (a) is, in fact, an analytic sentence: *A German (, whose characteristic feature is diligence,) is diligent.*

The second type are sentences with specific indicators:

(8) A Saxonian is considered taciturn.

This type of sentence can be described with the help of modal logic as follows. There exist worlds, treated as real, in which the judgment 'Saxonians are taciturn' is true. The speaker relates to these worlds but does not state whether his world is one of them, i.e. does not make it clear if the judgment is true for him or her.

The third type is similar but the speaker clearly states his or her opinion by using specific illocutionary expressions:

(9)   I have an impression that Americans are not different from us.

The fourth and last type can be called 'textual–linguistic' (*textlinguistischer Typ*), because in order to describe it one must relate to supersentential structures and the linguistics of text. It is represented by sentences such as (4) above, frequent in colloquial speech. One can also treat the following sentence as representative:

(10) (a)   He is German but he is very nice.

The stereotype is not expressed but contained implicitly in the meaning of the whole sentence and can be expressed as the following judgment:

(10) (b)   Germans are not usually nice.

The adverb *usually* indicates the reference of the sentence to a typical representative of the class of 'Germans'. Exceptions are allowed but the expected state of affairs is the 'normal' one. In her analysis of the last type, Quasthoff uses the notion of presupposition.

5   Two trends in linguistic research on stereotypes in Poland

In Polish linguistics, stereotypes are investigated along formal or semantic lines. The formal approach is represented by studies on stereotypes in phraseology. For example, Stanisław Skorupka makes an attempt to describe word combinations with regard to the degree of independence of the individual words. He identifies a distinct type, the so called 'fixed stereotypical combinations, entrenched in language in a certain form but without an added, extra meaning, i.e. basically preserving the meanings of individual components in the meaning of the whole' (Kurkowska and Skorupka, 1959: 158). The following examples are given: *czerwony jak burak* 'red as a beetroot', *gruby jak beka* 'fat as a barrel', *lekki jak piórko* 'light as a feather', *wysoki jak tyka grochowa* 'tall as a pea pole', *silny jak koń* 'strong as a horse', *(ubranie) jak psu z gardła wyjęte* '(clothes looking) like taken from a dog's throat', *(ludzie) podobni do siebie jak dwie krople wody* '(people) similar to each other like two drops of water'. These units are distinguished on the one hand from loose combinations, created online in context (*jeść jabłko* 'eat an apple' or *bardzo czerwony* 'very red'), and on the other hand from totally fixed expressions such as *pleść duby smalone* 'talk bullshit', *zalać sadła za skórę* 'be a nuisance to someone' (lit. 'pour fat under someone's skin'), *oddać wet za wet* 'an eye for an eye'.

A similar view can be found in the work of Andrzej Maria Lewicki, who defines pragmatic stereotypes as 'word combinations reproduced from memory', contrary to those which are 'synthesised' (Lewicki, 1976: 23). The distinction belongs to the fundamentals of contemporary grammar theory. It appears not only in relation to word combinations, but wherever we deal with constructing complex linguistic units from simple ones. It is usually the case that beyond the range of constructions resulting from an application of specific grammatical rules, there is a certain number of those which are either totally fixed (and so can be treated as simple signs) or tending towards fixation. Jespersen (1924) calls the secondary units 'formulas' (as opposed to 'free expressions'); Permyakov (1970, 1975) calls them 'clichés', 'printing plates' (what I have referred to as 'stereotyped texts') and includes in that category, apart from phraseologisms and proverbs, also 'larger' units of text (anecdotes, fables, stories and tales), as well as 'smaller' ones, i.e. individual words. Against this background, stereotypes can be defined as holistically fixed non-decomposable expressions, with an 'inner form' or 'etymological meaning' which gives way to the 'real' meaning as used by the speaker.[7]

A semantic conception of the stereotype, corresponding to its understanding in sociology and social psychology, was introduced by Walery Pisarek (1975) and Krystyna Pisarkowa (1976), according to whom 'stereotypes are the same as the semantic connotation of a nation's name' (Pisarkowa, 1976: 6). This approach to stereotypes situates the problem in the terminological context of linguistic inquiry. (It is true, however, that Pisarkowa's conception of connotation is too narrow: it is the emotionally-coloured semantic content accompanying the primary meaning of a name.[8]) The desire to 'linguisticise' the basically sociological notion of stereotype and to take note of strictly linguistic connotations, rather than solely object-related associations, induced Pisarkowa to apply two research methods: a questionnaire consisting of a few sentence types (a group of some forty students were asked to associate names of nations with adjectives such as 'phlegmatic' or 'disciplined', to provide names to go with epithets, to complement expressions of the type 'Chinese ...', or to define nationalities) and text analysis. She used lexicographic data on nationality names and checked what added, emergent meanings are provided for the entries *Cygan* 'Gypsy', *Kozak* 'Cossack' or *Szwab* derog. 'German' (lit. 'a native of Schwabia'), what meanings are associated with relevant adjectives (*po czerkiesku* 'the Cherkess way', i.e. 'in a disorderly, untidy manner') and verbs (*skozaczyć się*, lit. 'to Cossack oneself', i.e. 'to have a child out of wedlock'), what meanings are associated with nationality names in proverbs (e.g. *wmówić jak w Niemca chorobę* 'lead someone to believe something like lead a German to believe they are ill', i.e. do something easy, suggesting that Germans are hypochondriacs) etc.

The semantic understanding of stereotypes is also the foundation the of *SSSL* (1996–1999). Similarly to Pisarkowa's approach, stereotypes are interpreted in terms of connotation and described on the basis of texts as established combinations of at least two elements, with the logical structure of a judgment and with a sentence (or its equivalent) as its linguistic correlate. However, when working on the dictionary I thought it was unjustified to narrow down the conception of stereotype to the names of people (as is understandably the case in sociology) and returned to Lippmann's idea of an image in the head relating to people and things. A wider justification for this view can be found in the work of the American philosopher of language Hilary Putnam, the father of contemporary research on stereotypes.

6   Hilary Putnam's conception of stereotypes

In 1968, Hilary Putnam devoted a series of lectures at the University of Washington to the problem of stereotypes. These lectures became the basis for his essays 'Is semantics possible?' and 'The meaning of 'meaning'' (Putnam, 1975: 139–152, 215–271). An advantage of his approach is the possibility of linking the problem of stereotypes with that of reference, as practiced in contemporary linguistic semantics (cf. Lyons, 1977: chapter 7). For Putnam, 'in ordinary parlance a 'stereotype' is a conventional (frequently malicious) idea (which may be wildly inaccurate) of what an X looks like or acts or is' (Putnam, 1975: 249). He elaborates:

> [S]omeone who knows what 'tiger' means (or, as we have decided to say instead, has acquired the word 'tiger') is *required* to know that *stereotypical* tigers are striped. More precisely, there is *one* stereotype of tigers (he may have others) which is required by the linguistic community as such; he is required to have this stereotype, and to know (implicitly) that it is obligatory. This stereotype must include the feature of stripes if his acquisition is to count as successful. (Putnam, 1975: 250)

The set of features of a stereotype is found not in all exemplars of the class in question but in model ones, regarded by speakers as 'normal'.[9] The stereotype of gold, for instance, includes the feature 'yellow', although chemically pure gold is white (cf. Lippmann, 1961 [1922]: 81 on stereotype-based differences in seeing metals by chemists and non-chemists). The stereotype of a witch in onetime America said she had some dealings with the devil, caused diseases and death, etc. Stereotypes of this kind can hinder communication, though most stereotypes are detailed enough for communication to be effective.

Putnam considers the stereotype so understood to be a linguistically relevant phenomenon[10] and incorporates it in the description of word meaning, which he understands as a 'vector' which allows one to establish the extension of the word but which is something other than extension.[11]

Zbysław Muszyński looks at Putnam's approach against the background of contemporary conceptions of meaning:

> [A]n important aspect of Putnam's analysis is that the stereotype is understood as a theory of an object [...] As a result, no significant differences are postulated between scientific concepts and those connected with stereotypes based on folk knowledge. Both play the same role in relation to different conceptions of the world, depending on the views of the subject, i.e. a speaker of the language in which these concepts operate. The basic task of these theories is to explain, describe and order entities and phenomena with which humans have to do. (Muszyński, 1982: 24)

Putnam associates stereotypes with word meanings more than do Schaff or Quasthoff. He proposes to create linguistic means of establishing the content of stereotypes and a system of its presentation (this postulate, I daresay, may be realised by the cognitive definition, discussed in the next chapter). Putnam does not limit stereotypes to the names of people; on the contrary, he recognises its presence in, nearly, the whole lexicon of a language. He focuses primarily on colloquial speech, i.e. something that most fully exhibits the functions of language. Recognising the existence, in word meaning, of emotional and evaluative elements, as well as obvious falsehoods, resulting from faith, prejudice or subjectivism, Putnam is far from overestimating their role; indeed, he rather underscores the intention of a speech community to construct the image of a 'typical' object, a 'normal' tiger – this is a cognitive intention in relation to a folk, naive theory of reality. That the image is only partially true is irrelevant from the point of view of its function. This is in contrast to Schaff's focus on the defensive-integrative function of stereotypes.

Putnam's conception of stereotypes is connected with that of connotation, the way it is understood by John N. Keynes. Keynes treats connotation as a set of features associated with a term, the features one has in mind when using the term (this is subjective intension, as opposed to objective intension, i.e. the set of features common to the objects denoted by the term, or to conventional intension, i.e. a set of features mentioned in the term's definition) (Keynes, 1906: 327).

7   The stereotype and its variants: topos, formula, idiom

Let me now offer a brief characterisation of the research field at hand. A stereotype is a stable connection of meanings, i.e. one that is not created online but reproduced, entrenched in collective memory at the level of lexemic specificity. In stereotypes, there is no full correspondence between the semantic and formal plane of language. On this basis one can identify three variants of stereotype: topoi, formulae and idioms.

First, there are established combinations of purely semantic units, which are not yet accompanied by any definite form of verbalisation (topoi):

(11) (a)   Negroes do all the hard work.
    (b)   Shoemakers drink hard.
    (c)   Mazurians are born blind.

(12) (a)   A cuckoo can foretell the future.
    (b)   A magpie foreshadows the arrival of guests.
    (c)   When stars twinkle, it will be windy.
    (d)   A falling star means someone has died.

(13) (a)   One must not point one's finger at the sun.
    (b)   A brother should look after his sister.
    (c)   A good mother loves her child.

Views expressed in these sentences attribute certain characteristics to people or things (also to events, cf. (12) (d)). These characteristics are well-entrenched in the community of speakers of folk dialectal or colloquial Polish.

Sentences like the ones in (11) (a)-(c) are descriptive or quasi-descriptive; those in (12) (a)-(d) are based on beliefs and those in (13) (a)-(c) are normative. All contain judgments, most overt in the last set, which cannot be subjected to true–false evaluation: the convictions of the speakers are expressed by modals *must not, should not* or their equivalents. Convictions are the least conspicuous in (11) (a)-(c) but, as pointed out by Quasthoff and Putnam, the sentences refer not to whole classes ('every shoemaker') but to what are considered their 'typical' or 'exemplary' representatives. Thus, these sentences in fact contain a hidden subject: 'someone thinks that…'. The same pertains to sentences in (12) (a)-(d) and (13) (a)-(c).

The interpretation of all these types must include the cultural background of that 'someone' contained in the sentences' modal frame. Hence the multitude of expressions of the sort 'The Polish people believe that …', 'For the Polish people, …', or 'It is generally believed that …' in all kinds of ethnographic descriptions.[12]

Second, there are established semantic combinations of a stable formal shape (formulae):

(14) (a) *Murzyn zrobił swoje, Murzyn może odejść.*
          'The Negro has done what was expected of him and can go.'

　　 (b) *szewska pasja* 'white heat',
          lit. 'shoemaker's fury'

　　 (c) *zawzięty jak Mazur*
          'headstrong like a Mazurian'

(15) (a) *kukułcze jajo*
          'cuckoo's egg'

　　 (b) *patrzeć jak sroka w kość*
          'look like a magpie at a bone', i.e. without understanding

　　 (c) *liczyć gwiazdy*
          'count stars', i.e. 'undertake something unmanageable'

(16) (a) *jasne jak słońce*
          'as clear as the sun'

　　 (b) *(ktoś komuś) ni brat ni swat*
          '(someone is to someone else) neither a brother nor a matchmaker', i.e. there is no special relationship or bond between the two

　　 (c) *(taki) jak go matka zrodziła*
          'the way he was born', i.e. naked

　　 (d) *jaka mać taka nać*

'like mother like top leaves', i.e. the family is similar to the mother

There are, finally, purely formal combinations, without clear semantic motivation (idioms):

(17) (a) *wieszać psy na kim*
'slander someone', lit. 'hang dogs on someone'

(b) *rzucać mięsem*
'swear', lit. 'throw meat'

(c) *strzelić byka*
'make a big mistake', lit. 'shoot a bull/mistake'

(d) *zimno jak diabli*
'cold as hell'

(e) *idź do cholery!*
'go to the devil!'

(f) *(głupi) jak stołowa noga*
'very stupid', lit. 'stupid as a table leg'

(g) *ani w ząb*
'not in the least', lit. 'not by the tooth'

The distinction can be represented in diagrammatic form (Figure 5.1).

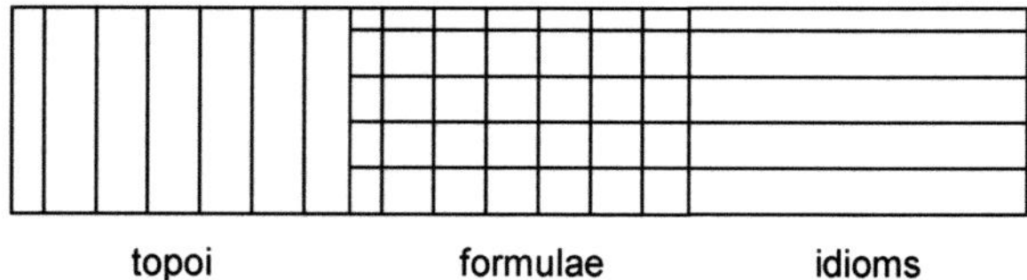

Figure 5.1 Meaning and form in topoi, formulae and idioms

In Figure 5.1 the vertical lines represent semantic combinations, whereas the horizontal lines represent purely formal links. The middle part is a combination of the two, the heart of the stereotype.

In the process of language change, topoi turn into formulae, which turn into idioms. For a linguist, the most important variant of the stereotype is the formula, extensively discussed in studies on phraseology. A formula, however, is a concept broader than a phraseological unit.

The problem of stereotypes is continued in the next chapter, in which I propose the conception of the cognitive definition.

Notes

1   The first important linguistic publication on the subject is Quasthoff (1973). The beginnings of linguistic research on stereotypes in Poland are Walery Pisarek and Krystyna Pisarkowa.

2   In this context, cf. especially Lyons, 1977: chapter 7.

3   In her later work, influenced by American cognitivists, Quasthoff appreciates the cognitive function of stereotypes by locating it at the very top of the hierarchy (cf. Quasthoff, 1989).

4   Let us note that in examples (2)–(3) it is only the very presence of an indeterminate 'stereotypical' meaning, different from the basic meaning, that is signalled formally; additional information about the content of one of the stereotype's components is only given in (4). In (5) neither type of signal can be found but it is easy to use the popular stereotype of a Scot and build sentences with its clear formal and linguistic exponents: 'My friend is very Scottish', 'He was a Scot to his family', 'He's Scottish but he's generous'. Quasthoff would probably treat sentences of this kind as evidence of the stereotype of a stingy Scot being a part of linguistic rather than merely pragmatic competence. But they may also involve mystification on the part of the speaker: the very fact of using, on a single occasion, a sentence with the contrary meaning is an insufficient proof for the existence of the presupposed stereotype in collective consciousness. The crucial feature of stereotypes does not reside in this or that sentential or textual structure but in the understanding of individual words, i.e. on the semantic plane, inseparable form linguistic competence.

5   Statistical research on stereotypes can be revealing in this respect. Some is discussed in Bartmiński (2007c).

6   Quasthoff does not differentiate between the two but they do result in a different modality of stereotypical images; cf. chapter 14 on the Polish stereotype of a 'typical' and 'true' German.

7   An example of the 'inner form' (Humboldt's term): Polish *miednica* 'washbasin' comes from *miedź* 'copper'. It denoted an object 'made of copper' and used for a particular purpose – but no longer does.

8   This conception of connotation can also be found in Quasthoff (1973), to which Pisarkowa refers, as well as in the work of Soviet and French authors (cf. Martinet, 1967; Komlev, 1976; Iordanskaya and Mel'chuk, 1980). Logicians of Mill's and scholastic traditions understand connotation as the content of a name different from its range, i.e. its denotation (cf. Lyons, 1977).

9   'Most stereotypes do in fact capture features possessed by paradigmatic members of the class in question' (Putnam, 1975: 260). The claim corresponds with Quasthoff's analysis of sentence (7) (a) above (*A German is diligent*).

10   'The theoretical account of what it is to be a stereotype proceeds in term of the notion of *linguistic obligation*; a notion which we believe to be fundamental to linguistics and which we shall not attempt to explicate here. What it means to say that being striped is part of the (linguistic) stereotype of 'tiger' is that it is *obligatory* to acquire the information that stereotypical tigers are striped if one acquires 'tiger', in the same sense of 'obligatory' in which it is obligatory to indicate whether one is speaking of lions in the singular or lions in the plural when one speaks of lions in English.' (Putnam, 1975: 251).

11 'My proposal is that the normal form description of the meaning of a word should be a finite sequence, or 'vector', whose components should certainly include the following (it might be desirable to have other types of components as well): i) the syntactic markers that apply to the word, e.g. 'noun'; ii) the semantic markers that apply to the word, e.g. 'animal', 'period of time'; iii) a description of the additional features of the stereotype, if any; iv) a description of the extension.

The following convention is a part of this proposal: the components of the vector all represent a hypothesis about the individual speaker's competence except the extension. Thus the normal form description for 'water' might be, in part:

syntactic markers	semantic markers	stereotype	extension
mass noun; concrete	natural kind; liquid	natural kind; transparent; tasteless; thirst-quenching; etc.	H_2O; (give or take impurities)

– this does not mean that knowledge of the fact that water is H_2O is being imputed to the individual speaker or even to the society.' (Putnam, 1975: 269).

12 The relationship between the topos and the (ethnic) stereotype is analysed in Quasthoff (1973; 68–69). The author distinguishes the two (stereotypes being thought of as judgements concerning groups of people) but points out a number of similarities between them: both have a certain content relating to reality; both have diverse variants depending on the environment; both arise independently of people's personal experience; neither has so far been distinguished in social sciences on the basis of their content and linguistic expression; both have, at least in the sociopsychological sense, largely statistical values. Similarly to stereotype, the topos recurs and is used by many people.

6 The 'cognitive definition' in the description of stereotypes

1 Introduction

In this chapter I discuss the conception of the 'cognitive definition' as it is used for the description of meaning in *SSSL*, but which can be used in any other dictionary of natural language.

The adjective *cognitive* (from Latin *cognosco* 'I come to the knowledge of') in the combination 'cognitive definition' has two functions. First, it means that the content of the definition is cognitive rather than 'purely' semantic in the sense adopted in structuralist semantics.[1] The cognitive definition aims to portray the way in which an entity is viewed by the speakers of a language, to represent socio-culturally established and linguistically entrenched knowledge, its categorisation and valuation. While recognising the need to distinguish between the linguistic and the encyclopedic dictionary (i.e. not to extend a description of language onto a description of the world), this approach does not set a firm boundary between so called linguistic and encyclopedic knowledge. The boundary is 'elastic': extralinguistic phenomena, such as customs and beliefs, certainly are part of meaning. Relating to Putnam's distinction between semantic markers and 'stereotypical' elements in a word's intension (cf. the previous chapter), one could say that the role of the cognitive definition is to *also* capture the latter. The defined entity is a 'mental object', a projection, not a reflection of the real-life artifact, although one can always compare the two and find similarities between them. But reflections of what are such 'objects' as the Pegasus or gnomes?

The second, less important reason for introducing the term *cognitive* is the desire to relate to the cognitive linguistic enterprise, which focuses on the problems of human ('natural') categorisation. This enterprise is related to the cognitivist trend in other branches of the humanities, such as psychology or sociology.

The conception of the cognitive definition is best seen in comparison to the taxonomic definition. In Doroszewski's *SJPDor* (1962), *wiatr* 'wind' is defined as 'a horizontal movement of layers of air in a certain direction, resulting from differences in air pressure' and *deszcz* 'rain' as 'precipitation in the form of water drops falling from above'. These definitions are scientistic and taxonomic. They are scientistic because they refer to elements of scientific rather than everyday knowledge; they are taxonomic because they attempt to unambiguously identify the denotatum from a superordinate class of denotata in accordance with the principles of logical classification. It is in order to preserve the taxonomic character of the definitions that the semantic components in the definientia are limited to the 'necessary and sufficient'. The scientistic nature of the definitions diminishes their descriptive value, especially in the case of older, highly polysemous vocabulary, characterised by rich derivation and phraseology.

Although useful in many respects, they do not help one interpret the way lexical units function in language and texts. They do not explain the semantic motivation of the derivatives. The definition of the archaic Polish *wietrznica* (from *wiatr* 'wind') as 'a light-hearted woman, inconstant in her feelings' has no apparent semantic link with the wind defined in purely meteorological terms. The expression *zmyć komuś głowę po ojcowsku* 'rebuke someone (lit. wash someone's head) in a fatherly manner' remains unclear if *po ojcowsku* 'in a fatherly manner' is explained as 'befitting a father; like a father would' and *ojciec* 'father' as 'a man who has a child' (more on the subject in Bartmiński, 1984; reprinted as 2006b: 35–41). Therefore, I propose to include in the definition also the word's connotations.

I use the term *connotation* in a broad sense, synonymous to 'content' or 'intension', and in contrast to 'denotation', 'range' or 'extension'.[2] I include in it both 'criterial' features and characteristic features (Putnam's stereotypical features). In analyses of texts I simply take note of the features for which there is linguistic evidence. These, upon closer scrutiny, may turn out to be occasional or coincidental. An important problem to solve is how to extract, from all the features of a given object found in linguistic data, the characteristic, criterial ones, entrenched in language and present in social awareness. The enterprise requires a methodical approach to the question of linguistic exponents of connotation, which constitutes the semantic content of the word and the linguistic image of the object associated with that word.

Another important characteristic of the taxonomic definition is its consistently hierarchical structure, in agreement with the logical principle of listing *genus proximum* and *differentia specifica*. Although programmatically precise, definitions exhibit an astonishing degree of leeway in the choice of the first element, the *genus proximum* responsible for initial classification. For example, *słońce* 'sun' is sometimes classified as a heavenly body, on other occasions as a gaseous sphere or as light. *Człowiek* 'a human' may be defined as a mammal, an animal or a rational creature. Surely, this first step is crucial for what happens next, what appears as necessary for distinguishing the object from other objects (more on this in Bartmiński, 1991a). The set of necessary and sufficient features of a human being must include: the order Primates, the family Hominidae, a biped, vertical posture connected with earth-bound lifestyle, a sizeable brain etc. A human being as an animal is characterised by thinking, speaking or tool production. A human being as a rational creature is mortal, in contrast to other rational creatures in the linguistic worldview, such as God, angels or the devil.

The choice of *genus proximum* imposes a certain categorisation and depends on the lexicographer's viewpoint and rationality, which make up a specific interpretive perspective for a holistic characterisation of the object. The perspective may be compatible with the consciousness of a given speech community or may be imposed on that consciousness from outside. Cognitive linguistics postulates that one assume the interpretive perspective adequate to the competence of the speakers of a given language or of its variety. Only then can a profound connection (through the word's connotation) between language and culture be revealed. Word meaning is a culturally determined interpretation of the world and definitions should bring this interpretation to the surface.

2 Examples

So what does the cognitive definition look like? In what way does it represent the cognitive content entrenched in language and the linguistic organisation of that content? Let me present two somewhat shortened examples from *SSSL*.

Example 1

STRZYGOŃ 'a ghost, spectre assuming various forms' (on the basis of folk stories and ethnographic records of folk beliefs)

i)   SUPERORDINATE CATEGORY: *strzygoń* is an evil spirit, a bogy

ii)   APPEARANCE: it looks like a phantom, ghost or nightmare; has double teeth, a pale face, blue marks on the back, blood behind the fingernails, closed eyes …

iii) CHARACTERISTICS: it is silent, malicious, importunate

iv)   ACTION: it gets up from the bed at midnight; wanders about the earth; steals apples from the orchard at night; eats wax candles from the altar; frightens, strangles, beats, bites and eats people

v)   TIME OF ACTION: it appears at night, midnight; disappears after midnight, when the cock crows

vi)   PLACE OF ACTION: it stays in a coffin, in a tomb, underground; is active in the church, in the orchard, at home, in the barn

vii) ORIGIN: a person born with two souls who received only one name at baptism

viii) MEANS OF NEUTRALISATION: for a *strzygoń* to stop frightening people, one must: put the dead body with its back up or cut its head and put it between the legs, or drive a nail into its head, or put a piece of paper with the name of Jesus under its tongue, or ask for the Holy Mass to be celebrated

Example 2

DESZCZ 'rain' (on the basis of texts of folklore, peasant dialects and ethnographic documentation)

i)   SUPERORDINATE CATEGORY: *deszcz* is water

ii)   APPEARANCE: it appears in the form of drops

iii) CHARACTERISTICS: it is fine (the drops are fine), *uprząść dratew z deszczyku drobnego* 'to spin twine from fine rain' (a formula of impossibility used in songs)

iv)   ACTION: *deszcz pada* it 'falls' (southern dialectal Polish *idzie* 'goes'); it falls with alternate strength, which is revealed through various verbal expressions: *deszcz mży* 'it drizzles', *kropi* 'spits', *roni* 'sheds drops', *pryska* 'splutters' vs. *leje* 'pours', *bije* 'strikes, beats', as well as through derivatives: it *pada* 'falls' – *popaduje* 'falls a little', *kropi* 'spits' – *pokrapuje* 'spits a little', *roni* 'sheds drops' – *porania* 'sheds a few drops', *pryska* 'splutters' – *popryskuje* 'splutters a little'; cf. also nouns: *mżawka* 'drizzle', *kapuśniaczek* 'Scotch mist' (lit. 'little cabbage soup') vs. *ulewa*, *leja* 'downpour'. According to traditional beliefs, spring rain impregnates the earth and brings about good harvest. *deszcz* causes mud, as in the proverb (*w jesieni*) *kwarta deszczu – korzec błota* '(in autumn) a quarter of the rain makes more than three bushels of mud'

v)   TIME OF ACTION in songs there are frequent references to Sunday morning, when the rain sheds an occasional drop (and when lovers meet), as opposed to the evening, when it pours (and lovers part); (a proverb: 'A morning rain, the anger of a virgin and the dance of an old woman do not last long')

vi)   EVENTS COOCCURING WITH *DESZCZ*:
      a) in the world of humans: love and tears; e.g. (in songs) *deszcz porania, dziewczyna wołki wygania* 'the rain sheds a few drops, a girl leads out her oxen'; *deszczyk pada, dziewczę biada* 'the rain falls, a girl laments';
      b) in nature: storm, lightning; clouds, dew, e.g. (in songs) *deszczyk pada, rosa siada* 'it rains, dew sits down'; *czarna chmura nastąpiła, deszcz leje* 'a black cloud has come, it pours';
      c) in the supernatural world: (in a song) the deceased father or mother come with the rain to the orphaned child; in folk beliefs: frogs and fish fall with the rain; (prohibitions and orders) when it rains, one must not plough or sow; it is good to plant potatoes, sow peas or to scythe; cf. the proverb: 'He who scythes in the rain, dries in fine weather'.

vii) PLACE OF ACTION: (in a song) *Deszcz pada po drobnej leszczynie, po białej brzezinie* 'It rains on fine hazel and on white birch' (the hazel and the birch are folk symbols of a girl; cf. the impregnating function of the rain above).

viii) AUGURY CONCERNING *DESZCZ* (entrenched in common beliefs) it will rain if (a) one can feel pain in the bones; (b) fire does not burn well, cattle yawn, a dog eats grass, fish thrash about, bees swarm to the hive, chickens bathe in sand; (c) kites (birds) want to drink, crows cry, swallows fly low; (d) the sun beats down, the sun is pale and sad, stars twinkle, in the morning the mist rises

ix) AUGURY BASED ON *DESZCZ*: the rain on the wedding day foreshadows unsuccessful married life

x) POWER OVER *DESZCZ*
   a) (in the beliefs from the Małopolska (Little Poland) region) the rain is brought about by *planetnicy*, also called *chmurnicy* (mythical creatures controlling the clouds, able to bring them in or disperse them);
   b) the rain is controlled by witches; a witch can stop the rain (i.e. by standing naked in front of the cloud) or bring it about;
   c) the rain is controlled by God himself or through St. Peter;
   d) the rain can be brought about by a human being if he or she: (a) kills a lizard or a snake and outs it in the sun; (b) deals with water in a certain manner: feeds it, pours out poppy seeds to the well, pours water into the grave of a suicide; (c) turns in prayer to God, the Holy Virgin, St. Peter; sings a proper religious song;
   e) the rain can be repelled by a person, if that person: sounds bells, puts the peel in front of the house, says the appropriate spell to the sun; phenomena opposite to the rain: fine weather, cf. (a fragment from a song) 'In fine weather he would tend pigs, in the rain he would romp about with me'; the sun, drought, heat[3]

As one can see, these definitions are very different from traditional lexicographic definitions.

The requirement of content adequacy, i.e. the inclusion of folk knowledge in the definition, means that the descriptive metalanguage must be the colloquial variant of standard Polish, with no elevated, bookish or scientific expressions. The requirement can be met by: i) analysing the entry word against the language system; ii) analysing the word in texts; iii) using questionnaires with native speakers, who, among others, propose their own definitions; iv) making references to sociological and ethnographic data, which pertain to the use of a given object in culture, to the behaviour of speakers in relation to the object and to the accompanying beliefs.

The requirement of structural adequacy means that on the basis of folk knowledge and all its components, the definition attempts to reconstruct the relationships between the components present in the collective consciousness of speakers. Above all, it rejects the limitations imposed on the definiens restricting the focus to distinctive features, i.e. those which are necessary and sufficient for the identification of the denotatum. Instead, it takes into account all the positive features established in the linguistic worldview.

Their set should be exhaustive. The definition, therefore, has to be rather long and so its internal organisation is of prime importance.

3   Characteristics of the cognitive definition

Let me now discuss in some detail the most important aspects of the cognitive definition as I see it.

The first striking structural feature of the colloquial conceptualisation of the world is revealed when one asks an informant questions such as 'What is the sun?' or 'What is fire?'. My informants offered two types of responses. They sometimes gave the superordinate category accompanied by the characteristic features of the object, e.g. for the sun the responses included 'a golden ball', 'a ball of fire', 'great light' or 'a heavenly ray'. Alternatively, they would not refer to any kind of superordinate class but would invoke characteristic features. For example, the question 'What is fire?' would be answered with 'There is no life without fire'; the question 'What is flint?' would be answered with 'Flint has such sharp edges'.

The case of a single-level definition is typical of certain portions of the lexicon, e.g. words pertaining to the 'first elements of the world', such as the sky, earth, fire, water and lightning; it is also to a degree typical of folk systematisation in general, which does not readily accept complex hierarchies. Colloquial (folk) varieties of Polish lack many superordinate terms, e.g. for a brother and sister, cheese and butter or even father and mother. The words *rodzeństwo* 'siblings', *nabiał* 'dairy products' and *rodzice* 'parents' (in folk varieties: *ojcowie* 'fathers') come from standard, literary Polish. Although folk and colloquial definitions of the cuckoo, rosemary or linden tree contain semantically superordinate taxonomic concepts such as a bird, herb or tree, equally frequent are partonomic definitions (of the type: a root is the underground part of a tree; the head is a body part; a wall is a part of a house); as well as functional ones (of the type: a plough is something to plough with; a spoon is something used for eating; an axe is a thing for chopping wood etc.).

The significance of functional and partonomic concepts in natural language has been investigated in a comparative spirit by Anna Wierzbicka, who claims that they constitute two important groups of concepts constructed differently than taxonomic concepts (Wierzbicka, 1994). Functional and partonomic concepts categorise reality in a peculiar manner, without complicating the vertical structure or building abstract hierarchical arrangements. Obligatory components of the cognitive definition are those which pertain to the object's function, origin, material it is made of, quality etc. The categorising factor, contrary to the taxonomic definition, is not obligatory, thanks to which the cognitive definition has a wider application extending onto the so called *indefinibilia*, including the 'first elements' such as the sky, earth or water.

The second noteworthy structural property of the folk linguistic view of the world is the establishment of more detailed relationships between the connotative components of a given word. The simplest of those is conjunction, co-occurrence of features, e.g. '*strzygoń* has double teeth' and '*strzygoń* has blue marks on the back' (cf. above). The order is free but it may be chronological, as in folk fairy tales; e.g. a definition of the stereotypical mother would include the following: 'the mother bears children'; 'looks after the child' (with the hyponyms: feeds, changes, rocks the cradle); 'the mother brings up the child' (with the hyponyms: gives advice, punishes, rewards); 'she marries her child' (with more details: she gives a duvet, a painted chest to her daughter).

Features are also linked in the cause-and-effect manner, e.g. '*strzygoń* frightens people'; 'people neutralise the creature'. Another kind of link may consist in references to sets or collections, e.g. augury concerning the rain and phenomena in the human body (pain in the bones), on the farm (fire, cattle, a dog), in nature (mist, swallows, crows) or in the sky (the sun, the stars). The ordering of the elements in this collection progresses from what is closer to humans to what is more distant.

Before I pass on to a characterisation of other properties of the cognitive definition, I would like to discuss the method of recording the definition's most important component, i.e. a judgment concerning a given object in the form of a sentence or its textual equivalent.

This method was already proposed in Bartmiński (1980). The idea was then confirmed in the work of Anna Wierzbicka (1985) and the work of psycholinguists, e.g. Trzebiński (1981). The approach I proposed in 1980 reflected the logic of the time, which devoted much attention to the structure and definitions of folk concepts. Two conceptions were especially inspiring: that of the 'entangled' definition and the fragmentary definition.

The 'entangled' definition, also called the axiomatic definition or the postulate-based definition, is a set of propositions ('postulates') which meets two conditions: it is non-contradictive (has a solution) and unambiguous (has no more than one solution). Such propositions define the meaning of the term in question (Ajdukiewicz, 1965: 79–82).

The conception of the fragmentary definition is developed by Tadeusz Pawłowski (1978) in relation to the work of Rudolf Carnap. Pawłowski applies the conception to an analysis of open concepts, typical of colloquial language and the humanistic jargon, with 'families of meanings'. The concepts, such as *gra* 'game', *język* 'language', *sztuka* 'art', *kicz* 'kitsch' or *powieść* 'novel', cannot be defined by means of ordinary definitions. Fragmentary definitions only provide a portion of the range of a term and establish the sufficient conditions for something to be an example of the concept. Pawłowski illustrates this by saying that if someone studies mathematics at a university, the person is a student. Asked which feature may be taken as the sufficient one, the scholar responds that the one found in the object unquestionably referred to by the term being defined – this is a typical object.

In this way we move on to the third property of the cognitive definition: the conception of a typical object, the key to this method of defining. It leads us to the trend in semantic research initiated by Eleanor Rosch, which uses the concepts of a prototypical object and a prototypical situation in which the object functions. In lexicographic practice, in the process of constructing a dictionary entry on the basis of hundreds of examples, the compiler has to look for the object's typical features. In other words, the multitude of the features attributed to the object in texts must be treated selectively. The cognitive definition will include stereotypical features. One of the criteria of stereotypicality is the recurrence of a feature; e.g. the rain is often referred to as 'fine', a frequent expression in folk songs is 'a fine rain falls on Sunday morning'. A feature can also be regarded as established by the very fact of appearing in folk texts, which are frequently repeated, reproduced, reiterated ('stereotyped texts'). Especially significant in this respect are proverbs, which are minimal texts and elements of the lexicon at the same time. If the definition of water contains the information that it quenches thirst, is brought from the well, is found in a river or falls as drops of rain from a cloud, the stereotypical character of the features is indicated by such proverbial expressions as 'There is no one to pass him a glass of water' (He is all by himself, with no help), 'Pour water to the well' (cf. 'Bring coals to Newcastle'), 'Much water has flowed in the river' (Much time has passed), 'It is raining as if from a bucket' (heavily).

The stereotypical nature of a feature is manifested above all in the way it functions in a sentence:

i)   it occurs as predicative complement in generic judgments of the type 'Gold does not rust', 'Fire purifies', 'Ghosts appear at midnight';

ii)   it occurs as a presupposition, i.e. in the semantic layer treated as obvious; in 'She was poor but honest' it is presupposed that poverty entails dishonesty.

The fourth and last property of the cognitive definition is a categorical, facet-based arrangement of the defining sentences. In the definitions above, the defining sentences are grouped into the following categories (facets):

for *strzygoń*: APPEARANCE, CHARACTERISTICS, ACTION, TIME AND PLACE OF ACTION, ORIGIN, MEANS OF NEUTRALISATION

for *deszcz* 'rain': APPEARANCE, ORIGIN, CHARACTERISTICS, ACTION, TIME AND PLACE OF ACTION, COOCCURING EVENTS, AUGURY CONCERNING THE RAIN, AUGURY BASED ON THE RAIN, POWER OVER THE RAIN

The selection and arrangement of facets must be different for different entries, though it is evident that some of them have a wider application (CHARACTERISTICS, ACTION, TIME AND PLACE, ORIGIN) than others (AUGURY). On the basis of this kind of organisation of the defining sentences, one may propose specific models of definition for specific groups of entries, such as the elements, heavenly bodies, wild plants, cultivated plants, wild animals, domesticated animals, professions, nationalities, tools, rituals, cultural practices etc.[4] The selection and arrangement of the facets should reflect the linguistic consciousness being studied; it should also introduce order to the data documenting the usage of the entry word. At this stage the cognitive definition stands a chance of becoming independent from individual definitions provided by informants as well as from the presence or absence of expressions in its categorising component. Even if water cannot be called an 'element', because there is no such expression in colloquial (folk) Polish, the facet-based selection and ordering of the defining sentences will be similar to that in the entries for fire, earth or air. This will help identify the systemic categorisation of the world in a given language.

Notes

1   The most complete version of a lexicographic definition based on the principles of structuralist semantics is the work of Apresyan (e.g. 1992).

2   This is the sense in which it is used by scholastics and John Stuart Mill. Cf. Lyons (1977: 175–176) and Majer-Baranowska (1988) for a survey of the interpretations of the term in the literature.

3   The same method of explication is used in Bartmiński and Żuk (2007) for the concept of RÓWNOŚĆ 'equality' (German *Gleichheit*).

4   A similar diversification of descriptive models is proposed for the Slavic ethnolinguistic dictionary by Svetlana Tolstaya and Nikita Tolstoy (Tolstye, 1984: 6–22).

7 Viewpoint, perspective, and linguistic worldview

1 Introduction

The 'linguistic worldview' conception functions in two variants. These can be described in a somewhat simplistic manner as 'subject-related' and 'object-related' and assigned to the terms *vision/view of the world* and *picture of the world* (German *das sprachliche Weltbild*), respectively.[1] A vision is necessarily someone's vision: it implies the act of looking and, by the same token, the existence of a perceiving subject. A picture, though also a result of someone's perception of the world, does not imply the existence of the subject to the same extent: the focus is on the object, i.e. that which is contained in language itself. This does not mean, however, that one can speak about someone's vision to the exclusion of the picture of the world that they possess. The latter arises in a more indirect manner (cf. e.g. the picture of the world typical of a child, a man in the street, a clerk or a European) and so does a classification of linguistic pictures of the world with regard to their authors (Serebrennikov et al., 1988: 32–35). The concepts of point of view and perspective, mentioned in the title, refer both to the 'vision' and the 'picture' of the world. The *SSSL* (1996–1999) constitutes a subject-related reconstruction of the linguistic worldview found in a specific cultural community traditionally referred to in Polish as *lud polski* 'the Polish people'.

In the present chapter, I elaborate on the subject-oriented variant of the concept at hand. I pose questions relating to the point of view and perspective taken by a virtual language speaker as they can be reconstructed from linguistic material. I also consider the question of how to use these constructs in analysing selected portions of Polish lexis.

Let me remind the reader (cf. chapter 3) that by linguistic worldview I mean the interpretation of reality encoded in a given language, which can be captured in the form of judgments about the world. The judgments can be either *entrenched* in the language, its grammatical forms, lexicon and 'frozen' texts (e.g. proverbs) or *implied* by them. A worldview is an *interpretation* or *projection*, rather than a reflection of reality. *Słońce* 'sun', *księżyc* 'moon', *woda* 'water', *wiatr* 'wind' and *ziemia* 'earth', *ręka* 'hand, arm', *oko* 'eye', *serce* 'heart', *nerki* 'kidneys', *kąkol* 'corn cockle', *bławatek* 'cornflower' or *pies* 'dog' are not mere labels denoting objectively existing things but expressions of definite semantic content (connotation), based on the segmentation and categorisation of phenomena performed by the human mind. Words 'portray' things mentally, rather than reproducing them in a photographic manner. Defining word meanings requires equal attention to perceptual features ('the cornflower is blue'), functional features ('the cornflower is a weed') and relational features ('the cornflower grows in corn'). The latter are connected with the human-induced relationship between things, between things and people, as well as with the human valuation of the things in question. The language-entrenched characterisation of things, sometimes referred to as an idea (Putnam, 1975), projection (Jackendoff, 1983), or creation (Kwaśnica, 1999), is best captured with the term *interpretation*. This term maintains a balance between epistemological objectivism (the world does exist and people can come to know it) and subjectivism (the world is perceived by humans in a specific manner). Thus, it underscores the active nature of human cognition and language in relation to the world.

2 Viewpoint and perspective

I understand 'viewpoint' or 'point of view'[2] as a subjective-cultural factor, decisive for the way an object is referred to, including its categorisation, the choice of the onomasiological basis for creating its name and the selection of features attributed to the object in specific utterances and entrenched in meaning. The point of view adopted by the speaking subject functions as a set of directives shaping the content of words and whole utterances. The importance of this factor in the eyes of speakers is manifested in the poem *The peasant's point of view* by the folk poet Kazimiera Sekuła:

> Romantics, dreamers with your heads in the clouds,
> for you daybreak lights burn in the countryside,
> the corn hums with sea-waves,
> silver twitters in brooks.
> Warm spring brings confusion to your heads,
> harasses you with uneasiness,
> plays an emerald green,
> tempts with a scent of jasmine…
> And to me it smells of dung!
> For you, summer blooms with cornflowers,
> smells of honey from the fields,
> a field of wheat shines with gold.
> To me it smells of the harvest sweat,
> as my bones ache.
> I do not write poems or learned books,
> how can I dream of wide expanses,
> when fields of corn are awaiting
> the toil of my hands.
> When the autumn sky blooms with scarlet for you,
> golden leaves are carried by winds,
> the Indian summer glitters with silver dew –
> I think of bread.
> So that no household in the country
> or city should be short of
> bread, milk or vegetables,
> so that poets could dream
> of the countryside in peace.
> (from the volume *Ojczyzna* (Homeland), 1987, p. 186; trans. A.G.)

I understand 'perspective' as a set of properties of the semantic structure of words, correlated with and, at least to a certain extent, resulting from a point of view. By identifying these properties, the receiver of the utterance recognises the point of view taken by the speaker. By and large, I use both terms (their Polish equivalents) in their dictionary meanings. According to *SJPDor* (1962), 'point of view' is 'a standpoint from which a person views a particular matter or thing' ('From the point of view of wildlife studies, a primeveal forest is a kind of forest in which biological systems develop spontaneously'). 'Perspective' (from Latin *perspectiva* 'optics') is 'a view opening onto something' ('A perspective opened onto a meadow mantled with yellow flowers'). 'View' depends on 'standpoint' and the latter can be recognised on the basis of the former.

Point of view and perspective are 'metalinguistic' inasmuch as they function above the grammatical and lexical-semantic resources of language, at the level from which its lower levels are controlled. One can say that in addition to the type of rationality, ontological assumptions, attitude and the axiological system, they belong to the most important factors of the differentiation of utterances into language types, genres and styles (Bartmiński, 1981, 1991b).

3   Examples

3.1   Źrenica 'pupil of the eye'

Let us consider the Polish names for the pupil of the eye. What ways of seeing the object and what interpretive perspectives are revealed in those names?

The basic contemporary term in standard Polish, *źrenica*, semantically motivated by the verb *spojrzeć, spozierać* 'look, take a look', expresses a tool-like nature of the object in the action of looking. However, the name is ambiguous in the sense of combining associations with a tool ('that by means of which one looks') and associations with the subject ('that which looks/the one who looks'). The ambiguity 'tool/subject' is absent from some peasant dialectal terms, *patrzydło, patrzydełko* ('that which one uses for looking') due to the suffix *-ydło* used in deriving tool names. Incidentally, they are internal calques of *źrenica* because, although based on different morphological material, they repeat the same pattern of tool naming, 'something used while doing something else'. Both terms, however, standard Polish and peasant dialectal, name the object from the *functional* point of view.

The Old Polish name for the pupil, *zienica*, is different. It is derived from the verb *ziać, ziewać* 'open' and so emphasises a characteristic of the object's appearance. It is motivated not from the functional but the anatomical, perceptual point of view.

Yet another viewpoint constitutes the basis for other peasant dialectal terms, *panienka* 'little girl', *lalka* 'doll' (in Kashuby *pupka* is used, from the German *Puppe* 'doll'[3]) or *człowieczek* 'little man'. Only when talking to someone and looking into the person's eyes (a requirement of the behavioural pattern of communication in folk and other cultures) is it possible to see a reflection of one's own image (a little man, a doll, a little girl) in the interlocutor's pupils. According to folk beliefs, a woman in whose eyes one can see a goat instead of a person is a witch. This group of names, therefore, is based on seeing the object in the social-communicative context and has a cultural basis.

The three types of point of view, entrenched in linguistic names of the pupil, differ in the degree of subjectivity (i.e. their dependence on the speaking subject). In *zienica*, which has the perceptual basis and is probably the oldest, it is nil. In other cases subjectivity is entrenched in different ways.

3.2 Other examples

An inquiry into points of view becomes especially important when applied to groups of linguistic expressions, e.g. the names of people, cultural artifacts and images, plants or animals. A consideration of a few examples is now in order.

Slavic ethnic communities achieved self-identification by referring to the family (*Serb* 'countryman'), the human being (*Chorwat/Croat* 'the real man'), the ability to communicate (*Słowianin/Slav* from *słowo* 'word' vs. *Niemiec* 'German' from *niemy* 'mute'). Thus, it was based on the conception of intra-communal 'familiarity', as opposed to 'foreignness' (Popowska-Taborska, 1990).

Folk names of basic genres of folklore, such as *bajka* 'fairy tale, fable' (from *bajać* 'tell stories; talk nonsense'), *pieśń* 'song (from *piać* 'sing; pray'), *zagadka* 'riddle' (from *zagadać* 'ask a question', from *gadać* 'talk') *opowiadanie* 'story' (from *opowiadać* 'pass information') are derived from appropriate illocutionary expressions and so name utterance types with regard to their communicative intention (Bartmiński, 1988b). A considerable portion of genealogical names alludes to the circumstances in which a given song is performed: *podróżniak* – a song sung *po drodze* 'on the road', *kołysanka* 'lullaby' – *przy kołysaniu* 'while rocking (a cradle)', *pieśń dożynkowa* – at the time of *dożynki* 'a harvest thanksgiving festival', *pieśń weselna* 'a wedding ceremony song' – at the time of *wesele* 'wedding ceremony', etc. (Adamowski and Żuraw, 1979).

Among the Polish names for ghosts and demons there is a high frequency of external, symptom-based terms, i.e. projections of human behaviour when dealing with an unknown, mysterious force, as well as of human organisation of the spatiotemporal environment. The general name, *duch* 'ghost', comes from the name for the movement of air while breathing. Specific names for demons are derived from their alleged activities (*odmieniec* 'the one who is/has become different', *latawiec* 'the one who flies'), perceived as unpleasant (*dusiołek, gniotek* 'the one who squeezes, squashes', *zmora* 'nightmare', *topielec* 'the one who has drowned', *strach* 'the one who frightens others'), as well as from the alleged consequences of these activities (*sporysz*, from *spory* 'big' and *sporzyć plon* 'to increase harvest'; *kaduk*, from the name of an illness, etc.). They are also derived from the places in which evil forces can be found (e.g. *boruta* and *borowy*, from *bór* 'forest'; *rokita*, from *wierzba rokita* 'the willow *Salix rosmarinifolia*';[4] *płanetnik*, from peasant-dialectal *płaneta* 'cloud'; *wodnik*, from *woda* 'water'; *pasiecznik*, from *pasieka* 'apiary'; *domowy*, from *dom* 'home') or from the time when they appear (*nocnica*, from *noc* 'night'; *południca*, from *południe* 'midday'). The indirect, symptom-based method of demon naming corresponds to the naming taboo in folk varieties of Polish, which requires that their actions be expressed by means of impersonal constructions: *chodziło* 'walk-IMPERSONAL-PAST', *tłukło się* 'bang around-IMPERSONAL-PAST', *coś było* 'something was', etc.

The names of the 'living dead' stand out in this category, motivated by the creatures' appearance: *strzyga, strzygoń* (from the Greek *striks* 'owl'), *upiór, wampir* 'vampire' (from *pióra* 'feathers', which an *upiór* was alleged to have in the armpits). Also conspicuous are the names of creatures which came into existence as a result of someone's 'abnormal' death: *poroniec*, from *poronić* 'miscarry'; *topielec*, from *utopić się* 'drown'.

In animal names one can find elementary observational criteria, which humans could resort to while dealing with the creatures at a very basic level. Jacobs (1958), whose book bears the telling title *Naming-Day in Eden*, enumerates the following: place of origin (cf. Polish *pekińczyk* 'Pekinese'); size (*wieloryb* 'whale', lit. 'a large fish'); eating habits (*mrówkojad* 'ant-eater'); a characteristic sound produced by the animal (*kwiczoł* 'fieldfare', from *kwiczeć* 'squeal'); shape (*pierścienice* 'segmented worms', from *pierścień* 'ring'); the manner of movement (*skoczek* 'grasshoper', from *skakać* 'jump'); colour (*szarak* 'hare', from *szary* 'grey') (Maćkiewicz, 1988).

The category of point of view can also be applied to phraseological units, usually of transparent internal semantic motivation (Pajdzińska, 1999, 1988). An analysis of somatic phraseological units in Polish peasant dialects reveals that nearly 90% of them are motivated by the function of relevant body parts (*wypuścić coś z ręki* 'to let something out of one's hand'; *rzucać się w oczy* 'to be eye-catching'; *ruszyć głową* 'to think', lit. 'to move one's head'), and only 10% by their topography and anatomy (*do góry nogami* 'upside down', lit. 'with the legs up'; *szeroki na palec* 'finger-wide', etc.) (Krawczyk-Tyrpa, 1987).

3.3 More comments on *źrenica*

Points of view also figure importantly at the level of word meaning. *SJPDor* (1962) provides the following definition of *źrenica*: 'a round opening in the eye's iris, whose function is to regulate the flow of light to optic nerve endings'. The structure of the definition incorporates both viewpoints revealed by means of onomasiological analysis: anatomical-perceptual and functional (the cultural viewpoint is absent here), but it also contains references to a certain type of knowledge about the object in question. This is scientific rather than colloquial knowledge: the pupil has a regulating function, the eye consists of optic nerve endings, etc. The content of the definition is not supported by the linguistic material found in the same entry of that dictionary, which contains the phraseological units *strzec jak źrenicy oka* 'to guard like the apple (lit. pupil) of one's eye', *być dla kogo źrenicą oka/duszy* 'to be like the apple (lit. pupil) of the eye to someone', *zamknąć źrenice* 'to close one's eyes (lit. pupils); die', *mgnienie źrenicy* 'a very brief moment', lit. 'a wink of a pupil', as well as colloquial and literary quotations. Both the linguistic material and intuition point to the importance of other types of knowledge in the semantic content of *źrenica*; the word should rather be defined along the following lines: 'the middle, dark, round part of the eye, considered as the most important, guarded and protected, because it is thanks to this part that we can see; the part we look at when talking to another person'. The 'denotative' component of the explication, i.e. the reference to the actual object, is the same in both definitions; what differs are certain 'connotative' components. For example, the academic definition omits to mention the fact that the pupil is treated as the eye's most valued part, even though it is this evaluative feature that constitutes the basis for the word's metaphorical extensions (in Polish). The scientific approach also deprives *źrenica* of its role in the *human* act of seeing but treats the act mechanistically in a depersonalised manner.[5] *SJPDor* (1962) totally ignores the socio-cultural fact of looking into the interlocutor's pupils, entrenched in folk dialectal Polish more strongly than in standard Polish. In short, depending on the viewpoint, the pupil receives a different 'portrait' or 'perspective', composed of different elements.

4 Viewpoint, perspective, and style

Viewpoint distinguishes meanings of words by directly determining the choice of the definitional basis, and indirectly through the selection of categories and the way they are realised.[6] For example, the definitions of *bławatek* 'cornflower', *kąkol* 'corn cockle' and *dziurawiec* 'St. John's wort' may be said to be based on the categories of 'flower', 'weed', 'herb', respectively, or on the more general category 'plant'. It depends on the point of view and has far-reaching consequences. The choice is decisive as to which features of the *definiens* can be considered as characteristic and what cognitive category they represent. Thus, it is decisive as to what hypothesis on the concept's cognitive structure (Wierzbicka, 1985) the definition will propose. *Bławatek* 'cornflower', categorised from the point of view of an average nature lover as a 'flower', must be defined with respect to its [appearance], [scent], [blooming season], [distribution], and maybe [use]. From the point of view of a farmer it is categorised as a 'weed' and defined relative to [the place where it grows], its [appearance], [harmful effects on human endeavours], and maybe [methods of uprooting]. From the point of view of a natural scientist it is categorised as a 'plant' and defined relative to the plant definitional schema. As can be seen, points of view are interwoven with human activity in various domains.

The conception of viewpoint also constitutes the basis for the stylistic identification of language variants and genre patterns. In Bakhtin's words, 'style presupposes the presence of authoritative points of view' (1984: 192), 'authoritative' meaning socially stabilised, recognisable and culturally important. The variety of points of view established in a given culture and language, and consequently the variety of language styles, is indicative of the richness of that culture. Colloquial style is anthropocentric, based on the multifarious and subjective view of the world of the so called 'simple people', whose predispositions and existential needs are the 'measure of things' in that view. Scientific style narrows the view to selected aspects of reality, rationalises and de-concretises the picture of reality, as well as depriving it of emotions and valuations. Official, formal style assumes a rational, normative and impersonal viewpoint (Bartmiński, 1981, 1991b, 1991d; Bakhtin, 1979).

The anthropological-linguistic category of point of view requires a more detailed characterisation as well as a typology based on historical linguistic facts and the notions of its variant, variety and style. I will not be proposing a typology of this kind here but will only mention the possibility of the perceptual, functional or cultural perspective, a purely descriptive or evaluative one, intellectual or imagistic, descriptive or normative. Points of view may coexist in harmony,[7] but on the other hand the language of science, technology or office is characterised by a specialisation of viewpoints and an elimination of their variety.

As already mentioned, the notion of point of view, decisive for a preliminary categorisation of a given object, shapes the perspective in which the object is shown in the linguistic worldview. Let us therefore pass on to the notion of perspective, defined above in a preliminary manner as a set of properties of the semantic structure of words.

More precisely, we are first of all concerned with a set of 'aspects' ('sides') of the object, which are taken into account by speakers in a non-arbitrary order, form specific configurations and constitute a profile of the concept in question. Secondly, we are concerned with the body of information provided about the object when viewing it from a given 'side'. Consider the following expressions: 'the biggest country with regard to population and territory'; 'interesting in the political sense but poor artistically'; '(someone is) a moral, professional, intellectual zero'. These express perspectives on the objects referred to. In analysis, I would like to associate perspective with the aspectual (categorical, 'facet-like') connections between the object's features, as well as with the number, sequence and global structure of these 'facets':[8] This is the linguistic-cultural vision of the object. In this sense, perspective depends on viewpoint, but at the same time various viewpoints may emerge within it.

5   Viewpoint and the cognitive definition

Needless to say, in individual cases those aspects of the object are emphasised which are considered important by speakers, i.e. those which constitute a (socially) established, internally coherent structure of the concept. It is those culturally and socially significant aspects that should be systematically included in lexicographic descriptions. As I have already tried to exemplify with *źrenica* 'pupil' above, this in practice is not the case. Let us now return to the problem and consider the Polish word *gwiazda* 'star', defined in *SJPDor* (1962) as 'a light-emitting heavenly body, composed of gasses, of a structure similar to that of our sun'. The competence of an average speaker of Polish, however, does not include information on the composition and internal structure of stars: this is specialised knowledge. Indeed, the very question of the objects' composition and structure does not even emerge. In order to replace the scientific definition with one based not only on colloquial knowledge of the world but also on the colloquial structuring of that knowledge (cf. Bartmiński, 1980, 1984, 1988a; Wierzbicka, 1985), we should include in the definition of *gwiazda* such aspects as its [appearance], [number], [place where seen], [time when seen] or [action]. These aspects should be filled with content corresponding to the colloquial, rather than scientific point of view, and therefore incorporate elements of people's beliefs. A definition adequately representing colloquial linguistic awareness of the speakers of Polish – in my terminology, the 'cognitive definition' – should therefore assume more or less the following shape: *gwiazda* is 'one of the many small lights in the sky, visible at night, which group into what are called *constellations*, and about which it is said: they shine, twinkle, light up, fade away, fall …'. In the folk explication one would also have to add at least the following: '… which are believed to accompany a person from birth to death and by their behaviour and arrangement to give clues as to people's fate' (cf. Niebrzegowska, 1990).

In Bartmiński (1980) I propose to reconstruct the semantic categorisation inherent in linguistic material and represent it by an adequate arrangement of the defining sentences in the context of language-encoded stereotypes. This conception also constitutes a proposal for a dictionary of Polish valuation terms (Bartmiński, 1987, 1989c). The idea, too, has been put forward in numerous cognitively oriented works on semantics. A well-constructed definition should contain systematically arranged information on the material, function, structure and causative actions of the object (Moravcsik, 1981). Attention is drawn to meaning schemata, which capture 'what is unsaid but might be said' (Tyler, 1978: 246); e.g. in the case of animals the schemata consist of such collection of features as attribution ('dogs have tails'), activity ('dogs growl, bite, bark'), relations ('dogs are similar to wolves, they are bigger than cats'), valuation ('dogs are faithful, dangerous'), etc. (Tyler, 1978, in Wierzbicka, 1985: 208–210). Different models of internal organisation are accepted for different types of entries, e.g. people (linguistic characterisation, events, special characteristics), demons (names, appearance, origin and transformations, place and time where seen and active), plants (names, beliefs and legends, modes of pictorial representation), animals (names, beliefs and legends of origin, transformations, demonic functions, bans and prohibitions, protection against, participation in events, representation on masks and in rituals, use in medicine), objects (names, precise description of events and situations), or events (names, time and place, participants, instruments and objects, motivation and semantics, verbal components of actions) (*ESSD*, 1984).[9]

The theory and practice of this method of explication (definitions of artifacts, animals and birds) has been most fully presented by Anna Wierzbicka. Let us consider a fragment of her explication of the entry for *cats* (1985: 167–8):

[CATEGORY] A KIND OF ANIMAL
[HABITAT] they live with people, in or near people's houses
[…]
[SIZE] small enough for a person to be able to pick one up easily with both hands
[…]
[APPEARANCE] they are soft and furry
they have a round head with pointed ears sticking out on both sides of the top of the head
[BEHAVIOUR] they like to be clean, and they lick their body to keep it clean

[RELATION TO PEOPLE] they can be useful to people because they can catch
and kill small unwanted creatures of a certain kind

For *birds*, the author adopts an explication schema composed of the following
facets (although she does not use the term herself): [CATEGORY], [HABITAT],
[APPEARANCE], [BEHAVIOUR], [SIZE], [RELATION TO PEOPLE]. For artifacts, such as *cup* or *mug*, the facets are: [CATEGORY], [PURPOSE], [MATERIAL],
[APPEARANCE], [SIZE], [USE]. The ordering of the facets is non-arbitrary; indeed,
it results form the internal logic of the concept (i.e. the appearance of cups or mugs
depends on the purpose for which they are made) and therefore the definitional schema
is also a hypothesis on the concept's cognitive structure. There exist whole sets of concepts whose definitions should be based on the same schemata. For Wierzbicka it is
important to distinguish between essential features of an object (introduced with the
formula 'imagining things of this kind people would say these things about them') and
non-essential ones (in which case the formula is: 'imagining things of this kind people
could say these things about them') (Wierzbicka, 1985: 32).

An important and difficult problem inherent in a facet-based description is how
to establish and name facets. The original idea to make use of Aristotelian ontological
categories of substance, quantity, quality, relation, place, time, position, state, action
and affection (Bartmiński, 1980: 21) met with resistance, including a rather serious
warning against cultural irrelevance (Bogusławski, 1988: 14–15). If such irrelevance
were the case, the basic principle of subject-related adequacy of the cognitive definition[10] would indeed be violated. Anna Wierzbicka, too, supports natural categorisation
in unambiguous terms. However, it seems that traditional Aristotelian categories did
not arise from a priori speculation but from an 'observation of how an average mortal
relates to the surrounding world' (Jodłowski, 2003: 12), and at least for this reason are
worthy of attention.

6   Tokarski's case study

Let us finally look at an interesting case study in Polish. Tokarski (1990) is a meticulous
analysis of the Polish expressions used in reference to people of low/high esteem. The
author is interested in the sources of these expressions and connotations inherent in
their evaluative use. He concludes that valuation of people encoded in Polish colloquial
metaphors is based on the opposition 'us – them'. On the positive side, one finds what is
'ours', 'human', 'European', 'Christian' and 'knightly', whereas on the negative side, there
are things 'alien', 'non-human' (typical of animals), 'non-European', 'non-Christian' and
'non-masculine' (feminine). However, one can look at Tokarski's data from a different
angle and ask what points of view and what aspects of the characterisation of people
surface in the data, i.e. what are the facets from which the views of people of low/high
esteem are built?

The terms collected by Tokarski, regardless of their origin, express value judgments
relative to the generally assumed [MORAL STANCE]. These are sometimes positive,

e.g. *kryształ* 'crystal', but mainly negative: *antychryst* 'antichrist', *diabeł* 'devil', *belzebub* 'Beelzebub', *szatan* 'satan'; *hiena* 'hiena', *szakal* 'jackal', *padalec* 'slowworm', *gnida* 'nit, louse', *ścierwo*/*męt* 'scum' (lit. 'carrion, dregs'), *zgnilizna* 'rotting flesh', *szmelc* 'junk', *gałgan* 'rascal' (lit. 'rag'), *łachman* '(human) wreck', *ścierka*/*szmata* 'scumbag, slut' (lit. 'rag'), *hycel* 'creep' (lit. 'dogcatcher'). A dominant position is occupied by value judgments based on [SOCIAL BEHAVIOUR], i.e. someone's behaviour towards others, differentiated in the following manner:

beton 'diehard' (lit. 'concrete'), *kapral* 'corporal', *karbowy* 'overseer of farm laboureres', *ekonom* 'steward (of an estate)', *kat* 'executioner', *oprawca* 'torturer', *rzeźnik* 'butcher', *pirat* 'pirate', *kacyk* 'cacique; jumped-up bureaucrat', *kanibal* 'cannibal', *potwór* 'monster', *wampir* 'vampire' ['cruelty'];

błazen, *clown* 'clown', *komediant* 'comedian', *iluzjonista* 'conjurer', *kabotyn* 'ham (actor), attitudiniser', *kuglarz* 'juggler; impostor', *bufon* 'buffoon', *jezuita* 'jesuit', *żigolak* 'gigolo' ['insincerity, lack of seriousness'];

jastrząb 'hawk', *kogut* 'cock', *sęp* 'vulture' ['aggressiveness'];

pachołek 'servant', *najmita* 'mercenary', *kramarz* 'huckster', *handlarz* 'trader' ['venality'];

piesek 'doggy', *świnia* 'pig', *kret* 'mole' ['cunning subserviency'];

zgaga 'bitch' (lit. 'heartburn'), *zołza* 'shrew', *przekupka* 'quarrelsome female vendor', *hetera* 'hetaera, shrew' ['vexatiousness, quarrelsome disposition'];

pomazaniec 'the anointed one', *książę* 'prince', *kapłan* 'priest' ['haughtiness'];

płaz 'amphibian', *bazyliszek* 'basilisk', *gad* 'reptile', *żmija* 'viper', *wąż* 'snake', *jaszczurka* 'lizard' ['falsehood'];

chorągiewka 'flag', *kameleon* 'chameleon' ['changeability'];

stonka 'potato bug', *szarańcza* 'locust' ['arduousness for the people around'].

The next aspects in line are:

[BEING ACTIVE/PASSIVE], also used mainly in the social sense: *król* 'king', *apostoł* 'apostle', *siewca* 'sower', *rycerz* 'knight', *reżyser* 'director', *sternik* 'coxswain', *impresario* 'impresario'; *manekin* 'dummy', *pajac* 'clown', *kukła* 'effigy', *robot* 'robot', *maszyna* 'machine', *mięczak* 'wimp' (lit. 'mollusc'), *kelner* 'waiter';

[POSITION AMONG PEOPLE]: *potentat* 'potentate', *purpurat* 'cardinal' (lit. 'one who wears scarlet'), *ciura* 'nobody, lightweight', *trybik* 'cog', *pionek* 'pawn', *zero* 'zero', *proch* 'dust', *płotka* 'small fish';

[PHYSICAL ADROITNESS/MALADROITNESS]: *akrobata* 'acrobat'; *ofiara* '(born) loser', *słoń* 'elephant', *koczkodan* 'vervet', *manekin* 'dummy', *kukła* 'effigy', *niedźwiedź* 'bear', *kobyła* 'gangling woman' (lit. 'mare'); *lew* 'lion', *tur* 'urus', *byk* 'bull';

[MENTAL ADROITNESS/MALADROITNESS]: *encyklopedia* 'encyclopedia'; *cymbał* 'dope' (lit. 'hammer dulcimer'), *bęben* 'drum', *trąba* 'bungler' (lit. 'trumpet'), *duda* 'bagpipe'; *gęś* 'goose', *cielę* 'calf' (animal), *baran/dudek/cap* 'fool' (lit. 'ram/hoopoe/billy goat'), *gawron* 'rook', *osioł* 'jackass', *bałwan* 'blockhead' (lit. 'snowman'), *lalka* 'doll', *robot* 'robot'; *analfabeta* 'illiterate person';

[RESOURCEFULNESS]: *jeleń* 'deer', *ofiara* '(born) loser', *chomik* 'hamster'; *fujara* 'dud' (lit. 'pipe'), *trąba* 'bungler' (lit. 'trumpet'), *duda* 'bagpipe', *cymbał* 'dope' (lit. 'hammer dulcimer');

[SOCIABLENESS]: *jaskiniowiec* 'caveman', *troglodyta* 'troglodyte', *cep* 'flail', *chomąt* '(horse) collar', *złób* 'trough'.

The following aspects are less conspicuous:

[APPEARANCE]: *liliput* 'liliputian', *karzeł* 'dwarf', *pigmej* 'pigmy', *pokurcz* 'eyesore, fright', *kościotrup* 'skeleton', *lalka* 'doll', *pałuba* 'awkward doll', *ropucha* 'toad', *szczurek* 'little rat';

[ATTITUDE TO WORK]: *wół* 'ox', *mrówa* 'ant-AUGMENTATIVE', *pszczoła* 'bee', *truteń* 'drone';

[EMOTIONALITY]: *kociak* 'kitten', *mimoza* 'mimosa', *jagnię/baranek* 'lamb', *owieczka* 'sheep';

[POSSESSIONS]: *parias* 'pariah'.

Once the 'inventory of aspects' has been established, one can proceed to investigate the relationships between individual aspects entrenched and revealed by the language user. For example, it is striking in the data that little moral value is attributed to what is of little material value.

7   Concluding remarks

What has been said here about viewpoint and perspective aims to show the importance of these concepts in research on the linguistic worldview. The latter is dependent on linguistic and cultural factors. Therefore, research should focus on revealing the conceptualisation of the world inherent in linguistic material, on identifying the formal, semantic and pragmatic exponents of the conceptualisation and on reconstructing on this basis the view of the human being and the world.

Notes

1   Zinken (2004a) uses the term *the linguistic picture of the world* to refer to what is here
    called *linguistic worldview*. Even though both presuppose the existence of the subject
    (albeit to different degrees), the notion transpires more clearly in the latter term. *World-
    view* is also used by Wierzbicka (e.g. 1988).

2   The two terms are treated here as synonyms, contrary to some other authors, who
    differentiate them for theory-internal reasons (e.g. MacLaury, 1997) or who show their
    different understandings in the literature on the subject (Tabakowska, 2004b).

3   Cf. also the English *pupil*, from Old French *pupille*, from Latin *pūpilla* 'little doll, pupil
    of the eye'.

4   An internet search yields the English names *creeping willow* or *slender willow*. However,
    they are uncertain, as the former is usually classified as *Salix repens*, and the latter as
    Salix gracilis. [translator's note, A.G.]

5   Cf. in this connection the following excerpt from Adam Mickiewicz's *Pan Tadeusz or
    the Last Foray in Lithuania*: *podróżny ... toczył zdumione źrenice po ścianach*, lit. 'the
    traveller ... rolled his amazed pupils over the walls' (*the young traveller ... viewed the
    walls in wonder's full attack*; Book One: 'The Farm'; New York: The Polish Institute of
    Arts and Sciences in America, 1962, trans. Watson Kirkconnell).

6   I am not interested here in polysemy, in which case systemic differences in a lexeme's
    meaning (but above all in its denotation) motivate those in categorisation: *kamień*
    'stone', 'figure in a game' or 'unit of weight'; *kania* 'kite' (bird) or 'parasol mushroom';
    kret 'mole' or 'mole plough', etc. Rather, I am focusing on names with the same
    denotation but different connotations, *depending on* different viewpoints and different
    categorisations, adjusted to the viewpoints.

7   The folk worldview is characterised by internal incoherence, or at least such are the
    findings of contemporary ethnolinguistic research. For example, in folk texts obtained
    in 1984 from middle-aged and elderly inhabitants of a few villages in the area of Biłgoraj
    in south-eastern Poland, 'one notices approaches typical of a variety of epochs and
    cultures' (Bartmiński, 1989a: 49).

8   The conception of a 'facet' is used in information science as a 'subcategory', as a 'group
    of classes of the same characteristics, corresponding to e.g. 'a kind of substance', 'a type
    of activity', etc. Facets can be grouped into categories' (*STIN*, 1979: 45). I use the term in
    reference to homogeneous sets of features attributed to the object of explication.

9   For dealing with Slavic mythological figures, a descriptive schema has even been
    proposed in the form of a detailed questionnaire consisting of sixteen major points and
    many subpoints (Vinogradova, Góra, Kabakova, Ternovskaya, Tolstaya and Usacheva,
    1989).

10 In Bartmiński (1980: 21) I say: 'We do not aspire to originality. On the contrary, good
    categorization is that which is the most banal, maximally approaching the experiences,
    feelings and intuitions of the so called 'simple people''.

8 Profiling and the subject-oriented interpretation of the world

1 What is profiling?

There are two basic ways in which the notion of *profiling* is used in the literature on semantics. One application has roots in American cognitivism (Langacker, 1991a, 2000), the other is present in the writings of Anna Wierzbicka (1985 and subsequent publications) as well as authors who relate to her work. In this chapter I will present the latter understanding, whose beginnings can be traced back to the first sample of *SSSL* (Bartmiński, 1980), tested on data from folk and standard varieties of Polish.

Before I move on to the differences between the two conceptions of profiling, let me mention the similarities between them, thanks to which both contribute to the same research area. The similarities are based on the analysis of meaning of certain language expressions within a wider context, which for Wierzbicka is the Fillmorian notion of a 'prototypical situation' (Wierzbicka, 1985) and for Langacker is the notion of a 'cognitive domain', corresponding to something that others call a 'frame' or an 'idealised cognitive model' (Langacker, 2000: 4–7). Within the realm of the anthropological model, closest to the present research, it is a set of notions relating to the concept of the *speaking subject* (*homo loquens*), composed of such 'subjective' elements as the type of rationality, knowledge about the world, system of values, and especially the subject-oriented viewpoint and the worldview motivated by this viewpoint. The description of meaning in these approaches is linked through a network of relationships to a certain background: the situation, a wider conceptual structure, or the 'subject's circumstances'. These, in turn, involve a number of factors connected with *homo loquens*, with his or her attitude and intentions, surfacing in text as, among others, the characteristics of genre, style and, at a more general level, as culture. The latter way of understanding the background opens new perspectives for 'holistic' descriptions. The idea of a 'subjective background' has important ramifications: it paves the way not only for the linguistic and conceptual system, for multifarious dependencies of language upon the situation of the speech event, but also for a revelation of 'relations between people's linguistic behaviour and their thinking, culture and the development of civilisation' (Lewicki, 1993: 623).

The subject-orientedness of the background present in descriptions of meaning is reflected in the terminology, including 'viewpoint/point of view', 'perspective', 'profiling', 'vision', 'picture', 'portrait', or 'aspect'. All of these terms imply the existence of the perceiving subject. In accordance with the tenets of ethnolinguistics, which opts for a subject-oriented reconstruction of culture from the linguistic basis, I start with the common intuition: a *profile* is understood here as a 'contour (outline), sketch, shape of something', and the verb *to profile* as 'to give the object a certain shape' (*SJPSzym*,

1994). In this understanding, profiling is a subjective (i.e. performed by the speaking subject) linguo-conceptual operation, which consists in shaping the picture of the object in terms of certain aspects (subcategories, facets) of that object: e.g. its origin, features, appearance, functions, experiences, events connected with them, etc., within a certain type of knowledge and in accordance with the requirements of a given viewpoint.

The notions of profile and profiling constitute the core of a whole set of notions, which includes the conception of viewpoint, aspect, experiential frame and scene. On a more general level, all these notions are assigned to that of the linguistic world-view. The factors which drive profiling are connected with the already mentioned subject-oriented categories: someone's rationality, someone's knowledge of the world, someone's system of values and point of view. They belong to a high level of linguistic organisation, on which there is obligatorily the figure of a human being as an interpreter and 'organiser of the scene' (Tokarski, 1991: 137). I will use examples to make these notions clearer.

A linguist embarking on a description of this kind first deals with a massive amount of data entrenched in various cultural codes: verbal, behavioural, mythological-ideological and subjective-symbolic. The data constitute the base within the experiential frame available to analysis.

The notion of the experiential frame, as understood here, is broader than those of the viewing frame or viewing field proposed in the cognitivist literature (Langacker, 2001). I would like to include in it not only what is seen and conceptualised in an act of cognition, but also what is culturally established in the form of ritualised behaviour, beliefs, emotions, valuations, etc. Also, the experiential frame contains what is contributed to experience by individual and social memory: the viewing frame, cognitive frame, semantic frame are all sub frames of the experiential frame. The work on *SSSL* (1996–1999) confirms the value of the experiential frame so understood: one is capable of capturing in this way the internal differentiation of linguistic and cultural worldviews, dependent on various codes, styles and speech genres. Our research on the Polish axiological lexis was only based on linguistic data, which did not allow for a characterisation of these internal complexities.

The data contained in the experiential frame undergo the process of specification in speech events in the process of scene construction. In contrast to the simplistic juxtaposition of system and usage, I propose to identify two stages of this specification: one in a specific speech event here and now, which results in a specific utterance (cf. Langacker's (2000: 6–7) immediate scope of conceptualisation) and the other one, recurrent in different instances of language use, at the level of social convention. As an illustration, consider the names for stars and constellations. An analysis of a great number of names of stars in folk Polish from the perspective of their onomasiological foundations (Niebrzegowska, 1996a) leads one to reconstruct two conceptual scenes: a 'religious' and a 'farm-related' one.

Venus may be called *Gwiazda Betlejemska* 'the Bethlehem star', the Orion is *Stajenka Betlejemska* 'crèche', Castor and Pollux are *Gwiazdy Trzech Króli* 'The Stars of Three Kings': thus a conventionalised 'Christmas' scene is at play. This is on the level of text linked with an appropriate recursive ('folklorised') fictionalisation superimposed on the neutral names. For instance, the stars in Berenice's Hair are in folk Polish called *Sito* 'Sieve'; the name is supplemented with a conventionalised text, which says that it is the sieve used by the three Magi to feed oats to their horses. Similarly, Aries and the Pleiades are said to be gifts from a shepherd to baby Jesus.

Other star names include *Młotki* 'Hammers', *Siekiery* 'Axes', *Sznury* 'Ropes', *Włócznie* 'Spears', *Kleszcze* 'Ticks', *Drabina* 'Ladder', *Słup* 'Pole' and *Krzyż Święty* 'Holy Cross' (Cygnus), which refer to the Passion of Christ. The scene is also evoked by the names *Gwiazda Matki Boskiej Bolesnej* 'The Star of the Sorrowful Mother', *Niewiasty* 'Women' and *Trzy Marie* 'Three Marys' (the three stars of Sagitta). Another collection of names, in turn, evokes the Last Judgement, yet another a scene from Nazareth, etc.

The 'farm-related' conceptualisation of stars has its widely known lexical exponents in the names *Wielki Wóz* 'The Great Wagon' (Ursa Major), *Woźnica* 'Wagoner' (Auriga), *Baby* 'Women-PEJ', *Kosiarze* 'Mowers', *Droga Mleczna* 'The Milky Way' and rests on the metaphor HEAVEN IS A BIG VILLAGE. In this case, too, it is not only names that constitute a semantically coherent collection but also certain events reported as folklorised tales. A classic example of such double articulations of the metaphor HEAVEN = VILLAGE (names plus tales) is Woyski's 'star teaching' in Book VIII of Adam Mickiewicz's epic poem *Pan Tadeusz*.

2 The role of facets

The key role in this conceptual system is played by the notions of aspect, subcategory or facet. These terms are often used interchangeably and mean more or less the same (although it would be sensible to differentiate between aspect in reference to the image of a given object and facet as a bundle of judgements making up the explication and grouping the characteristics of the object). I have decided to talk about facets; Langacker (2000: 4–7) and his followers talk in this context about a domain.

The notion of facet derives from other realms of scholarship. The conception of facet-based classification is used in the theory of information retrieval (Czerny 1981: 69–75), devised by the Indian bibliographer Shiyali R. Ranganathan (1933, 1951). In information technology a facet means 'subcategory', a group of classes with a certain characteristic, e.g. the material from which something is made, the type of activity etc. Facets may be grouped into categories (*STIN*, 1979: 45). The basic question relating to facets is whether they surface by being extracted from data or imposed from above as a network ordering the data and allowing for an easy comparison of various entries. A related question is whether facets are universal or specific to individual concepts and their sets.

In the first of these issues I have always been in favour of the type of classification which would 'approach the experience, feelings and intuitions of ordinary people, plebeians, representatives of folk culture' (Bartmiński, 1980: 21) and thus meet the requirements of subject-oriented reconstruction. Therefore, Aristotle's categories were proposed at a certain point, being – as Jodłowski (1971: 14) would say – the results of 'the observation of the world performed by an average person' (Bartmiński, 1980: 21).

When in 1980 I proposed a categorisation of definitional components, I was not certain what role the notion of facet would play in the cognitive definition. In fact, the role proved to be crucial, not only because the shift from a taxonomic definition (cf. its critique in Bartmiński, 1984) to the cognitive (Bartmiński, 1988a) or open definition (Bartmiński and Tokarski, 1993) has significantly extended the length of actual definitions and necessitated their internal organisation, but mainly because a facet-like arrangement opens exciting new vistas for showing the cognitive structure of concepts. Such exemplary use of facets (though without using this term) was made by Wierzbicka (1985), who showed the existence of definitional schemas in specific portions of lexis (names of artefacts or animals) and justified this theoretically. She identified taxonomic, functional, partonomic and collective concepts, as well as attributing to them separate definitional structures, both in categorisation and in the choice of facets. For example, for cups these would be purpose, material, appearance, size, use (Wierzbicka, 1985: 33–34), for mice – nature, origin, habitat, size, appearance, behaviour and attitude to people (Wierzbicka, 1993: 254–256). The possibility of using the same explicatory schema has been confirmed in the case of precious stones (Mazurkiewicz, 1989) or stars (Niebrzegowska, 1996a).

A certain set of facets is needed to interpret and compare national stereotypes. This includes: outlook on the world; appearance; attitude to people and life; traits of character and intellect; attitude to material goods (Bartmiński, 1995). For the characterisation of professions (peasant, manual worker and clerk) Andrzej Wejland (1989: 94) distinguishes slightly different aspects: feelings and attitude to people; the quality of and attitude to work; material status and attitude to material goods; one's situation in and attitude to life; religious and political views; education and customs; position among people; appearance and clothes.

However, the hypothesis that there are unified definitional schemata in the explications of entries from one semantic field must not be treated as a dogma. For example, a considerable distinctness in the facet structure can be observed in the national stereotypes of a German and Russian (the former was in 1990 categorised by Poles in terms of nationality, the latter in terms of ideology; cf. chapter 14) or in the stereotypes of a clerk and a peasant (the former being viewed in terms of his attitude to people, the latter in terms of his attitude to work; cf. Wejland, 1989: 95).

The categorisation of an object, the selection of facets in that categorisation, as well as the qualitative characterisations of the object within the facets together constitute what one may refer to as profiling. A profile is understood here not so much as a variant of meaning but a variant of the image of a given object, shaped through the selection of facets, their arrangement according to the rules of implication and the latter's content, linked with the particular type of knowledge. At the same time, it is a variant produced by a dominant factor. The creation of a profile is enmeshed in the mechanism of scene organisation at the level of an individual speech event or at the level of social convention.

3   Profiles and meanings

Before I move on to the relationship between profile and subjective (subject-dependent) viewpoint, let me turn for a while to the relationship between profile and word meaning. If we assume the most general understanding of meaning as a semantic correlate between a linguistic expression and reality, the following questions emerge:

i)   Do profiles and meanings belong to distinct, incommensurate interpretive planes?

ii) Is profile just another term for meaning, i.e. does the identification of profiles amount to polysemy?

iii) Do profiles exist within meanings?

A positive answer to i) renders considerations of ii) and iii) redundant; therefore, we must assume that both notions can be applied within the same semantic theory. This has been corroborated by analyses of a wide range of concepts in our work.

The answer to ii) is negative. Support for this conclusion comes from the domain of proper names, which are said to denote rather than mean, but which can be analysed in terms of profiling. For proper names are accompanied by a 'semantic correlate' which can be variously profiled: a reference to X may concern different aspects of X, depending on the speakers' attitudes and intentions. A diversification of this sort is shown in the case study of a German (cf. chapter 14) and other national stereotypes; it is also possible in the case of geographical names or the names of people, such as Napoleon, Kościusko etc. The names denote what they do and no-one doubts how to use them, but the associations they evoke – which do not correspond to meaning as traditionally understood – are strongly diversified at the level of what I described as subjectively and culturally determined profiles. I return to this below.

Question iii) receives a positive answer. Profiles function within meanings and are specific forms of shaping the base content of the latter. They differentiate the image of the prototypical object.

The mechanism of profiling can follow a few typical paths, involving components from various domains of word meaning. First, the value of a profile is connected with the choice of the categorising factor. Such is the case of the cornflower, which being categorised as a plant, flower, herb or weed, each time receives a different set of facets and different content within the set (Bartmiński, 1993a). The Polish *lud* 'a people', defined in the strict sense as 'underprivileged strata of society' and on a lower level categorised as a 'class' or 'social group', undergoes clear differentiation of content with regard to its [characteristics], [behaviour] and [symbols] (Bartmiński and Mazurkiewicz-Brzozowska, 1993a).

Second, variability need not occur at the level of superordinate categorisation but on a lower level. For example, *ogień* 'fire' in folk Polish is differentiated mainly with respect to the place of occurrence (*ogień niebieski* 'heavenly fire', *ogień piekielny* 'the fire of hell', *ogień czyśćcowy* 'the fire of the purgatory', *ogień domowy* 'home fire') (Szadura, 1996). The folk Polish understanding of *woda* 'water' is differentiated with respect to its use (as a drink, a hygienic product, medication or a magic lotion) (Majer-Baranowska, 1993).

The relationship between profiling and polysemy on the one hand and the categorising factor on the other is by no means simple or unidirectional. Do different categorisations establish different meanings? They do if different denotata are at play: e.g. *kania* 'kite' (a bird) and 'parasol mushroom', *żuraw* 'crane' and 'shadoof' etc. In each of these examples the whole defining schema is different because the cognitive structures of the concepts 'bird', 'mushroom' and 'mechanical device' are different.

However, the process of metaphorical extension does not allow for easy generalisation, since different categorisations need not disintegrate the semantic unity of the lexicographic entry. For instance, *baran* 'ram' and 'idiot', *młot* 'hammer' and 'blockhead', *klops* 'meatball' and 'washout' are treated in dictionaries jointly, as semantically homogeneous rather than separate entries. Therefore, are they not different profiles at a lower level of differentiation, something one might call 'hidden polysemy'?

Let us now consider the role of the word *as* (Pol. *jako*) in the contexts at hand and ask to what extent and in what uses it contrasts profiles with meanings. Are the contexts i) '*kania* as a bird and as a mushroom', ii) '*baran* as an animal and as a person' or iii) '*człowiek* (a human being) as a social creature and as a biological organism' semantically identical? Does the expression *as* merely switch the mode of seeing the object or does it 'highlight the function, a special character of something, a position or role played in relation to something else' (*SJPSzym*, 1994)? It seems that the 'highlighting of the function' is present in all the cases above but something else comes to the fore: there is a different treatment of the head. In i) and ii) the expression *as* is assigned to the head in the formal supposition (i.e. the latter is treated as a word). In iii), in turn, the head is taken in the material supposition, as a concept rather than a name. Only in the latter case can one talk about profiles.

In conclusion, one should state that different profiles are *not* different meanings: they are ways of organising the semantic content within meanings. They arise through derivation from an open set of semantic features within a meaning. Profiling is grounded in prototype conception. One may link the idea of prototype with that of profiling by assuming the existence of a prototypical profile and its derivatives.

4   The subject of profiling

The conception of profiling presented here has been important in allowing us to reconstruct semantic viewpoints, and in formulate hypotheses concerning the subject of such a viewpoint. For example, in the development of the stereotype of a German in Poland, there is a correlation with changing subjective viewpoints. In short, the model of a German as a stranger is constructed by an average, 'ordinary' person, the 'man in the street'; the model of a German as a *pludrak* (one who wears *pludry* 'skimpy trousers') – from the point of view of a Sarmatian (a member of the Polish nobility known as *szlachta*); the model of a German as an invader and enemy – from the point of view of a Polish patriot defending the country's independence; the model of a German as a war criminal – from the point of view of a victim of military brutality; and finally the model of a German as a diligent, rich and cultural European is constructed from the point of view of a young member of the Polish intelligentsia.

Similarly, a methodical analysis of the concept of *lud* 'a people' as it developed over the period of two hundred years has made it possible, by beginning with a detailed documentation of the word's usages in various text types along the principles of subject-oriented reconstruction, to identify the relevant viewpoints and their subjects. These subjects can then be characterised in terms of their social, political, economic and intellectual status (Bartmiński and Mazurkiewicz-Brzozowska, 1993a).

A description of this sort restores the link between linguistic and literary analyses, advocated by Tabakowska (2004b). Literary scholars have accumulated a huge body of knowledge relating to the construction of worldviews from different viewpoints. Three examples of literary works of this sort should suffice here: Stefan Themerson's grotesque *Professor Mmaa's Lecture* (the world seen through the eyes of termites), Jerzy Kosiński's *The Painted Bird* (a borderland community seen through the eyes of a child) and Günter Grass's *The Tin Drum* (the war described by an intelligent dwarf). A linguistic description of that sort becomes an anthropological one.

9 The subject's viewpoint(s) in language, text, and discourse

1 Introduction

The category of viewpoint or point of view (cf. chapter 7) is the common denominator for literary studies and new trends in linguistics; thus, it opens new vistas for cooperation within broadly understood philology. It locates philology, i.e. the science of words or the 'anthropology of the word' (cf. Godlewski, Mencwel and Sulima, 2003), in the context of contemporary culture, which undergoes a so called 'visual turn': a change of mode from verbal to pictorial.[1] From what is happening on the Polish scene, one may conclude that the category of viewpoint has a wide application in text analysis (any text, not only literary), but also in descriptions of language as a medium. The latter trend is represented by cognitive and anthropological-cultural linguists. An especially important field of inquiry in this respect is international and intercultural public discourse.

In the sphere of public communication, particularly sensitive are the following issues:

i)   the motivation of a particular viewpoint;

ii) the relationship between the attitudes, predispositions and interests of the subject and the quality of the worldview projected by that subject (cf. the folk proverb 'An organist can only see organs on the Moon');

iii) the relationships between different viewpoints.

The category of viewpoint was used in text analysis, more precisely in considerations of literary narration, by James (1934), Friedman (1971), Genette (1972, 1976) or Bakhtin (1979); German authors (e.g. Canisius, 1987) analysed it as perspective (*Perspektivität*); Uspensky (1973) analysed it in detail in literary and other works involving points of view on the ideological, linguistic, spatiotemporal and psychological plane. Uspensky's ideas were then taken up by Simpson (1993), who identified four types of viewpoint: ideological, spatial, temporal and psychological.

For some time now the category of viewpoint has also been present in linguistics. It has come to be particularly appreciated by linguists working at the interface of language and culture. In this context, the category has been considered a subject-related factor, determining the shape of the linguistic worldview and the way it is profiled in discourse. Profiling, in turn, is the creation of a subjective variant of the worldview constructed from a specific location and in a specific perspective (cf. chapters 3, 7 and 8 above).

Within the derivational conception of style, it was agreed (following Bakhtin) that viewpoint is a style-determining factor (Bartmiński, 1981, 1990c).

The issues relating to point of view figure importantly in Langacker's cognitive grammar and Tabakowska's CG-inspired research on translation (Tabakowska, 1993, 2004a), Przybylska's studies of prepositions (Przybylska, 2002, 2003), as well as works on literary narration (Kardela and Kardela, 2000; Głaz, 2004). Two relatively recent collections of papers dealing with point of view are Bartmiński, Niebrzegowska-Bartmińska and Nycz (2004a and b).

In the present chapter I would like to do three things. First, I would like to reconstruct the linguistic picture of the Polish concept of WIDZENIE (SEEING), together with its parameterisation entrenched in colloquial Polish, identifying in particular the role played by the category of viewpoint. Second, I would like to discuss the question of the subject of SEEING[2] in relation to viewpoint. Finally, I would like to consider what configurations of different subject-related viewpoints are possible or whether and how they can be combined.

2   The concept of seeing: an overview

The category of viewpoint and the whole conceptual sphere of SEEING may be investigated on the basis of systemic data (the lexicon and grammar, the established systemic conventions) and on the basis of texts. Language both classifies and preserves individual and communal experience.

Following the assumptions of the cognitive definition, I am looking not so much for the objective knowledge of how the human eye perceives the world as for how that perception is conceptualised by native speakers of Polish. In this type of reconstruction one can establish the aspects of a given phenomenon favoured by speakers, arrange them by facets and thus produce a parameterisation of the colloquial model of SEEING (as is done with other concepts in *SSSL* 1996–1999). In contrast to scholarly analyses, the cognitive definition is geared towards a description of colloquial, everyday conceptualisation, entrenched in the awareness of an average speaker.

Thus, the linguistic picture of SEEING differs from the scientific one, based on research in optics, physiology or experimental psychology (cf. e.g. Demidov, 1986). It is at the same time more objective and stable, regardless of the progress in science (this paradox was pointed out by Wierzbicka, 1993: 264; cf. also Apresyan, 1994). Scientific terminology is transferred from one language to another and aims to achieve universal value; it does not take into account what is particular to individual languages and cultures. Naive, everyday knowledge, relative to culture, is in some respects richer than scientific knowledge, and in others it is poorer. In short, it is different.

The general concept of SEEING (WIDZENIE) is expressed in Polish by a few dozen verbs and their derivatives: nouns, adjectives and adverbs. Let us look at the most important monolexemic items:

widzieć 'see', *widzieć się* 'see (and talk to) someone'; *niedowidzieć* 'be short-sighted, unable to see well', *przewidzieć* 'foresee';

widać 'one can see', *widnieć* 'be visible; be there to be seen';

derived nouns

widz '(passive) spectator', *krótkowidz/dalekowidz* 'a short-sighted/long-sighted person', *niewidomy* 'a blind person', *widzenie* 'eyesight', 'visit', 'vision' or 'hallucination';

do widzenia 'good-bye' (lit. 'to-seeing'), *widziadło* 'apparition', *widmo* 'phantom', *zwidy* 'mirage', *przywidzenia* 'hallucinations', *widowisko* 'spectacle, show', *widnokrąg* 'horizon', *czapka-niewidka* 'cap of invisibility', *widok* 'view', *widzialność* 'visibility', *widownia* 'audience, auditorium';[3]

widzimisię 'will, arbitrary discretion';

adjectives

widny 'light' (of a room etc.), *widoczny* 'visible', *widzialny* 'visible', *widomy* 'clear' (of a sign etc.);

adverbs in the function of modal operators

widocznie 'apparently, evidently'

patrzeć 'look' and its derivatives: *podpatrywać* 'peep', *popatrzeć* 'take a look', 'look for some time', *dopatrywać się* 'discern', *napatrzeć się* 'look long enough', *przypatrywać się* 'have a good look at', *wpatrywać się* 'gaze', *wypatrywać* 'look out for', *zapatrzeć się* 'fix one's eyes', *zapatrywać się* 'form a view of, be of the opinion that';

peasant folk dialectal *patrzydło/patrzydełko* 'pupil (of an eye)' (lit. 'that which looks'), *patrzałki* 'eyes' (lit. 'those which look')

postrzegać 'perceive' and its derivatives: *dostrzegać, spostrzegać* 'notice, catch sight of'

obserwować 'observe' and its derivatives: *zaobserwować* 'notice', *poobserwować* 'observe for some time', *obserwator* 'viewer, observer', *obserwacja* 'observation', *obserwatorium* 'observatory'

zerkać 'peek'

oglądać 'watch', *ujrzeć* 'see', *obejrzeć* 'watch' and their derivatives: *podglądać* 'peep', *przeglądać* 'look through', *przyglądać się* 'peer at', *rozglądać się* 'look around', *spoglądać* 'look', *spozierać* 'glance', *wyglądać* 'look out', *zaglądać* 'look in', *podglądacz* 'peeper', *oglądacz* '(active) spectator'

gapić się 'stare' and its derivatives: *zagapić się* 'stare long enough to lose control', 'not to look (where one should)', *pogapić się* 'stare for some time', *gap* 'bystander, onlooker'; *zoczyć* 'notice, see', *oczkować* 'ogle'

Each of these words (and not all are listed) refers to the global conception of SEEING (visual perception) and profiles it in a specific manner, underscoring some if its aspects and downplaying others, i.e. organising them hierarchically within an assumed perspective of viewing. A functional distinctiveness of individual expressions is manifested by the possibility of using them in sensible sentences of the following kind, in which the basic concept of SEEING is profiled in a variety of ways through the use of expressions which categorise it differently:

(1) *Widzowie siedzący na widowni oglądają (widzą?) widowisko.*
     'Spectators in the auditorium are watching (seeing?) a show.'

(2) *Widziadło znika sprzed oczu widzów.*
     'The apparition disappears from before the spectators' eyes.'

(3) *Obserwatorzy obserwują (oglądają) widowisko z pierwszych miejsc na widowni, skąd widzialność jest najlepsza.*
     'The viewers observe (watch) the show from the first row in the auditorium, where there is the best visibility.'

What are the basic parameters of the act of SEEING? Let us first refer to the treatment of the verb *widzieć* 'to see' in Polański's syntactic-generative dictionary of Polish verbs (*SSGCP*, 1980–1992). In the 5th volume, published in 1992, two meanings of the verb are distinguished. The first one, defined as 'react to visual stimuli; perceive; reconstruct, evoke in memory or imagination', is accompanied by a schema with three positions: an obligatory animate or human subject, an obligatory object (which can express a physical object or an event) and an optional adjunct introducing the instrument of seeing with an obligatory attribute, e.g. *na własne oczy* 'with one's own eyes', *jednym okiem* lit. 'with one eye', etc. (*Janek widzi Marysię/psa/ samochód* 'John can see Mary/a dog/a car'; *Marek widział, że mały czymś się gryzie* 'Marek saw that something was eating the little one'). The second meaning of the verb, defined as 'attribute something to someone; regard someone/something as someone/something else', is accompanied by a schema embracing a human subject, an object and a localiser: *Matka widzi w Henryku ideał* 'Mother considers Henry to be an ideal person'; *Ktoś w swojej pracy nie widzi sensu* 'Someone cannot see sense in their work'.[4]

Thoughtful seeing (seeing and understanding) is characteristic of humans and only them. It is poetically expressed in Wisława Szymborska's *View with a Grain of Sand*:

> We call it a grain of sand,
> but it calls itself neither grain nor sand.
> It does just fine without a name,
> whether general, particular,
> permanent, passing,
> incorrect, or apt.

Our glance, our touch mean nothing to it.
It doesn't feel itself seen and touched.
And that it fell on the windowsill
is only our experience, not its.
For it, it is no different from falling on anything else
with no assurance that it has finished falling
or that it is falling still.
The window has a wonderful view of a lake,
but the view doesn't view itself.
It exists in this world
colorless, shapeless,
soundless, odorless, and painless.
The lake's floor exists floorlessly,
and its shore exists shorelessly.
Its water feels itself neither wet nor dry
and its waves to themselves are neither singular nor plural.
They splash deaf to their own noise
on pebbles neither large nor small.
And all this beneath a sky by nature skyless
in which the sun sets without setting at all
and hides without hiding behind an unminding cloud.
The wind ruffles it, its only reason being
that it blows.
A second passes.
A second second.
A third.
But they're three seconds only for us.
Time has passed like a courier with urgent news.
But that's just our simile.
The character is invented, his haste is make-believe,
his news inhuman.

(trans. Stanisław Barańczak and Clare Cavangh; in Szymborska, 1995: 135–136)

In most general terms, an analysis of the lexical data allows one to identify the *act* of seeing, the *subject* and *object* of seeing; the relevant *bodily organ* and *instruments* which facilitate seeing, the *field of vision* and *visibility*, the first, second etc. *planes* and the *background*; the *angle* of seeing, i.e. the arrangement of the line of sight in relation to the subject-object line; the *location* from which something is seen (*vantage point*), the *viewpoint* and *perspective*.

What can be said about these aspects of seeing on the basis of linguistic data alone? I proceed to answer this question now.

3   Parameters of seeing

3.1 Preliminary remarks

In the conceptual field of SEEING, there are about a hundred verbs referring to the very act of visual perception. They profile the base conception in several ways, underscoring its various aspects. Let us disregard the less interesting distinctions into perfective and imperfective verbs, as well as punctual, durative and iterative (which distinctions pertain to most Polish verbs), and pay attention to a few other semantic contrasts.

First, certain verbs profile the event from the point of view of the observer, such as *ktoś widzi kogoś/coś* 'someone can see someone else/something', *ktoś obserwuje kogoś/ coś* 'sb observes sb/sth', while others only underscore the entity being perceived and hide the perceiving subject, e.g. *widać kogoś/coś* 'sb/sth is to be seen' (lit. 'see-IMPERSONAL sb/sth'), *coś widnieje w oddali* 'sth is visible/to be seen in the distance'.

Second, seeing can be good or bad. The verb *niedowidzieć* 'be short-sighted', 'be unable to see well', in contrast to *widzieć* 'see', signifies a situation in which seeing is hindered by a defect of the organ of sight, an obstacle or long distance. One may, for example, *niedowidzieć* in intense sunlight. SEEING can be graded: one can see like a cat, as if in a mirror/through fog, unclearly, something can be seen 'as if on the palm of one's hand (i.e. it is as plain as a pikestaff).

The third salient distinction pertains to passive vs. active reception of visual stimuli. Passive reception is expressed by the verb *widzieć* in sense 1 (*kot widzi po ciemku* 'a cat can see in darkness'; an active reception is expressed by the same verb in sense 2 (*ktoś widzi coś* 'sb can see sth') similarly *ktoś patrzy na/ogląda/obserwuje coś/kogoś* 'sb is looking at/watching/observing sb/sth' etc., *ktoś patrzy, ale nie widzi* 'sb is looking but does not see'.

Fourth, the act of SEEING may be thoughtless (*gapić się* 'stare', *gawronić się* 'stare' (lit. 'look at sth like a raven'), *patrzeć jak wół/cielę na malowane wrota* lit. 'look at sth like an ox/calf at a painted door', *jak kozioł na wodę* 'like a billy goat at water', *jak osioł na aptekę* 'like a donkey at a chemist's') or intentional (*patrzeć* 'look', *obserwować* 'observe'; *mieć oko na coś* 'keep a sharp eye on sth', *sondować coś/kogoś wzrokiem* 'probe sth/sb with one's eyesight').

In the latter case, and this is my point number five, the act of visual perception may be performed with a greater or lesser will and attention on the part of the observer: *wpatrywać się w kogoś/coś* 'gaze, fix one's eyes on sb/sth', *nie spuszczać z kogoś/czegoś oka* 'keep an eye on sb/sth'. Also, the person may focus on a specific point in space: *wbijać/ wpijać/wlepiać w coś wzrok/oczy* 'bore one's eyes into sth', *świdrować oczami/wzrokiem* 'pierce sb with one's eyes/eyesight'. It is also possible to do that thoughtlessly: *patrzeć jak sroka w kość/gnat* 'look like a magpie at a bone'.

Six, SEEING may be temporally profiled as short and superficial (*rzucić okiem* 'cast a glance') or long-lasting and in-depth (*przyglądać się* 'peer at', *lustrować* 'scrutinise', *oglądać* 'watch', *zapatrzeć się* 'fix one's eyes'). The latter can be enriched with an additional meaning of moving one's eyesight from one object to another (*popatrzeć* 'look a little; look at a few things', *pooglądać* 'watch a little, watch a few things', *wodzić oczami/śledzić kogoś/coś wzrokiem* 'follow sb/sth with one's eyes').

The act of perception my be accompanied by emotions manifested through the manner of looking: *wybałuszać ślepia/oczy/gały, wytrzeszczać oczy* 'goggle, gape' (i.e. to look in amazement and let it be known), *patrzeć jak w obraz/tęczę* 'look as if at a picture/rainbow', *sycić się widokiem* **or** *napawać/paść oczy/wzrok czymś* 'feast one's eyes on something', *wpatrywać się jak urzeczony* 'gaze spellbound', *strzelać oczami* 'cast happy glances' (lit. 'shoot with one's eyes'), *zerkać* 'cast a furtive glance' (i.e. look surreptitiously with interest, trying to hide it from others).

The specificity of the naive conceptualisation of SEEING does not, however, stop here. Interestingly, the relevant verbs jointly express sensory and mental meanings and additionally assume social meanings. This is a very important observation, also for the understanding of point of view. The ethnolinguistic description, based on natural language, respects the polysemy of words, in this case the polysemy of the terms from the domain of SEEING (all the verbs listed above have several meanings), and draws relevant conclusions. This is not always the case in studies influenced by Anglo-American cognitivism. For instance, in her very interesting work on the verbs of visual perception, Zawisławska (2004) only focuses on the sensory meanings at the expense of mental meanings, which evoke the cultural and psychological context.

Let us consider some usages of the verb *widzieć* 'see', given by dictionaries of contemporary Polish:

(4) *Ktoś widzi dobrze/źle/wyraźnie.*
'One can see well/badly/clearly.' (the quality of seeing)

(5) *Widział coś nieuzbrojonym/gołym okiem.*
'He saw something with his bare eyes.'

(6) *Widział go kątem oka.*
'He saw him from the corner of his eye.' (he viewed sb standing at the side)

(7) *Swoją przyszłość widział w różowych barwach*
'He saw his future in bright [pink] colours.' (imagined)

(8) *Widzę tę sprawę inaczej niż ty.*
'I see this matter differently from you.' (I have a different opinion on this matter than you)

(9) *Sam widzisz, że to nie jest takie proste.*
'You see yourself that it is no so easy.' (understand)

(10) *Nie widzę w tym nic złego.*
'I don't see anything wrong in this.' (I don't consider it wrong)

(11) *Był źle widziany przez ówczesne władze.*
lit. 'He was badly seen by the then authorities.' (the authorities were critical of him)

(12) *Jak widzi pani możliwość wejścia na rynek obcych banków?*
'How do you view the possibility of foreign banks entering the market?'
(how do you evaluate it?)

(13) *Nie widzieliśmy się od wielu miesięcy.*
'We haven't seen each other for months.' (have not had a chance to meet up and talk)

(14) *Transformacją dla językoznwcy najbardziej intrygującą jest przekształcanie się wrażeń zewnętrznych w obrazy, które widzimy 'oczyma duszy'.*

'For a linguist, the most intriguing transformation is that of external sensations transforming into images which we see 'with our minds' eyes.' (Doroszewski, 1982: 108)

The meaning of the verb *widzieć* in the examples above oscillates between a purely sensory meaning (as reception of visual stimuli, perception in (4), (5), (6)), an imagistic meaning (imagining something not being the case in (7)) on the one hand and on the other hand a mental (realising, accepting, knowing – (8), (9)), evaluative ((10), (11), (12)) and socially-communicative meaning (an encounter in (13)). Example (14) aptly summarises these differences.

This semantic differentiation is most fully documented in *USJP*, 2003, which lists nine meanings of the verb but only three of them have to do with sensory perception, one concerns a social context (meeting someone), while the majority refer to psychological and mental acts, such as recalling, realising, comprehending, regarding someone or something in a certain way or judging. With time, the mental meanings seem to be gaining more ground and beginning to predominate, which is a typical process in the verbs of 'visual perception'. The semantic and etymological correlation between the verbs *widzieć* 'see' and *wiedzieć* 'know' is non-arbitrary: seeing is considered as the most basic means of acquiring knowledge of the world.

The predominance of mental over sensory meanings is especially visible in phraseological expressions of the type *widzieć tylko własny pępek/koniec własnego nosa* 'only see as far as one's navel/the tip of one's nose' (not to be interested in the problems of others), *nie widzieć świata poza kimś*, lit. 'not see the world behind someone else' (be uncritical in one's admiration of someone else), *widzieć białe myszki* 'see white mice' (have hallucinations), etc.

The mental and social aspects of viewpoint are correlated with specific subjects. Even a blind person can be the subject; cf. the following example found on the Internet: 'By quoting this, you assume the point of view of the blind' (http://www.enter.pl/techno/archiwum.asp?id=1789; accessed March 13, 2008).

3.2 The object of seeing: real and imaginary

In the fundamental three-element model involving the subject, the act and the object, the latter is located in two spheres: in reality, i.e. the physical, sensual world, and in the linguistic-cultural world, an artifact of human cognitive activity. The real object of perception is presented in 'the other reality': in text, painting, cinema, television or on the computer screen. Thus, it becomes a *picture*, an *image*.

The transfer of the object from the physical to the cultural sphere takes place through its identification and interpretation in the act of naming. Both acts, theoretically distinct, are in fact closely intertwined.

It is a telling fact that Polish contains a number of synonymous expressions referring to the object of seeing: *obraz* 'picture', *wizerunek* 'image', *wizja* 'vision', *widzenie* 'vision, hallucination', *widziadło* 'apparition', *widmo* 'phantom'; also *zwidy* 'mirage' or *przywidzenia* 'hallucinations'. They differ with respect to the ontological status attributed to the object. Two extreme poles are established by the words *obraz* 'picture' and *przywidzenia* 'hallucinations'. *Przywidzenia* or *zwidy* 'mirage' are conventionalised names of such an object of seeing which according to the speaker only functions in the sphere of imagination, devoid of a real basis. Objects referred to with the words *widmo* 'phantom', *widziadło* 'apparition' or *wizja* 'vision' are close to that pole.

The characteristics of the *image* of the object (not those of the object as such!) allow one to draw conclusions about the subject of perception, as well as about the other components of the act (cf. Tolstaya, 2004). This is the path taken by linguists who inquire into the motivation of linguistic signs and reveal in this way the viewpoints assumed by the speaking subjects (Tabakowska, 2004a; Grzegorczykowa, 2004, Kurek, 2004).

3.3 The subject of seeing

In Polish, the subject of SEEING has several conventional names: *widz* '(passive) spectator', *obserwator* 'viewer, observer', coll. *oglądacz* '(active) spectator', *podglądacz* 'peeper', *gap* 'bystander, onlooker', to mention only a few. They stand in direct relationship to the corresponding verbs of SEEING: *widzieć* 'see', *obserwować* 'observe', *oglądać* 'watch', *podglądać* 'peep', *gapić się* 'stare'; they allow one to identify the repertoire of socially established and recognisable roles of the subject:

> *widz* '(passive) spectator': 'a person looking at something'; the noun only inherits a portion of the wide spectrum of the semantics of *widzieć*, namely purely sensory, not mental meanings;

> *obserwator* 'viewer, observer': 'a person observing something, looking at something carefully, following or investigating something'; this evokes active behaviour of the subject present in *obserwować* 'observe', *patrzeć* 'look', *przypatrywać się* 'have a good look at', *spoglądać* 'look', *dostrzegać* 'notice, catch sight of', etc.;

> *gap* 'bystander, onlooker': 'someone from the outside, accidentally present, not participating in a given event, looking at something thoughtlessly, staring at something'.

In colloquial Polish there are also names derived from certain verbs, such as *oglądać* 'watch', which have narrower, specialised meanings: *oglądacz* 'someone who watches something (pictures, films, TV series)' vs. *oglądacz zwłok* 'coroner'. A specialised character is a characteristic of the following items: *wizjoner* 'visionary' – someone who creates bold visions in their imagination, usually pertaining to the future of something, and presents them in their works; *naoczny świadek* 'eye witness' – someone present in a given situation, who can confirm and bear witness to what they have seen; *patrol* 'patrol' – a group of soldiers (or policemen) commissioned to perform specific duties, observe, search through a terrain (from French *patrouille*; in Polish it has also given rise to the verb *patrolować* 'to patrol').

The superordinate name of the subject of SEEING, which encompasses all the other nouns is the present participle *postrzegający* 'one who perceives' (lit. '(the) perceiving').

The names listed above profile the base conception of the subject of SEEING highlighting certain functions, properties and circumstances of SEEING:

i)   *widz* '(passive) spectator' receives visual stimuli passively, while *obserwator* 'viewer, observer', *oglądacz* '(active) spectator', *podglądacz* 'peeper' do it intentionally and actively; a passive reception of stimuli connected with thoughtlessness is a characteristic feature of *gap* 'bystander, onlooker', containing the feature of 'incidentalness', i.e. denoting a person who participates in a certain event accidentally, driven by unhealthy curiosity;

ii) a differentiation of the subject's profiles may take place with regard to the kind of sphere in which the perceived object is situated: in the domain of reality one uses the words *widz* '(passive) spectator', *obserwator* 'viewer, observer', *gap* 'bystander, onlooker', *podglądacz* 'peeper'; in the realm of imagination the word is *wizjoner* 'visionary';

iii) also important is the distinction between an external or internal position of the subject: the external position is expressed by *postronny obserwator* 'incidental observer', *podglądacz* 'peeper', *widz* '(passive) spectator', *gap* 'bystander, onlooker'; if the subject 'belongs' to the event, one may use expressions such as *obserwator-uczestnik* 'participant observer', *naoczny świadek* 'eye witness'.

In the light of linguistic material, then, the subject of SEEING is treated as someone who passively experiences visual sensations (*widz* '(passive) spectator') or who looks and actively uses the organ of sight (*obserwator* 'viewer, observer'). Both roles are taken as sensory and mental actions at the same time and are contrasted with passive and thoughtless behaviour (*gap* 'bystander, onlooker).[5]

Because SEEING is both a sensory and a mental phenomenon, the subject of SEEING is commonly associated with experiencing and thinking. A viewer, observer, perceiving subject readily assume the functions of an interpreter and commentator.

3.4 The instrument of seeing and aids to seeing

The eye (Pol. *oko*) as the organ of seeing is referred to in the expressions *widzieć coś na własne oczy* 'see something with one's own eyes', *nie spuszczać z oka* 'not to take one's eyes off (sb/sth)', *wlepiać oczy* 'fix one's gaze', *mieć oko na coś* 'keep a sharp eye on sth'. The word gives rise to *zoczyć* 'see', *oczkować* 'look coquettishly'. The instrumental function of the eye is present in the folk peasant expressions *patrzałki* 'eyes', lit. 'the ones that look' and *patrzydełko* 'pupil', lit. 'the one that looks', which formally resemble the names of other functional objects, such as *zapałki* 'matches' or *szydełko* 'crotchet hook', respectively. The Polish terms for the pupil allow one to identify three types of conceptualisation of the object: functional (*źrenica*, motivated by the verb *spozierać* 'glance'), anatomical (*zienica* from *ziać* 'open') and communicative-cultural (folk peasant *lalka* 'doll', *człowieczek* 'little man', *panienka* 'girl', from the image of the speaker reflected in the interlocutor's eyes) (Bartmiński, 1990c: 112–113).

In phraseological units the functions of the eyes are extended even further. The organ is treated as something else: as a weapon (*strzelać oczami* 'cast happy glances', lit. 'shoot with one's eyes', *sztyletować wzrokiem*, lit. 'dagger with one's eyesight', *wbijać wzrok* 'bore one's eyes into sth'), as things to throw (*rzucić okiem* 'cast a glance'), as a drill or awl (*świdrować oczami/wzrokiem*, lit. 'drill with one's eyes/eyesight', *patrzeć świdrem/ szydłem*, lit. 'look with a drill/awl'), as a needle (*przeszywać wzrokiem/spojrzeniem* 'look piercingly', lit. 'pierce with one's eyesight/look'), as eating utensils (*jeść oczami* 'eat with one's eyes', *pożerać wzrokiem* 'devour with one's eyesight') or as another body part, e.g. an arm (*objąć spojrzeniem* 'glance around', lit. 'embrace with one's look', *wychwycić/ pochwycić coś wzrokiem* 'catch sight of').

The organ of sight can be aided by an additional instrument, such as glasses, a magnifying glass, spyglass, telescope, microscope, binoculars, visor or infrared receiver. The instrument may change the colour of the thing seen: *widzieć coś przez różowe okulary* 'see sth in bright colours', lit. 'through pink glasses'.

The organ of sight may be imperfect. Someone may have *bielmo* 'leukoma' over the eyes, i.e. the person may be blind to facts; they may also have *klapki* 'blinkers', i.e. they only see in a narrow-minded manner. When the leukoma or *łuski* 'scales' fall from sb's eyes, they realise the true value of something. One can also, in the mental sense, *zamydlić komuś oczy* 'pud suds into sb's eyes', i.e. mislead them.

The expression *nie widzieć świata poza kimś/czymś* 'be uncritical in one's admiration of someone else', lit. 'not see the world behind sb/sth', refers to a situation of excessive attention being paid to a person or thing and not enough attention to other important things which should be noticed in the field of vision.

3.5 Field of vision, visibility

The field of vision has its established lexical exponents in the form of the following expressions: *widok* 'view', in the sense 'the region seen, filled with details' (*USJP*, 2003); *jak okiem sięgnąć* 'as far as the eye could see', *widnokrąg* or *horyzont* 'horizon', in the sense 'the line at which the sky seems to touch the earth; the boundary of the field of vision'.

SEEING or visibility can be good or bad (easy or difficult). SEEING can be hindered by obstacles. The first and natural obstacle is darkness, which contrasts with light. We say *ciemno choć oko wykol* 'pitch dark' (lit. 'so dark that one could poke one's eye out') or *jak w grobie* 'as in a grave'. Thanks to lighting objects become *widoczne* 'visible'. The very ability to see is described with modal adjective *widzialny* 'that can be seen', whose antonym is *niewidzialny* 'invisible'.

The field of vision may be fairly large, in which case the subject concentrates on many objects at the same time (a macro-view): *obrzucić kogoś/coś wzrokiem*, lit. 'throw one's eyesight over sb/sth', *toczyć wzrokiem* 'look around' (lit. 'roll one's eyesight over sth'), *ogarnąć wzrokiem/objąć spojrzeniem* 'glance around' (lit. 'embrace with one's look'), or on a single object selected from the ground (a micro-view): *utkwić wzrok w czymś/ wpatrywać się w jeden punkt* 'fix one's sight on sth/on one point', *przyuważyć / zauważyć / spostrzec / zaobserwować / dojrzeć / wypatrzeć / wychwycić* 'notice'.

The object in the field of vision may be situated a long or short distance away from the subject: *widzieć z daleka* 'see from afar', *posyłać wzrok*, lit. 'send one's sight', *spojrzenie w dal* 'a look into the distance', *sięgać wzrokiem/oczyma daleko przed siebie*, lit. 'reach far with one's eyesight/eyes', *widzieć tylko koniec własnego nosa/pępka* 'only see as far as the tip of one's nose/navel'. The adjectives *dalekowzroczny* 'longsighted' and *krótkowzroczny* 'shortsighted' contain a salient evaluative element, connected with their mental meanings 'characterised by foresight' and 'lacking in foresight', respectively.

3.6 Foreground and background

Everyday linguistic consciousness identifies different 'planes' or 'grounds': the foreground and the background. *ISJP* (2000) includes the following information in the entry for *plan* 'plane': 'A close, distant etc. plane in a picture or theatrical stage is a group of objects or persons salient due to their proximity to the viewer'. *Pierwszoplanowy* 'in the foreground' in reference to elements of a picture, film, shot etc. are 'those in the first plane', and *drugoplanowy* 'in the background' are literally 'those in the second plane'. Anything located further than the object seen is called *tło* 'background, ground': 'objects, people, scenery etc. located behind what we can see in front of us'. An example: *Topole, żuraw studzienny, sztachety płotu ledwie odcinały się od tła* 'Poplars, the crane and the fence were barely seen against the background'.

3.7 The angle of seeing

The basic linguistically entrenched pattern of visual perception is the interpersonal model, when the object of seeing is the interlocutor, with whom the speaker establishes eye contact. This prototypical situation is referred to with expressions such as *oko w oko* 'eyeball to eyeball', *twarzą w twarz* 'face to face'; or *patrzeć komuś prosto w oczy* 'look someone straight in the eyes'. When the object is not a person, there is a metaphorical extension of the prototypical scenario: *stać twarzą do przedniej części obiektu* 'face the front (or: face) of an object', *stanąć przed czołem budynku* 'stand in front of (lit. in front of the forehead of) a building', *en face*; also *zajść od tyłu* 'walk up to something from behind', *z boku* 'from the side', *z lewej/prawej strony domu/samochodu* 'from the left/right side of the house/car (cf. Przybylska 2002).

In contrast to looking straight, we have *zezowanie* 'squinting', *patrzenie spode łba* or *wilkiem* 'glowering' (lit. 'looking from below the head' or 'in a wolf-like manner'), *widzenie/patrzenie kątem oka* 'seeing from the corner of one's eye', *patrzenie pod pewnym kątem* 'looking at an angle', *patrzenie krzywo/krzywym okiem* 'looking askance', all involving the avoidance of eye contact. This kind of personal communication is taken as abnormal, one that violates the rules of politeness and indicates communicative insincerity. Hence, it may provoke a hostile behaviour towards the interlocutor.

3.8 Point of observation, viewpoint

The category of viewpoint (or point of view) is a 'node' in the conceptual sphere of SEEING: it links the subject, the act and the object of SEEING.

The conception of viewpoint is sometimes used interchangeably with point of observation or the observer's position (Rzepkowska, 2004; *PSWP*, 1994–1998, vol. 35, defines it as 'the place from which someone or something can be observed'). But viewpoint is anything but equivalent with point of observation. The latter has a purely physical, sensory meaning and refers to the place (or perhaps time) at which the subject is located and performs sensory operations (sees, looks at, observes the object). Viewpoint involves a mental aspect, prototypically connected with the human subject, who not only observes but also conceptualises (identifies, categorises and interprets) the object, in order to finally name it. In this way, the subject processes sensory data into a linguistic and cultural picture of the object. (More on viewpoint below.)

3.9 Perspective

The word perspektywa 'perspective' is a Latin borrowing (via French); in dictionaries it is defined through the word *widok* 'view' ('an open, extensive view' in *USJP*, 2003; 'a wide view' in *PSWP*, 1994–1998). It is a complex notion, existing at a level higher than field of vision, angle of seeing or observation point and additionally containing the sense of directionality: a perspective may open up, extend; it may be extensive, wide, distant or blurred; an obstacle may close or cover the perspective. In contrast to unidimensional viewpoint, perspective is two- or even three-dimensional: it begins in the observation point and, through the line of sight, links the subject with the object(s) in the field of vision. Although in Polish it is often used interchangeably with point of view (one can see something from the point of view or perspective of a bird or frog), the two notions should definitely be distinguished.[6]

4   The role of viewpoint vis-à-vis other parameters of seeing

4.1 From the sensory to the mental and social meaning

Let us return to the distinction between point of observation and viewpoint. These fundamentally different categories are nevertheless related, similarly to the different meanings of the verb *widzieć* 'see'. If point of observation is merely a physical location from which someone sees something (Langacker calls it *vantage point*), viewpoint is a place or position in an extended, cognitive sense. SEEING is treated here not only in a sensory fashion but above all mentally, as a metaphorical extension from visual perception to understanding. In this way one moves on from the spatial and temporal plane (as in Awdiejew, 2004; Habrajska, 2004; Rzepkowska, 2004; Kudra, 2004 etc.) to the psychological, axiological and social plane.

The dominance of the mental meaning of viewpoint, including its psychological and axiological aspects, is confirmed by Polish lexicographers, who define *punkt widzenia* as 'someone's standpoint on an issue' (*SJPDor*, 1962), 'standpoint, opinion on an issue' (*USJP*, 2003), 'the way in which one sees various matters and evaluates them' (*ISJP*, 2000).

The mental and social understanding of point of view dominates, too, in contemporary Polish writing. For example, someone (the subject) 'assumes', 'formulates', 'represents', 'presents' or 'explains' their point of view. One may get to know someone else's point of view, try to understand it, share or support it. People's viewpoints may be convergent or close; they may overlap. Different points of view may be mutually exclusive or clash. In accounts of debates, e.g. on the enlargement of the EU, there are references to forcing or imposing one's point of view.

The purely sensory meaning of SEEING need not necessarily imply, though it may admit, cognitive activity. But the mental, metaphorical meaning necessarily does. This component is clearly present in the meaning of *obserwować* 'observe' and in the derivatives of *patrzeć* 'look' (*wypatrzeć* 'notice', *podpatrzeć* 'peep', *rozpatrzeć* 'consider' etc.). One must note, however, that the basic sensory meaning is in contemporary usage far from obsolete.

4.2 Viewpoint and the category of subject

A viewpoint is always *someone's* viewpoint. Literary texts emphasise an individual, idiosyncratic, unique viewpoint, but in public discourse the speaking subject is easily generalised, viewed as a representative of a group or an organised community. A typical, collective subject emerges, for example:

> May 26, 2004 Warsaw (PAP – Polish Press Agency). Józef Oleksy, the speaker in the Polish parliament, thinks that the speech of the German chancellor Gerhard Schroeder, delivered in Warsaw on Wednesday, was very interesting and represented the chancellor's point of view on the current developments in

> Europe and on the continent's future [...] 'It is only natural to expect that the
> German chancellor should speak from the position of Germany', says Oleksy.
> (http://euro.pap.com.pl; accessed May 26, 2004)

Such a generalised subject is identified through references to the viewpoint of the mother, the interlocutor, the consumer, the blind people etc. Bringing into relief the subject representing a particular point of view usually goes hand in hand with juxtapositions of subjects, points of view and worldviews dependent on them, e.g. those of the defendant and the judge, the head of a hospital ward and a patient, the parents and the child, the seller and the buyer, the attacker and the victim etc.[7] (cf. Piekot, 2004 for a discussion of the opposition between private and public perspective).

The most frequently mentioned generalised subjects in contemporary Polish public discourse include:

i)   the nation; there are specific, peculiar, usually contrasted viewpoints: Polish vs. German vs. Russian vs. Ukrainian; Iraqi vs. American; Palestinian vs. Israeli/Jewish etc.

ii)   a supernational community: the European point of view;

iii)   a group of people identified with regard to their sex: the male/female point of view;

iv)   an age group: the point of view of children/teenagers/adults/;

v)   a social group in a given environment: the point of view of students/the nobility/the youth (cf. Niewiara forthcoming);

vi)   members of a profession: the point of view of peasants (cf. Kurek, 2004)/ teachers/an average driver/a judge/a businessman/a manager;

vii)   an advocate of a given ideology: the Western/Eastern/citizen's/leftist/conservative point of view.

Through metonymic shift, a viewpoint may be attributed to a particular scholarly discipline or an institution. The human subject is in such cases positioned in the background, though not eliminated. (Sometimes the subject is hidden behind an attribute: the viewpoint may be auctorial, private, individual, personal, particular, global, general, one's own (mine, ours) or someone else's (theirs, yours), clear, interesting, optimal, dominant, evolutionary, religious or lay, practical or theoretical, official or unofficial).

One often deals with a depersonalised viewpoint, with a purely technical treatment of the category. The prepositional phrase *z punktu widzenia* 'from the point of view of' can then be replaced with *patrząc od strony* 'looking from the perspective (lit. side) of' or *ze względu na* 'with regard to' (examples come from the corpus of the Polish national daily *Rzeczpospolita*): *z punktu widzenia teorii / systemu / celu / budżetu / analizy / biznesu / bodźców / banku / długoterminowego wzrostu / rynku kapitałowego / rynku pracy / przepisów ustawy o podatku dochodowym / analizy technicznej / historii sztuki aktorskiej* 'with regard to the theory / the system / the aim / the budget / the analysis / business / the stimuli / the bank / long-term profit / capital market / job market / the act on income tax / technical analysis / the history of acting; *z architektonicznego punktu widzenia* 'from the architectural point of view'.

In Polish social exchange of ideas nowadays, genuine debate is being replaced by subjective opinions. Therefore, the conception of a 'neutral point of view' has emerged, one in which the speaker/writer presents controversial views without taking sides with any of them. Such is the conception promoted by the online free encyclopedia Wikipedia (www.wikipedia.org). However, this conception met with substantial criticism, which is hardly surprising. It is simply impossible to eliminate the subject as an observer and conceptualiser, or even as an 'organiser of the scene' (Tokarski, 1991). An objectivist treatment of viewpoint, in turn, may mask the factual arbitrariness of certain judgments.[8] Texts produced by subjects from their unique points of view my also be valuable as personal testimonies, may articulate collective experiences and as such be of value for historians (Pomorski, 2004; Elm, 1997).

It is important, therefore, to realise at this stage that the opposition between an individual and a collective subject does not correlate with that between a unique and a typical viewpoint or between a subjective and objective viewpoint.

4.3 Relationships between viewpoints: their diversity and dynamics

A successful communicative strategy must address the issues of the coexistence of various viewpoints in text and discourse: their complementation, overlap, inclusion or total disjunction. There is a widespread opinion that a multitude of viewpoints enriches knowledge as well as revealing novel aspects of old and known phenomena. A contrary opinion exists, too: the multitude may cause misunderstandings, install communicative barriers or even engender conflicts.

Let us consider typical cases in which:

i)   the same subject changes his/her point of view, constructs a new picture (profile or profiles) of the same object or event and produces the effect of multidimensionality;

ii)   different subjects perceive the same object, reveal its different aspects, which produces on a higher level a more complex, fuller picture of the object;

iii)   points of view of two subjects overlap, one encapsulating the other;

iv)   two (different) subjects, while assuming their respective points of view, construct incongruent, contradictory and irreconcilable pictures.

The most interesting domain in which one may observe relationships or an 'interplay' between different viewpoints are literary texts. The diversity of the subjects of SEEING and of the concrete roles they assume (of a viewer, observer, interpreter, commentator, recorder of facts or a judge) lies at the very foundation of the diversity of viewpoints and enables the writers to use them in a multitude of ways. Literary critics have analysed the issue thoroughly, identified the techniques of narration, described how one moves from the plane of the narrator to that of the protagonist, etc. (e.g. Uspensky, 1973).

4.3.1 The subject changes the point of observation

A variable location of viewpoint, in the sense of a spatial observation point, and the effects of such a situation, is a phenomenon well-known to photographers.:

> When you try to photograph children for the first time, you tread on an unknown territory. Only sometimes do you assume the point of view of the child's eye. Most of the time people assume the point of view of adults and look down. But if you really want to enter the world of children, you must get down to their level, to look at them eye to eye. Sometimes the photographer lies flat on the ground, sits on the floor or crouches. It is a simple method of taking very agreeable pictures which tell a child's story. (http://www.agfa.imagecenter.pl; accessed in 2003)

The technique of seeing or showing the same object from different positions is called 'multicamera registration':

> One of the exceptional, perhaps the most important features of DVD is the possibility of synchronic registration (and viewing) of the same event from many points of view (multicamera registration). The viewer may change his or her viewpoint at any time by selecting a different camera. A click is all it takes: the viewpoint changes but the event develops uninterrupted. (http://cis.art.pl/PODWORKO/AKADEMIA/FILM/V-02/V02–5.html; accessed July 10, 2007)

If viewpoint is treated mentally, rather than physically (in the spatial and temporal sense), unlimited options open up before the subject to portray and interpret one and the same event. As an example, consider Antoni Pawlak's 'Parallel lives' in the afterword to his 1998 book *A zmarli tak lubią podróże* ('The dead like to travel'). The author produces a humorous account of three ideologically different versions of his own life:

> I was born in 1952 to:
>
> a) a family of progressive working intelligentsia;
> b) a traditional and profoundly religious family, unable to accept the forcefully imposed authorities;
> c) a family of regular intelligentsia.

In April 1968, as a pupil at the 6th Lyceum in Gdańsk, I joined the Socialist Youth Association because

a) factious Zionists, responsible for the so called 'March events,'[9] convinced me that my duty as a citizen of the People's Republic of Poland is determined and unambiguous support of the policy of the Polish United Workers' Party;

b) in the wake of the failure of the student liberation movement, I realised that within the structures of the existing system only Wallenrodism[10] may aid Poland's efforts to regain sovereignty;

c) maturity came to me as a girl late for a date: all my friends enrolled and so did I. [...] (*Gazeta Wyborcza*, a Polish national daily, April 4–5, 1998)

The case well exemplifies the category of an 'ideological viewpoint' (cf. Uspensky, 1973 and Simpson, 1993).

4.3.2 Different subjects, different construals of the same object

A contrasting case is when different subjects observe the same entity but speak about that entity differently, revealing its different aspects or differently evaluating the same features. All of this produces an effect of multidimensionality, complexity and mysteriousness. A juxtaposition of the accounts of eye witnesses talking about the same person or event, a frequent situation in a court of law, is also a readily used literary device.

In Czesław Miłosz's *Road-side Dog* (1999, first Polish edition 1997), Paul transforms the objectified 'Tale of a Convert' into a bundle of divergent subjective opinions of his friends about the man, which gives the figure an intended indeterminacy. Similarly with Conrad's *Lord Jim*: the deplorable deed of the captain, who abandoned the ship with people on board, is discussed by many individuals but remains unsolved and enigmatic. Different points of view and different images of the protagonist are in such cases complementary. In novels, the narrator may also shift the viewpoint from one character to another: in each of them it opens up a different perspective, encompassing different objects or events. Uspensky (1973: 90) illustrates this with a scene from Tolstoy's *War and Peace*: subsequent portions of narration are constructed from the point of view of Pierre, Natasha, Nikolay etc. and as a result 'the narrative breaks into a series of apparently separate descriptions, each of which is narrated from the point of view of a different person'.

As is well-known, contemporary novels avoid the 'talkativeness of the omniscient narrator' and willingly cede his viewpoint to a specific character. According to Henry James, the originator of the point-of-view technique in novels, the contemporary novelist must constantly make a tremendous creative effort in order to enter the world of his own work (after Friedman, 1971: 112). A narration limiting the omniscience of the author and relying on the limited knowledge and sensitivity of a character (thus,

1st-person narration) is the most reliable and the most highly valued, as it 'presents' the character, rather than being a 'story about' that character (Friedman, 1971: 120). Giving voice to various subjects, representatives of different points of view, sensitivities and systems of valuation is a feature of good journalism, represented by, for example, Ryszard Kapuściński. The technique introduces the reader into the world of the reporter, the world of the eye witness and the world of the characters.

4.3.3 Co-occurrence, crisscrossing or overlap of viewpoints

A crucial case for our discussion is the co-occurrence, crisscrossing or overlap of viewpoints within the same text. Let us first consider what happens when one deals with two hierarchically organised states of consciousness. In her work on epistemic verbs, Danielewiczowa (2004) shows that the co-occurrence or crisscrossing of viewpoints is in a way 'foreseen' by the meanings of the verbs such as 'know', 'think', 'understand' or 'realise', which contain information about two states of consciousness: of the author-controller and of an epistemic subject. The two states are hierarchically structured and can occur in the utterance of one speaking subject, e.g. in epistemic statements with objects expressing events: 'I know I can do it'; 'I think I have not made a mistake'; 'I suppose he knows it'; 'In my opinion [I think], I have been wrongly accused'.

Danielewiczowa writes that one of the most characteristic features of epistemic predicates with sentential objects is dual subjectivity, because these predicates introduce information about the epistemic state of a given object, but also necessarily provide information about the state of knowledge of the person who uses a particular verb.

We might also come across cases which I call an 'empathetic encounter of two subjects', as in genuine dialogue. The encounter brings about a revelation and empathetic closeness of two personalities, two points of view. They can both be revealed in the same text. An exponent of the relation of coexistence, empathy and understanding is free indirect speech, as in Wisława Szymborska's poem *Pietà*:

> In the town where the hero was born you may:
> gaze at the monument, admire its size,
> shoo two chickens from the empty museum's steps,
> ask for his mother's address,
> knock, push the creaking door open.
> Her bearing is erect, her hair is straight, her gaze is clear.
> You may tell her that you've just arrived from Poland.
> You may bear greetings. Make your questions loud and clear.
> Yes, she loved him very much. Yes, he was born that way.
> Yes, she was standing by the prison door that morning.
> Yes, she heard the shots.
> You may regret not having brought a camera,
> a tape recorder. Yes, she has seen such things.
> She read his final letter on the radio.

> She sang his favorite lullabies once on TV.
> And once she even acted in a movie, in tears
> from the bright lights. Yes, the memory still moves her.
> Yes, just a little tired now. Yes, it will pass.
> You may get up. Thank her. Say goodbye. Leave,
> passing by the new arrivals in the hall.

(trans. Stanisław Barańczak and Clare Cavangh, in Szymborska, 1995: 51)

The tourist-narrator, dominating over the whole scene, does not invalidate the viewpoint and the characteristic reactions of the protagonist but includes them into his or her emotional sphere. The distinctness of both subjects is very clear. Under the apparent coolness and routine behaviour of the narrator, there is a carefully masked sensitivity, full of discretion and sympathy. There is an insurmountable distance between the mother, suffering with dignity and humility over the loss of her son and fulfilling the obligation to remain within the tight 'visit' scenario. Płuciennik (2004) refers to the same author's *Cat in an Empty Apartment* as an example of 'assuming someone else's perspective':

> Die – you can't do that to a cat.
> Since what can a cat do
> in an empty apartment?
> Climb the walls?
> Rub against the furniture?
> Nothing seems different here,
> but nothing is the same.
> Nothing has been moved,
> but there's more space.
> And at nighttime no lamps are lit.
> Footsteps on the staircase,
> but they're new ones.
> The hand that puts fish on the saucer
> has changed, too.
> Something doesn't start
> at its usual time.
> Something doesn't happen
> as it should.
> Someone was always, always here,
> then suddenly disappeared
> and stubbornly stays disappeared.
> Every closet has been examined.
> Every shelf has been explored.
> Excavations under the carpet turned up nothing.
> A commandment was even broken,
> papers scattered everywhere.

What remains to be done,
Just sleep and wait.
Just wait till he turns up,
just let him show his face.
Will he ever get a lesson
on what not to do to a cat.
Sidle toward him
as if unwilling
and ever so slow
on visibly offended paws,
and no leaps or squeals at least to start.

(trans. Stanisław Barańczak and Clare Cavangh, from Szymborska, 1995: 189–190)

The subject may also engage in an internal dialogue with his or her own self. An individual may entertain more than one viewpoint and yet retain his or her self; cf. Catullus' *Odi et amo* (Poem 85), Hamlet's *To be or not to be* or Mikołaj Sęp-Szarzyński's (a Polish sixteenth century poet) *Peace – happiness … frail, inattentive, split within.* Such is the characteristic of an internally dialogic personality. The same subject may see the same object from various points of view, in various perspectives, noticing its different sides and combining e.g. its sensory and ethical aspects. A dual take of this kind may give the impression of an internal dialogue, as in Czesław Miłosz's poem *An Honest Description of Myself with a Glass of Whiskey at an Airport, Let Us Say, in Minneapolis*:

My ears catch less and less of conversations, and my eyes have weakened, though they
    are still insatiable.
I see their legs in miniskirts, slacks, wavy fabrics.
Peep at each one separately, at their buttocks and thighs, lulled by the imaginings of
    porn.
Old lecher, it's time for you to the grave, not to the games and amusements of youth.
[…]
(trans. by Robert Hass and Czesław Miłosz)

The subject, as it were, 'takes two looks': sensory and axiological, puritanical. He feels both young and old, yields to 'erotic appetite', desires to engage in ecstatic closeness, but at the same time restrains himself, driven by the feeling of decency and guilt. All the time, however, he remains a sensual, world-loving moralist, engaged in an unceasing dialogue with himself and controlling his experiences. Many of Miłosz's late poems embrace two temporal perspectives: current and historical. Facts are continually enriched with memories of the past.

Finally, the same text may reveal a harmonious split of imagination; harmonious because seeing the same object in many ways may be a sign of the strength of imagination and intellectual plasticity of the one who looks. Consider the following excerpt from Martin Buber's (1970) *I and Thou* (orig. *Ich und Du*, 1923):

I consider a tree.

I can accept it as a picture: a rigid pillar in a flood of light, or splashes of green traversed by the gentleness of the blue silver ground.

I can feel it as movement: the flowing veins around the sturdy, striving core, the sucking of the roots, the breathing of the leaves, the infinite commerce with earth and air – and the growing itself in its darkness.[...]

I can overcome its uniqueness and form so rigorously that I recognise it only as an expression of the law – those laws according to which a constant opposition of forces is continually adjusted, or those laws according to which the elements mix and separate. I can dissolve it into a number, into a pure relation between numbers, and eternalise it.

Throughout all of this the tree remains my object and has its place and is time span, its kind and condition. [...]

This does not require me to forego any of the modes of contemplation. There is nothing that I must not see in order to see, and there is no knowledge that I must forget. Rather is everything, picture and movement, species and instance, law and number included an inseparably fused.

Whatever belongs to the tree is included: its form and its mechanics, its colors and its chemistry, its conversation with the elements and its conversation with the stars – all this is its entirety. (Buber, 1970: 57–58)

5   Cognitive and political motivations of viewpoint

Let us finally consider the factors motivating the choice of viewpoint. The contemporary Polish usages (*poznawczy punkt widzenia* 'the point of view of acquiring knowledge; the cognitive viewpoint'; *kulturowy / społeczny / historyczny / polityczny punkt widzenia* 'the cultural / social / historical / political point of view') signal a relationship between viewpoint and various spheres of human activity. Especially conspicuous are the desire to know the truth; the sphere of broadly understood culture, with a major role played by aesthetic, ethical and hedonistic values, the problems of beauty and fiction, imagination and play; or the sphere of political activity, set to a defense of individual and group interests.

Different viewpoints assumed by the same subject can be harmonised, as is the case in the excerpts from Miłosz and Buber above, in a scenario of 'knowing oneself' and the world around. Different viewpoints dramatise the use of language, they produce the effect of moving in a clearly established direction along the axis of the subject's changeable sensitivity and imagination. The clarity of the direction is brought about by the cognitive, epistemological intention.

The situation is different if what motivates points of view is not a quest for knowledge but politics. A good example is given by Yevgeny Tarle, who mentions the evolving ways of reporting Napoleon Bonaparte's advance in Parisian press during his 'hundred days'. The first message was: 'The Corsican monster has landed in the Gulf of Jouan'; the second: 'The cannibal advances towards Grasse'; the third: 'The usurper entered Grenoble'; the fourth: 'Bonaparte occupied Lyon'; the fifth: 'Napoleon approaches Fontainebleau'; and finally: 'His Imperial Majesty is expected today in his faithful Paris' (quoted after Uspensky, 1973: 21–22).

Contemporary political discourse is rife with contrasting viewpoints in inter-ethnic dialogues. It is enough to recall the dramatic, endless Polish–German debates concerning the Centre Against Expulsions,[11] Polish and Jewish versions of the Jedwabne massacre,[12] Polish and Ukrainian views on the massacre of Poles in Volhynia.[13] One can appreciate the significance of collective viewpoints motivated not so much by the quest for the truth as by the gravity of stereotypes and attempts to defend true or alleged national interests.

If the difference in viewpoints motivated by the desire to obtain knowledge can be reconciled through the concept of truth, the diversity of politically or ideologically oriented points of view is much harder to overcome. To do that would mean to be able to reconcile what look like irreconcilable interests.

Notes

1   For example, the victory of the visual paradigm over the "linguistic turn' so loudly trumpeted by twentieth-century philosophers' is discussed by Martin Jay (1996: 3), an American historian of ideas.

2   For the sake of simplicity, the English gloss SEEING will be used instead of the Polish WIDZENIE but the reader is advised to always bear in mind that it is the Polish concept that is being analysed here. [translator's note, A.G.]

3   It is interesting that the English terms *audience* and *auditorium* make reference to aural rather than to visual perception.

4   Phraseological units receive a separate treatment in the dictionary: *widzieć coś w czarnych/różowych barwach* 'see something in black/bright colours'; *widzieć coś oczyma wyobraźni* 'see something in one's imagination' (lit. with one's imagination's eyes); *nie widzieć świata za kimś/za czymś* 'think all the world of someone' (lit. 'not to see the world behind someone'); *widzieć tylko koniec własnego nosa* 'not to see further than the tip of one's nose'; *kogóż to widzą moje oczy?* 'and who do I see?' (lit. 'and who do my eyes see?').

5   Langacker differentiates between a 'viewer' and a 'conceptualizer' but notes a close link between them, as 'certain aspects of conceptualization are understood metaphorically in terms of visual perception' and 'perceptual experience represents a special case' of conceptualisation (2000: 204). In her survey of Langacker's views, Tabakowska (1995: 59–61) uses the terms *viewer* (*the subject of conceptualization*) and *conceptualizer*, the

relationships between the sensory and mental planes being interpreted as metaphorical extensions (the 'viewing metaphor'). But in Tabakowska (2004a), the author subjects the category of the viewer (who registers what falls within his or her purview) and the observer (who consciously chooses his or her observation point) to that of the conceptualiser. Zinken (2004b) considers one more distinction: between an external observer and a 'subject shaping the world'. Awdiejew (2004) and Habrajska (2004) treat the sensory observer as a grammatical category. Kudra (2004) juxtaposes the category of the observer with that of the commentator, which is located on the mental plane and definitely goes beyond the conception of SEEING.

6   In Langacker's cognitive grammar, perspective is defined as 'an aspect of construal that subsumes such factors as vantage point, orientation and subjectivity/objectivity' (Langacker 1991b: 551). In another view, perspective embraces a 'spatial organization of the scene', with an 'arrangement of the subject and object relative to each other' and an 'orientation of the whole arrangement in space' (Tabakowska, 1995: 70) but also point of view, which can also be 'a point in time' (Tabakowska, 1995: 71). Perspective is also defined as an aspectual characteristic attributed to the object (or the object's image as a semantic structure), correlated with and, at least in a certain sense, resulting from point of view (Bartmiński, 1990c: 112).

7   'They are educated and qualified lawyers, psychologists, nurses, medical doctors or even administrative officials employed by the hospital, and fulfil their duties as spokespersons on a voluntary basis. 'I consider it important that what I do is not a fiction. Of course, the point of view of the ward doctor and a patient will always be different', says Grażyna Kieszniewska, the spokesperson of patients and a nurse in a hospital in Sieradz.' [http://www.esculap.pl; accessed June 2005].

8   Cf. the discussion among German historians on the crimes of fascism, synthesised by Theo Elm in the following way: 'The scholarly tone of the debate is indicative of amazingly positivist thinking. However, one cannot say that adherence to objective scholarship hindered the development of subjective worldviews, which was a one-time strong conviction of Max Weber. On the contrary, the abstract rationality of scholarly research seemed to contribute to the arbitrariness of judgments [...]. In this way, the content of scientifically established historical facts turned a historical debate into a political one.' (Elm, 1997: 215).

9   A political crisis in Poland in March 1968, involving student protests and an anti-Semitic atmosphere in the Polish government, which resulted in the enforced emigration of several thousand Polish Jews.

10   An attitude represented by Konrad Wallenrod, the protagonist of Adam Mickiewicz's narrative poem bearing the same title (1828). 'The patriotic poem tells the story of Konrad Wallenrod, a Prussian, who sought refuge in Lithuania, where he was reared among the people's mortal enemies, the Order of Teutonic Knights, who becomes the order's Grand Master and deliberately leads the Knights to military disaster. Bound by patriotic dictates (of which he has been reminded by an old bard) and nurtured on imperatives of vengeance, Wallenrod faces a tragic choice; shorn of love and honor, he ends in suicide.' (wikipedia.org; accessed July 10, 2007) The poem was inspired by the figure of Konrad von Wallenrode (ca. 1330s–1393), the 24th Grand Master of the Teutonic Knights, serving between 1391 and 1393.

11   Documenting the forceful emigration of Germans from parts of Eastern Europe during the Soviet offensive towards the end of WWII. To be erected in Berlin (http://en.wikipedia.org/wiki/Centre_against_expulsions; accessed May 2, 2008).

12   A massacre of Jews from the town of Jedwabne (now north-eastern Poland), now
     officially recognised by the Polish Institute of National Remembrance to have been
     'committed directly by Poles but inspired by the Germans' (http://en.wikipedia.org/
     wiki/Jedwabne_pogrom; accessed May 2, 2008).

13   Conducted in 1943–1944 as an act of 'ethnic cleansing' against Polish civilians (http://
     en.wikipedia.org/wiki/Massacre_of_Poles_in_Volhynia; accessed May 2, 2008).

10   The stereotype of the sun in folk Polish

1   Introduction

1.1 The cultural background

The Polish stereotype of SŁOŃCE 'sun' inherits many features from the past. In early cultures, the sun was worshipped as a cosmic force, a manifestation of a supernatural power, or even as a god. The cult of the sun was practised in ancient Egypt (the god Ra with the symbols of a boat, a shield with a snake, an eye, a falcon and a scarab), in Babylonia (Shamash), Persia (Mitra), Greece (Helios riding in the sky in a chariot drawn by white horses). In India, since the time of the Vedas, the sun and light have been considered as epiphanies of being, immortality and fecundity. Cults of the sun have also been found in Mexico, Peru and Australia. Israelites, too, worshipped the sun (2 Kings 23:5.11), in spite of official prohibition (Deut 4:19). The cult of the sun was brought to Rome by the Roman legions from Persia around the year 100 A.D. The 25th of December was celebrated as *Dies nativitatis Solis invicti*, the day of birth of the invincible Sun. The early Christian Church assimilated the cult and gave it a new meaning by choosing that very day for Christmas: in the Bible Christ is called 'the rising sun' (Luke 1:78). Christian temples were oriented to the east, towards the sun.

In Old Slavic there were two gods associated with the sun: *Swaróg*, the god of the sky/heaven, and *Swarożyc*, the god of fire. In Slavic folklore the sun belongs to one mythological sequence with the day, sky/heaven, east, fire and life, whereas the moon belongs with the night, earth, west, water and death. This is compatible with Indo-European tradition, which links the sun with light and the sky/heaven.

The linguo-cultural picture of SŁOŃCE presented here is based on the nineteenth and twentieth century documentation of Polish folk culture (including 60 volumes of Oskar Kolberg's *Lud*, 23 yearly issues of *Literatura Ludowa*, 78 issues of *Lud*, 30 issues of *Łódzkie Studia Etnograficzne*, 23 issues of *Orli Lot*, 48 of *Polska Sztuka Ludowa*, 20 of *Wisła*, 18 of *Zbiór Wiadomości z Antropologii Krajowej* and 283 other publications), as well as field work of the Lublin ethnolinguistic team conducted from 1960 to 1994.

1.2 The background of standard Polish

Four meanings of *słońce* 'sun' are distinguished in standard Polish:

1   'The light in the sky during the day';
2   'Shine, warmth';
3   'An insolated place';
4   'Sunny weather'

This diversity is most conspicuous when one considers the expressions of the type *poruszać się za słońcem* 'move with the sun (as it traverses the sky)' (meaning 1), *robić coś o słońcu/za słońca* 'do something when the sun shines, in daylight' (meaning 2), *chodzić po słońcu* 'walk in sunlight' (meaning 3). The meanings can be treated as profiles of the same base image, connected through metonymy. Meanings 2–4 are derived from the first, basic meaning. Meaning 4 is a generalisation of the first three, cf. example (31) in section 4: Documentation.

In accordance with the assumptions of the cognitive definition, I present below the meaning of SŁOŃCE in the whole network of syntagmatic and paradigmatic relationships in different, crisscrossing semantic fields. I divide the description into two parts, the explication and the documentation of basic motifs.[1]

2 Explication

The Polish word *słońce* (in folk dialects also *słonie*, *słonio*) has close counterparts in other Slavic languages (Russian *so!ntse*) and generally Indo-European languages (Latin *sol*, French *soleil*, English *sun*, Lithuanian *sáulé*). Etymologists link the term to the Proto-Indo-Iranian *svar* and Avestan *súvar* 'shine, sky, sun', as well as to the name of the Old Slavic gods *Swarog* and *Swarożyc*. All these terms are derivable from the Proto-Indo-European root **sau-/*su-* 'shine'. It is this component of meaning that is the most conspicuous in Polish words derived from *słońce*: *słonecznić się* 'glitter, sparkle in the sun', *osłonecznić się* 'brighten', *rozsłonecznić się* 'light up, brighten up', *słoneczny* 'sunny', *słonecznica* 'sunbeam' or 'photophobia'; the verb *nasłonecznić* 'warm (something) up, lighten (something)' also strengthens the connection between the sun and warmth.

The diminutives of *słońce* have an ameliorative meaning: *słonko*, *słoneczko*, *słoneńko* (the Lublin region), *słonyszko* (the Kashubian region). One can even come across forms typical of animal offspring: *słoniątko*, *słończę* 'young sun; young elephant' (in Linde's dictionary, *SJPLinde*, 1807–1814). The latter form is also used in the Silesian name of the so called St. John's bread: *słończęta*.

WHAT IS SŁOŃCE? The sun is perceived as a light in the sky, a ray or beam from the sky; more rarely as fire, a ball of fire, a spark from the sky (example (8) (c) below) – thus, as sources of warmth (example (4)). It is interpreted mythologically in accordance with the archaic image of the sky as a dome. The sun is a hole in the dome (the stars are smaller holes), it is the sky's window. The sun is also treated as the eye of God, who can see everything from above. For contemporary non-mythological rationality, these interpretations are metaphorical.

In the folk picture of the world, metaphorical extensions of the sun include a golden ball or, in a new-year carol (example (17)), a ball of gold, dug out by the boar from beneath the roots of a fir tree. Other metaphorical representations of the sun include an oak, bird, dove, ladybird, horse, or, in a symbolic manner, a circle or an egg.

In a secondary sense, the sun is treated metonymically, similarly to standard Polish, being detached from the source: as elusive shine or brightness (example (38)); as an insolated, golden place (example (32)); as an element of weather (brightness, warmth), along with the wind and frost (example (3)).

Słońce is a component of a complex image of the sky (cf. *jak słońce na niebie* 'definitely', lit. 'as the sun in the sky'), portrayed in riddles as a farmer on the heavenly field (the moon is a farm-hand and the stars are cattle; example (1)). The central position of the sun is also visible in the riddle about the sun as a tree (an oak), the boughs of which reach down to every house (example (2)). In written peasant poetry one finds an image of the world as a house, with the sky as the roof (example (42)). It is lightened by the sun and the moon.

In the folk picture of the world, the sun makes up a minimal collection with the moon (cf. examples (4), (5), (16), (18), (28), (35), (39), (40)). In folklore, the sun and the moon are treated as a pair of people: an admirer and the girl he admires (example (16)), a husband and wife, or two brothers with stars for sisters. In the extended collection, the sun and moon are usually accompanied by the stars, e.g. in a Lenten song the sun, moon and stars mourn the death of God (example (19)). The sun and the stars are ornaments worn by the Virgin Mary (example (35)).

There are also paradoxical collections with a magic power. One of them consists of two lights (the sun and the moon) visible during the day at the same time – one should not sow flax or wheat then (example (43)). Another magic collection is one with the shining sun and the rain (example (15)): in the Poznan region one says then that a wolf is laughing.

The sun functions in four oppositions:

i)   as a light during the day it is opposed to the moon, which shines at night (the opposite features: day/night and work/rest) (example 5)); the opposition is an aspect of a larger one, between good and evil, God and the devil, since according to a cosmological myth the sun was created by God and the moon by the devil, who stole a piece of the sun for the purpose;

ii)   as a source of health it is opposed to diseases in magic spells (examples (11), (12));

iii)   as something bright it is opposed to dark spots (example (6)), clouds (example (27)), shade (example (33)), darkness (example (38));

iv)   as something warm it is opposed to cold water (example (34)), frost, fog (example (26) (b)) or dew (example (7) (a)).

The sun comes from God, as does the whole world (example (41), (34)). In a nursery rhyme, a ladybird is sent to heaven or to Jesus to bring the sun.

APPEARANCE. The most important, dominant feature of the sun, its brightness, is entrenched in the phraseological expression *jasne jak słońce* 'as clear (bright) as the sun, obvious'. The sun may also be described as golden, rose-coloured (at dawn), red (at sunset) or blood-coloured (before a battle).

VALUATION. The sun is maximally positive, which is expressed with stable attributes (holy, beautiful, nice) and ameliorative diminutives (cf. above), or in intratextual and intertextual sequences. It is called a heavenly (example (8) (b)) or a permanent treasure (example (8) (c)).

The sun performs three basic ACTIONS: it i) moves, ii) shines and iii) heats things. A separate category is iv) the behaviour of the sun as a living creature in fables.

i)   The sun rises (examples (7) (a), (9)), goes out (example (11)), sets (examples (9), (10), (20), (27)) etc. Sunrise and sunset are linked in folk thinking with the idea of the beginning and end (example (45)).

The direction of movement together with the sun used to guarantee participation in the cosmological order, so it was observed in farm work, as well as in ritual and magical practices. Ploughing and sowing began at dawn and proceeded west, so that corn could grow well. In Podlasie (eastern Poland) family land was divided in accordance with the movement of the sun: the oldest son received the easternmost plot and then the allotment proceeded in the direction in which 'the sun travelled in the sky'. A wedding company should follow the sun, 'as the sun goes', so that the newlyweds would do well 'like the sun in the sky'. In a wedding song the sun goes in a circle when a girl goes to a wedding (example (22)). The opposite direction was taken in funerals and in casting spells to cure diseases.

On some days the sun is believed to behave in a peculiar manner: it plays and dances at dawn on Easter, on the day of Annunciation and on St. Paul and St Peter's day. On St. John's day it plays around in many colours, as a rainbow, or walks like a quail; it jumps on Christmas and Annunciation; bathes on Christmas, on Sundays and during a wedding (example (23)).

ii)   The sun shines; cf. the proverb 'The sun shines everywhere in the same manner'. The sun shines for, on or over someone (examples (26) (a) and (b), (27)), in which case that person is happy; hence the curses: 'May you not see the sun any more', 'May you not see a single sunbeam'; 'May the sun not shine for you!' (example (28)). The places where the sun does not shine (a grave, rock, mountain, forest, water) are dead; this is where diseases are exiled (example (12)). Positive actions are expressed by the formula: 'the sun gilds the earth'. The sun is believed to stop shining when the world ends. A solar eclipse is treated as a harbinger of doomsday.

iii)   The sun heats the earth and the world. It purifies and cures; burns everything that is wrong, kills diseases and restores health. The sun is called upon in spells against illnesses (examples (11), (12)). These are causative actions, in which the sun represents masculinity and insemination: the earth gives birth (example (41)), there is no life without the sun. There is a song in which a girl grazes her oxen on a meadow (a poetic formula expressing a sexual intercourse) when the sun is hot (example (30)); her garland withers away, becomes pale (she loses her virginity). The sun also beats down; it is blazing and scorching, burns without flames.

iv) In tales from the Kraków and Poznań regions the sun is a living creature: it has a house or a wonderful palace on a high mountain, a farm; it lives with its sister and mother. In a Lublin tale, it administers justice to someone who has harmed a poor peasant.

The sun has emotions like a human being: it is joyful on the Feast of Annunciation and at Easter (because of Christ's resurrection); it cries on All Souls' Day. In songs it is portrayed as sad, crying or angry: it is sad when lovers do not sleep together (example (40)), after Christ's death it cries together with the moon, stars, clouds, lightning, streams, rivers, water springs, angels and holy ghosts after Christ's death.

It has been recorded several times that there is a peculiar, mythical relationship between the sun and the snake (viper). It is widely believed that when a viper looks at the sun, it can drink the sun's shine and take away its strength. The body of a killed viper had to be buried in the ground because the sun may get angry or set bloody-coloured, there may be hail and rain, the sun will be ill, it may smoulder or go dark. The sun bows to the person who buries a snake or a viper.

People's BEHAVIOUR TOWARDS THE SUN is that towards a living creature. Prayers to the rising sun were still noted in the twentieth century (examples (8) (a) and (b)), sometimes in the form of poetic 'hymns to the sun' (example (8) (c)). They were (still are?) accompanied by appropriate religious-like behaviour (kneeling down and crossing oneself, reported in 1984). The Kashubian end-of-the-day prayer goes: 'Oh, sun, thank you for letting us end the day so happily'. It is followed by making the sign of the cross over the sun, fields, the farm and on oneself.

The cult of the sun is also recognisable in bans on pointing one's finger at the sun (so that its eyes are not poked out), cursing and swearing in its presence, standing with one's back towards it, urinating, throwing rubbish or even looking in its direction.

One tells the TIME of the day and year according to the position of the sun in the sky (a proverb says: 'The stars and the sun are the best clock'). The movement and position of the sun determines, in traditional culture, the time of work and rest (example (5)). The times and directions determined in this way are sunrise and the east (Pol. *wschód* for both), noon (midday) and the south (*południe*), sunset and the west (*zachód*). Midnight and the north (*północ*) are established through contrast with midday and the south.

A proverb says that on Saturday there must always be a little sunlight. In Catholic tradition this day of the week is devoted to the Virgin Mary, who dries Jesus' nappies or her own coat, wet from the tears of the orphans whom she takes care of or of the souls in purgatory. In historical songs about the battle between Jan Sobieski and the Turks (1683) (a later variant: between Marshal Piłsudski and Bolshevist Russia in 1921), the sun, asked by Mary to do so, shines three hours longer (example (35)).

The formulae localising the sun have in fact temporal meanings: 'the sun is high' means that there is still daytime, the time of work; 'the sun is low' means that dusk and the time of rest is approaching (example (25)). Similarly the formulae 'a man-high sun', 'a poplar-high sun', 'a two-poplar-high sun' have locative-temporal (chronotopic) meanings.

On the basis of the sun's appearance one can FORETELL future events. The future well-being of the household is determined on the basis of the sun's appearance, its presence or absence on specific days of the year (cf. the proverbs 'If on the Palm Sunday the sun shines, barns, barrels and nets will be full'; 'If in April the sun shines, the farmer will not be poor'). No sunlight on the day of the wedding forecasts a difficult life to the newlyweds. A red sun forecasts war, death and hunger. A halo around the sun or a pale sun forecasts rain. Other proverbs include: 'If on St. Mark's Day the sun is hot, a downpour usually follows'; 'The sun is hot before a storm'.

The sun is a symbol of perfection (example (6)), the highest good (examples (8) (b) and (c)), well-being (examples (7) (a) and (b)), truth (e.g. in the proverbs 'The sun cannot be covered with a sack', 'Don't say anything against the sun'), happiness ('life full of sunshine, though sometimes stormy') or freedom ('our homeland will finally see sunlight').

In Christmas carols the sun is a symbol of Christ: 'The Magi run to the dark crib and pay homage to the Sun hidden under the shadow of the body'. Religious songs also contain the biblical motif of a woman clothed with the sun (Rev 12:1), i.e. the Mother of God (example (37)). Metaphorically, the sun is evoked in reference to a person in lullabies ('Go to sleep my daughter, my sun') and in love songs ('Where there is the sun, there is my love').

In the folk dream book the sun usually signifies something good: health, joy or good weather. The rising sun forecasts long life, while the setting sun forecasts short life or the death of a family member. The sun may also signify fire and storm. If it appears in a girl's dream, it forecasts a suitor.

In folk ornamentation the sun is SYMBOLISED by a circle, also in the form of a rosette. In a new-year carol from the Lublin region it is symbolised by a ball of gold, dug out by a boar from beneath a fir tree and made into a cup (example (17)).

The most important life-giving functions of the sun are symbolised by an egg and a snake. An egg, similar to the sun in its shape and colour,[2] symbolises the beginning and source of life (cf. magic spells in example (13)). A snake, resembling a sunbeam (which is usually drawn as a wavy line), is connected to the sun through its associations with the inseminating phallus (cf. comments on the sun and the snake above).

The sun is also symbolised by an oak (example (1)), a horse (example (38)), a ladybird (examples (14) (a) and (b)) (in Silesia also called *słoneczko* 'little sun'); in songs it is symbolised by a bird and a dove, in a riddle by a farmer. In religious ritual songs (example (22)) and prayer books (example (10)), the sun can be associated with a girl or a virgin (also with the Virgin Mary). In a wedding song the bride is the sun and the bridesmaids are the stars (example (24)).

The plant associated with the sun is the sunflower, which, as a proverb has it, 'turns around following the sun'.

An important feature of the sun is the fact that it rises and sets, as well as the location of these events. This is the theme of the next section.

3   Sunrise/east and sunset /west

The words *wschód* 'sunrise; east' and *zachód* 'sunset; west' symbolise two concepts: the beginning/end of the day (the time when the sun rises/sets) and the places where the events happen.[3] The two characteristics are regularly associated with positive or negative emotions, as well as with numerous practices and beliefs.

The time of sunrise is associated with light and day; it is preceded by the dawn, evokes positive feelings or joy (cf. diminutives in a song: *Świętego Jana raniusieńko zesło słuneńko jaśniusieńko* 'On the morning-DIM of St. John's Day the sun-DIM rose very bright-DIM'), marks the beginning of an activity. To say that 'the sun rises for someone', means that the person is doing well. In folk love and wedding songs a typical event at dawn is an encounter of the lovers: the beloved one appears at sunrise on Sunday morning. Traditional beliefs treat the moment of sunrise as magical: it is good at the time to do things relating to the treatment of illnesses (collect herbs, cast spells on diseases, especially those affecting the eyes and skin), to protection and to ensuring fertility and good harvest. Farm work is also effective at that time of the day (sowing millet or wheat, hoeing cabbage); it is good to wash oneself in water from a river (especially on Good Friday and Good Saturday). However, it is also the time when witches are active.

The way sunrise looked like was used to forecast the weather or, on some days of the year, to predict the quality of the harvest.

Sunset is associated with the approaching darkness and night: it is the time when work is finished and one gets ready for sleep (cf. 'Hush, the sun is setting; close your eyes and sleep, my daughter'). In folk songs sunset is when one awaits the beloved one. In ritual songs it is when the maiden's garland is exchanged for the nuptial coif.

Sunset generally evokes negative emotions ('The sun sets behind the viburnum forest, cold dew falls on the cherry orchard'); it forecasts an uncertain future ('The red sun sets behind the green wood; poor soldiers, Silesian warriors go for a bloody battle').

According to traditional beliefs, the sunset is also a magical moment: the time after sunset was considered the time of the devil, witches and the souls of the departed. This led to numerous prohibitions, e.g. one could not lend, borrow or sell things, perform certain jobs or collect herbs (in the Kashubian region).

On the basis of what the setting sun looked like, people predicted the weather and future events.

In the realm of beliefs the times of sunrise and sunset are contrasted but not necessarily symmetrically. The time of sunset, associated with darkness and inactivity, evokes sadness, while the belief that the souls of the dead return and the devil is more powerful at night results in fear and consequently in prohibitions. In contrast, there are no such prohibitions resulting from sunrise, which is associated with brightness, the beginning of daytime activity, expectation of encounters and suchlike – all this evokes positive emotions.

One finds more symmetry in directional meanings of *wschód* and *zachód*, i.e. 'east' and 'west', respectively. The difference in the position of sunrise and sunset, between winter and summer, is reflected in the mirror-like differentiation of descriptions: a small/short/winter sunrise/sunset vs. a big/long/summer sunrise/sunset.

However, several activities exhibit preferences towards the east, which is reflected by the word *wschodniować* 'orient oneself relative to sunrise' (*SJP*, 1861).[4] Altars in churches and windows in houses were located on the eastern side, people sat at the table facing the east, at weddings a holy picture was hung above the newlyweds on the eastern side etc. In Podlasie (eastern Poland) the first handful of the harvest was to be laid on the ground towards the east. These beliefs and practices can be found in the whole Slavic territory (Tolstoy, 1995: 445).

The west as a direction was not so significant in traditional cultural practices.

4 Documentation[5]

Riddles

(1) 'A wide field, numerous cattle, a horned farm-hand, a rich farmer.' (The sky, the stars, the moon and the sun)

(2) 'An oak is standing in the middle of the village, its boughs reaching down to each house.' (The sun in the sky)

(3) 'Which is the strongest: frost, the sun or the wind?' (The wind, because frost cannot bite without it, and the sun is not scorching hot when it blows)

(4) 'St. Ursula spread pearls, the moon knew about it but did not tell, the sun rose and collected them.' (Dew, dried by the sun)

Proverbs

(5) 'Sleep by the moon, work by the sun.'

(6) 'He who hates his neighbour will see spots even on the sun'; a variant: 'To look for spots on the sun.' (Find faults with what is good)

(7) (a) 'Before the sun rises, dew will eat out the eyes.' (Before good times come, evil will do harm and bring destruction)

(b) 'The sun will shine on our doorstep, too.' (Good times will come for us, too)

Prayers

(8) (a) 'I greet you, sun, so that I could work through the day happily.'

(b) 'Welcome, rosy sun, heavenly treasure, which shines on us, poor people on earth. You are so beautiful and shiny, sent directly by God. May Jesus Christ be praised for you.'

(c) Welcome, shining sun,
hot rays come from you.
Welcome, sun, a permanent treasure,
you heat mountains and rocks for us.

> Welcome, sun, in the heavenly mansion,
> you heat the earth and the sea for us.
> Welcome, sun, heavenly spark,
> you heat the whole globe.
> (The folk poet Rozalia Grzegorczykowa)

(9)   'Oh, God, who orders the sun to rise and set, who gives dew and rain to the thirsty land, who clothes meadows with grass, who makes the corn grow in the field, who feeds birds of the air, who decorates flowers – have mercy on us.' ('The litany for God's blessing on the harvest', said during the Easter procession on horses in Pietrowice Wielkie, the Opole region)

(10)   'On Sunday morning the sun rises, the Virgin Mary walks through the sky holding her little Son by the hand.' (A morning prayer)

Children's spells and rhymes

(11)   'The sun looms from behind the mountain, and you disease go out from under the skin'; a variant: 'The sun goes behind the mountain – and you, disease, go to the hole!'

(12)   (to chase away erysipelas) 'Oh, red skin, come out! Go to the mountains, to the forests! The sun does not shine there, birds do not fly there. Die forever!'

(13)   (to chase away clouds and rain) 'Shine, sun, shine! I will give you an egg when the hen lays it in the oak wood. Take the egg to the paradise, let the souls rejoice!'; a variant: 'Come out, sun, I will give you a white egg!'

(14)   (a)   'Ladybird, ladybird, go to Jesus to get the sun.'

   (b)   'Sun, fly to the sky, bring us good weather or rain.'

(15)   (a)   'It is drizzling, the sun is shining, a witch is making butter.'

   (b)   'It is raining, the sun is shining, Baba Jaga (a witch) is chasing children.'

Speeches

(16)   'As the night is sad without the moon and the day without the sun, so are you, young man, sir, without a girlfriend.'

Carols

(17)   A boar digs out a ball of gold (i.e. the sun) from under a fir tree: 'What will these hogs be doing? They will be digging under the fir there. They dug and dug and they dug out balls of gold. What will we do with them? We will take them to the goldsmith. He will make a golden cup, a golden bottle out of them. Who will drink from the cup? Lord Jesus himself when he goes caroling.'

(18)   'Let us praise the king, born today in Bethlehem. The sun and the moon serve him day and night.' (From Pomerania)

Lenten songs

(19) 'Cry, sun, cry, the monthly ring, and you stars pour your graceful light over the grave of the king of the heavenly capital.'

Songs for the harvest and the harvest festival

(20) 'Set, sun, when you are about to do so, 'cause my legs hurt from tending and following the cattle.'

(21) 'Harvest rye and remember Jesus. A girl harvested it when the sun was bright.'

Wedding songs

(22) 'The sun goes in a circle, our Mary goes to her wedding.'

(23) 'Early on Sunday morning the sun bathed. Mary was trying to catch it, she fell herself to the sea.'

(24) 'The bride among maids as the sun, the brightest among the stars.'

Love songs

(25) 'The evening is approaching, the sun is low; we will now part, my (dear) company.'

(26) (a) 'The sun shines for some, for me it is always sad; fate is stable for some, it is cruel to me.'

(b) 'The sun shines beautifully for some, for me there is only fog and frost.'

(27) 'For some the sun shines and sets behind the mountains, for me, the unhappy one, it hides behind the clouds.'

(28) 'May the sun not shine for you! Once you did not want to marry me.'

(29) (a) 'The moon is shining, the sun is hot, my heart longs for my beloved.'

(b) 'It is raining, the sun is hot, my heart longs for my beloved.'

(c) 'A quiet wind is blowing, a warm sun is shining; Kate is smiling at John through the window.'

(30) 'In summer, in summer the sun was hot, a girl tended oxen in the meadow.' (A repetitive incipit of a love song, which forecasts a rendezvous)

(31) 'When it shines and the weather is fine, come, Johnny, to my garden.'

(32) 'A dove flew over a green oak. It sat on the porch, in golden sunlight, and spread its tail.'

(33) 'The sun, the earth gave me joy, but a girl led me to the shade.'

(34) 'Old like a log, cold like water; young like a feather, hot like the sun.'

Historical songs

(35) 'The sun shines three hours longer than usual, as willed by the Virgin Mary, so that our soldiers can finish off the victorious battle: Virgin Mary, how are we supposed to fight when the sun is setting and it is too late to get ready for battle? I have told you that for my sake the sun will shine three hours longer for you.' (About the king Jan Sobieski and the Turks, 1683, or Marshal Piłsudski and the Bolshevist Russian army, 1920)

Short, occasional songs

(36) 'The sun, the inn, two God's gifts, a Kraków-dweller cannot live without them. The sun feeds him, the inn entertains him. May God, people praise you for this.'

Religious songs

(37) 'Hey, a maid is coming along clothed in the sun and stars.' (The Virgin Mary)

Tales about stupid people

(38) 'A stupid man built a house. Not a window or anything. He goes waving his hat, driving the view into the house, the sun. What are you doing? Why, I have built a house but it is dark, I'm driving the sun in.'

Unbelievable stories

(39) (a)   'A woman carries the sun in a bucket.'

(b)   'A woman catches the sun with a sieve and covers it with her apron.'

Written peasant poetry

(40) Among the July fields
goldened
by the sound of the scythe
a song comes to life.
The sun rolls
a huge loaf of bread,
holiness is toil
then it flows down […]
Reapers return
with an ear of corn in the heart.
A farmer carries the sun
on his shoulder.
(Władysław Sitkowski)
(41) Your fields
are like an ear of wheat:

golden,
jingling.
A huge sun
rolls about on them
on a July afternoon,
like a horse in the meadow.
(Jan Pocek)
(42) The ceiling,
the dome of the sky,
the walls
are the four quarters of the globe.
The moon at night
and the sun during the day
is a bulb to me:
such is my hut.
(Marian Karczmarczyk)

Personal reports

(43) 'My folk paid attention if there was the sun and the moon in the sky during the day, and if so, they did not sow flax, for they say it will be destroyed by disease. And wheat, too, but that might not be true for there were such black ears. They say if there are two lights in the sky, the sun and moon; they paid attention.'

(44) 'The sun, why, everybody knows, is a great light given by God, which warms us and the earth gives birth and life under the sun and all is good.'

(45) 'The world begins where the sun rises and it ends where it sets. And beyond, nothing can be seen, there is no world there.'

Notes

1   Context is a motif understood as a thematic segment of text. It embraces components which make up a stable verbal and/or semantic combination. Thus, documentation becomes an index of motifs found in various genres of folklore.

2   Even though the yolk might seem more similar to the sun, the latter is symbolised by an egg as a whole.

3   There are, then, two oppositions: temporal and spatial. The third meaning present in standard Polish, namely 'the countries and cultures in the East and West', has not been attested so far in peasant folk dialects of the language.

4   Cf. also the English *orient oneself*, *orientation*, *disoriented* etc., which come through Old French from Latin *orientum*, *orientem* (nom. *oriens*) 'the rising sun, the east, part of the sky where the sun rises'.

5   All references to the sources of examples have been omitted, but can be found in *SSSL* (1996, vol. 1–1: 119–157).

11 The Polish stereotype of the mother: towards a cognitive definition

1 Background

In the Polish linguistic worldview, the mother occupies a high position in the axiological, family-oriented, national and religious sense. MATKA (MOTHER)[1] is a rich concept, based on a universal experiential basis, common to many cultures and languages. It usually occurs with other basic existential concepts, such as HOME, FAMILY, LAND or NATION. The Polish conception of the mother, however, also contains certain peculiarities reflecting the specific characteristics of the history of the Polish nation. The symbolic formulae of that tradition are: *rodzona matka* 'mother by birth', *ziemia matka* 'mother-earth', *Matka Polska* 'Poland the Mother' (łac. *Mater Polonia*), *matka Polka* 'the Polish mother' or *Matka Boska* 'God's Mother' (the Virgin Mary).

The conception of the mother has been approached by semanticists of different methodological orientations: structural and cognitive. In Manfred Bierwisch's structural componential analysis, MOTHER is assigned eight semantic features. The positive ones include 'living creature' [*Lebewesen*], 'human' [*Mensch*], 'female' [*weiblich*], 'older' [*älter*], 'related by direct kinship' [*verwandt*], [*direkt verwandt*]; and the negative ones (expressing lack of something) are 'not in the same generation' [*-gleiche Generation*] and 'non-male' [*-männlich*] (cf. Bußmann, 1990: 398, referring to Bierwisch, 1969: 67).[2]

The cognitivist approach makes use of the notions of type and of an Idealised Cognitive Model (ICM). Lakoff (1987: 74–76) analyses the meaning of MOTHER in terms of prototypical and non-prototypical cases. He questions the existence of a semantic invariant and assumes that the concept cannot be unambiguously defined by means of necessary and sufficient conditions. He distinguishes several models of MOTHER:

> the birth model (basic): 'the female[3] who gives birth';
> the genetic model: 'the female who contributes the genetic material';
> the nurturance model: 'the female adult who nurtures and raises a child';
> the marital model: 'the wife of the father';
> the genealogical model: 'the closest female ancestor'.

Some scholars, such as Anna Wierzbicka, have subjected Lakoff's analysis to severe criticism. Wierzbicka regards the approach as carrying 'little conviction' because it overlooks the crucial point that 'foster mothers, adoptive mothers, genetic mothers, surrogate mothers, and so on are not 'mothers' on a par with 'biological mothers'' (Wierzbicka, 1996: 154). She says:

Without a modifier, the word *mother* ('X is Y's mother') refers clearly to birth-givers, not to the donors of eggs, providers of wombs, caretakers, or fathers' spouses'. The author also notes (on the same page) that Lakoff 'overlooks the syntactic – and hence the semantic – difference between *my real mother* (either birth-giver or caretaker) and *a real mother to me* (caretaker only). Furthermore, he overlooks the fact that the test with *real* is not semantically reliable. For example, sentences such as *he is a real man* or *she is a real woman* may refer to the speaker's views or prejudices about men and women which have no basis in the semantics of the words *man* and *woman*. He doesn't appreciate the implications of the fact that the expression *biological mother* would be used only in contrastive context, and that normally (without a contrastive context) one would not say *she is a biological mother*, whereas expressions such as *foster mother, adoptive mother*, or *surrogate mother* are not restricted to contrastive contexts. (Wierzbicka, 1996: 154)

The author ends her highly critical passage with a comparison:

To treat 'biological mothers' as being on a par with 'surrogate mothers' or 'foster mothers' is a little like saying that there are two kinds of horses: biological horses and rocking-horses (or that there are two diverging 'models of horsehood': a biological model and an artefact model); and that we cannot define a *horse* as 'a kind of animal …' because a rocking horse is not a kind of animal at all. (Wierzbicka,1996: 155)

Wierzbicka's definition of a mother couched within her Natural Semantic Metalanguage contains the biological, sociological and psychological components of the concept:

X is Y's mother. =
(a) at one time, before now, Y was very small
(b) at that time, Y was inside X
(c) at that time, Y was like a part of X
(d) because of this, people can think something like this about X:
'X wants to do good things for Y
X doesn't want bad things to happen to Y'
(Wierzbicka, 1996: 155)

2   The mother in the linguistic system of Polish

2.1 Lexicographic definitions

Lexicographic definitions of the Polish word *matka* 'mother' (*SJPDor*, 1962; *SJPSzym*, 1994; *PSJP*, 1998; *SWJP*, 1996) distinguish seven or eight meanings of the word, of which the basic one is 'a female who has her own child (children), regarded in relationship (or with respect) to that child'. The definition meets the conditions of semantic representation, as specified by structural semantics (Grochowski, 1993): it contains the categorial (essential) features, characteristic of all referents in the category of mothers, i.e. [1] 'being a female' and [2] 'having a child'.

The first feature, however, is more important than the second. The sentence *Ann is a mother but she is not a female* is definitely unacceptable, which shows that being female is crucial for being a mother, but the sentence *Ann is a mother but she doesn't have children* may be acceptable (she had but no longer has, etc.). Similarly, the sentence *Ann is a mother but she did not bear any children* may also be acceptable, though someone familiar with the details of artificial insemination may object by saying that she is merely an egg cell donor, whereas the inseminated egg cell matured in the womb of another woman. It is probably true that this is specialised knowledge, not common, folk knowledge, but even within common knowledge there is a certain degree of shading of the roles played by the mother towards her child (the social nature of the mother is reflected in the Polish proverb 'The mother is not she who has given birth, but she who has raised'). If, then, the 'core features' are those which cannot be negated at all, at the risk of an expression becoming nonsensical, 'being a female' is definitely one of them. Within feature [2], in turn, the very *relation* to the child is obligatory but its manifestations allow for variation. Perhaps it should be expressed in terms of alternatives: 'has given birth to/supplied the genetic material/ has/nurtures ...'.[4]

The definition restricted to the necessary and sufficient features of a mother distinguishes mothers from the superordinate category of women, aims to locate the concept of MOTHER in the semantic system of a language and is taxonomic in nature. As such it is very incomplete: it contains very few unquestionable features identifiable with the contradiction test, too few to account for the functioning of the concept and the usage of the corresponding word(s) in language.

In the folk linguistic intuition and communicative practice the mother is someone more than the person who has given birth to (or has etc.) a child. For an average speaker, the mother is endowed with positive, socially agreed-on characterisation, containing not only the 'vital' features (i.e. obligatory in all mothers and obligatorily absent from non-mothers) but also 'typical' features, relevant in the semantics of the word, its relationship to other words and its usage in texts (Bartmiński, 1984: 19). These features are ascribed at the level of social semantic norm to 'all true' mothers[5] (as opposed to 'bad mothers'): they constitute a linguistic image, a stereotype of the mother. Related questions are those of the boundaries of the set of features which compose the stereotypical image, the openness of the set and its internal structure.

Let us now try to propose a systematic juxtaposition of the features but at the same time acknowledge the fact that due to the dynamic and open nature of meaning it can only be incomplete and approximate.

2.2 Word-formational derivatives, semantic derivatives, metaphors

It is relatively easy to identify the relevant features in word-formational derivatives of *matka*: *matkować komu* 'to mother someone', *mamka* 'wet-nurse', *matecznik* 'lair', *po matczynemu* 'in a motherly way'. The expressions show that the meaning of *matka* also includes the features [3] 'looks after', [4] 'breastfeeds', [5] 'provides shelter' and [6] 'is tender and loving'.

Numerous diminutives as forms of address, in turn, provide evidence for the attitude of tenderness and affection in the other direction, i.e. on the part of children to their mother (*SJPDor*, 1962 lists *mama, mamcia, mameczka, mameńka, mamuchna, mamula, mamunia, mamuńka, mamusia, mamuśka; matczysko, mateczka, mateńka, matuchna, matula, matuleńka, matulka, matunia, matusia, matuś*): one's mother is [7] 'treated with fondness and tenderness'.

Such an attitude towards the mother is corroborated by the existence, on the other (negative) pole of expressiveness, of vulgar terms of abuse referring to someone's mother: the culture demands that one's own or another person's mother be respected.

Semantic derivatives and metaphorical uses of *matka* provide evidence for the existence, in the concept's structure, of features absent from dictionary definitions but activated in the process of creating new meanings.[6]

The meaning of *matka* as 'a nun, especially one with higher functions in the order', as well as the expression *matka przełożona* 'Mother superior', point to a yet another feature: [8] 'occupies an important position in a group'. The meaning 'the most important player, the leader in team games', allows one to view this position not merely as 'important' but as [8a] 'the most important'.

2.3 Word combinations and phraseological units

Fixed word combinations listed in dictionaries corroborate the features identified so far in the connotative aspect of the meaning of *matka*, as well as showing their further elaboration and modification:

> *matka chrzestna* 'godmother' – 'one who accepts the responsibility of moral care over the person being baptised' [3]; also: 'a female performing a symbolic act of naming a ship etc.' (*PSJP*, 1998);

> *mleczna matka* 'wet nurse' – 'a female breastfeeding someone else's child' [4];

> *komisja matka* 'mother committee' – 'a committee whose task is to decide upon candidates in an election' [2];

> *samolot-matka* 'mother aircraft' – 'a big cargo aircraft with another, small and fast aircraft on board, which leaves the big aircraft in the air, the big aircraft then landing or returning to the base' [5];

> naut. *statek-matka* 'mother ship' – 'a big ship supplying a smaller ship with fuel, food etc. at sea' [3], [5], [8];

infml. *kaseta matka* 'mother cassette' – 'a cassette from which copies may be made' [2];

Phraseological units, in turn, characterise the mother-child relationship in greater detail:

powtarzać co jak za panią matką 'to repeat exactly, obediently' (lit. 'as one would after the mother') – implies two kinds of judgement: [9] 'the mother teaches children' and [10] 'children obey the mother';

jak matkę kocham 'I swear to my mother' (lit. 'as much as I love my mother') – an oath, presupposing that [11] 'one loves one's mother';

(zbić kogoś) tak, że go rodzona matka nie pozna 'to beat someone black and blue' (lit. 'to beat someone so that their mother would not recognise them') – presupposes that [12] 'the mother will recognise her child in any situation', because she is attached to and loves the child.

From the perspective of an outside and critical observer, the relation is modelled by the following units:

(ktoś) jeszcze matce za cycek nie podziękował, lit. 'someone has not yet thanked their mother for her breast' – breastfeeding is treated as obvious (cf. feature [4]) and [13] 'the child should be grateful to the mother for her care';

(ktoś) trzyma się matczynej spódnicy 'someone is tied to their mother's apron strings' (lit. 'someone is holding on to their mother's skirt') – a feature similar to [5];

maminsynek 'mother's boy' – 'a boy who is not self-reliant and who stays in his mother's care for a long time'; a feature close to features [3] and [5].

The set of features extractable from linguistic data is probably larger, as is the list of the relevant phraseological units: e.g. I omit the ones based on 'giving birth', such as *nadzieja matką głupich*, lit. 'hope is the mother of the stupid', or *potrzeba jest matką wynalazków* 'necessity is the mother of invention'.

As one can see, semantic features extracted form linguistic data constitute a set, organised internally through mutual implications as a syndrome. Among them are both specific features and more general features based on the specific ones, e.g. from 'to give birth' derives the generalised 'bring into existence' (mother committee). There are general but particularised features ('feeds', 'breastfeeds'); basic and semantically derived (consecutive) features at the same level of generality, e.g. 'caring' and 'busy'; finally, there are features close to one another or even identical but differently named, e.g. 'tender and loving' [6] vs. 'warm' and 'feeling' (in LSQ-90; cf. 'Key to questionnaires'). The identification of the internal ordering of content makes it possible to talk about the 'cognitive structure of the concept' (Wierzbicka, 1985).

2.4 Etymology

What is the role of etymology in semantic explication? An inquiry into the etymology of *matka* reveals a fundamental bond between the mother and the child. Both the form and the meaning of the word have been shaped from the position of the child, for the words *matka* 'mother' and *mama* 'mummy' come from the language of children (*REW*, 1950–1958) and are based on the root *ma-, which in its phonological structure realises the fundamental opposition of closure/openness, the first one to appear in child speech.

The rich content of the stereotype of the mother is also modelled from the perspective of a child, either immature and still in the mother's care, or grown-up and independent but preserving the 'family memory'. The child's viewpoint constitutes the basic, though not the only, semantic profile of the mother.

3 The mother in questionnaires

The understanding of *matka* by an average speaker of Polish can be investigated by means of questionnaires. Answers to the following questions can be sought: Which components of meaning are recognised more widely? In what order are they mentioned? What configurations of components can be identified? What is the typical semantic and syntactic conventionalised valency of the word, etc? One can investigate the content of the stereotype, measure the entrenchment of its components, as well as inquire into their judgment and valuation. In this way one can access the sphere in a word's meaning referred to by Coșeriu (1988: 297–302) as the 'social norm'.

I discuss here some of the results of two questionnaires concerning the stereotype of the mother administered to native speakers of Polish in the 1990s.

3.1 The problem of the definition

The respondents of LSQ-90 were asked to describe the meaning of *matka* – the simplest but one of the most important questions in linguistic questionnaires. Their spontaneous responses were not only taxonomic (a 'female', a 'person', the one who has 'given life' or 'birth') but in half of the cases also typological, pointing above all to basic social functions of the mother in relation to her child: a person 'who gives birth to, nurtures and raises', 'who has given birth to a child and looks after him/her', 'who manages the home' etc. The students also projected an image of the mother from their own perspective: 'nurtures my soul and stomach', 'one who has given birth to me and brought me up', 'one who has brought me up, though has not given birth to me', 'one who loves us with an everlasting love' etc. All these characteristics can be accommodated within the realm of the already mentioned features.

3.2 The 'typical' and the 'true' mother

In the questionnaires discussed here (see the description in 'Key to questionnaires'), two questions were clearly directional and concerned the features of a 'typical' mother (LSQ-90) and those of the 'true' mother (AXL-90). The questions contained these expressions explicitly. Let us first juxtapose some of the results.

The question in LSQ-90 concerning the features of a 'typical' mother yielded almost forty features, including many not extracted from the systemic data. Can we simply add them to the set of features at our disposal at the moment? Warnings against a too easy solution of this sort (Wierzbicka, 1993) seem sensible. One certainly needs some kind of verification procedure, the simplest of which is statistical verification. The most frequently used features are listed in Table 11.1:

Table 11.1 The most frequent features of a 'typical' mother (LSQ-90)

No. of respondents	Features
48	loving (children, her family)
21	caring, protective, overprotective
18	understanding
17	good
9	thoughtful
8	tender
6	with a feeling/sensitive nature, very dear
5	busy
4	warm, full of warmth, with parental warmth
3	devoted

This set of the most frequently mentioned characteristics of the mother includes certain new features, above all [14] 'understanding' (maybe under the influence of a Polish hymn to the Virgin Mary about the 'Mother who understands everything') and [15] 'busy'. Certain other features are semantically derived from the basic ones as their generalisations, e.g. [16] 'good' (derived from 'looks after', 'is tender and loving', 'provides shelter'), [17] 'with a feeling nature' (from 'tender and loving'). The statistics of those features are not unambiguous, as they cannot be broken down into sharp categories.

Another analysis of statistical data has yielded the so-called unidirectional correlation principle: a high statistical rank of a feature implies its linguistic (semantic) relevance, but a low rank does not imply linguistic irrelevance (Bartmiński, 1988b: 103–104). The principle, together with the conception of meaning as an open structure (Bartmiński and Tokarski, 1993), allows for the enrichment of the set of stereotypical characteristics of the mother with at least these four social and psychological features.

In another questionnaire (AXL-90), a question about the features of the 'true' mother yielded almost a hundred descriptors, the most frequent of which are given in Table 11.2.

Table 11.2 The most frequent features of the 'true' mother (AXL-90; N = 103)

No. of respondents	Features
66	loving (64% of respondents)
43	protective
22	understanding
20	dedicated
19	thoughtful
17	good
9	devoted, tender
8	setting an example
6	eager to assist, warm

Ninety other features were given less frequently, including about seventy used only once.

New features were added to the already established ones and the relative rank of those changed in comparison to the question about a 'typical' mother. In the first ten we have three new features: [18] 'dedicated', [19] 'example to follow' and [20] 'eager to assist'. It is noteworthy that the first three positions are in both lists occupied by the same features: 'loving', 'protective' and 'understanding'.

A comparison of the results of LSQ-90 and AXL-90 allows one to recognise a significant influence of the modifiers 'true' and 'typical' on the nature of the features obtained. In the case of the 'true' mother, the set skews towards an exemplary image (what a true mother should be like) and so is idealised, whereas in the case of a 'typical' mother it is free from idealisation and skews towards pure description (what a mother really is like, e.g. 'busy'). For the ontology of stereotype this is a matter of prime importance. Stereotypical thinking contains a mythological element, i.e. an image of what *should be* is superimposed onto that of what *is*.

3.3 A single association and the 'but'-test

A similar group of respondents (students) were given (twice, in 1980 and 1990) yet another task: to supply the one word which best characterises the mother. 170 respondents used almost 60 expressions and in both cases the top two positions were occupied by the same words, 'love' and 'goodness', which characterise the mother relative to her social functions (results are discussed in Panasiuk, 1990).

Open-ended questionnaires seem relatively more valid, as they do not involve suggestions on the part of their authors, in contrast to the sometimes used closed questionnaires, in which respondents are given a list of features and asked to perform tasks with them, e.g. to associate them with categories of people (cf. Pisarkowa, 1976; Kapiszewski, 1978 and others). Interesting vistas are opened by questionnaires asking one to complete texts. For example, in LSQ-90 the model of an opposite sentence was used: respondents were to verbalise features *opposite* to the stereotypes they entertained, i.e. to construct sentences with *presupposed* stereotypes. The sentence 'Ann is a mother but …' could be completed with 'she does not love her children', 'she does not look after the home and family', 'she doesn't know how to look after the children', 'she is cruel' – these are characterisations opposite to the 'normal' ones (in the respondents' opinions). In this way the features already identified in the image of a stereotypical mother were corroborated, above all those relating to the mother's social function and attitudes: 'loves her children', is 'thoughtful', 'protective' and 'tender' (Olechnowicz, 1990).

3.4 Characteristic objects

Another question in LSQ-90 concerned the *objects* characteristic of a mother (Olechnowicz, 1990: 93–97). These turned out to be highly conventional objects, connected with the kitchen and food: pots (34 respondents out of 150), kitchen utensils, rolling-pin, rag (duster), tenderiser, bucket, kettle, apron, pan, shopping bag, washing machine, washing powder, sewing machine, knitting needles, wool etc. The set is closely related to the typical activities of mothers, such as shopping, doing the laundry or sewing, and with her most important social role in relation to children: the provider of food, caretaker and educator.

Interestingly, students only marginally referred to the mother as one who looks after a baby: the characteristic objects from this domain include a cradle, pram and nappies, each mentioned but a few times. Similar observations can be made for money matters (the objects: money, a purse). Equally weak is the image of the mother as a woman who looks after herself, who takes care of her looks and elegance: lipstick, facial cream and hand cream.

3.5 Conventionalised semantic valency

Questionnaire-based research on the adjectives *matczyny, -a, -e* 'mother's, motherly', a part of LSQ-90, supplied additional details. Almost a hundred respondents used 50 nouns, the most frequent of which are listed in Table 11.3.

Table 11.3 Nouns used as reaction to the prompt word *matczyny, -a, -e* 'mother's, motherly' (LSQ-90)

No. of respondents	Features
43	heart
27	love
17	hand(s)
6	problem to solve; goodness
5	smile
4	feeling
3	warmth; apron; care; concern, thoughtfulness
2	protectiveness; instinct; anxiety; voice; home; milk

This stage of research revealed the role of specific, generally established linguistic expressions, which serve as labels for already known characteristics: 'mother's heart' is a metaphor of tenderness and love, 'mother's hands' is a symbol of care, work and thoughtfulness, 'mother's smile' is an expression of acceptance etc. The image of the mother's body (the heart, hands, face), just like that of home, is a derivative of her functions; a semiotic picture. The third set directly names the attitudes of the mother towards others: love, goodness, care, concern, anxiety and feeling.

As can be seen, various data elicitation techniques continue to corroborate a certain fundamental set of the characteristics of the mother in social consciousness. The centre of this set gradually becomes clearer and clearer, the boundaries remain open. It is an uncountable set, although not indeterminate: subsequent features are to an extent predictable on the basis of the already known ones. It has a concentric, radial structure.

4   The image of the mother in texts

When one investigates how the word *matka* functions in texts, the richness and variety of data renders its global characterisation virtually impossible. The image of the mother in specific instances of use depends on the accepted model of reality and knowledge of the world but also on the ideological orientation of the author, his or her communicative intention and the text's genre.[7]

Subject-related factors yield various profiles of the mother (cf. Bartmiński and Niebrzegowska, 1998). Folklorised stereotyped texts, a social property in wide circulation, containing common and rather traditional knowledge, are markedly different in this respect from individual, one-off texts, whose intention is to convey a novel or controversial message. Irrespective of this global diversification of texts, it is important how the word *matka* is used in a given context: in a generic manner (in reference to all mothers) or in a unique manner (in reference to a specific mother). A selection of texts only will be discussed.

4.1 Proverbs

Proverbs constitute a special category of text. They codify social knowledge in its popular variant and model collective behaviour. They express realistic ascertainment, relating to private and collective life, as well as advice, frequently formulated in the imperative mood from the objective, panhuman perspective. As a rule, and this is extremely important, they express generalised, generic judgments pertaining to all mothers. In *NKP*, 1978 (vol. II) one can find proverbs corroborating the already identified stereotype of the mother as someone who

'loves children', e.g. 'Every mother holds her children dear' (1696);

'looks after her children and nourishes them': 'Where children have a mother, their heads are beautiful' (1861);

but also containing new elements, as a result of which the mother (the proverbs come from various times and contexts):

[21] 'punishes and beats her children': 'Blessed are the mothers who punish their children for wrongdoing' (1902); 'The mother is agreeable to one, even if she resorts to beating' (1806); 'The mother beats but teaches' (1878); 'Whoever disobeys their mother will go to prison' (1894);

[22] 'is the only one and irreplaceable for the children': 'It is not that the husband's wife dies, it's the children's mother' (1902); a similar sense is expressed by the proverbs 'A mother is a mother, a stepmother is a stepmother' (1632), 'You will never find another mother' (1894), 'You cannot buy yourself a mother' (1620), 'When the father dies, the child is a half-orphan, but when the mother dies, the child is fully an orphan' (1894);

[23] 'transmits her features to the child' – 'Like mother, like daughter' (1579), 'Like tree, like bark', 'Like loaf, like crust', 'Like drill, like hole' etc. Proverbs partially in disagreement with those, suggesting a reverse situation of a lack of similarity, are much rarer: 'The mother is one way, the daughter is another' (1913), 'Different children of the same mother' (1632);

[24] 'accepts unconditionally': 'Everyone is beautiful to their mother' (1894);

[25] 'is self-sacrificing, disinterested': 'One mother can provide food for ten sons but ten sons will not provide food for one mother' (1568); 'Whatever the mother has, she makes her children take it' (1745) and 'The mother gives, while the stepmother asks the children if they want it' (1649).

The most interesting semantically is the still popular nineteenth century proverb 'The mother is not she who has given birth, but she who has raised' (1819), which radically reappraises the traditional characterisation of the mother, placing the 'additional' features higher than the basic, categorial ones.

4.2 Patriotic poetry

Polish patriotic literature of the nineteenth century produced the emergence of a vivid ideological stereotype of the Polish mother (cf. Adam Mickiewicz's famous poem *To a Polish Mother*, 1830), derived from older stereotypes of Poland the Mother and Mary, the Mother of God. It is a variant of the stereotype which can be described as a 'pattern to follow', set in an ideal-oriented, deontic modal frame: it says what a mother should be like. A mother's social role has been narrowed down to the National Programme; the Polish mother is someone 'admirable, good, caring and fertile, but also a patriot; one who gives birth to and raises the defenders of the homeland, as well as protecting national values' (Monczka-Ciechomska, 1992: 95). The Polish ethos of maternity stems from the cult of the Virgin Mary, characteristic of Polish Catholicism, which produces a combination of the ideal with the tragic: the Polish mother sacrifices (should sacrifice) her children for the great national cause and therefore her maternity involves (and must involve) suffering. She is (to be) 'the guardian of morality, full of goodness and dedication; someone who offers her love and the purity of her heart to others, a Christian virtue' (Monczka-Ciechomska, 1992: 96).

4.3 Sermons

Similarly, though on a different, more universal axiological basis, the idealised image of the mother as the example to follow is propagated in Catholic sermons. The dominant features of the mother here are love, protectiveness and dedication. They are postulated features and the role of the resultant image is to aid catechesis. Consider the following quotes:

> No-one can replace the mother, who gives birth, nourishes and raises. No-one can replace the heart of the mother at home; the heart which is always there, which always waits there. (John Paul II, Częstochowa, Poland, June 6, 1979)

> The mother not only waits for her children in her home but follows them wherever they build their own homes. (John Paul II, June 4, 1979)

> The state of not-being-free in love is never experienced as bondage; a mother who is 'bound' to the bedside of her ill child does not experience it as bondage but as affirmation and fulfillment of her freedom. It is then that she feels most free. (John Paul II, June 4, 1979)

> A child's life begins under the mother's heart. It is the mother who takes pains to bring the child to the world, and then it is parents who do the same to raise him or her. (Jerzy Popiełuszko,[8] February 26, 1984)

This idealisation is justified by the Catholic doctrine and springs from the cult of the Virgin Mary; it exploits the cult's vitality but also helps maintain it. At the same time, sermons contain an anti-pattern, the image of a bad mother who kills her unborn children.

4.4 Folk songs

The stereotype of the mother in folk songs exhibits a fair degree of peculiarity (cf. Jagiełło, 1980). The image arises in a family or a small local community and has an elaborate facet-like structure (the social, psychological, everyday-life and cultural aspects).

The mother in folk songs gives birth to, nurses, raises and looks after a child but also [26] 'manages the home' and [27] 'gives advice to the children'. The roles of the birth-giver and caretaker are described in terms of more detailed activities: she rocks the cradle, keeps vigil, nourishes, clothes; she is at home, by the cradle; she is tender; her attributes (in the sense of artifacts) are the cradle, bread and the dress she gives to the child. As an educator she is well-wishing and attentive; she punishes and rewards the child; as a caretaker, she [28] 'teaches her daughter how to work' and [29] 'marries her'; as an administrator she [30] 'gives orders', 'makes her children work', 'scolds', 'beats', [31] 'is strict', 'uses a stick'; as an advisor, she counsels her son, helps her daughter-in-law, and she is [32] 'wise'.

This song-derived stereotype of the mother is based on semantic features of wide social circulation but also includes its own peculiar characteristics. Apart from the psychological aspect, the social and everyday-life aspects are also quite strong. Folk songs present the basic image of the mother in an objectified perspective. In popular belief, the mother functions in opposition to the stepmother and the mother-in-law, whose stereotypical images are decidedly negative, the dominant features being hostility and estrangement, e.g. *traktować coś po macoszemu* 'to treat something badly, unjustly' (lit. 'like a mother in law'), *być od macochy* 'to be omitted' (lit. 'to come from the stepmother') or the Silesian proverb *teściowa jest zimną matką* 'the mother-in-law is a cold mother'.[9]

5   Final remarks

The above is a sample analysis of the linguistic stereotype of the mother in Polish. It leads to the following conclusions:

i)   A combination of various research methods (analysis of the linguistic system, references to the linguistic intuition of speakers, analysis of texts) allows one to reconstruct the multidimensional image of the entity in question, to uncover the socially stable base set of the features of the mental object in question.

ii) Each of the sources has its own limitations. If the set of features meeting the structural criteria (the contradiction test) is rather poor, that obtained through questionnaires is much more comprehensive and includes dozens of elements. My research procedure is to use a variety of complementary types of data.

iii) The greatest number of characteristics can be extracted from texts, the smallest from the language system. The number of features is inversely proportional to the degree of their linguistic entrenchment.

iv) All the features attributed to the mother identified in the present study (and perhaps not only those) may be said to constitute the social semantic *norm* of the word *matka*. Many of them are not irremovable (a sentence 'X is a mother but does not have the feature [3]–[28]' is non-contradictory) and therefore not criterial, core or categorial in the sense adopted in structural semantics. Some of them, however, are treated as *more* important than categorial features, as shown in the proverb 'The mother is not she who has given birth, but she who has raised'. There are many more of these features, e.g. 'loves her children', 'nourishes', 'looks after' them etc.: they are ascribed to all 'typical', 'normal', 'ordinary' or 'true' mothers. A denial of characteristic features, required by the social model of the mother, allows one to talk about 'bad' mothers, called to the bar of public opinion.

v)   The components making up the semantic content of the stereotype have a radial and zonal, sector-like organisation. The semantic core is surrounded by features of various degrees of entrenchment (stereotypisation). The boundaries of this set are open.

vi) The set of characteristic features is established within the realm of a certain experiential base; it is ordered and structured by speakers relative to their points of view and communicative strategies. The structuring can be accounted for with the help of the notions of viewpoint, perspective and facet-like feature arrangement. The concept of MOTHER is internally structured in a non-arbitrary fashion. A narrow set of basic categorial features ('female', 'in a certain relationship to the child: giving birth/looking after/ bringing up/ …') is superimposed with subject-oriented typical entrenched and configured sets of features, pertaining to the mother's attitudes, her social functions in relation to the child and family, her typical 'living space', the objects she typically uses or the treatment she receives from her kin. A selection of such aspects and the manner in which they are filled with content are decisive as to the stereotype's cognitive structure, its variants or profiles.

vii) Different variants of the stereotype of the mother, in which the base content is profiled in alternate ways, function in texts, their genres and ideological types. For example, the song-based profile of the stereotype consists of a bundle of characteristics on three planes: biological, everyday, social and cultural. The characteristics are projected from the perspective of a close-knit community whose core is the family and relatives. It endows the mother with the roles of the birth-giver, caretaker, housewife, someone who rocks the cradle, keeps vigil, nourishes, clothes the child and who typically deals with the cradle, bread, the child's dress and a stick. The mother is characterised by love, care and responsibility for the home and family. This profile is different from that obtained in student questionnaires, which arises from the viewpoint of a young person who has already left home but has yet not set up his or her own home. The mother is viewed as someone closest, beloved, good.

viii) I assume that the content of the stereotype is also shaped by people's socially normalised *conduct* towards the mother, contained in the cultural base of the language. It constitutes what Peirce calls the *final interpretant*. Custom-entrenched conduct is that of showing respect to the mother, reflected – or extended – in 'linguistic etiquette', i.e. in the ways of talking about people. The customary respect in talking about the mother is a cultural norm one has to know to understand terms of abuse. To disparage someone's mother is the most serious insult, not only in Polish tradition. Also the proverb 'Have I killed the mother or father or what?', which amounts to 'Why do I have to suffer so much?', contains a cultural presupposition that a certain type of conduct (matricide) is a heavy crime.

ix)   The stereotype of the mother reconstructed here is a linguocultural fact of the Polish linguistic worldview, the subject of anthropological linguistics (ethnolinguistics). The analysis allows one to empirically verify Lakoff's (1987) conception and the different import of the partial models he distinguished. Above all, it allows one to establish their 'semantic capacity', internal logic and interconnections. In the view of the analysed data, the most important is the nurturance model, whereas the birth and the genetic models are not yet distinguished in Polish.[10]

The base set of the characteristics of the mother, a part of the experiential frame of a language, is profiled relative to the subject's viewpoint and system of values. As a result, one deals with various aspects of the image of the mother.

Let us recall that in student questionnaires one of the basic functions of the mother, that of a caretaker, was recognised only marginally (a cradle, pram and nappies as characteristic objects are mentioned but a few times). Equally weak is the status of the mother as the one who manages the family finances or who is mindful of her good looks. The category of viewpoint, indeed, seems to play a significant role here. It is worthwhile, then, to ask in what perspective and by whom the mother is being perceived in a particular case.

The following aspects (facets) can be recognised in the characterisation of the mother: biological, psychological, social (relation to other people), ethical and connected with everyday life. A facet-based arrangement of the features reveals a greater importance of the social aspect relative to others (cf. again the proverb 'The mother is not she who has given birth, but she who has raised'):

The superordinate category:
[1] 'is a female'

biological aspect:
[2] 'has a child' [= gives birth]
[4] 'breastfeeds'
[23] 'transmits her features to the child'

social aspect:
[3] 'looks after'
[20] 'assists'
[5] 'provides shelter'
[8] 'occupies an important position in a group'
(8a) 'occupies the most important position'

[9] 'teaches her children'
[21] 'punishes and beats her children'
[27] 'gives advice to the children'
[28] 'teaches her daughter how to work'
[10] 'children (should) obey the mother'
[13] 'the child should be grateful to the mother for her care'

socio-psychological aspect:
[6] 'is tender and loving'
[16] 'good' (← 'looks after', 'is tender and loving', 'provides shelter')
[24] 'accepts one unconditionally'
[7] 'is treated with fondness and tenderness'
[11] 'one loves one's mother'

aspect of everyday life (behaviour):
[26] 'manages the home'
[30] 'gives orders, drives one to work, scolds, beats'
[15] 'is busy'
[22] 'is the only one and irreplaceable for the children'
[12] 'will recognise her child in any situation'
[29] 'marries her daughter'

psychological aspect:
[17] 'is emotional' (← 'tender and loving')
[14] 'is understanding'
[32] 'is wise'
[31] 'is strict (her instrument is a stick)'

ethical aspect:
[19] 'sets an example to follow'
[18] 'is dedicated'
[25] 'is self-sacrificing, disinterested'.

The selection of aspects and specific characteristics is decisive for the profiling of the linguocultural image of the mother in social discourse. The different profiles are constructed from the points of view of different speaking subjects: a child, an adult, the family, a local community, the Church. The profiles may arise in discourse and be subordinated to social conventionalisation depending on the axiological assumptions and communicative aims of the speakers. All profiles, nevertheless, are anchored in the base set of features, which I have attempted to reconstruct in this chapter on the basis of a variety of sources: the language system, texts and questionnaires.

Notes

1   Whenever possible, the English word will be used for the sake of simplicity. The reader must bear in mind, however, that it is the Polish concept (and word) that is being analysed here, unless the context or references suggest otherwise. [translator's note, A.G.]

2   The set seems to contain some redundancy; cf. the equivocal features 'female' and 'non-male'.

3   Lakoff uses the word *person* in the birth model but *female* in the other models. I use the latter option consistently.

4   Dictionaries also give other meanings of the Polish *matka*, derived from the basic meaning: 2. 'the female of animals; the one that has offspring'; 3. 'in some insects, e.g. bees: the female capable of reproduction; the queen'; 4. 'something that supplies sustenance, nurturance, care etc. (e.g. mother-earth, mother ship)'; 5. 'the title of certain nuns, especially those with higher functions'; 6. 'the most important player, e.g. in rounders'; 7. inf. 'one's own wife, an elderly woman, usually in the country'. (Newer dictionaries, e.g. *ISJP*, 2000; *USJP*, 2003, add: 'the female who has given birth to and usually raises a child'.)

5   Various authors, e.g. Lakoff (1987), talk about 'real mothers'. However, the present approach aims to clearly differentiate the notion of a(n) (statistically) average mother (what a mother really is like, for which I use the term 'typical'), an exemplary mother (what a mother should be like, termed 'ideal') and the type of person a mother is and should be at the same time (for which 'true' seems to be a better word than 'real').

6   The separate metaphorical and derived meanings in *SJPDor* (1962) I treat jointly.

7   For example, Barbara Pietkiewicz's 'Raport' in the Polish weekly *Polityka* of March 9, 2002, entitled 'Matki i córki: trudne związki' (Mothers and daughters: difficult relationships), informs of a widespread attitude of young women in the 1970s, especially in France, characterised by contempt towards mothers as 'transmitters of the oppression of women': 'Their main vocation was – the daughters would say – ironing, cleaning, frying, polishing, washing and cooing so that their husbands are fully satisfied'. These views are expressed in such books as Yvonne Knibiehler's *La révolution maternelle: femmes, maternite, citoyennete depuis 1945* (1997), Gianni Monduzzi's *Manuale per difindersi della mamma* (1991) etc. The author of 'Raport' states that 'Poland, populated with mother-Poles, has never seen a contestation of mothers as 'transmitters of oppression'', which does not mean that certain types of mothers have not been distinguished linguistically and stigmatised for overprotectiveness (cf. the expressions *kwoka*, lit. 'brood hen' or *matka toksyczna* 'toxic mother' etc.).

8   A Catholic priest from Poland, associated with the Solidarity movement and murdered by the intelligence agency in 1984.

9   The anti-pattern of a bad mother can among others be found in 'From the Hill Fields', a song performed by The Saint Nicholas Orchestra, a folk band from Lublin, Poland.

10   The situation might have changed since the 1990s, when the research was conducted.

12 The Polish DOM (house/home) in its physical, social, and cultural aspects

1 Introduction

DOM (in the sense of 'house') is a favourite topic of children's drawings. It has walls, doors, windows, usually also a chimney with smoke coming out as a sign of people living in the house. But the image of DOM also includes invisible characteristics, carries certain values and functions as a cultural symbol, i.e. it also means 'home'.[1] In this chapter I investigate the various dimensions of DOM, the nature of its content and the way it functions in general discourse.

The concept of HOUSE/HOME is universal, pan-European, supernational,[2] but also culture-specific. It is universal because it constitutes the centre of a person's world, the place from which the person views reality. Lurker (1990) notes that when at home a person feels as if in the centre of the world. Indeed, the home is a symbol of the world as such. Herder (1986), in turn, describes the home as a symbol of the universe, cosmic order and the human body. The concept is a universal motif of folklore worldwide, also common in literature, philosophy, journalism and politics. But it is also culture-specific because cultures mould it according to historical circumstances and within a given system of values.[3]

In the Polish context, DOM functions as a physical object but also as a social, national and cultural value. It is tied up in a network of semantic relationships with the concepts MOTHER, FAMILY, POLAND or HOMELAND. DOM in Poland is the 'stronghold of national identity'. Can this conception survive in the face of Europeisation and globalisation?

The cultural model of the 'Polish home' (cf. Prokop, 1992) took its shape in the nineteenth century, when Poland did not exist as an independent state (1795–1918). Social and patriotic functions were taken over from the then hostile state institutions by the family. The home and family became the mainstay of the national spirit against Germanisation and Russification. In the communist period of 1945–1989 its role was also to protect and preserve religious values.

The idyllic image of the Polish house or in fact a nobility manor house, extolled by Adam Mickiewicz, Henryk Sienkiewicz and others, was severely criticised for opportunism and intellectual infertility already towards the end of the nineteenth century.[4] However, the jeopardy to the existence of the nation during World War I and World War II contributed to the maintenance of the home as a 'national stronghold' conception. In the final stage of the communist system, which was engaged in a long but losing battle with the Polish national and religious tradition, a respondent of the questionnaire for the monthly *Znak* (no. 390/391, 1987) wrote: 'It is not administrative or social structures, not clubs, pubs and school ties (as in England), not military tradition (as in Prussia)

[...] but the family home [...], the neighbourhood and friends that in the historical perspective is the mainstay of Polish identity'.

Why, then, did Polish voters in the 2007 parliamentary elections reject the right-wing League of Polish Families, whose programme is based on the apotheosis of national and family tradition? Is it the case that without the communist ideology, the national myth opposing that ideology with the tradition of the 'Polish home' and the 'God-based family' has no *raison d'être*? What picture of DOM is now present in the Polish linguo-cultural space, in the Polish linguistic worldview? What changes have taken place and are still in progress? As in the case of MOTHER, I will try and reconstruct the picture on the basis of systemic, questionnaire-based and textual data.

2   *Dom* in dictionaries

The lexicographic treatment of *dom* is of very low quality: the definitions are poor and fragmented into too many separate meanings. *USJP* (2003) lists six (clearly dependent and linked) meanings of *dom*:

   i)   a house for living;
   ii)   a flat, apartment, the place where one lives;
   iii) the family; the apartment and the household;
   iv)   the family matters;
   v)   the family line; dynasty;
   vi)   a public, social, trade etc. institution usually localised in a separate apart-
         ment of building: also: the building where it is located; a firm or company.[5]

These definitions (as well as those in other dictionaries) strive towards objectivity, 'matter-of-factness', devoid of people's subjective feelings and values, without references to what a house or home is *for them*. The definitions do not contain 'connotations', whose value has been identified on numerous occasions (Bartmiński, 1984, 1988a) and without which the description of the perceived and conceptualised world is incomplete (Chlebda, 1993).

Let us dwell a little on the question of the dimensions (parameters) of DOM. The fragmented lexicographic accounts seem to corroborate an important (preconceptual?) feature of DOM, namely is multidimensionality. They describe it in the physical sense (as a building), in the social sense (a community of people) and in the functional sense (family matters or an institution). These are by no means separate dimensions; on the contrary, they make up a conceptual whole with different aspects. The multidimensional nature of DOM is especially pronounced in parts of the dictionary entry other than the definition, such as in the typical collocations with *dom* or in examples of the word's usage.

The physical aspect is present in a few dozen units, such as (cf. *PSWP*, 1994–1998): *zbudować/zburzyć dom* 'build/destroy a house', *sprzedaż/ubezpieczenie domu* 'house sale/insurance', *drewniany dom/dom z cegły* 'a wooden/brick house', *dom wielopiętrowy* 'a multi-storey house'; *niski/wysoki dom* 'a low/tall house', etc.

The social aspect is recognisable in: *założyć dom* 'set up a home', *wynieść z domu dobre wykształcenie* 'receive good education at home', *głowa domu* 'head of the household', *przyjaciel domu* 'friend of the family', *pan/pani domu* 'host/hostess' (lit. 'the master/mistress of the household'), *pojechać gdzieś całym domem* 'go somewhere with the whole family' (lit. 'the whole home'), *postawić cały dom na nogi* 'wake up everyone at home' (lit. 'stand the whole home on the legs'); the proverb: 'Woe to the home where the cow butts the bull' (i.e. it is bad when the woman is the head of the household).

The functional aspect is present in: *dom letniskowy* 'holiday house', *dom wczasowy* 'guesthouse', *dom noclegowy* 'lodging house', *dom studencki* 'student hostel' (lit. 'students' house'), *dom opieki społecznej* 'institution' (lit. 'the house of social care'), *dom towarowy* 'shopping mall' (lit. 'goods house') etc. *PSWP* (1994–1998) gives as many as fifty examples of that type. They suggest that one is staying at a given place only temporarily, e.g. in a guesthouse (*ergo*: the real *dom* is for permanent residence), that the inhabitants of the place do not own it, e.g. at a student hostel or an institution (*ergo*: one usually owns the house one lives in), or that the building is set for a specific purpose, e.g. a shopping mall (*ergo*: a real house is for living).

In textual usages of *dom* an important explicit or implicit role is played by axiology. It surfaces explicitly in e.g. *wszędzie dobrze, ale w domu najlepiej* 'there is no place like home'; implicitly in e.g. *być panem we własnym domu* 'my home is my castle'. Axiology is present in all aspects of *dom*, also in its specific characteristics. This corroborates Krzeszowski's (1994: 32) view that Lakoff and Johnson's preconceptual image schemas are equipped with an additional 'plus-minus' parameter.

We can investigate the specific features subjectively attributed to *dom* on the basis of the word's derivatives, oppositions to the concept, the mechanisms of metaphorisation and etymology. We will look at these in turn.

3   Derivatives of *dom*

The derivatives of *dom* include features of vitality and hedonism: the feeling of security, freedom and pleasure. The meanings of *domowy* 'of home', *po domowemu* 'as it is/as one would at home', *jak w domu* 'like at home' oscillates between the purely informative and the qualitative, with a positive attitude to the home, its atmosphere, well-being of the people who live there etc. (cf. e.g. *urządzić coś po domowemu* 'organise something as one would at home', *czuć się jak w domu* 'feel at home'). The expression *ubrany po domowemu* 'dressed in clothes to wear at home' also means 'casually', 'informally', 'comfortably'.

4   Oppositions

The multiaspectual nature of DOM is very strongly revealed in oppositions, in which it is viewed in relation to people, as physical space, but also a social and 'subjectivised' space. The fundamental opposition between DOM and the world is based on the distinction between 'close' and 'distant', 'internal' vs. 'external', as well as on the psychosocial notions of 'familiar/ours' vs. 'foreign/alien'. DOM is close, ours, familiar and friendly; the world is distant, alien and dangerous (cf. the proverbs 'Let him who feels well at home not roam the world', 'Let us praise the world but stay at home', 'No place like home'). Antonyms of *dom* also include: the inn or hotel (cf. the proverb 'This world is not our home but our inn'); the street and the forest (hence the prohibition, in Eastern Poland, to whistle at home, expressed with the formula 'Don't whistle at home, you're not in the forest'). Being at home, living there is a basic, elementary experience of a human being. The saying 'We are cold, hungry and far from home' evokes two basic functions of DOM: to provide food and warmth.

Proverbs also contain a clear social juxtaposition of being at home and staying somewhere else, where 'at home' means 'at one's own place, among one's folk': 'At home you do as you want, at someone else's place as you should'; 'Peas at home are better than meat at someone else's place'; 'Peas or cabbage at home are better than a fat hen when one is at war'.

5   Metaphorisation

Thanks to the richness of its axiological content, the image of DOM and those of its parts are used as source domains in metaphorical references to people or their bodies, or to Poland, Europe and the world.

5.1 The body as DOM

DOM can serve as a reference frame for understanding the human body or clothing (treated purely functionally or evaluated). The relevant descriptive-functional metaphors include: 'The eye is a window to the heart' (1620) or 'The eye is a window to the mind' (1632; usually the eye is the soul's reflection, from Latin *Oculus animi index*); 'The world is a dress, the home a shirt' (1859, Aleksander Fredro). The understanding of the body as a person's DOM can be found in everyday phraseology: *ktoś nie ma wszystkich w domu* 'someone does not have everybody at home' means 'someone has gone out of their mind'; *ktoś ma dobrze/źle pod sufitem* 'someone is well/badly furnished under the ceiling' means 'is (is not) sensible'; otworzyc wrota 'to open the gates' means 'to open one's mouth'. In student jargon one can refer to a woman's breasts as 'balconies'.[6]

The BODY AS HOUSE metaphor may be evaluated negatively because both the body and a house can restrict one's freedom. A Polish sixteenth century poet Mikołaj Sęp-Szarzyński wrote:

> Our house-this body, for fleeting delight,
> Heedlessly envying the spirit its might,
> Will not cease striving to fall for ever.
>
> (*Sonnet IV*, trans. Michael J. Mikoś)

However, in one of Czesław Miłosz's poems the body does not obstruct the flow of thought and sensations:

> The purpose of poetry is to remind us
> how difficult it is to remain just one person,
> for our house is open, there are no keys in the doors,
> and invisible guests come in and out at will.

('*Ars Poetica?*', 1968, trans. Czesław Miłosz and Lillian Vallee)

5.2 The homeland as DOM

DOM is traditionally made use of while referring to Poland as the homeland in the spatial, social and axiological sense (cf. chapter 13). In fact, the operating principle here is metonymy rather than metaphor, the home being a portion or aspect of the country. Consider the following examples:

> The nation, not surprised, raised its head: [...]
> The whole Poland is its home.

(Artur Oppman, 1925, trans. A.G.)

> When they come to set your house on fire,
> The one in which you live – Poland

(Władysław Broniewski, *Bayonets Ready*, 1939; trans. Adam Gillon and Ludwik Krzyżanowski)

> We did not write the Bible, as Jews did
> we did not beat Persians, as Greeks did
> in the four walls of the simplest homeland
> we swore fidelity to field poems

(Jan Pocek, a folk poet)

Consider also the electoral slogan of Aleksander Kwaśniewski, a former Polish president: 'Poland: the home of all Poles'.

A 1992 questionnaire administered to students showed that as many as 37% of them were ready to use the word *dom* to illustrate their conception of the homeland. One of them said: 'A synonym of the homeland is *dom*, though a bigger one. The home is associated with warmth and goodness. The homeland evokes similar feelings. To be in one's homeland is to be at one's own place, at home' (Kloskowska, 1993: 50).

5.3 Europe as DOM

In present-day public discourse Europe is called *dom*. Józef Tischner, a Catholic philosopher and theologian, writes:

> One can often hear today that Europe is to be 'the common home of Europeans'. The metaphor of the 'common home' is a metaphor of freedom. It suggests that the new European freedom is to be like the freedom one has at home, in a place where one actually feels 'at home'. (Tischner, 1998: 229).

When Mikhail Gorbachev talked about 'the European home', he had in mind security and well-being more than freedom, but he too talked about it in axiological terms and evoked the values commonly associated with the home. Before Poland's accession to the EU in 2004, the 'European home' meant a community of spiritual values. This axiological view united right-wing and left-wing circles, irrespective of the different motivation and expectations of the two sides.[7]

5.4 The world as DOM

The conceptualisation of the whole world as DOM is rooted in the Bible.[8] Jan Kochanowski, a Polish Renaissance poet, translated the beginning of Psalm 12 as 'Save me, oh you builder of the heavenly *dom*', which follows the biblical tradition. Jan Czyński (nineteenth century) wrote about the 'great builder of the world'; similarly, Franciszek Kniaźnin (also nineteenth century) exhorted to 'renew the construction of the world'. Kazimierz Brodziński (early nineteenth century) views the loss of this broad perspective as a great misfortune, saying that the world used to be home, but then the home became the world. However, even in the times of national dependence, Cyprian Kamil Norwid (nineteenth century) thought of the world as his home/house: 'I pay rent to the world' (*My Country*, 1861; trans. Adam Czerniawski). The conception of the world as home, connected with he idea of brotherhood and 'the family of nations', can easily be found in nineteenth century humanistic and cosmopolitan discourse.

The treatment of the world as the home is reflected in poetic formulae with the adjective *domowy* 'domestic; of the home': 'How much do I owe you, the trees of my home' (Adam Mickiewicz, *Pan Tadeusz*, Book Four, 42);[9] 'Niemen, the river of my home' (Mickiewicz, *To the Niemen*, 1822);[10] 'the rocks of my home' (Stefan Żeromski, *Wind from the Sea*).

The conception of the world as home is still present in folk culture. Let me discuss this in some detail.

In the folk conception the world (the universe) is actually *identified* with *dom* and the roof is the sky. Mircea Eliade traces the emergence of this conception back to the Neolithic Period but its examples can be found on all levels of culture. This home-as-the-world (the world-turned-home) is viewed as a sensitive and compassionate place, whose important part is mother earth, united in a cosmic hierogamy with father sky.

A question arises whether we are dealing here with a metaphor or with a mythical image. The 'myth' interpretation is suggested by a peculiar folk rationality (animate nature) and bidirectional mappings (the world is the home but the home is also the world). The treatment of the home/house as the world in Slavic cultures is emphasised by Albert Bayburin (1983), who says that the division of the house into an attic, the living space and the cellar is analogous to the division of the universe into the sky, earth and underworld. The manmade house replicates the structure of the cosmos on the human scale; it is a microcosm of sorts.

Let us notice, however, that the two conceptualisations (the world as the house/home and the house/home as the world) are not cognitively equivalent, nor are they equally interesting. The image of the world as a huge house or village is based on simple anthropocentrism and rather anachronistic sociomorphism. To extrapolate close images onto the distant world is to strip the latter of its portentous aspect, to fulfill one's need to be at home, to protect oneself against the dangerous and the ominous. But it also limits one's knowledge of reality to the subjective; reduces the object to familiar categories.

Not so when the home/house is conceptualised as the world. In this case new perspectives open up and the house assumes cosmic dimensions. When the roof and attic are equated with the sky, the living space with the earth and the cellar with the underground, it is something more than a simple structural analogy: it introduces the house into the conception of *axis mundi*, enriching its characteristics with cultural and axiological dimensions. It makes room for the world, that is, for what is distant, new and unfamiliar. In southern Poland the act is symbolised by a special Christmas tree wafer decoration, called 'the world', which after the holiday is crushed and added to corn seeds for a better harvest. The idea of hospitality and readiness to accept someone from 'the world' is expressed in a still very popular Polish proverb 'A guest in the home is God in the home' (first record 1618).

5.5 The mother tongue as DOM

This metaphor is especially dear to poets, writers and emigrants, and can be found in the work of Cyprian Godebski (eighteenth–nineteenth century), Juliusz Słowacki (nineteenth century), Artur Oppman (nineteenth–twentieth century), Julian Tuwin (twentieth century) or Czesław Miłosz (twentieth century).

The material aspect of DOM is captured from the perspective of human needs: biological (warmth), social (security and closeness to another person) and psychological (intimacy). This functional, or in fact axiological, aspect of DOM is revealed most clearly when parts of the house are evoked, for the metaphor can also operate on its parts:

- the walls protect people against cold and separate them from the outside world;

- the roof protects them against rain;

- the doorstep and the front door set the boundary between what is inside and what is outside; they also enable people to cross the boundary in both directions;

- the windows let the sunlight in and provide access to the world.

The functional principle introduces the personal perspective and integrates people with objects.

Literary descriptions of houses in the work of Adam Mickiewicz (the mansion in Book I of *Pan Tadeusz*), Stefan Żeromski, Maria Kuncewiczowa or Melchior Wańkowicz are strongly subjectivised and serve to characterise the inner states of protagonists.

In questionnaires (Byc, 1993) the parts of the house are ordered according to importance in the following way: the kitchen, room, bathroom and toilet (the latter two often combined). The ordering corresponds to the hierarchy of functions: eating – sleeping – excretion. The most important objects are the table (because the family gather around it for meals and conversation) and the bed. Next in line is the TV set (especially for blue-collar workers), religious paraphernalia (a crucifix, pictures of God, the Virgin Mary and saints),[11] the stove (only for country dwellers, who are familiar with fire in the house), and occasionally books.

6   Etymology

The inseparability of the three aspects of DOM, physical, psychosocial and functional (axiological), is confirmed by etymological analysis (Ivanov, Gamkrelidze, 1984: 741–743). It shows that *dom* has old, Proto-Indo-European roots, present in Greek (*dómos*) and Latin (*domus* 'house', 'home' or 'family'; *dominus* 'host'); it comprises the notions of 'building', 'home/place to live' and 'family, clan', and is etymologically related to the Greek *demo-* 'build' (hence the Polish *demiurg* and English *demiurge* – the builder or artificer). Already the Indo-European root **dem-/*dom-* probably had a complex meaning 'a place to live for a group people connected through social and family ties' (Ivanov and Gamkrelidze, 1984: 742).

The links between the physical, social and cultural dimensions are also present in other languages. Biblicists mention the existence of a similar, multiaspectual conception in Jewish tradition: 'to construct a home is not just to build its walls, but it is to establish a hearth and to beget a lineage and to pass on to them religious teaching and examples of virtue' (Léon-Dufour, 1967: 245). The Hebrew word *bana* evokes the notions of building a house and setting up a family.

7   The importance of values

The Polish image of DOM is dominated by psychosocial and axiological features. Experimental, questionnaire-based research which provides access to the colloquial conceptualisation of DOM was conducted in 1990 and 2000 among students in Lublin,

Poland (a hundred respondents each time; cf. Bartmiński, 2006a; Żywicka, 2007: 52). Similar results were obtained in both cases: asked to provide the characteristics of the 'true home', the students mentioned (in this order): the family, love, warmth, the place one returns to, understanding, security, community, trust, friendly atmosphere, help, support, peace, respect. The results have been replicated in other studies. For example, Fleischer's respondents to his 1993 and 2000 questionnaires concerning Polish 'collective symbols', used the same concepts and expressions, with a strong axiological load: the family, warmth, love, security, care, peace, quiet, shelter, children, building, place to live, parents (mother, father), joy, happiness, friendship, community, hearth (Fleischer, 2003: 122). Fleischer places DOM at fourth position in the hierarchy of Polish collective symbols, behind love, family and friendship.[12] This is a higher position than in German (also investigated in Fleischer's study), but in both languages the valuation of house/home is decidedly positive (Fleischer, 1998: 325).

All these data point to the importance of values in the Polish colloquial stereotype of DOM. The values make up a complex described as 'family atmosphere' or 'hearth' (in the psychosocial domain) and 'safe haven' or 'one's own place' (the domain of everyday life). One may say that the Polish DOM is an ideological stereotype, a cultural pattern. Because the pattern exists in colloquial language and thinking, one may assume that it belongs to the common cultural ground, in the sense of van Dijk (2002). This also explains its stability and relative (though not absolute) resistance to change in the face of transformations of the Polish society.

8   The multidimensionality of DOM

Let us finally consider in what way one may describe the multidimensional conception of DOM so as not to dissociate its aspects or lose the many features through which it is characterised and valuated. A semantic description of this kind may be constructed according to the principles of the cognitive definition, in an attempt to arrive at the fundamental components of meaning (cf. chapter 6). The definition would thus contain judgments well established in the community, repetitive 'stereotypical motifs'.[13]

The basic stereotypical motif defining DOM is composed of three concepts which appear in dictionaries as its superordinate categories (hyperonyms): BUILDING, PLACE TO LIVE and FAMILY.[14] They are combined into a semantic gestalt, whose parts imply one another: the place, the event and the participants in the event. The whole has a certain functional independency; it is recognisable as a 'semantic standard' in the system of language and in social convention (Hjelmslev's or Coşeriu's 'norm'). (In Awdiejew and Habrajska's (2004: 43) communicative grammar, a 'semantic standard' is an 'intersubjective generalised representation of the ideational image, with a predicate-argument structure'.) Furthermore, it can be formalised as the sentence [A FAMILY LIVES IN A BUILDING]. This base stereotypical motif is the first interpretant of the conception of DOM.

But there also exist a number of motifs derived from the base, which are included in dictionaries in the entry for *dom* as fixed phraseological units: *zbudować/wznieść/*

wyremontować/zburzyć dom 'to build/construct/redo/destroy the house', *kupić/sprzedać/ wynająć dom* 'to buy/sell/let the house', *opuścić dom* 'to leave home/the house', *powrócić do domu* 'to return/come back home/to the house' etc.

The basic motif and the derived ones can be further elaborated on by means of substitution, paraphrase or elaboration. Substitution can be exemplified by: 'Peasants live in huts' →'Farmers live in detached houses' → 'Landholders live in manor houses' → 'Aristocrats and businessmen live in palaces' → 'Terrible townsmen live in terrible flats' (from a poem by Julian Tuwin, first half of the twentieth century). Examples of paraphrase include: 'Someone lives in house' → 'Someone likes being in a house'; 'Someone has a house' → 'Someone own a house/The house belongs to someone'. Finally, sample elaborations are: 'Someone has a house' → 'Someone has bought/built a house'; 'Someone lives in a house' → 'Someone leaves their house/home' → 'Someone returns to their house/returns home'. In effect, a whole operating system arises.

Stereotypical motifs are potential components of text, in which they are combined in sequences (plots) according to the rules of text construction. The possibilities of text construction by means of base stereotypical motifs are theoretically limited only by pragmatic, historical and cultural factors. Textual analysis enables the identification and description of the motifs.

It is practically impossible to embrace with one's research the whole universe of texts concerning DOM but it is possible (cf. Bartmiński and Żuk, 2007) to pinpoint the significant ideological types of discourse, within which the basic image of the home/ house is profiled from a given perspective and according to an assumed system of values. In a rudimentary manner, one may distinguish the following types of public discourse about the Polish DOM:

- Christian (Catholic): the patriarchal home;

- national: the home and family as the stronghold of national identity (the idea of 'the Polish mother');

- emigrant: the feeling of alienation; nostalgia;

- liberal: the open house;

- left-wing: the home and family are subordinated to the community;

- feminist: the house as a prison (the woman is the involuntary stay-at-home); domestic violence.

One of the basic dilemmas around which reflection about DOM is centred is the choice between staying at home with one's family, in an environment which is friendly and safe but which restricts one's personal freedom, and leaving the home, taking personal challenges and the risk of solitude. A poetic expression of this dramatic choice can be found in one of Bolesław Leśmian's poems (early twentieth century), who in his own peculiar way capitalises on the motif of Odysseus:

<table>
<tr><td>

Niegdyś dom mój ochoczy i świat za dąbrową

Porzuciłem, by dachu nie mieć ponad głową,

I siebie porzuciłem gdzieś na skraju lasu

Bez pomocy, bez żalu, bez śpiewu, bez czasu

I biegłem tam, gdzie burza, mrok i zawierucha,

By serce niepokoić i narazić ducha –

Tak się chciałem utrudzić i krwią własną zbroczyć,

Żeby istnieć wbrew sobie i ból swój przekroczyć.

I minęło lat wiele – i po latach wielu –

Marnotrawiąc dróg tysiąc – dotarłem do celu

I pieśniami nade mną rozbrzmiały niebiosy,

Powiększyły się kwiaty, zolbrzymiały rosy –

I zgaduję, że z płaczem, po własnym pogrzebie,

W opuszczoną bezdomność powracam do siebie.

</td><td>

I once left my eager home and
the world beyond the oak woods

so that I wouldn't have a roof
over my head,

And I left myself at the wood's
edge

Without help or grief, or singing,
or time

And I ran where there was storm
and darkness

To disturb my heart and
jeopardise my spirit –

I wanted to tire so much and
shed my blood

so that I would exist in spite of
myself and move beyond my pain.

And many years have passed,
and after many years

I reached my destination, having
wasted a thousand ways

And the heavens broke out
singing above me,

Flowers and dew grew

And I guess that, crying, after
my own funeral,

I return to myself into my
abandoned homelessness.

</td></tr>
</table>

This is a vision of an individual but it is deeply entrenched in tradition. The image of DOM is that of a warm and secure place but not of the hearth or the stronghold of national identity. Instead, one finds an individual determination to go out to the world beyond, to experience uneasiness and darkness, to face the enormity of the world and to accept suffering as the price for the acquired wisdom, for the knowledge one has of the world and of oneself. Returning home is interpreted as returning to oneself. I am my own home; you are your own home. One cannot escape or abandon the home so understood. The material aspect of DOM (i.e. the house) is not foregrounded but does not disappear: it constitutes the necessary background against which one witnesses the dramatic change of the protagonist. The protagonist is liberated from the bondage of idyllic congeniality and matures to the state of bitter awareness of himself and the necessity to build his own identity.

Notes

1   The Polish word encompasses the English notions of 'house' and 'home' (as well as being unique in its own ways) and I will use the Polish word throughout the chapter, except when the context allows or requires otherwise.

2   In 1987 I visited an ethnographic museum in Milwaukee, WI, USA, where there was an exhibition of houses (the buildings with their interior, furniture etc.) in different cultures of the world. The European house (from Spain to Russia) was treated as a coherent, historically shaped type, different from the African, Asian, American etc. house.

3   I have in mind here the basic, colloquial variety of language, which in comparative research figures as the most important.

4   Prokop (1992: 52–53) suggests that the dispute reflected the tension between gregariousness, a 'herd instinct' of sorts, and individualism, both inherited from the times of the Republic. The Polish house was built at the intersection of the two roads, which is why its walls are cracked from shocks. But, Prokop continues, it will survive: national memory restores its glorious moments.

5   In my opinion the practice of splitting the global image into distinct senses may obliterate the colloquial conceptualisation because it separates elements which in the speakers' consciousness may interpenetrate. They may be distinguished only in context, depending on the speaker's perspective.

6   The use of the human body as the source domain is very common, as evidenced by numerous metaphorical extensions of the words for a hand, finger, leg, foot, ear, the head, mouth, nose, tongue etc. However, as the source domain in referring to the house/home it is very rare, a notable exception being the pan-Slavic name for a window, *okno*, derived from *oko* 'eye'.

7   However, an interesting difference emerged in Polish public discourse of the 1990s. Grzegorz Żuk (2004) observes: 'An analysis of metaphors suggests that Europe is considered 'ours' by the clergy, who also think that Poles deserve to be there. But the lay, leftist journalists view themselves and other Poles as mere guests. The two viewpoints are connected with two profiles of Europe: the bishops see Europe as a cultural formation in which Poland has been continuously present since the tenth century, but the leftist journalists see it as an institution, the European Union which Poland is still to join'. (Poland accessed Europe in 2004.)

8   Consider the following quote: 'For the people of the Old Testament, man is an integral part of nature. Not a stranger, an intruder or 'penitent', sent to a hostile planet to suffer, atone for his sins and through good deeds deserve eternal life. Man came from the earth, received his name from it (the Hebrew for the earth is *adama*); the earth feeds him, the earth is his home and homeland. This is where he is 'at home'. Between him and nature there is full harmony, as was in the paradise, with complete solidarity between man and animals. At this point the Bible fully parallels primitive cultures.' (Filipiak, 1993: 31).

9   Trans. mine [A.G.]. Watson Kirkconnell's rendering of the line does not contain a reference to the house/home. [translator's note]

10   Trans. mine [A.G.]. Peter K. Gessner translates it as 'river of my youth' (http://infopoland.buffalo.edu/classroom/mickiewicz/poem.html; accessed April 20, 2008). [translator's note]

11 In the 1980s and 1990s people would more and more often hang the picture of John Paul II in their homes.

12 On an earlier list based on data from 1993, DOM was the 11th positive value (Fleischer, 1998: 326).

13 A similar effect is achieved by Anna Wierzbicka (1994) by means of 'cultural scripts'.

14 Such is the case in e.g. a dictionary of synonyms, *SS* (1993). The category BUILDING includes, apart from *dom*, Polish counterparts to 'edifice', 'tenement house', 'block of flats', 'high-rise', 'skyscraper', 'office building', '(railway) station' and suchlike. The category PLACE TO LIVE includes 'apartment/suite', 'hotel', 'address'; the category FAMILY mentions 'household', 'clan/family line', 'relatives', 'married couple', 'parents', 'children'.

13 The Polish OJCZYZNA (homeland): its base stereotype and ideological profiles

1 Introduction

Homeland is a pan-European ideological stereotype (Wandruszka, 1990). Polish sociologists and historians view the Polish conception of homeland (OJCZYZNA) as an ideological image, an idea in the canon of Polish national culture, a 'synthesis of the culture's prime values' (Kłoskowska, 1991: 52). It is a 'lofty' word and concept. It is present in public discourse, especially in the discourse of the Catholic Church, in education and politics (a Google search for *ojczyzna* on March 10, 2008, yielded about 2,500,000 hits), but is almost totally absent from everyday speech. Moreover, in contemporary youth subcultures it may be treated critically and even rejected.

The concept of homeland has a long tradition all over the world. The starting point in the process of the formation of the Polish concept was, similarly to other European cultures, the Latin *patria*, connected with home, the father (*pater*), inheritance after the father (*patrimonium*) and later with the institution of the state. The Latin word and the structure of the Latin concept is continued in Romance languages and as a conceptual model it has been calqued into German (*Vaterland*), Russian (*otechestvo*, from *otets* 'father'), Ukrainian (*batkivshchyna*, from *bat'ko* 'father'), Bulgarian (*tatkovina*, from *tatko* 'father'), Lithuanian, Hungarian and others. At the same time, as revealed in the 1992 research on the concept in twelve European countries (Bartmiński, 1993), individual national cultures have modified and adapted the concept to their own needs and local traditions. A common component, however, is the obligation to protect the common good, associated with the family home, the state, sometimes the nation, in accordance with Horace's formula *Dulce et decorum est pro patria mori*.

In Poland, the broad conception of homeland was known to Latin medieval chroniclers, Gallus Anonymus (twelfth century) and Wincenty Kadłubek (thirteenth century). Piotr Skarga, the author of the famous sermon 'On the love of homeland' (1597) used the images of Poland, then a multiethnic state, as a mother who takes care of everyone and as a ship which 'carries us all'. When Poland was subjected to foreign powers (1795–1918), Romantic poets created great Tyrtean poetry, synthesised in Karol Libelt's passionate patriotic manifesto 'On the love of homeland' (1844).

It is this variant of the Polish understanding of homeland that is contrasted by Anna Wierzbicka (1997) with the German *Vaterland* and Russian *rodina*. By employing her Natural Semantic Metalanguage, she shows significant differences between the three concepts. She identifies nearly thirty characteristics in the Polish concept: the country of my birth, the country to which I belong, which is not like other countries, which is unhappy, which has done a lot of good for me, for which I want to do good things, which is treated in a similar way by other people with whom I am one (because we act and feel in the same way and because we are as if a portion of that country), etc. Wierzbicka shows that many of those features are missing in the German concept of *Vaterland* (birthplace, being unhappy, the moral duty of compassion), which is according to her characterised by one's obedience to one's country and by superiority over other countries.

The variant described by Wierzbicka is certainly basic and representative of Polish culture, but it is also at least partly historical, originating in the nineteenth century. True, it is still present in Polish public discourse but slowly becoming obsolete. Many different conceptions of homeland and of the relationship between a person and their homeland have recently emerged – I will discuss them in this chapter.

In fact, the first reformulation of the conception of national homeland appeared already in the nineteenth century; then in the twentieth century and now the concept is undergoing further ideologically driven transformations. Homeland is a 'matter of argument' by nature. The differences are even manifested in its contemporary lexicographic definitions, let alone in journalistic or political discourse. What is the core of these discrepancies? What components of the concepts are subjected to debate?

It seems that the discrepancies arise because the concept of homeland is a very complex one, although it is not a 'conceptual cluster' in the basic understanding of the term. A cluster may be unpredictable, while homeland has a clear and to a degree predictable internal cognitive structure. It contains a stable part, the semantic core, as well as variable parts. Relatively stable are its very dimensions or aspects: physical, social, institutional, cultural (axiological), while their selection, hierarchy and content are variable. The range and quality of what is variable depends on the communicative and cultural context, but above all on the speaker's intentions and system of values (cf. chapter 4 above). I will try and describe both what is stable and what is variable in terms of the conceptual base and its profiling (cf. chapter 8).

2   The Polish conception of homeland in dictionaries

The dictionary representations of the base features of the concept of homeland are incomplete. The most important post-World War II Polish dictionary, *SJPDor* (1962), defines *ojczyzna* in a rather reserved manner as 'the country of one's birth in which one's compatriots live', without any note of cultural or axiological connotations. It is only in the examples, especially of phraseological units, that one finds hints as to the relationships between a person and their homeland or as to the prevalent or even obligatory patterns of behaviour: *bronić ojczyzny* 'to defend one's homeland', *walczyć/przelać krew/umrzeć za ojczyznę* 'to fight/shed blood/die for one's homeland', *synowie ojczyzny* 'the sons of the homeland'. These are all patriotic and heroic scenarios, inherited from the times of partitions, uprisings and wars. The experience of exile and emigration is reflected in the expressions *druga/nowa ojczyzna* '(one's) second/new homeland'.

Mieczysław Szymczak's dictionary (*SJPSzym*, 1994, first published in 1978), compiled when Poland was a socialist state, adds two ideological components: being a citizen and being a member of the nation (homeland is 'a country where one was born, of which one is a citizen or to which one belongs through national bonds'). Later dictionaries reproduce this definition to a large extent.[1] However, the exemplification of the homeland in *SJPSzym* is different from that in *SJPDor*: it highlights the notions of an independent, free, liberated country, though the phraseology remains in the sphere of fight, struggle and service for the country (later dictionaries add the notions of love (*SWJP*, 1996) and a return to the homeland (*USJP*, 2003)).

A radical enrichment and extension of the linguistic worldview of homeland came with *PSWP* (1994–1998), which also includes the following notions: 'to live out of one's homeland', 'to be the national pride', 'God, honour, homeland', 'the Europe of homelands' (a slogan for the regional aspect of the united Europe), 'one's little homeland' (the region thought of as one's native land), as well as important quotations from the literature: 'Sacred love of our cherished homeland' (Ignacy Krasicki, eighteenth century); 'Lithuania, my fatherland' (Mickiewicz, *Pan Tadeusz*, Book I; nineteenth century, trans. Watson Kirkconnell); 'A free homeland give us back/bless for us, our Lord' (Alojzy Feliński, nineteenth century); 'he is from my homeland, and is a human' (Antoni Słonimski, twentieth century). The dictionary also gives eight proverbs which reflect the traditional ethos of sacrifice for one's homeland, but also the attitude of self-interest ('One's homeland is where there is good living') and criticism ('Homeland on every lips but the hearts are frozen').

The differences in the representations of homeland in dictionaries point to the existence of hidden controversies and make one think about the choices being made, the boundaries of the leeway and the nature of the changes. The Polish concept of OJCZYZNA will now be subjected to careful analysis within the framework of the cognitive definition.

3   What do speakers think?

The validity of lexicographic solutions may be verified by referring to the linguistic intuitions of contemporary Poles through questionnaires and analyses of the books on school compulsory reading lists.

The question 'What in your opinion constitutes the essence of a (true) homeland?' was asked to university students in Lublin, Poland twice: in 1990 (102 respondents) and in 2001 (101 respondents). The answers received were rather similar: one's birthplace and origin; the place to which one returns willingly; the country where one lives; the home to which one can always come back; the national community with which one feels a spiritual bond; the people of the same language and culture, the people one considers close; history and tradition; well-being and the feeling of security, freedom and the ability to work, care for the well-being of the citizens; love of the place, people and customs; emotional bond and nostalgia (Bartmiński, 2006: 340–347). Great importance was attached to the spatial, geographical understanding of homeland: the place where one is born, lives and returns and to which one feels a certain emotional attachment. The responses were mainly given in the 1st person: 'I was born here', 'our roots are here', 'my friends live here', etc. There is also an important component of high moral or ethical values, ideals and the common good. Language, culture and history occupy a high position but, contrary to expectations, religion does not and is mentioned only marginally.

Over the ten-year period a certain statistically measurable shift could be observed: the everyday criteria weakened (place of residence, security, work), while psychological and social ones strengthened (love, emotional bond, nostalgia, the feeling of unity). Another tendency has also appeared, if only weakly: a link between the homeland and the state (with references to its flag, coat of arms, anthem and citizens).[2]

4   A poet's view

Let us consider the poetic image of the homeland in the poem *homeland's face* by Tadeusz Różewicz, a Polish twentieth century poet:

> homeland is the country of childhood
> one's birthplace
> this is the little, closest
> homeland
> the town
> street house backyard
> first love
> the forest on the horizon
> the graves
> in childhood one learns about
> flowers herbs corn animals
> fields and meadows
> words fruits
> homeland is laughing
> at first homeland is close
> within arm's reach
> it is only later that it grows
> bleeds
> hurts
>
> (trans. A.G.)

In the poem, a significant role is played by the very personal, emotional bond between a person and their homeland. The bond has a physical, spatial aspect (the city and country with its wildlife) and a social aspect (the first love, the living and the departed). Secondly, the 'space of the homeland' is treated as dynamic, multidimensional and concentric; it is organised according to the logic of one's life and personal development: the horizon expands from the close and known to the distant and new.

How many 'identity circles' are opened up by a dynamic understanding of the Polish homeland? Are there only two of them: the 'private' and the 'ideological' homeland (by analogy to the German *Heimat* vs. *Vaterland* and Russian *rodina* vs. *otechestvo*, as proposed by Stanisław Ossowski in his famous 'A sociological analysis of the concept of homeland' (Ossowski, 1946)? In my opinion, there are many more. But Ossowski is right in saying that homeland is a relational concept. Just like the concepts of mother, father, brother or sister can only be described as such in relation to someone, a homeland is necessarily someone's homeland. To explicate the content of the concept means to describe it within a larger configuration in which the subject remains in a certain relationship with the object. The following questions arise: What is the nature of the object? Who is this subject such that he or she remains in a relationship with the object and considers the object his/her own? What kind of relationship is it?

5   The various dimensions of homeland

The multitude and elasticity of the 'identity circles' is best seen in the basic spatial dimension of homeland. For the majority of contemporary Poles, the homeland is their country, their place, shared with people one considers close, it is the national territory. However, it is not *always* the country. There is also a narrower understanding of homeland in the spatial sense, as one's home, patrimony, home town and region. On the other hand, homeland can also be extended onto Europe and the whole world. A peculiar status and clear religious overtones can be attributed to the 'heavenly homeland'.

Consider the following selected examples of the usage of the word *ojczyzna*:

HOMELAND AS THE HOME

> A university professor: 'In my home village near Kraków the family home is called *ojczyzna*. This was for many years the only meaning of the word. It meant the home. Simply the home.' (Styczeń and Balawajder, 1986: 74).

> In peasant folk dialects and folk songs one meaning of *ojczyzna* is still associated with the father (*ojciec*): it is the patrimony, something inherited from the father: 'Maciek has died, may he go to heaven, / And I will live on his *ojczyzna*.' Similarly in a poem by folk author Józef Baran: 'The sun goes down behind the barn / and over *ojczyzna* – *ojcowizna* (fatherland – patrimony)' (more on this in Bartmiński, 1990b).

HOMELAND AS HOME TOWN or VILLAGE

> 'In Welęszyn, his *ojczyzna*, he built a church of stone' (from the Old Polish period)

> '*Ojczyzna* is for me not a country or state, not Poland. It is my district, housing estate, street or home. The place from which I draw all kinds of values most profusely' (Olgierd Budrewicz, a journalist, writer and globetrotter, *Przekrój* 43, 1992)

'*Ojczyzna* is not a country, it may be for example a village' (a student respondent in the 1990 questionnaire)

HOMELAND AS ONE'S HOME REGION OR NEIGHBOURHOOD

'A highlander will miss his *ojczyzna* even if he's in Kraków' (*Wierchy*, 1931: 5), i.e. not far away, the city of Kraków being about a hundred kilometres from the Tatra Mountains

An expert on plebeian culture, Czesław Hernas (1973: 7), says: 'The conviction that one's region is the centre of one's *ojczyzna* is an extended form of understanding property and ownership, something in between homeland and patrimony'.

Czesław Miłosz, in turn, says: A homeland-state (*ojczyzna-państwo*) is too much and when Vincenz thought of a Europe of homelands he had in mind small territorial units, such as his beloved Hutsul region inhabited by Ukrainians, Jews and Poles. [...] And as Vincenz remained rooted in his Carpathians all his life, so am I – or at least my imagination – faithful to Lithuania'. (1985: 32)

Olgierd Łukaszewicz (an actor): 'Silesia is my *ojczyzna*, even though my parents do not come from there' (an interview in *Dziennik Lubelski*, March 3, 1993)

Kashubians in this sense use the term *tatczyzna*, lit. 'dad's land': 'Kashubian *tatczyzna* has been given to the Kashubian people by God' (the peasant writer Bolesław Jażdżewski, 1992: 12)

Of course, the basic and most frequent understanding of *ojczyzna* is its reference to the national territory, the country, Poland. This has been confirmed in many studies, e.g. Agnieszka Kłoskowska's questionnaire from 1991 (cf. Bartmiński, 1993).

EUROPE as homeland was close to Poles in the prime time of the Polish Republic, its 'golden age' (sixteenth century). At present, it rather appears in liberal and right wing discourse (Żuk, 2004). The conception of a 'European homeland' promoted by Pope John Paul II (cf. his 2005 book *Memory and Identity*) is contested by certain circles in the Catholic Church (the Redemptorist Tadeusz Rydzyk and his radio station 'Radio Maryja') or even openly rejected by radical right-wing parties.

It is in a way paradoxical that the world is a better candidate for the homeland than Europe (or such was at least the case in the early 1990s). This attitude is not new. The seventeenth century poet Wacław Potocki writes: 'The virtuous man has the whole world for his homeland' (*Syloret*); the nineteenth century poet and playwright Aleksander Fredro says: 'The whole world is my homeland, all the people are my brothers' ('A New Don Quixote'). Respondents to questionnaires provide answers in the same spirit.

HEAVEN

'I have a homeland in my father's place, with God, in the infinity of time and space.' (Józef Bohdan Zaleski, a nineteenth century poet)

The conception of heaven as homeland has a biblical origin,[3] and projects this conception onto the future: 'For here we have no lasting city, but we seek the city that is to come' (Hebrews 13:14).

One can say, then, that the 'space of the homeland' in Polish collective imagination subsumes seven concentric circles of various degrees of importance and salience: i) one's home; ii) one's home town or village; iii) one's closest vicinity or neighbourhood; iv) one's home region; v) the country; vi) Europe; vii) the world. It is the country that occupies the dominant position.

The spatial dimension of homeland is correlated with its social aspect. The concentric organisation of space is paralleled by a conceptually similar linguistic organisation of human communities: the family (or people), neighbours and countrymen, the tribe (now obsolete), the nation, the whole of humanity. The linguistic exponents of this organisation include: terms for family members and relatives (father, mother, son, brother, sister, uncle, cousin etc.), *sąsiad* 'neighbour', *swojak* or *krajan* 'someone from the same neighbourhood or close vicinity', *ziomek* 'someone from the same region', *rodak* 'compatriot', and finally *człowiek* 'person; human being' or *bliźni* 'any person; neighbour'.

Human communities are differentiated in the realm of culture and language, as well as social institutions, such as marriage, family (in the legal sense), county, local government, social organisations, state, international organisations, the United Nations etc. The multidimensional understanding of homeland was most fully explicated by the nineteenth century philosopher Karol Libelt.

The role of the state in the Polish understanding of homeland, which took its shape in the period of political dependence (nineteenth century), is relatively insignificant,[4] the role of the cultural component is much bigger. For decades culture was the main criterion of Polish national identity, mainly in the domain of literature (Adam Mickiewicz, Henryk Sienkiewicz, Eliza Orzeszkowa – in the nineteenth century the Poles' language was their homeland) but also in the domain of customs, rituals and generally traditional folklore. In the period of national dependence, national identity was also upheld through religion, which helped in a way 'demarcate' the predominantly Catholic Poles from the Orthodox and Protestant invaders.

Of all cultural exponents, the zonal diversification along the 'home – world' axis is best realised in language, for apart from the standard, national, super-regional and codified variety of Polish, there exist local dialects, sociolects, 'professiolects' or 'famililects'.

The spatial, community-related and institutional spheres are linked to the domain of values. The repondents in the AXL-90 questionnaire (Bartmiński, 2006) agreed on the values they considered important with a fair degree of consistency. For the home and family these were: warmth and understanding, peace and tranquility and the feeling of security; for the country and nation: independence, patriotism, solidarity, common culture and history; for the world and humanity: peace, cooperation, solidarity, unity. There exist values constitutive of communities, which the philosopher Władysław Stróżewski (1981: 294) calls 'entrusted values' (cf. chapter 2). It is thanks to those that the community acquires its identity and achieves its aims.

These correlations are represented diagrammatically in Figure 13.1.

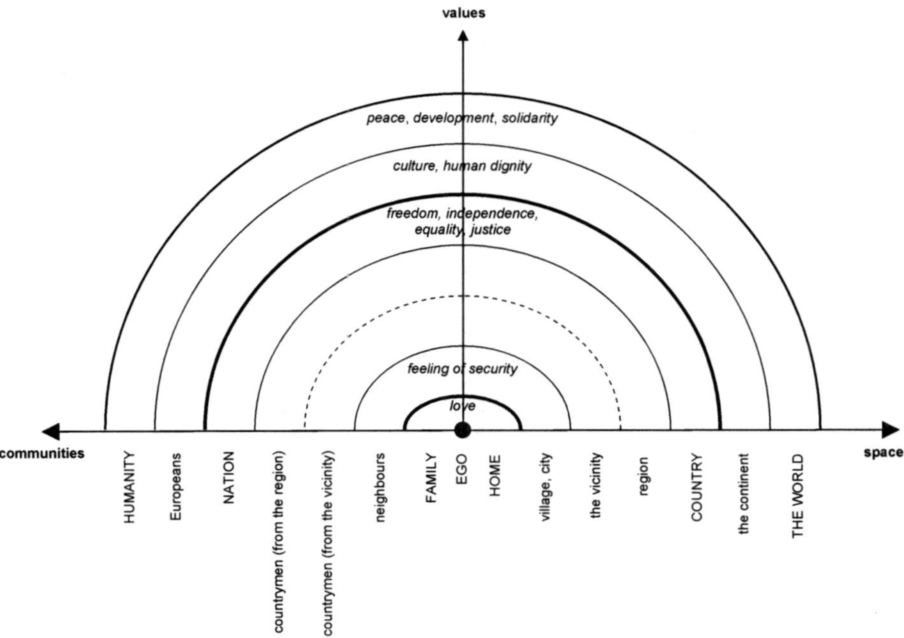

Figure 13.1. The Polish OJCZYZNA 'homeland': components of the conceptual structure

But do these dimensions of the Polish image of homeland, together with their multilayered structure, constitute its full characterisation? They do not. The Polish understanding of homeland also contains something else, something that unites and breathes life to all the concept's components. That something is, incidentally, also present in other languages and cultures, especially those originating in agrarian communities: it is the conception of homeland as the mother.

The mother is treated as the central point of the conceptual sphere of homeland and functions as its prototype, in the ordinary rather than the technical (e.g. Rosch's) sense of the word, i.e. as its archetype, followed in its subsequent usages and metaphorical extensions. The concept of the mother unites all the dimensions of homeland:

i)   spatial, for the mother's body is the first natural environment and literally 'the place of origin' of a person;

ii) communal, for the relationship between persons is the fullest and existentially primary in the case of a child and its mother;

iii) cultural, for the mother's words, behaviour, attitudes, beliefs and valuation are the first 'spiritual world' for a person, the world of moral patterns and norms.

Moreover, the child–mother relationship most fully reveals the specificity of the person–homeland relationship because one does not choose one's homeland: it is 'given' (Józef Tischner, a Polish twentieth century philosopher). To receive that gift, with all its good and bad aspects, is to act according to one's personal feeling of emotional attachment and responsibility. The analogy between a person's attitudes towards the mother and the homeland has been expressed in a particluarly apt way by the film director Krzysztof Zanussi: 'One's homeland, like one's mother, has its vices and is no better than the others, except that it is our own' (*Tygodnik Powszechny* (a Polish weekly), no. 43, 1984).

6 The profiles of the Polish homeland

6.1 The role of values

Debates on the conception of homeland and patriotism in the age of globalisation and unification, especially intense in Polish electoral campaigns, reveal the concept's plasticity. New interpreatitions and variants of the concept emerge continually: ideological, national or even nationalistic, but also civic and regional variants. The driving forces behind the process are values. Values determine how the selected ideological components are configured; they establish what portion of the geographical and social space is considered 'ours'; they organise the components into a hierarchy. Depending on what he or she considers as close and dear, a Pole's homeland is the country, Europe, the world, region, neighbourhood or home; it is the national or the local culture. Values determine the horizon of one's aspirations and the range of one's responsibilities.

Let us try to establish what ideological profiles (variants) are created on the basis of this general, schematic conceptual sphere of homeland. The profiles arise around certain dominant components, such as the home (and the family, marriage, love, warmth etc.), one's neighbourhood or region (with its wildlife, friends, customs or dialect), the country and nation (the state, the nation's culture and history), Europe or the world. Institutions and elements of culture can also function as dominants. We may refer to the different profiles depending on what is the dominant in each case.

6.2 The family-and-home profile

The family-and-home profile of homeland is linguistically well-entrenched; cf. *gniazdo rodzinne* 'family nest', dom rodzinny 'family home', *dom ojcowski/ojców* 'forefathers' home', *ojcowizna* (Kashubian *tatkowina*) 'patrimony'. The family-and-home variant is the place of birth or origin. The dominant characteristic is the feeling of security and acceptance, being in one's own place, with one's closest family and relatives, the mother and father, brothers and sisters, sons and daughters, grandparents and grandchildren. The centre of that community is the mother; the keywords are *łono* 'womb' and *kolebka* 'cradle' or 'birthplace'.

The parts of the home and house which figure as important in this profile are: the doorstep, walls, windows, the roof and the fire (*ognisko domowe* 'hearth', plus the chimney and the smoke). Then there is the furniture (especially the table and the bed), as well as the places where one works (the garden and fields): they assume the generalised meaning of places one knows and treats as one's own. They are metaphorised in phraseological expressions: *przekroczyć próg czyjegoś domu*, lit. 'cross the doorstep of one's house' ('come into the person's house'), *przyjąć kogoś pod swój dach* 'take someone under one's roof', *powrócić na łono rodziny*, lit. 'return onto the family's womb' ('to the family'), *tęsknić do domu* 'miss one's home', *zasiąść z kimś do stołu* 'sit with someone at the table' etc. These are collective, familiar and culturally established scenarios of behaviour.

Adjectives derived from the names of people and objects connected with the home and family do not only mean 'belonging to or associated with someone' but also have evaluative meanings: *macierzyński* – 'motherly' and 'caring'; *ojcowski* – 'fatherly' and 'solicitous'; *braterski* – 'brotherly' and 'helpful', *siostrzany* – 'sisterly' and 'cordial'; *familijny* – 'typical of a family', i.e. 'loose, unceremonial, cordial'; *po domowemu* – 'like at home', i.e. 'with liberty, informally', etc. The adjective *ojczysty* in connection with the nouns *dom* 'home', *gniazdo* 'nest', *zagon* 'field' means 'of a family' but also strikes a positive emotional chord.

In contrast to the home and family there is the (alien and distant) world as the opposite pole in a people's living space (cf. chapter 12).

The family-and-home type of homeland is the prototypical variant because of its interpretive function relative to other variants. Its components (parts of the home/house and family members) are the interpretants of 'macro' homelands, described in terms of the former: *pod polskim dachem* 'under the Polish roof', *dom europejski* 'the European home', *pod dachem nieba* 'under the sky's roof', *Matka-Polska* 'Poland the Mother', *ojciec narodu* 'the nation's father', *bracia rodacy* 'brothers and compatriots', *wszyscy ludzie braćmi* 'all people are brothers' etc.

6.3 The local homeland

The local homeland, since the emergence of the regionally and locally organised 'Solidarity' movement in 1980, and as a result of the revival of local patriotism and democracy, is also called 'a little homeland'. From the perspective of the centralised, city mentality it is belittled as 'backwater' and an 'out-of-the-way' place. It is contrasted with 'foreign lands', the 'great wide world', or treated as the first and necessary step in an individual's participation in the wider, national social life. Should one limit one's life to the local context, they can be labelled as 'parochial' and 'narrow-minded'.

The axiological basis of the local homeland is the ideal of individual self-fulfillment through participation in creative formation of the local community, through the common interests of the people living and working together (so that the community controls the individual), as well as through an emotional bond with the closest social and natural environment. Apart from the family and relatives, the local homeland also embraces friends and neighbours as 'the ones who live here', 'the people from the vicinity'. A new and progressively more popular slogan is the protection of the natural environment, which includes not only the traditional fields and forests, huts and villages, the home town and its streets, clean air, water and soil but also the local culture with its customs, rituals, attire, dialect and folklore. Furthermore, the cultural image of the local homeland contains local institutions, workplaces, the school and the church. In town it includes 'my street' and 'my disctrict'; in the country 'my village with its mayor', 'my county with its administrator and institutions', usually also 'my parish', 'the parish church and the rector' etc.

The local homeland is viewed in opposition to the whole country and may receive negative valuation. The Polish words *prowincja* 'the provinces' and *prowincjonalny* 'provincial' are derogatory, though *regionalny* 'regional' is neutral. Similarly, *regionalizm* 'regionalism' means 'acceptance of one's region; social movement promoting its development' or 'a regional linguistic expression', whereas *prowincjonalism* 'provincial attitude' refers to an attitude characterised by focusing on one's region without regard to or interest in broader horizons.

The idea of regionalism in its positive sense refers to one's emotional attachment to a particular region's history and culture, and after the revival of administrative self-government in 1989 also to topical regional economic and social matters. Regions become more and more political (Żywicka, 2007).

A significant role in the linguistic-cultural picture of regions is played by natural landmarks, such as mountains and rivers, as well as manmade ones, especially towns. Both categories give rise to names of regions, cf. *Powiśle* 'the part of town on the other side of the Vistula river (*Wisła*)', *Poznańskie* 'the Poznań region', *Lubelskie* 'the Lublin region' etc.

Polish regional communities have lost the terms *plemię*, *szczep* 'tribe' or *współplemieniec* 'tribesman'. However, the names of inhabitants of a given region are still very much used: *Poznaniak* 'someone who lives/comes from the Poznań region', *Kaszuba* 'a person from the Kashubian region', *góral* 'highlander' (from *góra* 'mountain'). In colloquial usage they may acquire stereotypical features.

Regional culture along with regional media determines the social perception of regions. A relatively recent phenomenon is 'regional literature'.

State or Church institutions (voivodships and dioceses, respectively), established and modified in a top-down manner, correlate with the centuries-old regional traditions only to a limited degree.

6.4 The national homeland

The national homeland is the basic profile of the concept. It took shape in the nineteenth century, the time of national uprisings, after the collapse of the multiethnic Polish Republic. As I have already mentioned, it is this variant that Wierzbicka (1997) contrasts with the German *Vaterland* and Russian *rodina*. It is closely related to the family-and–home variant, the connection being especially visible in the semantics of the adjective *ojczysty*, which can mean 'parental, related to the family' (e.g. one's home or village) and 'national' (language, history). It is not only that the conception of the national homeland arose from the family-and-home variant as its prototype, but also

Poland's history was such that the home and family became the stronghold of national life, when none was possible politically.

The semantic dominant in this profile is the 'nation' composed of one's 'compatriots' (in the narrowly nationalistic sense one would talk about ethnically 'true Poles'), but more and more often of 'citizens'. The nation is treated as a collective subject, with aspirations to freedom and independence, with its own sovereign state, a state-controlled economy and national culture. In the face of globalisation and Europeisation,[5] the proponents of the national homeland redefine the concept of a nation. Its understanding in contemporary political discourse oscillates between the nineteenth century objectivism (common origin and history) and the present-day importance of subjective awareness (the feeling of belonging to a cultural, political and civic community) (cf. Puzynina, 1998).

The spatial dimension of the national homeland is the country of Poland as a territory inhabited by the Polish nation. The dominance of the localistic understanding of that variant is visible in such expressions as 'in/to/from the homeland' or 'to visit/leave the homeland', which (contrary to Wierzbicka's view) are anything but archaic.

The attitude to the national conception is modelled linguistically through a series of phraseological units, among which *ojczyna matka* 'homeland our mother' and *synowie ojczyzny* 'homeland's sons' can be treated as the base. Both units code first of all one's duties towards the community, manifested also in such formulaic expressions as 'to love/defend the homeland', 'to fight/save/shed blood/die for one's homeland' or 'to serve the homeland'. At the other extreme, the notion of 'the homeland's traitor' is associated with a stigma. In everyday colloquial thinking, however, the heroic ethos is being supplemented with or even replaced by the attitude of claims and pretences: what my homeland should give and do for me (Bartmiński, 2006).

The national homeland is sacred, which is why the word *ojczyzna* is frequently capitalised, as in *na ołtarzu Ojczyzny* 'on the homeland's altar'. The love of one's homeland is elevated to the rank of a national programme. (This conception is critically reviewed in Jan Józef Lipski's 1981 famous work; cf. below).

6.5 Homeland as a state

The Polish conception of homeland as a state is for historical reasons rather weak. It foregrounds the sovereignty of the state above local interests. It is close to what Russians understand by *otechestvo* and Germans by *Vaterland*: one must serve, defend, sacrifice oneself and work 'for the good of the homeland'. The spatial dimension is identified with state borders and the community is composed of 'citizens' obliged to defend the state. After a period of dominance of an ideological state and the now rejected 'socialist homeland', contemporary variants of homeland as a state are liberal-democratic; they evoke Poland's multiethnic heritage and propose the programme of 'civic patriotism'.

6.6 The public and cultural variants

Two other conceptions of homeland, the public (social) and cultural homeland, are less coherent and unequivocal, though in a sense they are close to each other.

The public (or social) homeland is based on the notion of 'common good' for the 'civic community' which inhabits the country and is organised as a state. It grants equal rights to ethnic minorites and promotes cultural pluralism. In the view of Gustaw Herling-Grudziński,

> [t]he idea of public homeland [...] includes attachment to land, people (not all), the history and culture of the country, appreciation of its tradition, identification with its aspirations (not always and not all), readiness to serve and to sacrifice oneself, should the need arise. And last but not least, it includes participation in the country's social and political endeavours. We are entering the domain of 'society' here and abandon the Romantic ideal of a 'nation'. (Herling-Grudziński, *Tygodnik Powszechny* (a Polish weekly), no. 10, 1992)

The cultural homeland, a conception orginating from the times of political dependence and still present at all levels of educational discourse, is founded on the importance of the national heritage, i.e. the nation's language, customs, literature and art. This is where humanist values belong, such as the idea of freedom/liberty, justice, solidarity and human rights.

7   The profiles in public discourse

How do all these profiles of homeland function in public discourse? In the concentrically organised semantic space of the Polish homeland, one can observe a transfer of characteristics and values along the axis linking features of the same category (from the home to the country and the world, from the mother and family to neighbours, friends and the nation) and across categories (e.g national culture, the state, community, territory).

The cultural and public profiles well agree with the regional and family-and-home profiles, as well as with the national, but not nationalistic, profile.

However, the transfer is accompanied by diversification and even confrontation. A sharp ideological contrast can nowadays be observed between the national conception in its nationalistic and xenophobic version, as promoted by the nationwide radio station 'Radio Maryja' and the daily *Nasz Dziennik*, and the liberal and Universalist conception of a social, public and civic homeland.

The original rejection of national obligations by the socialist movement, as expressed in *The Communist Manifesto* ('The working men have no country', 1848) is still present on left-wing Internet sites (e.g. www.lewica.pl). A more radical manifestation of the rejection of the whole ideology of homeland can sometimes be found in youth magazines.[6]

However, the narrow and xenophobic understanding of the national homeland is also countered by the Christian Universalist and European humanist conceptions, expressed, e.g., by Cyprian Kamil Norwid (a nineteenth century Polish poet) in his poem *My Country*, and the already mentioned Jan Józef Lipski in his 1981 essay 'Two homelands, two patriotisms'. Let me close by quoting these authors:

Cyprian Kamil Norwid, *My Country*

Those who say my country means:
Meadows, flowers and fields of wheat,
Hamlets and trenches – must confess
These – are her feet.
The child – not snatched from his mother's arms;
The youth – at her side will grow;
And she leans on her adult son:
These – are my laws.
My country has not risen *here*;
My body antedates the Flood,
My spirit soars over Chaos:
I pay rent to the world.
No nation fashioned or saved me;
I recall eternity's span;
David's key unlocked my lips,
Rome called me man.
I fall on the sand to wipe with my hair
My country's blood-stained feet:
But I know her face and crown
Radiant like the sun of suns.
My ancestors have known no other;
Her feet with my hand I used to feel;
I often kissed the peasant sandal strap
Round her heel.
They needn't teach me where my country lies;
Hamlets, trenches and fields of wheat,
Flesh and blood and this her scar
Are her print, her feet.

(Paris, January 1861; *Selected Poems*, Anvil Press, 2004, trans. Adam Czerniawski)

Jan Józef Lipski, 'Two homelands, two patriotisms':

The world of values from whose perspective one must look at the problem of homeland is above all, though not exclusively, the world of moral values. The ethical concepts of our culture have been mainly shaped by Christianity. [...] I think that chauvinism, national megalomania, xenophobia, national egoism and hatred of all that is foreign cannot be reconciled with the Christian obligation to love one's neighbour. It is possible, though, in the case of patriotism. Just like a special kind of love in the family need not and should not stand in the way of the love of the neighbour, so the love of the nation must follow the same moral norm. Patriotism originates in love and must lead to love: any other form of patriotism is its ethical deformation. Therefore, the 'love of everything Polish' is a frequent formula of national, 'patriotic' stupidity, for things Polish include the ONR,[7] pogroms in L'viv, Przytyk and Kielce [...], pacification of Ukrainian villages, the Brest trials,[8] the Bereza Kartuska detention camp[9] and the camp for Jewish soldiers in Jabłonna in 1920 – and all that within a mere two decades of our history. Patriotism is not only respect and love of tradition but also a cruel selection of the tradition's elements, an obligation to make an intellectual effort. (Lipski, 1981; quote from Lipski, 1992: 139–140)

Notes

1   E.g. *SWJP* (1996), *PSWP* (1994–1998) and *USJP* (2003). The ideological additions have been omitted in *ISJP* (2000), which says: 'Our homeland is the country where we have been born, with which we have an emotional and cultural bond and where we usually live'. I omit here the derived sense of homeland as a country of the origin of something: 'Italy is the homeland of Baroque', 'The homeland of the elephant is Africa' etc.

2   In a slightly different questionnaire from the year 2000, Michael Fleicher identified similar associations with the homeland: Poland, country; patriotism; state; nation; home, family home, land, territory; honour; family, one's origin or birthplace; tradition; community; love; land and graves; history, culture; mother (Fleischer, 2003: 128).

3   The Old Testament stresses the connections between humans and the earthly world, as has been attested in many primitive cultures.

4   In 1844 Libelt wrote: 'Without political independence there is no state but there is homeland – and this makes an enormous difference'.

5   In his speech of Jan 15, 1959, the French Prime Minister Michel Debre used the term 'Europe of homelands' (Markiewicz and Romanowski, 1990: 169).

6   Consider the following passage from an anonymous article published in the magazine *QQRYQ*, no. 6, probably from 1986: 'Patriotism. (Attention! Struggle against dirt!). Everyone is obliged to love the homeland. They sell you this shit since childhood. The homeland must be the guiding idea of every righteous person. But I do not love the homeland. Surely, I am a Pole in the sense that I was born here, I speak the language etc. But what else? Do I become better if I participate in patriotic shows? How many people treat it seriously anyway? Patriotism begins to resemble a monumental façade with nothing behind it, something terribly artificial, pompous, the main weapon in the arsenal of the system's propaganda. We must reject it! Let us strive to a panhuman, supernational consciousness. In every, even the most tolerant patriot, there is a subconscious aversion to other nations and the conviction that 'we are better'. Fuck that! Let us just be people; no boundaries necessary. All that is good in our tradition is *bigos* [Polish traditional cabbage stew, A.G.] and pickles. Do not be fooled by silly images. Fight with the shit behind all this. No feelings or emotions give the smart asses the right to control

our lives!' (I thank Michael Fleischer for pointing out and making this article available to me.)

7   The National Radical Camp, established in 1934 and made illegal after three months, characterised by its anti-semitic and fascist program.

8   Trials of representatives of the centre-left political opposition (1931–1932).

9   For political prisoners, 1934–1939.

14 Changes in the Polish stereotype of 'a German'

1 Introduction

The new political situation in Central Europe has revealed significant diversity, complexity and – which is surprising – instability of inter-ethnic relations. Problems of the social reception of these relations, the functioning of traditional ethnic stereotypes and the formation of new ideas about one's neighbours can be seen as a challenge for cognitive sociology, psychology and linguistics. If stereotypes are functions of not only general psychological and social needs but also of cultural factors, such as changing aspirations and values, one may expect them to evolve together with those aspirations and values.

These questions are especially relevant in the case of the heavily painful historical relations between Poles and Germans, their colloquial understanding and scholarly description. To what extent are the stereotypes of the past valid now? Do the changes affect the base set of features considered for years to be typical of Germans or are they merely novel configurations of features within the old characterisation, relative to new perspectives and communicative intentions? In what perspective(s) are Germans perceived by Poles now, how does this perception compare with the past or with the perception of other nationalities?

I will present the results of research on the stereotype of a German among students in the city of Lublin between 1990 and 1993. With a population of around 350,000 (2007) and several higher education institutions, Lublin is an important academic centre. The city is situated in eastern Poland, about 500 kilometers from the German border, so the city-dwellers' opinions about Germans are necessarily based more on hearsay and popular belief than on personal exposure (although the latter has become much more frequent recently). The student community, in turn, as the most dynamic and promising segment of the opinion-forming intelligentsia, is composed of people from various social groups and may be considered as the society of eastern Poland in miniature.

2 Theoretical assumptions

The theoretical and methodological basis of this research is a linguistic conception of stereotype, discussed at length in chapter 5. Stereotypes are inextricably linked with natural language, although they can also be communicated non-verbally, e.g. through caricature. Stereotypes in everyday language are primary and superordinate in relation to the opinions expressed in literature and journalism: the colloquial style dominates over other styles derived from it. It has been noticed that 'a stereotype [...] finds its way to literature from the outside' (Mitosek, 1974: 62). This, certainly, does not rule out the creativity of artistic texts and their ambition to influence social consciousness.

Cognitive and emotional components of stereotypes are not all equally stable and, as a consequence, not equally significant: changes in emotional values take place more quickly; those in the descriptive content are slower. Jasińska-Kania (1991) describes a multidimensional evolution of emotional attitudes to other nationalities, depending on the latter's standard of living, political system, ideology or religion (similar means better), the number of students, the genres of films shown on TV, the behaviour of political leaders and so on. In the relatively short period of time between 1975 and 1991 the attitude towards e.g. Russians and Romanians changed from positive, until 1989, to very negative in 1991, while the attitude towards Germans changed from very negative to significantly less negative (Jasińska-Kania, 1991: 156; Wilska-Duszyńska, 1992: 100–101) and even to that of acceptance, especially among educated people (Nowicka, 1991: 172).

More stable is the cognitive, descriptive content of stereotypes, which is my main focus. In accounting for it, however, I am inquiring not so much after the 'kernel of truth' (or falsehood) inherent in stereotypes as after interpretations of a given object, its characterisation relating to the basic cultural contrasts 'us – them' or 'one of us – alien (other)'. This characterisation is in its nature ethnocentric: in its deepest layer it also subsumes a picture of ourselves as the frame of reference for perceiving others (Benedyktowicz, 1988).

3   Method

Our method was the use of questionnaires, which were administered four times, twice in 1990 and twice in 1993. Open and closed questionnaires were used, composed of several kinds of questions. These were prepared and administered in the Department of Polish, Maria Curie-Skłodowska University in Lublin (LSQ-90, SD-93, URB-93 and AXL-90; more information in the 'Key to questionnaires').

The answers received are treated as texts representing a specific genre with a clearly delimited communicative intention and communicative situation, and even common structural features. The responses amount to a short anthology of texts characterised by triple unity: of the theme, of the generalised sender and of the generalised receiver. The texts yield to the analytical methods of semantics, lexicology, phraseology and linguistic statistics.

4   A German in the light of LSQ-90

LSQ-90 was concerned with national and family-related stereotypes. The part devoted to the stereotype of a German contained the following questions and tasks:

i)   What meanings does the expression 'a German' have?
ii)   Provide words you use instead of 'a German'.
iii) What features, in your opinion, best characterise a typical German?
      (What is a typical German like?)
iv)   What features, in your opinion, characterise an exemplary German?
      (What should an exemplary German be like?)
v)   Enumerate objects characteristic of a German.
vi)   Fill in the gap: 'X is a German but ...'
vii) Add a noun you associate with the adjective 'German': '(a) German ...'
viii) Add the verb to the expressions '... like a German' and '... the German way'
      and explain the meaning of those expressions.
ix)   What proverbs about Germans do you know?
x)   What anecdotes about Germans do you know?

I will discuss the results in a somewhat different order. 149 respondents took part in
the study. A preliminary analysis can be found in Gasek (1990) but I have reanalysed
the data independently and omitted a few dubious records.

4.1 Definition of 'a German'

In defining a German the respondents frequently disregarded the principles of logic,
which, however, is not particularly relevant for the identification of the stereotype
as a subjective view of an entity. Most frequently (in almost 50% of cases, 72 out of
149) they 'correctly' used 'nationality' as the superordinate category. But in one third
of cases (42) the broader category of 'location' was used: 'a neighbour from behind
the Oder', 'our western neighbour', 'an inhabitant of Germany', etc. In only slightly
fewer cases (33 respondents) the political category of 'citizenship' was mentioned: 'a
citizen of Germany', 'a citizen of one of the German countries', 'a citizen of the German
Democratic Republic or the German Federal Republic'. Some respondents combined
different categories: 'a citizen of Germany, someone of the nationality inhabiting the
territory west of Poland', etc. Also used were certain non-definitional (non-categorial)
synonymous characterising expressions, of which a few referred to history and ideology: 'fascist', 'capitalist', 'the German race' but also 'enemy', 'a Pole's enemy', 'occupier',
'soldier' (cf. below).

It is interesting that the categorisation of a German was systematically different
from that of a Russian, defined most frequently in political terms ('a citizen'), then in
terms of location ('an inhabitant of ...') and only then in terms of nationality ('someone
of Russian nationality') (Czarnocka, 1990).

4.2 Synonyms of 'a German'

Two traditional synonyms of *Niemiec* 'a German' dominate: *Szwab* (81 respondents, i.e. 54%) and *Szkop* (27 respondents or 18%). Both are negatively charged and semantically opaque. The third one in line is the Russian loan word *Germaniec* (24), expressive and hostile in tone, or the historical and neutral *Germanin* (4) or *Prusak* 'an inhabitant of Prussia' (5). Citation-names were also used in this function: *Deutschland, Deutsch, Jung*.

A significant portion of the synonyms of *Niemiec* are proper names: *Helmut* (10), *Fryc* (7), *Adolf* (4), *Hans* (4), *Franc*. As exponents of distance and aversion one can mention expressive derivatives of the basic term: *Niemiaszek* (2), *Niemczysko* (3), *Niemiacha, Niemra* (for women). More telling are ideological terms as an echo of WWII: 'fascist', 'sadist', '(little) Hitler', 'Hitlerite', 'a member of the Gestapo', 'SS-man', 'kings of Europe', 'Nordic', 'a citizen of the Reich', as well as of the post-war order: 'a citizen of the GDR', 'a citizen of the FRG'.

Interestingly, common characterising expressions were provided, such as the most frequent 'hard worker' (7) but also 'philosopher', 'a person of high culture', 'a dutiful/ principled person', 'a human', 'a person from behind the western border', 'foreigner'.

4.3 What is a 'typical' German like?

Respondents to LSQ-90 provided a hundred features characterising a 'typical' German. The features listed in Table 14.1 were mentioned most frequently (in four or more cases). Here and elsewhere derivatives and lexical synonyms are counted together with the basic form and included in parentheses. Sometimes, in and outside tables, the same feature is given in the nominal, adjectival or verbal form.

Table 14.1 The most frequently mentioned features of a 'typical' German in LSQ-90. N=149

No. of references	Features
45	hard-working (likes work)
24	thorough
17	calculating
15	pedantic
13	cool (cold)
12	orderly (loves order)
11	disciplined
10	stickling
8	solid thrifty dutiful cunning (sly)
7	punctual haughty (putting on airs) false unyielding (stiff) dry

No. of references	Features
6	composed
	wily
5	rich
	clean
	proud
	arrogant
	possessive (desires power)
4	serious
	economical
	conscientious
	precise
	self-confident
	resourceful
	hostile

Almost two-thirds of the features are positive. The features 'hard-working' and 'thorough' come to the fore. Their stereotypisation index (Si), understood as the percentage of the frequency of the two most frequent expressions in the sum of frequencies of all the expressions used[1] is 18.16. This is a very high value, identified only in very strongly stereotyped names of people in Polish, such as *warszawiak* 'inhabitant of Warsaw' (the features 'con artist' and 'conceited'; Si = 67), *szewc* 'shoemaker' ('drunk' and 'given to swearing'; Si = 27) or *poznaniak* 'inhabitant of Poznań' ('stingy' and 'thorough'; Si = 14) (Bartmiński, 1988a: 101).

From what *point of view*, from what *side* is a German characterised? Let us extend our investigation onto all expressions used by the respondents.

Table 14.2 The features of a 'typical' German arranged by aspect on the basis of LSQ-90. N = 149

Aspect	No. of features	Sum of feature frequencies	No. of respondents	% of no. of respondents in N	Examples of most frequent features
everyday life	24	166	96	64.40	hard-working, thorough, orderly
psychological	32	89	66	44.29	unyielding, serious, proud, cool, dry
social	24	98	61	40.94	calculating, disciplined, stickling, haughty, false, hostile
physical	8	18	13	8.79	
cultural	5	9	9	6.04	
ideological	5	6	6	4.03	
political	2	3	3	2.01	
Total:	100	380			

It turns out that the features given as the first reaction to the questions were connected with everyday life: 'hard work' and work-related 'precision', 'thoroughness', 'pedantry', 'solidness', 'scrupulosity', 'conscientiousness', 'love of order' (*Ordnung muß sein*), 'good organisation', 'dutifulness', 'thrift', 'good management', 'punctuality'. A German is said to be 'systematic', 'resourceful', 'rich', 'wily', 'caring about himself/herself'; he/she is 'a business person' and 'likes beer'. These features are definitely positive and express approval and respect.

The second significant group of features were psychological and intellectual ones: 'ambitious', 'unyielding', 'stiff'; 'lacking in understanding', 'obstinate', 'resolute', 'self-confident', 'opinionated'; 'conceited', 'proud', 'arrogant'; 'cool', 'cold', 'having a detached outlook', 'cold-blooded', 'dry'; 'individualistic'; 'naive'; 'taciturn'; 'envious', 'mistrustful', 'cunning', 'sly'; 'mundane', 'boring', 'obtuse', 'with no fancy', 'with no sense of humour'. These features express distance and are characterised by negative emotional colouring.

Interestingly, certain contradictory features appear with a similar (low) frequency: 'calm', 'restrained' and 'fanatical'; 'composed' and 'quick-tempered'; 'stupid' and 'wise'.

Some features have an ethical aspect, such as 'honest'.

The third position is occupied by characterisation of social behaviour: 'disciplined', 'loyal', 'keeps his word'; 'docile', 'blindly obedient'; 'respecting hierarchy and regulations', 'stickling', 'overzealous as a legalist'; 'rough'; 'possessive', 'desiring power', 'putting on airs', 'with aversion towards Poles'; 'aggressive', 'haughty', 'despising others'; 'calculating', 'stingy'; 'false', 'mendacious'; 'indifferent to others'; 'mean', 'hostile'. Valuation-wise, the features in this category are either neutral or pejorative, although a few respondents used positively-charged descriptions: 'friendly', 'nice to friends', 'helpful'.

In contrast to this, a German was rather poorly represented from the physical point of view in terms of appearance and behaviour ('blond-haired', 'red-haired', 'with a protruding belly', 'tall'; 'wearing a uniform', 'statue-like'; 'noisy', 'vociferous', 'loud'; 'clean') or with respect to his/her manners ('well-mannered', 'well-educated'; also 'foul-mouthed', 'callous').

The political dimension was also weakly manifested ('devoted to authorities', 'respecting authorities and state', 'law-abiding'), as was the ideological aspect, with decisively negative associations ('believes in the power of his nation', 'chauvinistic', 'wants to rule the world', 'racist', 'Nazi').

The greater or smaller importance of individual aspects naturally results not from the respective numbers of features but the frequencies with which features in a given aspect are evoked by respondents. The frequencies, an exponent of the entrenchment of features, are significantly higher in the everyday life, psychological and social aspects than in others, as shown in Table 14.2.

4.4 The image of an 'ideal' German

To ponder over the image of an 'ideal' representative of a nationality may seem super-fluous and nonsensical, but it is not. In LSQ-90 questions were asked in a parallel fashion about the characteristics of a 'typical' German (Russian etc.) and of an 'ideal' (exemplary, model) German in order to establish the degree of the 'sensitivity' of respondents to the manner of questioning but above all in order to arrive at the differently coded stereotypes. We were interested in the nature of the distinction, should it emerge in the first place. The procedure was based on the hypothesis of a mirror image of a real picture with values being switched to positive (and with positively marked values being maintained). The hypothesis was confirmed both in the case of a German and of a Russian.

129 respondents of LSQ-90 mentioned a total of 83 features of an 'ideal' German, among which the ones given in Table 14.3 were the most frequent.

Table 14.3 The most frequent features of an 'ideal' German. LSQ-90. N = 129

No. of references	Features
22	hard-working honest
14	friendly
11	tolerant
8	well-mannered
7	neighbourly
6	non-nationalistic
5	merry cheerful peace-loving pedantic
4	patriotic humane

Table 14.4 The features of an 'ideal' ('exemplary') German arranged by aspect (LSQ-90; N = 129)

Aspect	No. of features	Sum of feature frequencies	No. of respondents	% of no. of respondents in N	Examples of most frequent features
social	29	77	64	49.61	friendly (14) tolerant (11) neighbourly (7) peace loving (5) humane (4)
everyday life	15	49	33	25.58	hard-working (22) pedantic (5)
ethical	8	30	28	21.71	honest (22)
psychological	11	21	20	15.40	merry (5)
ideological	10	20	19	14.03	non-nationalistic (6) patriotic (4)

Aspect	No. of features	Sum of feature frequencies	No. of respondents	% of no. of respondents in N	Examples of most frequent features
cultural	3	10	10	7.75	well-mannered (8)
physical	6	7	7	5.43	
political	1	1	1	0.75	
Total:	83	215	greater than N because one or more features were given by a respondent		

As one can see, the image of an 'ideal' German contains the already familiar features 'hard-working' and 'pedantic'. At the same time, there also emerge certain characteristics in the form of, one might say, 'postulates'. These above all concern social behaviour ('friendly', 'tolerant', 'neighbourly', 'peace-loving', 'humane'), ideology ('patriotic', 'non-nationalistic') or to an extent psychological attitudes and reactions ('merry', 'cheerful'). It is easy to see that they are based on certain negative features in the image of a 'typical' German ('hostile', 'possessive', 'calculating', 'arrogant', 'haughty', 'nationalistic', etc.) and constitute its opposite, positive side.

In this context it is interesting that respondents should frequently use negative constructions: an 'ideal' German 'is not …', 'is anti-…', is 'less (of a consumer)', is 'more (humane, peace-loving)'.

At the same time, those respondents whose characterisations of typical representatives of different nationalities (a German, Jew, Pole) were clearly contrastive to one another, projected close images of the 'ideal' representatives. For example, one in eight participants responded to questions about a Jew, German and Pole in exactly the same way. Some even formulated *expressis verbis* the general requirement of 'being a human', with the leading role played by the features of 'honesty', 'tolerance' or 'kindliness'. Some noted that 'good traits are not linked to a nationality' and an exemplary human being 'should have the same virtues regardless of the nationality', etc.

The aspect-based (or facet-based) structure of the image, seen from the ideal-oriented perspective, underwent a characteristic if slight modification: the dominant position is now occupied by the category of social behaviour, relation to other people and nations. Additionally, the image of an 'ideal' German was endowed with an ethical aspect.

4.5 What is a 'true' German like?

A stereotypical judgment is not a simple generic judgment on all the tokens of a given type. Its important characteristic is an enrichment and subjective relativisation of the quantifiers 'all' or 'every' by adding the modifier 'true', which changes 'All Scots are stingy' to 'All true Scots are stingy'. The adjective 'true' plays a key role in the mechanism of stereotyping concepts (Quasthoff, 1973; Bartmiński, 1988c; Wejland, 1991). Therefore, apart from questions about a 'typical' and an 'ideal' representative, a separate question about a 'true' representative was also answered. It was not decided, however, whether that meant 'as is' or 'as should be', leaving it to the respondents to solve this potential ambiguity (the ambiguity is only potential, for at the level of colloquial thinking it need not exist). This time, again, the idea was to observe the consequences of the use of this additional word. These consequences were minor.

The image of a 'true' German was sought in AXL-90, which only contained one, context-free question. 103 students from Lublin responded, providing 153 features occurring 336 times altogether. Table 14.5 presents the top fourteen with the number of occurrences, but we are in fact interested in all the features provided (the data were broken down by Jolanta Urban and checked by myself).

Table 14.5 The features of a 'true' German according to AXL-90. N = 103

No. of references	Features
31	hard-working (26 times), working well; devoted to nothing but work; enthusiastic about work; well-organised at work (2)
18	thorough (15); doing one's work thoroughly; showing care and attention to everything around; accurate; orderly (8); keeping things in order (5); likes order (3); showing aversion to chaos; leading an orderly life
10	clean (cares about cleanliness) pedantic
8	speaking fluent German has blue eyes
7	brutal
6	conscientious
5	disciplined (4); disciplined at work
4	resolute chauvinistic stubborn systematic

As one can see, the top of the list is exactly the same as in the case of a 'typical' German: the features 'hard-working' and 'thorough' reign supreme, though with a lower stereotypisation index of 11.61 (as opposed to 18.16 for a 'typical' German). Two other features of a higher rank in both lists are 'orderly' and 'pedantic', next in line are 'clean', 'conscientious' and 'disciplined', which also occur in both, though in different positions.

However, the complete list of features of a 'true' German differs from the list of those for a 'typical' German in a few points. The former is longer: it contains about 150 features, as opposed to around 100 for a 'typical' German. This may indicate that the respondents were not as sure of the answers they gave. Several new features appeared; two of them, 'has blue eyes' and 'speaks fluent German', are of high frequency. Note that they concern appearance and language, i.e. the elementary, traditional, not to say primeval criteria for identifying nationalities. Today, these criteria are obsolete, totally inadequate in a complex situation of interracial cohabitation and the use of foreign languages: they are in a way 'mythological'. But it appears that they have not been forgotten and are very much present in a certain mode of thinking about people.[2] The introduction of the word 'true' into the questionnaire, then, triggers in colloquial thinking and language the propensity to in a way mythologise things, to take note of features not evoked by the adjective 'typical'.

The dominance of the everyday aspect is maintained, as is the stable status of its features, but the image of a 'true' German is richer in its ideological aspect (links with fascism, attachment to the *Heimat*), its historical and political aspect (possessiveness, warlike spirit), but above all its cultural aspect (attachment to tradition, language and national customs).

Let us, then, consider the aspect-based alignment of a 'true' German (Table 14.6).

Table 14.6 The features of a 'true' German by aspect on the basis of AXL-90. N = 103

Aspect	No. of features	No. of uses of features	No. of respondents	% of no. of respondents in N	Examples of features
everyday life	26	117	62	60.20	hard-working, thorough, pedantic
social	21	63	49	47.57	disciplined, brutal, possessive
psychological	34	59	39	37.86	conscientious, stubborn
physical	15	54	31	30.10	with blond hair, with blue eyes
ideological	23	39	30	29.12	chauvinistic
political	15	22	19	18.44	
cultural	15	25	18	17.47	speaks German
locative	4	7	6	5.82	
Total:	153	336			

As one can see, a 'true' German receives a fuller, multidimensional characterisation, as compared with a 'typical' German (Table 14.2), not only from the point of view of everyday activities or attitude to work, not only from the social and psychological side, but also in the physical aspect (appearance) and in much broader ideological, historical, political and cultural aspects. This image of Poland's western neighbour is different from that of a Russian, in whose characterisation (in the same questionnaire) the ideological and physical aspects predominate.

The juxtapositions of the features of a 'typical', 'ideal' and 'true' German very clearly illustrate the importance of this type of qualification for establishing the content of stereotypes. At issue, naturally, are not only researcher-induced effects but the communicative status of stereotypical images and the way they are filled with content depending on the modal frame of a given statement. Stereotypical images prove sensitive to the modifiers 'typical', 'ideal' and 'true', though with the exception of 'everyday life' features, such as 'hard-working', 'thorough' or 'clean'. The variability concerns not so much individual features as the whole cognitive structure understood as a set of hierarchically ordered aspects (Wierzbicka, 1985).

4.6 Presupposed features (outside the bounds of modifiers)

It is interesting to find out what happens when the cognitive sphere is not limited by any of the modifiers, 'typical', 'ideal' or 'true', and which method of description used so far can be confirmed.

A group of students were asked to complement the sentence: 'X is (a) German but he/she ...'. To do that, they needed to invoke the stereotypical characterisation of a German and supply a feature contrasting with it. The responses included: 'is not thrifty', 'is poor', 'has Polish friends' etc., in a necessary but unwitting and involuntary manner relating to a certain stereotype. What image(s) is, or are, subconsciously accepted as a presupposition?

A total of forty two features were used, largely amenable to grouping into the now familiar arrangement. Table 14.7 lists the features used more than four times.

Table 14.7 The features most frequently presupposed in the formula 'X is a German but ...'. (LSQ-90; N = 142)

No. of references	Features
26	hard-working
17	clean
13	thrifty
10	likes order
7	likes beer
6	doesn't get drunk doesn't like Poles
4	punctual hostile fascist

Which of the previously composed characterisations with an overt modifier does this one approximate most closely? Out of the ten most frequent features, nine coincide with those of a 'true' German (the non-matching one being 'doesn't get drunk'), eight with those of a 'typical' German (the non-matching ones being 'doesn't get drunk' and 'fascist'), while only one coincides with those of an 'ideal' German. This finding lends support to the hypothesis that the modifier 'true' plays a special role in the semantic structure of stereotypical images.

Table 14.8 The features presupposed in the formula 'X is a German but . . .' by aspect (LSQ-90; N = 142)

Aspect	No. of features	No. of respondents providing the features	% of the number of respondents providing the features in N	Examples of features
everyday life	14	75	54.03	hard-working, thrifty, likes order, likes beer, doesn't get drunk, punctual
social	8	20	14.40	doesn't like Poles, hostile, disciplined
physical	3	19	13.00	clean
psychological	8	14	10.00	
ideological	5	10	7.04	fascist
political	3	3	2.11	
locative	1	1	0.70	
Total:	42	142		

The new features 'doesn't get drunk like a Pole' and 'is inhospitable' can perhaps be explained by the fact that the opposite sentence activates the traditional matrix of comparing nations,[3] as a result of which Germans are contrasted with drinking and hospitable Poles.

This list of features is significantly shorter than the ones previously discussed, which can be accounted for by the emphasis on the everyday aspect.

4.7 'The German order': conventional collocability of the adjective *niemiecki, -a, -ie* 'German'

One of the instructions in LSQ-90 was formulated thus: 'Supply the noun that comes to mind in connection with the adjective *niemiecki, -a, -e* 'German''. The 146 respondents who performed this relatively easy task provided a total of 60 nouns (Table 14.9).

Table 14.9 Nouns collocating with the adjective *niemiecki, -a, -ie* 'German'. (LSQ-90; N = 146)

Aspect	No. of nouns	No. of uses	Nouns in the order of appearance
everyday life	17	103	order (59), punctuality (8), thoroughness (8), beer (5), pedantry (5), car (4), hard work, systematicness, tidiness, (German) shepherd (2 each), precision, good management, prosperity, cassette player, TV, VCR, manor farm (1 each)
social	6	29	discipline (15), rigour (10), aggression, possessiveness, desire for power, rule
psychological	3	12	arrogance (9), composure, fanaticism
military	7	12	army (4), uniform (3), officer, soldier, coat, helmet, trampling boots
cultural	9	12	school (3), culture (2), philosophy, literature, poetry, Romanticism, dictionary, language, accent (1 each)
physical	2	10	cleanliness (9), beautiful appearance
political	9	9	wall, population, republic, affairs, politics, political parties, ideals, law, system
ideological	6	8	race (2), revisionism (2) Europe, *Drang nach Osten*, fascism, imperialism
other	1	1	quality
Total:	61	196	

Twelve expressions were used relatively frequently, three or more times, and one of them, namely 'order', was much more frequent than all the others, having been provided by 59 respondents (40.5%). The next in line are: 'discipline' (15), 'rigour' (10), 'arrogance' (9), 'cleanliness', 'punctuality' and 'thoroughness' (8), 'pedantry' and 'beer' (5), 'car' (4), 'school' and 'uniform' (3).

When looked at from the point of view of its content and aspectual nature, the expressions again appear as mainly referring to the everyday sphere of life, everyday activities and behaviours, eating or work, or to social attitudes ('discipline', 'rigour'). The proverbial 'German arrogance' (Pol. *niemiecka buta*) is lower in the list than expected. Instead, a relatively high position is occupied by formulaic, half-fixed expressions from the military sphere: army, uniform, soldier etc. There are few cultural associations (and only in students of the humanities) or, surprisingly, ideological ones: the infamous German revisionism was only mentioned twice.

4.8 'To work like a German'

Another instruction in LSQ-90 was as follows: 'Supply a verb to complement the expression 'like a German' and explain the meaning of the whole'. 126 respondents performed the task.

Most frequently the expression 'like a German' was associated with 'work' to yield e.g. '*works* like a German' (45 out of 126 respondents, i.e. 36%). It was explained with a fair degree of consent as 'solidly, thoroughly', sometimes with the additional characterisation as 'slowly but effectively', 'very accurately', 'persistently', 'systematically', 'efficiently' or with valuation, e.g. 'conscientiously', 'in a solid and reliable manner', 'honestly'. One respondent wrote: 'Germans are famous for their diligence'. 'It is their most common national characteristic', added another. The sentence 'works like a German' was considered obvious and self-explanatory, which is why 7 respondents did not comment on it at all. The phrase 'hard-working like a German' appeared 7 times.

No other verb was evoked with nearly the same ease. The next most frequent ones were only used five times: 'to clean (something) like a German' (explained as 'thoroughly', 'well, solidly') and 'to behave like a German' ('arrogantly' (3), 'loudly, in a boorish manner' (2)).

A few other verbs appeared only once but they are also noteworthy, being interpreted in the spirit of the already familiar characterisations. For example, 'to manage something like a German' was taken to mean 'solidly, thoroughly'; 'to think like a German' – 'to the point'; 'to fight like a German' – 'to blindly obey orders'; 'to serve like a German' – 'to be devoted to a cause till the end'; 'to live like a German' – 'to lead a peaceful life'; 'to buy like a German' – 'thoughtfully'; 'to count like a German'[4] – 'with no clear idea in mind'; 'to drink like a German' – 'showing good manners, without causing trouble'; 'to speak like a German' – 'noisily', 'using a lot of words, incomprehensibly; to jabber'. A respondent also used the expression 'shouts like a German at a Bundestag meeting'.

Some respondents combined the expression 'like a German' with an adjective rather than with a verb. In order of frequency these were: 'thorough' (10), 'orderly' (5), 'solid', 'obedient', 'proud' and 'cruel' (3), 'dutiful', 'arrogant' and 'perfidious' (2), 'thrifty', 'pedantic', 'punctual', 'honest', 'head-strong', 'stubborn', 'insidious', 'cunning' (1 each).

4.9 What is done the German way?

A similar task in LSQ-90 consisted in supplying a verb to the expression 'the German way' and explaining the whole thus obtained. 89 responses were solicited.[5]

The construction '*work* the German way' was used 23 times and explained as 'thoroughly', 'well', 'without long breaks', 'without producing trash', 'with precision', 'honestly', 'with good manners, ethically', 'conscientiously, in an orderly fashion', 'solidly'. Sometimes the construction was left unexplained, which suggests that it was considered obvious. Table 14.10 lists the responses in order of frequency.

Table 14.10. What is done the German way? (LSQ-90; N = 85)

No. of references	Features
6	clean – 'thoroughly', 'clean up/out'
4	manage something – 'in an orderly manner, displaying exemplary management and discipline', 'with thrift', 'carefully, prudently'
3	rule – 'like in a strong-arm regime', 'with discipline', 'according to regulations'
2	think – 'precisely', 'consistently', 'coherently' walk – 'haughtily' wage war – 'in a cruel, ruthless way', 'with careful premeditation'
1	exploit – 'subject others to oneself' live – 'comfortably, keeping a high standard' order (someone to do something) – 'concisely, up to the point' drink – 'beer' be cruel

4.10 Objects characteristic of a German

In LSQ-90, 135 respondents mentioned objects characteristic of a German, mainly articles of everyday use, which adds to the already established predominant tendency of viewing Germans from this perspective (cf. Table 14.11).

Table 14.11. Objects characteristic of a German on the basis of LSQ-90 (N = 135)

No. of references	
136	articles of everyday use: • foods (76): beer (59), beer mug (2), mug of beer (7), bottle of beer, can of beer, sausage (3), Bockwurst, pork chop, cheap chocolate • car (42): car (12), luxury car, Mercedes (13), Trabant (7), Volkswagen (6), BMW (2), Audi, Wartburg • toiletries and cleaning products: soap (3), broom, brush, hoover, watch (3), good watch, wallet full of money, gold-rimmed glasses, sports equipment, bike, razor, book, one's own cottage, garden
42	militaria and historico-political symbols, esp. connected with WWII: uniform (13), rifle (12), swastika (4), arms (4), helmet (2), tank, eagle, Iron Cross, Knight's Cross, knee-high boots, black (high-upper, shining) shoes; Berlin Wall (2)
37	elements of attire and appearance: Tyrol hat (2), hat with a tassel, hat, Tyrol cap, shorts, elegant attire, nice duds, nice clothes, blond hair (9), fair hair (4), red hair (6), red noggin, blue eyes (3), big belly (3)

5 Changes in the polish stereotype of a German. Profiles and cultural-historical influences

The results of studies conducted with the relatively homogeneous community of students reveal that the stereotype of Poland's western neighbour has recently undergone significant changes. The direction, tempo and intensity of these changes can be identified on the basis of the rather substantial literature on the subject. Their mechanism can be interpreted with the conception of the 'base set of features', the features giving rise to 'profiles', understood as subject-oriented, culture-determined variants of the stereotype, selecting and hierarchically structuring the elements of the base in various ways.

Four periods can be identified in the development of the Polish stereotype of a German:

i)   the Old-Polish period: until the loss of independence by Poland in 1795 (Bystroń, 1980 [1924]);

ii) the period of partitioning and struggle against Germanisation, culminating in regained independence in 1918 (Wrzesiński, 1992);

iii) the interwar period, extending onto WWII and the first post-war years (Chałasiński, 1935; Pisarkowa, 1976; Święch, 1977; Niewiara, 1992a and b; Wrzesiński 1992);

iv) the period of the rise of new relationships and images; this process acquired momentum with the emergence of the Solidarity trade union and even more so after the union started to exert influence on Polish social and political life (*Der Spiegel*, 1991; Gruszczyński, 1992; Urban, 1993; Szymański, 1993).

The images of a German were differently profiled; their linguistic picture was also somewhat different in different periods, which can be detected in the Polish lexis, established characteristic features, phraseology and proverbs.

a) The oldest layer of Polish folk mythology, strongly coded in folk and popular culture, includes the image of a German as the prototype of a 'stranger'. This image rests on the elementary cultural opposition 'us – them' and is manifested in e.g. the Medieval legend of Wanda who did not want to marry a German. The semantic dominant of this oldest variant of the stereotype of a German is exposed in the very name: the Polish *Niemiec* 'a German' comes from *niemy* 'dumb', in the sense 'incomprehensible, impossible to communicate with' (as opposed to *Słowianin* 'Slav', from *słowo* 'word', i.e. someone with whom it is possible to communicate). Even today the words *szwargot* 'jabber' (noun) or *szwargotać* 'to jabber' are used in reference to the German language, meaning 'speak in a way difficult to understand'. There are numerous anecdotes, songs or stories ridiculing the German language or the inability of the Germans to 'talk normally', like 'we do' (Bystroń, 1980 [1924]: 338–341). Linguistic 'foreignness' is entrenched in the folk proverbs 'Try and talk to him when he's a German', 'Every German is a misfit', 'Sitting like at a German sermon', 'Were it not for the *der-di-das*, I would be a German' (*NKP*, v. II, 1970).

The model of a German as a 'stranger' also assumed, in folk and popular culture, mythological features, based on the basic opposition 'good – bad'. Germans were thought to possess demonic or devilish features, as in the proverbs 'Wherever a German puts his foot, the grass won't grow' or 'A servant of a German is paid by the devil' (1894). The devil was represented as a German, which is expressed in the proverb 'He fell in love like the devil with German attire'. The attire meant was short, 'skimpy'; cf. the expression 'skimpy like a German', also in Adam Mickiewicz's ballad: 'A a skimpy one, a real German'. At the same time Germans were denied human features (e.g. 'A good man, though a German', Artur Oppman, a nineteenth/twentieth century poet).

However, similarly to the idea of the devil and in order to 'tame' the alien and hostile folk image of a German, the latter was also equipped with comic, jocular and mocking features.

b) A German as *pludrak* (one who wears *pludry* 'skimpy trousers'). In the 'high' culture of the Old-Polish period, a German was predominantly viewed from the point of view of the gentry (Bystroń, 1980 [1924]; Lück, 1938) and associated with the following striking features:

- a different appearance (skimpy trousers called *pludry*, hence the nickname *pludraki* 'those wearing *pludry*'; a hairtail called *harcop*);

- a different cuisine ('potato eaters');

- a different culture, language and religion (cf. the proverbs 'Every German is a heretic, Calvinist, Lutheran'; 'You're a Lutheran, not a man');

- a different attitude to life: stinginess ('Not even a fly can have enough food with Germans'), thoroughness.

In this context, it is understandable that the following quatrain from Wacław Potocki's *Moralia* became very popular:

Poles and Germans never lived in sincere peace,
Poles are offended by vanity, Germans by freedom.
Hence the saying that as long as the world exists
Germans will never be brothers to Poles.

Some features of Germans, however, receive respect; cf. the proverb 'Learn reason from Germans and virtue form Poles' (*NKP*, 1978; proverb dated 1898).

On the whole, the general outlook on Germans in the Old-Polish period was 'unfriendly, sometimes outright disrespectful or contemptuous, at best hesitantly neutral or else aimlessly satirical' (Bystroń, 1980 [1924]: 335). Bystroń emphasises, and this view is important for the present study, that 'the opinion comes from the gentry man, who considered himself a candidate to the throne and treated the German colonist, city-dweller or even the German gentry man in a foreign contingent with disrespect; the opinion was upheld by the Polish townspeople and peasants, regarding the successes of hard-working and thrifty Germans with hatred' (Bystroń, 1980 [1924]: 335–336).

c) Germans as enemies but also representatives of high culture; this ambivalent stereotype of a German arose in the nineteenth century. Mitosek (1974: 73) notes that 'the increase in aversion on the part of Poles towards Germans paralleled the rise of Prussian hegemony', as a result of which Prussia gradually represented the whole of Germany. In the course of the nineteenth century Prussia and the Teutonic Knights gradually began to be identified with things German and, accordingly, the following features began to dominate in the characterisation of Germans (Wrzesiński, 1992: 750–762): ruthlessness, lack of understanding or respect for others, brutality, egotism, a plundering spirit, the cult of strength, preoccupation with material things, megalomania, hypocrisy, inclination to retaliate, cruelty, contemptuousness, use of violence, vanity, appreciation of strength, warlike spirit, possessiveness, opinionatedness, treacherousness, savagery. It is in the nineteenth century that the expression *niemiecka buta* 'German arrogance' became established and began to reign supreme in the stereotype of a German at the time.

At the same time, as noted by Wrzesiński, 'regardless of the conviction of permanent conflict with and threat from the Germans, Poles nearly always viewed them, even in moments particularly ominous for their own national identity, as a community of high culture and civilisation' (Wrzesiński, 1992: 713). German culture and civilisation of that period were fascinating mainly to the educated layers of Polish society. Wrzesiński notes that if German virtues 'were always associated with civilisation, culture and organisation of everyday life', vices were linked with politics (Wrzesiński, 1992: 719).

d) Germans as oppressors is an image constructed from the point of view of the victim of the Nazi aggression. WWII corroborated the negative elements of the traditional stereotype and redefined the positive ones so that they revealed another, ominous face: thoroughness, obedience or love of order. The stereotype of Germans as enemies, identifiable in the Polish war literature, denies them the possession of human features (Święch, 1977: 236). The lexis used in referring to Germans animalises and reifies them. 'On the one hand, the oppressors were associated with wild beasts, craving for murder, on the other they resembled cogs in a horrible and efficient machinery of crime' (Szarota, 1978: 150). Simultaneously, from the linguistic point of view, the image of a German is viewed in terms of oppositions between European culture and Germanic barbarism, a state of law and Prussian lawlessness, Christian values and paganism, God and Satan, human and animal, mental health and insanity.

Krystyna Pisarkowa's research in the community of students in Kraków (in 1970–1971) shows that the experience of the war left a permanent trace in the collective memory of Poles. The most frequently used synonyms of a German fitted well into the war tradition ('criminal', 'occupier', 'oppressor', 'Hitlerite', 'member of the Gestapo', 'SS-man', 'evil-doer', 'sadist', 'barbarian', 'bandit', 'shouter', 'despot', *Übermensch*, *Szkop* or *Szwab* 'a German (derogatory)', 'cruel man'), although positive characteristics, typical of earlier periods, were also revived ('clean', 'thorough', 'scrupulous', 'diligent', 'practical', 'solid', 'economical', 'thrifty'). In the post-war period the old proverbs attributing quarrelsomeness, stinginess or hypochondria to Germans ('Make someone believe something like make a German believe they are ill') were no longer current. Of the 24 features of a German identified by Pisarkowa, half are negatively valuated and express fear ('cruel', 'stern', 'ruthless'), reserve ('cold', 'indifferent', 'irreconcilable', 'stubborn'), anxiety ('insidious'), disrespect ('without taste', 'without fancy'), and half receive positive valuation, expressing trust ('obedient', 'disciplined', 'solid and reliable', 'hard-working', 'practical', 'precise and exacting', 'keeps his word') and even liking ('emotional').[6]

Some sociologists even claim that when two German countries existed side by side and the socialist propaganda of friendship between Poland and the German Democratic Republic was rather intense, a split stereotype of a German emerged. One 'portion' of it related to people from 'democratic' Germany, peace-loving and friendly towards Poles, the other to those from the Federal Republic of Germany, rich fascists and retaliators (Kwilecki, 1978). With time, an unexpected (at least from the official point of view) revision of judgments took place: western Germans began to be perceived as decent, Europeanised and cultural, those from the east as lazy, nationalistic and given to drinking (Gruszczyński, 1992: 12). A 1991 questionnaire in *Der Spiegel* corroborated this difference (eastern Germans being perceived as more self-confident, lazy, provincial, less ingenious or resourceful etc.).

e) A German as a European. Research in the early 1990s (*Der Spiegel*, 1991; Urban, 1993; Bartmiński, 1994; Szymański, 1993) point to a new phase in the functioning of the stereotype of a German in Poland. New aspirations in Polish society cause a 're-profiling' of the traditional image, especially among the younger generation, with aspects of a developed civilisation being foregrounded (such as good management or social discipline). Accordingly, the valuation of a German tends to become more positive. While completing the sentence 'I like the fact that Germans are ...', respondents in Jolanta Urban's (1993) questionnaire most frequently referred to traits of character ('hard-working', 'thorough', 'orderly', 'dutiful', 'punctual'), everyday life ('wealthy', 'orderly', 'well-organised') and attitudes to work ('good at management', 'enterprising'). The attitude of Germans to other people and nations was evaluated negatively ('nationalistic', 'possessive', 'aggressive', 'introvert').

The (positive) everyday-life features also surfaced as dominant among the list compiled with the semantic differential method (Bartmiński, 1994; Urban, 1993): 'hard-working' (84%), 'enterprising' (82%), 'thrifty' (76%), 'wealthy' (74%). The following features, however, also ranked high: 'nationalistic' (82%), 'proud' (75%), 'clean' (74%), 'patriotic' (70%), 'well-educated' (64%), 'intelligent' (55%), 'head-strong' (54%).

Let me briefly recapitulate. In the history of the stereotype of a German one may identify certain socially established points of view, which give rise to various models, such as:

a)   the point of view of the 'man in the street': the model of a German as a 'stranger';

b)   the point of view of a gentry man, whose views were shaped by Sarmatian culture: a German as *pludrak*;

c)   the point of view of a Polish patriot defending the nation's jeopardised independence: a German as an invader and an enemy;

d)   the point of view of a victim of military violence: the model of a Nazi German criminal;

e)   the point of view of a young representative of the intelligentsia, looking for a place for him- or herself in the contemporary world: the model of a German as a hard-working, rich and cultural European.

6 Conclusion

The Polish linguistic and cultural tradition contains a certain rather stable set of 'base' features attributed to Germans in different periods, expressing distance, the feeling of otherness or 'alienness', but combined with a certain degree of interest and respect. The base is profiled in different ways depending on specific historical conditions. It is untrue that stereotypes are permanent and inflexible: Changes in the stereotype occur at different levels of its structure.

It is important to differentiate external, surface and objective changes from the ones which are internal and subjectively-motivated (in the sense of being dependent on the attitude of the cognising subject). The former consist in reflections of simple historical processes, examples of which are aspects of attire (a skimpy tailcoat) or eating habits (potatoes). The latter, much more interesting, comprise the basic *criteria* of describing people and are manifested by a change of the point of view or perspective in which the 'other' (the 'stranger') is perceived. They depend on the aspirations of the conceptualisers and their system of values, thus revealing certain features of the cognising subject(s). A consequence of changes in the criteria of description is both a modification of the profile (the aspectual or facet structure) of the image and a reconstruction of valuation, which, as we have seen, is different in different aspects. Leszek Kołakowski (2004: 203) remarks: 'Stereotypes teach us about those who believe in them as much as about those they refer to'.

Notes

1   Calculated in the following way: where F1 = 45, F2 = 24, Total = 380.

2   The high rank of 'language' in traditional cultures while identifying nationalities is manifested in the etymology of the names of many ethnic groups, e.g. *Łemkowie* (the Ruthenian/Lemkish people) from *łem* 'only', *Bylacy* (an ethnic subgroup of Kashubians) from *byl* 'was', *Chmaki* (a Ukrainian ethnic group in the Lublin region, characterised by the use of the *-chmo* ending in 1st p. pl. verbs, e.g. *bylichmo* 'we were'), *Przeki* (a colloquial term for Poles in Belarus and Ukraine) from the prefix *prze-*, as in *przesadzać* 'exaggerate' or *przemyśleć* 'think over' etc.

3   Cf. e.g. the proverb 'Every Italian is a doctor, every German a merchant, every Pole a hetman'.

4   I.e. 'backwards', for instance *fünfundzwanzig* 'five and twenty'.

5   The most frequent were verbs of speaking, which results from the ambiguity of the Polish expression *po niemiecku*: 'the German way' or '(in) German'; hence *mówic po niemiecku* means 'speak German'.

6   One can include here features expressing respect ('resolute', 'bold', 'proud', 'serious').

15 *Prawica* 'right wing' and *lewica* 'left wing': profiles in contemporary discourse

1 Introduction

The semantic development of the Polish words *prawica* and *lewica* is an interesting example of the influence of the system of values professed by a given community on the semantic content of words, the internal organisation of that content and lexical usage. The meanings of *prawica* (now predominantly 'right wing' in the political sense) and *lewica* ('left wing') were for a long time clear and straightforward: the right side (hand) vs. the left side (hand) (recorded in Polish dictionaries since the fifteenth century). The valuation imposed on the two meanings was also clear and universal and is in fact preserved in colloquial and folk Polish to this day: 'good' for *prawy* 'right' and 'bad' for *lewy* 'left'.

2 A historical view

Since the eighteenth century the words have been used in the political context of revolution, progress, equality, justice etc., and have gradually begun to lose their primary meanings, which today are perceived as 'bookish', 'elevated' or 'old-fashioned' (*SJPDor*, 1962). They are also losing their traditional and universal valuations. To the forefront have gradually come the political categories of 'party' or 'sociopolitical trend'. This has been paralleled by an axiological conversion of the expressions, a reversal of their values. *Lewica* 'the left wing', *lewicowy* 'of the left wing' and *lewicowość* 'leftism' have acquired positive valuation, while *prawica* 'the right wing', *prawicowy* 'of the right wing' and *prawicowość* 'rightism' have changed from positive to negative.[1] It was only when the conceptions of progress and rationalism began to be questioned in the face of the twentieth century totalitarianisms that the two-century-long fascination with leftist views declined.

All in all, speakers of contemporary Polish inherit two expressions which were once (approximately until World War II) associated with a specific content, clear etymology and transparent axiology, but whose present-day semantics is vague. The expressions, according to many authors, have lost their unequivocal reference and are no longer useful as descriptions of social reality. Instead, they have become, as have other ideological stereotypes, tools drawn on in political debates.

An ordered presentation of the semantics of *lewica* and *prawica* is given in *SJPDor* (1962), which first lists the political meaning (*lewica*: 'the progressive, radical sociopolitical trend; progressive radical political parties; progressive, radical faction of a party, organisation or society'; *prawica*: 'a conservative party or faction'), then 'the group usually seated in the left part of the parliament', and finally the concrete, somatic and spatial meaning (*lewica*: 'the left hand'; *prawica*: 'the right hand'; in the expressions *po/na lewicy/prawicy* 'to/on the left/right side').

3   Semantic looseness

This arrangement of categorisations portrays, in the reverse order, the historical development of the meanings of *lewica*: from the name of the sides of the human body, via a reference to the surroundings in relation to a given side (already in the fifteenth century), then the group of deputies to the eighteenth century French National Assembly sitting to a particular side of the speaker and representing a radical political programme,[2] to the name of any group representing views similar in spirit to those of the French Revolution. These historical links between the components of the meaning of *lewica* (and, in a parallel fashion, of *prawica*) have not been totally obliterated in contemporary Polish and some dictionaries include them in one entry (though the meanings 'a side of the body' and 'a political orientation' only share the general aspect of spatiality). The reversal of the valuation of *lewica* and *prawica* results from the influence of the enlightened ideology and the pressure from the 'language of politics' and its idiosyncratic principles, on colloquial language. A co-occurrence of two interconnected changes: metaphorisation (from 'a side of the body' to 'political orientation') and axiological conversion, has produced a rift in both the historical and contemporary data.

Thus, the words *prawica* and *lewica* exhibit semantic looseness, manifested among others in journalism:

> What is the left and what is the right today if the extreme right orientation, wielding power here and there, has taken oven the augmented political attributes of a reactionary state? (Kisielewski, 1983: 53)

> The emergence, in the 20th century, of totalitarian political systems (communism, fascism, national socialism) and the seizure of power by totalitarian parties rendered the division into the right and left wing more complex. (Karpiński, 1985: 126)

> The conceptions of the political left and right, after forty years of communism, only have a historical significance. They refer to two ideological traditions, distant from our contemporary experience, which once focused on diverse systems of values. (Cywiński, 1986: 14)

Stefan Kisielewski writes about 'emotionally frozen traditional linguistic clusters, such as the left and the right' (1983: 164); Teresa Bogucka (1990) expresses her disapproval of 'anachronistic formulae' and 'traditional labels of left and right', Andrzej Romanowski (1989) states that the 'left-right distinction mystifies reality rather then describing it'.

Leszek Kołakowski, the author of the famous essay 'How to be a Conservative-Liberal Socialist', in which he shows the fuzziness of political divisions, views the left-right schema as 'fuzzy, overgrown on both sides with lies, rife with excuses and 'failures to mention". The author uses the method of 'implication *ad absurdum*':

> Aah, so you're a leftist? That is, you worship Stalin, pray to Mao-Tse Tung and Pol Pot, [...] Hohxa's Albania is your model and Ceauşescu your idol?

> But why, you consider yourself a rightist! Which simply means you love Hitler, wish Jews to be gassed, worship Pinochet's police at the top of your voice, revolt against the South African government when it wants to abolish racial laws. Your heroes are Batista, Somoza, Trujillo and Marcos, you dream of a return of the Persian shah and maybe even want to bring back the stakes? (Kołakowski, 1990: 6)

Semantic looseness was characteristic of the idiom of propaganda in the People's Republic of Poland (1945–1989) in periods of intense political struggle. Michał Głowiński notes the following in his diary, with the date of September 14, 1968:

> In official propaganda there is a great confusion in the use of the words *lewica* and *prawica*. The Czech emancipation movement is referred to as the right wing, though Czechs themselves, as far as I know, used the term in reference to Novotny's[3] supporters. But three months earlier, during the French student revolt, the intellectual left was treated with contempt as a serious threat to communism. The terms as such are a matter of fluctuating linguistic convention. I would not be surprised to read that the intellectual left is the worst kind of fascist Zionist right. The usage is arbitrary; everything can change depending on one's whim or on the circumstances. (Głowiński, 1990: 6)

These and similar views show that *lewica* and *prawica* are rich in semantic content and variously understood. I would especially like to pinpoint a certain type of difference, connected with the problem of conceptual profiling and a source of a peculiar 'covert polysemy'.

4   Towards a systematic presentation

From the commentaries on the political left and right wing one can extract a set of characteristics which may be thought of as the defining features of the concepts.[4] The features pertain to specific aspects of concepts, organise those concepts from different perspectives and may be combined into 'bundles' I call facets. The grouped explicatory sentences tell us what VALUES are characteristic of the political left and right, what the relevant BELIEFS and ATTITUDES to social facts are, the relevant PROGRAMMES, METHODS OF ACTION and what PEOPLE share these ideas. Table 15.1 presents the juxtaposition.

Table 15.1 *Lewica* 'left' and *prawica* 'right' contrasted

	The characteristics of *lewica* 'left wing'	The characteristics of *prawica* 'right wing'
VALUES	liberty, equality, brotherhood social justice people, humankind, a people reason	law and order independence God, the Church, homeland, Poland, nation, state, family, person
BELIEFS	humans are the source of morality	God is the source of morality
ATTITUDES	sensitivity to human suffering disregard of the current laws social combativeness / rejection of national wars pacifism	respect of law cult of tradition, unwillingness to implement changes social cooperation acceptance of strength, cult of strong authority social amicability / acceptance of war as a means of solving international conflicts
PROGRAMME	attempt to effect changes ('progress') attempt to institute international communities ('internationalism') attempt to institute equal laws ('democracy') defense of the weak ('social care', 'protective state', 'social security') attempt to institute common property struggle against unemployment	attempt to preserve the present states of affairs ('conservatism') efforts to strengthen the national community acceptance of elites, i.e. unequal financial status of citizens the right to private property acceptance of free market, competition-based economy acceptance of unemployment limitations of the role of the state
METHODS OF ACTION	collective action violence ('revolutionary terror')	individual action strong authority based on the law
PEOPLE	delegates on the left side of the parliament members of the socialist and communist parties	delegates on the right side of the parliament Catholics

Historically, the oldest definitions of *lewica* and *prawica* were formulated with reference to the political PROGRAMME (cf. Wierzbicki, 1985). This category began to lose importance as the sociopolitical reality started to change and the ideologies of the Polish left and right were being modified. Many programmatic components underwent modification, e.g. the attitude to religion, to the Catholic Church or to the nation. New components and questions appeared, e.g., that of the attitude to abortion, Jews or to the idea of self-government.

One can observe a clear shift in the self-definition of *lewica* from the category PROGRAMME to that of ATTITUDE, with the latter playing a progressively greater role. Jacek Kuroń, a Polish politician and human rights activist, writes:

> [I]n the left – right divide, personal traits complement political and spiritual factors. [...] People with a strong tendency to express themselves through the experiences of others may be willing to join the left wing (as long as it is in opposition), especially its anarchistic and revolutionary variants. They are drawn by a strong urge to implement radical changes, by sensitivity to suffering and by predilection to opt for conflict, disrespect of law and order in the name of justice and freedom. (Kuroń, 1990: 368–369).

Apart from ATTITUDES, an important role is played by the category of VALUES, especially in the apologetic variants of *lewica* and *prawica*, including negative valuation of these concepts. For example, *lewica* is associated with populism, a demagoguery of claims, 'just distribution of poverty', cosmopolitism etc. *Prawica* is described as excessively preoccupied with God and the homeland and associated with rampant religiousness and market liberalism, with clericalism, nationalism, chauvinism and militarism.

The dominant role is played by the aspect PEOPLE: programmes and attitudes are identified on the basis of the lives of specific individuals. The relevant expressions are: 'a Polish Catholic', 'a true Pole', 'Jewish masonry', 'Catholic left'.

Thus, with respect to various means of profiling and different aspectual dominants, four conceptual variants can be identified:

programmatic (dominant aspect: PROGRAMME)
attitudinal   (dominant aspect: ATTITUDE)
personal   (dominant aspect: PEOPLE)
axiological   (dominant aspect: VALUES)

In this way the conception of profiling can be used to disentangle at least some of the intricacies of these semantically complex words.

Notes

1   In the political idiom of the left-wing, there has been a further differentiation into the positive *lewica, lewicowy, lewicowość* and the negative *lewactwo* 'the ultra-left-wing', *lewacki* 'of the ultra-left-wing', *lewackość* 'ultra-leftism'. This distinction reconstructs the nature of the old opposition of *prawy* 'right' vs. *lewy* 'left'.

2   In the nineteenth century the expression began to be metaphorically used in reference to similar groups in other parliaments.

3   Antonín Novotný, president of Czechoslovakia and General Secretary of the Czechoslovakian Communist Party in the 1950s and 1960s.

4   I understand defining features as categorial and typical features. I do not embrace the distinctions into 'essential' and 'secondary' features, or analytic and synthetic ones, for these cannot be drawn without a degree of uncertainty.

16 Varieties of fate: the Polish *los* and *dola*; the Russian *sud'ba*

1 Introduction

The Polish concepts of *los* and *dola*, pertaining to the human condition, destiny and existence, belong to the category of cultural key-words. The inspiration to deal with the subject of the Polish *los* and *dola* as well as the Russian *sud'ba* has come from a very interesting study by Anna Wierzbicka ('Fate and destiny'), published in her 1992 book *Semantics, Culture and Cognition*. My remarks here partly develop Wierzbicka's ideas and partly oppose them. I will start with a presentation of her views.

2 Wierzbicka on *sud'ba* and *los*

Wierzbicka asks what the words referring to human fate in Russian (*sud'ba*), Polish (*los*), German (*Schicksal*), French (*destin, sort*), Italian (*destino, sorte*) and English (*fate, destiny*) mean for speakers of these languages as *nations*. She points to the lexemes' sociocultural and historical correlates and looks for the features which distinguish these concepts. For example, she draws a sharp contrast between the Russian *sud'ba* and the Polish *los*. The contrast, says Wierzbicka, is caused by different folk philosophies of life and man, a different history, culture, and different 'characters' of the nations.

The Russian *sud'ba*, an important concept in Russian culture, has power over people. It is a force independent of human will; it does not assume that human life has a sense or a value but that it is subjected to external forces from another world. *Sud'ba* implies that one should humbly yield to what has been decided by those forces (etymologically it derives from *sudit'* 'think, judge', *sud* 'judgment') and in that sense it is close to the Latin *fatum* (meaning 'that which is said, divine oracle, destiny', from *for, fari* 'say, speak'). Russian proverbs with *sud'ba* have fatalistic overtones, they advise to expect something bad rather than good and suggest that the best one can do is humbly and passively subject oneself to *sud'ba*: 'Whatever *sud'ba* decrees, be it just or unjust, will come to pass'; 'To each his own *sud'ba*'. *Sud'ba* is 'implacable' or 'inevitable'; it is also anthropomorphised ('in the hands of *sud'ba*'), it has a will ('by the will of *sud'ba*') etc. Wierzbicka seeks the origin of this attitude in Russian history, religion and culture, in the despotism of some and absolute submission of others, in the typically Russian humble acceptance of suffering, based on the Orthodox ideal of 'holy resignation', and on eastern fatalism.

In contrast to this idea of passive and humble submission to the decrees of forces more powerful than humans, the Polish conception of *los*, says Wierzbicka, is based on a different philosophy. The word *los* is used in the context of a lottery, in which people draw lots (*losy*). One's *los* is not controlled by anyone; it may be good or bad but it is always unpredictable: one can only win a good *los*; hence the fixed expressions *ironia losu* 'los's irony', *kaprys losu* 'los's whim', *uśmiech losu* 'los's smile'. In the word's semantics there are no traces of submission, resignation or humble acceptance; on the contrary, it contains a dose of optimism and a belief in the inexhaustible possibilities of the lottery of life.

The phraseology of *los* suggests that a person may shape his or her life by challenging fate (*wyzywać los*) or by actively cooperating with it (*zrobić los* 'to make the fate', *zrobić świetny/wielki los* 'to make a great fate'). A person may also wait for his or her chance to come (*zdać się na los szczęścia*). In general, the phraseology has rather active overtones. According to Wierzbicka, this can be explained by the pro-Western orientation of Polish culture (glorification of freedom, active attitude towards life), its Catholicism (stress on a person's free will) and national history, full of political upheavals, spectacular victories and painful defeats. The author writes: 'In some ways […] the Polish *los* is closer to the Roman *fortuna* than to the Roman *fatum*. [..] [T]he Russian concept *sud'ba* leans more toward a *fatum*-like interpretation' (Wierzbicka, 1992: 76).

This elegant juxtaposition, however, also has weak points, one of which is actually mentioned by the author herself. Wierzbicka admits that the understanding of *los* which she discusses in not exclusively and typically Polish: it is based on the tradition of the nobility and intelligentsia, not on the folk or peasant tradition. In a marginal but important remark, she notes that 'Polish folk culture viewed human life not in terms of *los* but in terms of a different concept, *dola*' (Wierzbicka, 1992: 103). Having mentioned that, though, Wierzbicka considers *dola* relatively insignificant in standard Polish and does not discuss it. This, I think, is a mistake. On the one hand, one can readily agree with the view that 'in Poland, the spread of the idea of *los* to the entire population can be regarded as a symbolic expression of the spread of the 'noble ethos' and of its identification with the national ethos' (Wierzbicka, 1992: 103). But on the other hand, the concept of *dola* has a stable position in the Polish language and functions not only in folk dialectal Polish but also in standard Polish. In the standard literary variety, *dola* is a language-internal counterpart of *los*, contrasting with it semantically in the same way in which the Russian *sud'ba* does. This contrast cannot be motivated by the specificity of the Polish national character; it rather results from a different understanding of the situation of humans, characteristic of another, 'plebeian' cultural formation. It also has a rich cultural background (Arutyunova, 1994; Symotiuk, 1996). I will present data on the basis of which one can reconstruct the linguistic picture of *dola*, in accordance with the principles of the cognitive definition (cf. chapter 6).

3   The polish *dola* and *los*

Dola and *los* function, often interchangeably, in the same semantic field, which in Polish is composed of a few semantically connected elements. In the entry for *los*, *SWB* (1971) includes three words: *dola*, *przeznaczenie* 'destiny' and *fatum* 'doom, fate'. *SS* (1993) provides more synonyms and arranges them in two sets:

i)   *LINIA ŻYCIA* 'the life's line', *dola, położenie* 'situation', *stan* 'state', *koleje życia* 'life history', *bieg wydarzeń* 'course of events', *opatrzność* 'providence', *przeznaczenie* 'destiny', *predestynacja* 'predestination', *fatum* 'doom, fate', *gwiazda* 'star', *łaska boża* 'God's favour';

ii) *FORTUNA* 'fortune', *przypadek* 'chance, coincidence', *zrządzenie (losu)* 'a stroke of fate', *traf* 'luck, chance', *zbieg okoliczności, splot wydarzeń, koincydencja* 'coincidence', *zbieżność* 'convergence'.

One can easily notice that the two sets involve contrasts between a line and a point, a state and a change, between passive and active. The central elements in the first set are *dola* and *fatum* 'doom, fate'; in the second set these are *traf* 'luck, chance' and *fortuna* 'fortune'. This observation in itself is enough to realise that Polish contains not only the concept of *los* but a greater number of semantically related concepts, contrasted in the national discourse, and *dola* does not only belong to the folk variety of the language.

Los is a relatively late, eighteenth century borrowing of the German *Los* (with a change of meaning), which has replaced an earlier borrowing from Latin, namely *fortuna*. *Dola*, on the other hand, is an indigenous word, present in East Slavic languages, some West Slavic languages and in Bulgarian. *Los* is documented to have existed in Polish since the eighteenth century, *dola* since the seventeenth century.[1] *SFPW* (1990) distinguishes between the two items very clearly in terms of their frequency: *los* is used 71 times per 10,000 words, *dola* only 4 times. However, both unquestionably belong to contemporary standard, literary Polish; they are recorded in basic meanings without qualifiers and are used in lexicographic definitions. For example, *SJPDor* (1962) defines *los* by *dola* ('*los: dola*, one's life history, course of events moving towards a result') and vice versa ('*dola*: a person's *los*; situation, state'). In *PSWP* (1994–1998) the words treated as synonymous to *dola* include *los*, but also happiness, condition, situation, state, life's history, while those synonymous to *los* are first of all *dola*, and then situation, event, fact, incident, life's history, chance, coincidence, unpredictability, destiny, doom, inevitability.

It is interesting that *dola* often appears in definitions of *los* in the latter's contextual, phraseological uses; e.g. *PSWP* (1994–1998): 'come to terms with one's *los* – come to terms with one's *dola*'; 'risk an uncertain *los* – risk an uncertain *dola*'; 'curse one's *los* – curse one's *dola*', etc. This function of *dola* as a definiens of *los*, contrary to the suggestions of its low frequency, points to its high position in the lexical system of contemporary standard Polish.

4   The semantics of *dola*

Let us now try to synthetically characterise, without the division into folk and standard Polish, the semantics of *dola* in terms of the cognitive definition. Let us consider what perspective it is based on and what kind of experiencing and speaking subject it is projected by.

The Polish *dola* has formal and semantic equivalents in other Slavic languages. *SEJP* (1952–1982) mentions Slovak *dol'a* 'fate, share, cut', Ukrainian *dolja* 'fate, luck', Russian *dolja* 'part, share, cut, fate, destiny' and Bulgarian *dola* 'part'.

Etymologically, *dola* is connected with two groups of words: on the one hand with *dzielić* 'deal' and on the other hand with *dołać, podołać* 'manage', *zdolny* 'able', *niedołęga* 'oaf'; with Old Church Slavonic *odoleti* and Russian *odolet'* 'to defeat'. Sławski's *SEJP* (1952–1982) traces the Slavic data to the Old Slavic **dol-ja* and similarly Vasmer (*REW*, 1950–1958) juxtaposes it with the Latin *dolare* 'trim off (with an axe)' and Lithuanian *dalia, dalis* 'part'. Finally, the Indo-European root **del-* is taken to mean 'separate, cut off, hem, finish, work up'.

The dominant feature is that of distributing with a result; *dola* is seen as a result of distribution, a share one gets. This meaning of the word is especially well documented in Polish sociolects, such as the criminal jargon: *dola* is something one receives after the booty is split. In the jargon of drug addicts, *dola* is a portion of a drug (cf. also the colloquial expressions *otrzymać swoją dolę* 'get one's share'; *wypił swoją dolę i oddał butelkę drugiemu* 'he drank his share and passed the bottle to the next person' (*SJPDor*, 1962)).

Dola functions in the opposition *dola : niedola* 'good and bad times' (cf. *zostać z kim na dolę i niedolę* 'be with someone through thick and thin', *towarzysz doli i niedoli* 'one's companion through thick and thin' (*PSWP*, 1994–1998)).

The understanding of *dola* as a result of the act of dealing something implies that there is someone who assigns a portion of a larger whole to each person or can decide about the allocated part. The owner of *dola*, the implied agent of the action, is basically hidden in standard Polish but very much present in folk varieties of the language. Consider the following proverbs (*NKP*, 1978): 'One's *dola* changes with God's will'; 'As you call upon God, such is your *dola*'; 'The lazy one lies down and God prepares his *dola* for him'; 'Whomever God defends will not drown in bad *dola*'. In folk wedding songs *dola* comes from God, Jesus or the Virgin Mary and is treated as a synonym of happiness. God is a feeling Being, who can be asked for favour and kindness, which is what happens at a wedding: 'May God, who deals *dola*, bless you'; 'May God bless you and give you a good *dola*'; 'Mary, apologise to your mother (father, brother, sister), if you got her (him) angry; if you do not, you will not have *dola*'; 'I will apologise to you, my mother, if I got you angry; maybe I will have a better *dola* from God'; 'Oh, my powerful God, give me *dola* (or: happiness), 'cause I'm going to bondage'; 'May God bless you and give you good *dola* (*doleńka* – diminutive). If God gives good *dola*, glory to you God; if he does not, oh my God!'

God as the giver of *dola* appears in folk songs in eastern Poland (the Lublin region, Masovia) and a similar motif is found in Ukrainian songs: 'Let them ask God and raise their hands, for a good *dola*, a happy hour'. An impersonal *dola* is inexorable but the *dola* in the hands of God can be influenced by turning to God, examples of which are the wedding songs above.

Dola can affect individuals or whole communities: the subject-participant is perceived in both personal and social or national terms. In standard Polish there are two fixed, frequently used expressions relating to communities: *chłopska dola* 'peasant's *dola*' and *polska dola* 'Polish *dola*'. In both cases the people's fate is hard. The motif of undeservedly cruel and hard *dola* was especially frequent in patriotic Polish writings of the nineteenth century. In his poetic drama *Forefathers' Eve* (Part III), written after the collapse of the November Uprising of 1931, Adam Mickiewicz pitied the Polish nation's *dola*, which drives it to only one kind of heroism: that of bondage. Tadeusz Komar wrote after the collapse of the January uprising of 1863:

> Polish children in Olomouc
> In sorrow, misery and bondage,
> Like free falcons in a nest
> We await the Polish *dola*.

(quoted in *KC*, 1975: 155, 18; trans. A.G.)

Stefan Żeromski in *The Rose* presents the following dialogue:

> 'Tell me, what kind of standard am I supposed to be under together with an advocate of conciliation or a national democrat, who belittle everything that I got so many wounds for? What do I have in common with them, apart from my language?'
> 'The Polish *dola*'.
> (quoted in *KC*, 1975: 613, 18; trans. A.G.)

The other typical participant of the hard *dola* in Polish literature is the Polish peasant. This was especially pronounced in the work of socially engaged poets, particularly in the nineteenth century. Maria Konopnicka wrote: 'Peasant *dola*: grey' ('From meadows and fields', quoted in *KC*, 1975: 167, 12). Wiktor Gomulicki, in turn, lamented:

> Oh you, peasant *dola*, you are, too, goldened
> And blued by the hard work of poets,
> [...] But he who strips you off the false embellishments,
> will see a mark of suffering on your face
> And that you are ugly, dark and miserable.

(*KC*, 1975: 98, 2; trans. A.G.)

If the Polish *dola* was portrayed as dramatic and peasant *dola* as hard, the *dola* of the Polish nation accepting responsibility for the homeland was seen as outright tragic. This is reflected in Jan Kasprowicz's *The Book of the Poor*:

> You died far away from your kin
> Fighting for someone else's cause,
> An alien violence exiled you,
> Cruel and bloody *losy* [fate-PL].
> You, a child of the Polish people,
> The land rich in misfortunes,
> I remember your young heart,
> Overflowing with the homeland's *dola*.

(*KC*, 1975: 132, 9; trans. A.G.)

The bad Polish *dola* was associated with political subjection, bondage, and wars, the peasant *dola* with hard work and poverty: 'The hard, grey *dola* of the poor' (Artur Oppman, in *KC*, 1975: 382, 9); 'A poor man is never happy with his *dola*' (Adam Naruszewicz, in *KC*, 1975: 320).

Dola receives a different treatment in folk texts. In songs, a 'miserable *dola*' is connected with one's personal situation, which depends not so much on wealth but on interpersonal relationships, especially in the family. The fate of a girl who is not allowed to marry is miserable ('Miserable *dola*! They forbid me to marry, and I am getting old; they have no regard'), as is that of a girl whose lover leaves to fight for the national cause ('If it is your will to go and fight – my *dola* is miserable! Why do you punish me? What will I do without you? How unhappy I am!') or who 'breaks her drum and loses her geese', i.e. loses virginity before marriage ('The drum is broken, the geese are lost; oh, unhappy me, what have I done? She laments and cries: my *dola* is so miserable!'). A miserable *dola* is also that of a husband physically abused by his wife, as well as that of a wife whose extramarital affair is discovered. But complaining about one's *dola* is considered futile; cf. the proverb 'Do not lament your *dola* before people, as you will only sadden your friend and make your enemy happy' (*NKP*, 1978).

At the same time, *dola* is viewed as something unchangeable, unyielding to a person's will, established forever. This is expressed in the proverbs 'You cannot change your *dola*' (*NKP*, 1978); 'The human *dola* is like a bird: it will come and go and it is futile to make it stop by' (Maria Konopnicka, *NKP*, 1978).

Dola is anthropomorphised: it is thought to have intentions regarding people though the intentions are not known. It is mysterious, one cannot predict its actions: '*Dola* will give what it will' (Konopnicka, *KC*, 1975: 169); 'Oh, you *dola*, / You go with the wind, / You sow flowers for some, / And scythe them for others' (Konopnicka, *KC*, 1975: 169). These actions are, in general, unfavourable to people: 'We don't know what stick *dola* is cutting out for us' (*NKP*, 1978); 'The good *dola* will change faster than the bad one' (*NKP*, 1978).

5   The valuation of *dola*

The valuation of *dola* deserves a separate treatment. One can observe axiological liability and directional changeability in this respect, a transfer from positive through neutral to negative valuation, i.e. from acceptance of one's *dola* to complaints, aversion and internal defiance.

A positive valuation of *dola* is manifested in the above-mentioned opposition *dola: niedola* (lit. 'non-*dola*'); it is also positively evaluated in many folk usages. In the most archaic cultural tradition *dola* as a gift from above could have been associated with the giver, i.e. God (Ivanov and Toporov, 1987; Arutyunova, 1994). On the other hand, it is also viewed as underspecified and capable of occurring with either positively or negatively charged adjectives, e.g. *dobra/zła dola* 'good/bad *dola*' (*SJPDor*, 1962); *szczęśliwa/nieszczęśliwa dola* 'happy/miserable *dola*' (*PSWP*, 1994–1998).

The negative valuation of *dola* is, it seems, dependent on the social and cultural context: it matters whose *dola* is considered. The *dola* of a lord or master is fortunate, that of a people is not. The oldest proverb with the word *dola* in *NKP* (1978) comes from the writings of the rich magnate Andrzej Maksymilian Fredro: 'One's own *dola* can make everyone happy' (dated 1659). Similarly, a positive connotation of *dola* is found in Sebastian Petrycy's translations (dated 1609) of Horatius's poems: 'Our ancestors settled on this land and took this *dola* with God's will'. On the other hand, authors who write the 'peasant way', view and evaluate *dola* differently, as a force hostile to humans: 'The wind shatters the woods, and *dola* shatters people' (Konopnicka, *NKP*, 1978); 'dog's *dola*' (Władysław Orkan, *NKP*, 1978). One's *dola* on earth is basically hard and difficult. Juliusz Słowacki in his 'Response to the *Psalms of the Future*' contrasts the earthly *dola* with a child's life on the moon (*KC*, 1975: 455,5). It is striking that in folk texts, especially in ritual songs, *dola* is not portrayed as necessarily bad but as something given, something that one must accept, manifested in folk diminutives of *dola*: *doliczka, doleńka*.

6   People's attitude to *dola*

We now come to the next interesting question, that of people's attitude to their *dola*. In contemporary standard Polish *dola* is treated in the same way as in the folk variety, as independent of and uninfluenced by people, unknown and unknowable: 'You will not ride around your *dola* on horseback' or 'You will not ride on horseback around what is destined/predetermined' (*NKP*, 1978); 'You sleep and your *dola* grows' (you don't know what your *dola* has in stock for you) (*NKP*, 1978). *Dola* stands above humans, governs their life and fate. One can lose but not change one's *dola*; *dola* can make one happy or unhappy. As already mentioned, however, the Old-Polish tradition of the nobility was different in this respect: seventeenth century authors (Fredro, Petrycy) used the concepts of a positive *dola*. Even as late as in the eighteenth century, Adam Naruszewicz, a typical representative of the Enlightenment and rationalism, believed that people can influence their *dola*:

> That our *dola* goes along the wrong path
> Is due to our own actions.
> Decency is a certain forecast of happiness.
> We lament our fate because we want it to be such.

(Adam Naruszewicz, *Forecast for the year 1775*; in *KC*, 1975: 318; trans. A.G.)

A demise of this optimistic conception of *dola* took place in the nineteenth century as a result of a merger of the connotations of the Polish and the peasant *dola*. It is not surprising that *SWJP* (1996) suggests in the very definition of *dola* that it refers to a difficult situation, unfavourable to a person.

7   Conclusions

Summing up, one must conclude that contemporary and older data reveal a coexistence of two parallel concepts in Polish: *dola* and *los*. They are equivalents and maybe even continuators of the Latin *fatum* and *fortuna*.[2] It is only when considered jointly that they reveal the internal differentiation of one linguistic and cultural picture of the world.

The conception of *los*, brilliantly contrasted by Wierzbicka with the Russian *sud'ba*, is projected by someone who believes in the possibility of influencing his or her life, someone who is free from the incapacitating feeling of external determinism, someone active and bold. The conception of *dola* is projected from the point of view of someone who understand the multifarious limitations of his or her condition and who accepts the situation he or she cannot change.

Both these conceptions are well-known in the Polish language; they are both well-entrenched in Polish tradition, history and culture. They also have counterparts in other languages and cultures (Arutyunova, 1994). The conception of *los* had its prototype in the figure of the Polish nobleman, but with time also an insurgent, lancer, legionary, dissident or intellectual, for whom the human ideal is someone courageous, a desperado and daredevil, a bold risk-taker – this ideal is realised in the Polish ethos of insurgency. The conception of *dola*, on the other hand, is built around the historical prototype of the Polish peasant, a plebeian, or now around the so called 'simple person'.

The two conceptions correspond to two contrasting attitudes to life, both of them well-known in Poland and other societies. To understand human life as *dola* is by no means out of place in contemporary Poland, nor is it anything specifically associated with peasant thinking. What is more, it seems to be growing in importance, as indicated by *PSWP* (1994–1998), a modern dictionary of Polish. The presence of *dola* in contemporary Polish makes one look at Wierzbicka's sharp Russian-Polish contrast from a different perspective. What is contrasted with *sud'ba* is the Polish *los*, but not the Polish *dola*. The causes of this contrast must be sought in social aspects, in people's attitudes and sociologically determined aspirations, rather than in the mythical national character (a category which is often criticised nowadays; cf. Berting and Villain-Gandossi, 1995).

Finally, it is interesting to consider the reasons for the liveliness of *dola* in contemporary Polish. It seems to be socioculturally motivated both in the 'peasantisation' of Polish society and in the characteristics of the Polish transformation of the 1990s, initiated in 1989 by the victory of the essentially folk Solidarity movement. The 1990s were on the one hand a period in which the traditional, romantic, noble national ethos became anachronistic, in which the ideal of a desperado and a daredevil, mentioned by Wierzbicka, turned into a new cultural pattern, that of an effective pragmatist, a calculating businessman, a trader and organiser. On the other hand, a sizeable portion of the society, not partaking of the benefits of the transformation, remains within the realm of the traditionally plebeian understanding of *dola* as something forced by external circumstances, uninfluenced by the person concerned. In this context *dola* is brought about by someone else's clandestine action, often distrustfully interpreted by 'simple people' as mysterious and unfavourable to them.

Notes

1   There is no entry for *dola* in the dictionary of Old Polish, *SStp* (1953–2003), or the dictionary of sixteenth century Polish, *SPXVI* (1966–1999). Linde in his early nineteenth century dictionary (*SJPLinde*, 1807–1814) quotes *dola* in Sebastian Petrycy's early seventeenth century translations of Horatius's poems.

2   Incidentally, the Latin items are also borrowed into Polish and function side by side *dola* and *los* as distinctive Latinate words.

17 The conception of the linguistic worldview in comparative research

1 Introduction

The conception of the linguistic worldview (cf. chapter 3), deriving from the ideas of Wilhelm von Humboldt, Edward Sapir and Benjamin Lee Whorf, has currently found its advocates in ethnolinguistics in Poland, Russia and the Czech Republic. Over the last quarter of a century, several books with the concept of 'linguistic worldview' in the title have been published.[1] This conception could add a new dimension to Slavic comparative research and help initiate a dialogue with new research trends of anthropological-cultural linguistics and cognitive linguistics, but above all with the dynamically developing intercultural semantics.

At the same time, analyses inspired by the linguistic worldview conception show that the value of comparative research rises tremendously if not limited to phenomena within a specific genealogically-determined branch or group of languages, such as Slavic, or to the traditional comparative-historical paradigm. It stands a better chance of development if based on the conception of language typology, language relatedness, *Sprachbund*, European and global community – such research is topical for it may help diagnose difficulties in intercultural communication and contribute to overcoming those difficulties.

The linguistic worldview conception is semantic, anthropological and cultural in nature. It is based on the assumption that language codes a certain socially established knowledge of the world and that this knowledge can be reconstructed and verbalised as a set of judgements about people, objects and events. The knowledge results from the subjective perception and conceptualisation of reality by the human mind; it is anthropocentric and relativised to languages and cultures. In contrast to the restrictive structuralist view, the knowledge of the world belongs to the realm of semantics, being entrenched in the very fabric of language, primarily in the meanings of words but also in grammar.

I understand lexical meaning in an integral way, as something that embraces both the 'hard core' and the broad 'soft' peripheries. These encompass what Apresyan (1994) or Iordanskaya and Mel'chuk (1980) describe as 'cultural connotations' and exclude from linguistic semantic description. Contrary to those authors, I argue for the relevance of cultural connotation to semantic description in Bartmiński (1984).

The whole semantic richness of a word may be portrayed through the cognitive definition (see chapter 6), which aims to reflect the way in which an entity is viewed by the speakers of a language, to represent that knowledge, its categorisation and valuation, established socio-culturally and accessible through language. The cognitive definition provides information on what an x is, what it looks like, how it functions, where and in what quantities it can be found etc. The questions are addressed through bundles of characteristics, communicated as stereotypical judgments and arranged in the definition in subcategories. i.e. facets.

Grzegorczykowa (2001) devotes a whole chapter to the conception of the linguistic worldview and the methods of its reconstruction. For her, the conception is a very promising one in comparative semantic research (Grzegorczykowa, 2001: 162) and the work of Anna Wierzbicka is quoted as an example. Despite a substantial number of publications on the linguistic worldview, when Stanisław Gajda (2000) proposed to include the conception in his comparative research on Slavic languages, the scholars he invited to cooperate were faced with the question of how the notion can be operationalised to the benefit of the field so as to yield measurable results one could treat in a synthetic manner (Chlebda, 2000; Bartmiński, 2000).

In formulating certain observations and proposals in this respect, I will refer to ethnolinguistic findings. In my opinion, the most comprehensive and at the same time methodologically coherent attempt to reconstruct a linguistic and cultural worldview, based on the anthropological-cultural and cognitive conception of language, is the dictionary of folk stereotypes and symbols (*SSSL*), compiled in Lublin, and published since 1996. It makes little difference that the dictionary is based on data drawn mainly (though not exclusively!) from one variant of Polish, namely folk Polish, because theoretical and methodological solutions proposed on the basis of one variety can be applied to other variants, e.g. to the standard variety. They can also be used in comparative research.

2   *Tertium comparationis*

However, let us first recall that in all comparative endeavours the key role is played by the standard for comparison, a *tertium comparationis* (TC), since 'the feature selected as the TC determines the type of judgments pertaining to the objects being compared, and as a consequence it also determines the procedures of observation, the experiments, the type of inferencing etc.' (Bogusławski, 1994: 15). Therefore, statements about the objects of comparison should characterise those objects according to the same criteria and should belong to the same logical class.

Let us then ask what functions as TC in comparative Slavic research: a word, a thing (object) or a concept, if one is to maintain Ogden and Richards' tripartite distinction? How are the three elements treated in the linguistic worldview model?

A word (lexical item) as the *tertium comparationis* is unwaveringly the point of departure in etymological dictionaries, multilingual dictionaries of specialist terms or translational bilingual dictionaries. Dictionaries of this kind juxtapose equivalents of a word in various languages and may also provide its meanings in a semasiological description. The meanings are given in a maximally concise manner. Language atlases follow the same principles. For instance, the Slavic Linguistic Atlas (*VOLA*, 1965) contains information about the meaning and distribution of lexemes, their phonetic and morphological starting-point variants, as well as the meanings of the relevant Proto-Slavic units. Similar information can be found in all Polish dialectological questionnaires.

The maps which arise in this way portray lexical and partly semantic differentiation of genealogically related words in the different languages.

An illustration of this type of comparative procedure may be the entry for *dunaj* in *SGP* (2004, vol. VI-19: 459–461) or *SP* (1984, vol. V: 92–94). The information one finds there concerns the lines of development of the Proto-Slavic forms **dunavъ* and **dunajъ* in all Slavic languages and of numerous derivatives in the names of rivers and places (*Dunajec* (Danube), *Dunajek, Dunajowice* etc.). Hypotheses are also offered of the word's origin from the German **Donawi* and its later history (borrowings from Slavic languages to Lithuanian, Hungarian and Romanian). The author of the entry concludes: 'The name of a big river, which played an important role in Slavic folklore, was as usual transferred onto other rivers, as well as onto common nouns meaning 'deep water' or 'river' in general'.

In studies couched within the linguistic worldview conception, the descriptions of *dunaj* are more exhaustive: they record not only the word's form and basic meaning but also its rich linguistic and cultural connotations. Yudin (2004a) discusses numerous linguistic analyses of *dunaj*, makes use of the rich documentation of the word in various genres of Russian, Ukrainian, Byelorussian, Polish, Czech and Bulgarian folklore, and favours the hypothesis that the word in Slavic and partially Baltic languages has become a common noun, referring to an unknown river, deep water, the sea, backwater, a brook etc. He also goes much further and shows the word's usage and functions in texts of folklore, magic spells, love songs and wedding songs – in short, he reconstructs its cultural meanings.

It appears that *dunaj* functions in texts from different Slavic languages in a similar fashion. Compare the similar motifs in folk songs:

> Polish: winds throw a girl's chaplet into the *dunaj* – the girl is mature enough to marry; a girl swims across the *dunaj* – she leaves her home to be with her chosen one.

> Ukrainian: winds come from the *dunaj* and seize a girl's chaplet; a girl lets her chaplet flow on the *dunaj* to the one she loves.

> Czech: a girl addresses the wind in the following way: *Zafoukej, větřičku, z Dunaje, at' ta zima brzy roztaje* 'Blow, wind, from the *dunaj*, may the winter pass quicker'.

> Moravian: lovers talk on the banks of a *dunaj*, the girl washes her feet on one side, the boy gives water to his horse on the other, after which the boy swims across the *dunaj* to his girl and often drowns (a similar motif can also be found in Bulgarian songs).

A comparison of stereotypical textual motifs of this kind, which acquire parallel symbolic meanings in various Slavic languages, allows one to reconstruct the image of *dunaj* as a prototypical river (and generally water), the centre of the mythical world, as well as a road which both divides and unites people.[2]

In an onomasiological approach, choosing the object for the TC opens another research perspective, and allows one to show the diversity of names and conceptualisations of the object behind those names. The comparative procedure is relatively straightforward in the case of objects unambiguously identifiable on the basis of extra-linguistic empirical observation, such as the sun, stars, the elements, plants, animals or body parts. It is more difficult in the case of artifacts, such as clothes, prepared foods, kitchen utensils etc., very different in different cultures and environments. The most problematic are components of the spiritual culture, such as political, social or moral concepts and ideas. These are mainly untranslatable, specific to individual cultures and languages. Let us consider some examples.

The Polish term for a colourful bow sometimes visible in the sky after rain is *tęcza*, deriving from the word for a cloud (cf. Russian *tuča*) via metonymic shift. East Slavic terms, however, have different origins: Ukrainian *veselka* is derived from the adjective *veseliy* 'joyful' and Russian *raduga* is composed of *ra-*, the first element of the word *radost'* 'joy', and *duga* 'arch': an arch of joy (because of sunshine after a storm). The French *arc-en-ciel*, English *rainbow* and German *Regenbogen* are motivated by the shape of the object and connect it with the rain. A similar basis can be found in the Czech *duha* and Lithuanian *vaivorykštė* (etymologically closely connected with the root **uer-* 'twist, bend'). But synonymous Lithuanian folk terms also evoke the whole linguistic and cultural worldview, the beliefs which constitute the word's motivation: *Laumės juosta* 'Launa's ribbon', *Dievo juosta* 'God's ribbon', *Smakas* (a name based on the image of a mythical dragon drinking water), *straublys* 'snout, trunk' and others (Laurenkienė, 2004).

The description of *tęcza* in *SSSL* contains the following information: a rainbow is multicoloured (cf. the adjective *tęczowy* 'multicoloured' and *tęczować* 'sparkle with many colours'); it is treated like a living creature with two mouths and a neck, which drinks water from rivers, moves clouds, pulls in green frogs, can suck in a person and throw them on the ground; it is delightful (cf. *patrzeć w kogoś jak w tęczę* 'to look up to someone', lit. 'look at someone as one looks at a rainbow'; *ładny jak tęcza* lit. 'beautiful as a rainbow') but may also invoke anxiety or fear; it sleeps in winter. It is only against the background of these beliefs that one can explain why the rainbow in Polish folk dialects is also called *smok* 'dragon', or *pijawka* 'leech', both names evoking the image of sucking and drinking.

Comparisons of 'the same' object with the aim of reconstructing their linguistic worldviews in specific languages unfailingly lead to the conclusion that the linguistic worldview is never a simple reflection or a 'photograph' of the object but its portrait or interpretation.

In this way we arrive at the most important but also the most difficult group of examples, namely those in which TC is the meaning, i.e. the mental object, the concept or a cultural artifact, such as HOME, BREAD, MOTHER, FATHER, BROTHER, UNCLE, SIN, HOMELAND, FREEDOM etc. Such research is similar to onomasiological analyses and is sometimes treated jointly; however, it also has its own tradition.

The choice of meaning as TC is the most dubious and problematic. Meaning, or the correlate between the name and the object (thing) cannot be unambiguously identified, is very sensitive to subjective modulation, changeable and indeterminate, even open-ended. The problems begin with the establishment of the boundaries of meaning, the number of their components, their status (central or peripheral), or the mutual relationship between multiple meanings of the same word. For example, where the Russian *SD* (1995–2004) has one entry *boloto*, the Polish *SSSL* (1996–1999) has two: *błoto* 'mud' and *błota* 'marshland, swamp'. When the comparison takes into account a greater number of languages (Johannes Schröpfer's onomasiological dictionary (*WVB*, 1979) contains data from eighty seven), it becomes only sensible to limit the description to the necessary and minimal core. However, the linguistic worldview conception opts for maximal meaning, i.e. one that includes not only taxonomic (necessary and sufficient) features but *all* the linguistically and culturally relevant features.

Is it thus possible to establish a TC with any degree of precision? Two methodologically acceptable solutions can be proposed. The first one is based on the concepts common to the members of a sufficiently broad international community, the second one utilises a universal semantic metalanguage, independent of particular languages and cultures.

The TC in some studies is a certain general concept, accepted in a specific cultural sphere, e.g. the Mediterranean. For instance, in works concerning the conception of FREEDOM/LIBERTY (Abramowicz and Karolak, 1991), HOMELAND (Bartmiński, 1993b) or FATE/FORTUNE (Arutyunova, 1994) in different languages and cultures, references are made to the 'source' Latin concepts of LIBERTAS, PATRIA, FATUM/ FORTUNA, which gave rise to the later concepts of *wolność, ojczyzna, dola/los* (Polish), *svoboda, rodina, sud'ba* (Russian) or *Freiheit, Vaterland* and *Schicksal* (German).

A similar procedure can be found in analyses of the concepts of HOME (Sawicka, 1997) or ANGER (Duszak and Pawlak, 2003) in a number of languages and cultures in the world, also beyond the Mediterranean sphere of influence. For many researchers, the 'source' concepts constitute an adequate common denominator and point of reference for comparative cross-linguistic analyses.

The other option, that of a universal semantic metalanguage, is represented by Anna Wierzbicka, who has been applying her Natural Semantic Metalanguage to cross-cultural semantics for many years (cf. Wierzbicka, 1992, 1996, 1997, 1999; Goddard and Wierzbicka, 2002). Wierzbicka proposes a methodologically very precise description of the semantics of SOUL, FATE, HUMILITY, COURAGE (1992) or FRIENDSHIP, FREEDOM and HOMELAND (1997) in several languages. She reveals semantic components common to many languages and those which are specific to a single language – and all that in connection with the history of specific nations. Wierzbicka usually attempts to show the untranslatable concepts peculiar to specific cultures, such as the Russian *duša, sud'ba, toska*, Japanese *amae, giri* and *enryo*, or Australian English *chiack, yarn* or *shout*.

Structural semantics has given rise to comparisons based on the conception of lexical-semantic fields, i.e. not only of single lexical items but sets of those. The hierarchical structure of lexis allows for an easy and natural transition from units at the basic level to those at the superordinate level: from the Russian *toska*, Polish *tęsknota* and German *Angst* to the field of emotions, from specific colours to the whole colour domain, from *podanie* 'legend', *kawał* 'joke' and *chiack* to the field of speech genres etc. In doing that one is able to establish conceptual superordinate categories of extensive semantic ranges. Thus, comparisons are performed between whole categories rather than merely between their individual components (cf. e.g. Grzegorczykowa and Waszakowa, 2000–2003; Dubisz, Porayski-Pomsta and Sękowska, 2004).

The structuralist semantic tradition also embraces comparative studies whose aim is to reveal superordinate semantic and semiotic oppositions between units of language. In Tolstoy's ethnolinguistic dictionary (*SD*, 1995–2004) these are: up-down, right-left, front-back, even-odd (number), human-animal etc. The theoretical foundation was laid by the semioticians of the Tartu school (their classic linguistic application is Ivanov and Toporov, 1965). The third volume of *SD* (1995–2004) contains seven such oppositions: covered-uncovered, new-old, male-female, young-old, beginning-end, first-last plus the general, overarching notion of 'semantic oppositions'. The use of the common semiotic background enables one to arrive at synthetic conclusions, relating to several languages and cultures, at a high level of generality.

Comparative analyses regardless of their starting point and the assumed TC may be based on minimal or maximal, comprehensive definitions; they may restrict the comparison to isolated units or take note of the 'values' they acquire through functioning in a broader semantic field. One can thus identify several types of comparative analyses, regardless of the basis and methods of comparison or the structure of the definitions (Table 17.1).

Table 17.1 Types of comparative analyses

The basis (Tc)	Type of description	Type of definition
LEXICAL ITEM	in isolation	minimal or maximal (cognitive)
	in the lexical-semantic field	minimal or maximal (cognitive)
OBJECT	in isolation	minimal or maximal (cognitive)
	in the lexical-semantic field	minimal or maximal (cognitive)
MEANING	in isolation	minimal or maximal (cognitive)
	in the lexical-semantic field	minimal or maximal (cognitive)

Any type of comparative analysis can fare well without the linguistic worldview conception but in fact all of them come together in that worldview. Let us notice that the term 'linguistic worldview' is composed of three elements, each referring to a different apex of the semiotic triangle: 'linguistic' evokes words (meaningful and referring to objects); 'view' evokes an image (concept or meaning), a subjective construct correlated with the word and the real-life object; 'world' evokes reality, if only virtual.

The linguistic worldview conception allows one to ask questions in a certain order: What do units of language tell us about the conceptualisation of reality performed by a given language community? What content is coded by the meanings of those units?

What are the criteria for linguistic categorisation of real-life objects and events? The most important question is: what social and cultural experiences are preserved in language, what kind of collective mentality does it express?

3   Linguistic worldview and comparative research

I now move on to a rather brief presentation of my second point, with which I would also like to close these divagations: comparative research should not be limited to related languages but should extend beyond the traditional comparative-historical paradigm. It should be practised as contrastive research, based on the notion of typology and *Sprachbund*. Such research may today have practical application and help in intercultural communication.

The accession of Poland and a few other Slavic states to the European Union has created a new political, social and cultural space, in which a new multinational communicative community is slowly emerging. The multilingualism of the EU is a difficult problem, not only practically or financially. The adoption of one common language (English) or, which is only a theoretical possibility, of the principle of equality of all national languages with the documents functioning in all of them in a parallel fashion, is only a partial solution. The problem lies in the different understandings and connotations of certain seemingly equivalent words, without which public discourse is impossible, such as the following English items and their counterparts in other tongues: *nation, people, society; nationalism, patriotism, chauvinism; freedom, independence, sovereignty, separatism; work, volunteer work, unemployment; progress, conservatism; tradition, heritage; home, homelessness; family, concubinage; sexism, feminism; loyalty, servility; tolerance, compromise, aggression* etc. The differences in their connotations in different languages may and already have led to misunderstandings. It is obvious that the words expressing these concepts in different languages contain, especially in the sphere of 'weak' connotations, many language-specific elements. The methodology of the linguistic worldview conception allows one to identify, reveal and describe those elements.

Which concepts should one investigate within the framework of the linguistic worldview enterprise? I address this question in Bartmiński (2001a) and propose a certain thematic scope of the endeavour. I propose to deal with at least six issues, in accordance with the basic model of linguistic communication: WHO is communicating, WITH WHOM, WHERE, WHEN, WHAT FOR and HOW? I postulate that the following be compared:

i)   the expression of collective identity – who are 'we' (self-stereotypes);
ii) the perception and linguistic construal of others – who are 'they' (heterostereotypes of one's neighbours);
iii) the conceptualisation of ones place, location in the world;
iv) the conceptualisation of the communal time in which we live;

v)   the values, declared and actually functioning, in 'our' social world
       (communal, social, national);
vi)   the means and types of expression, according to the criteria of style and genre.

I consider the most urgent task in comparative typological research to be the initiation of cross-cultural analyses of the terms of valuation, or perhaps more broadly: of the semantics of the sociopolitical and ethical lexis. Those who question the existence of a pan-European axiological canon may not be totally right, but discrepancies in the understanding of such concepts as DEMOCRACY, HUMAN RIGHTS, JUSTICE, SOVEREIGNTY, FREEDOM or HOMELAND are a fact of life. It is expedient that in this day and age the discrepancies be recognised.

A comparative axiological dictionary need not contain many entries but they should be culturally relevant.[3] In my opinion, the research must embrace the following issues:

i)   key political concepts, including many '-isms': FREEDOM/LIBERTY,
       INDEPENDENCE, DEMOCRACY, TOTALITARIANISM, LEFT
       AND RIGHT WING, SOCIALISM, COMMUNISM, REVOLUTION,
       INTERNATIONALISM, CAPITALISM, COSMOPOLITISM, GLOBALISM,
       TERRORISM, REGIONALISM, LOCALISM, SELF-GOVERNMENT,
       STATE, AUTHORITY, TRADE UNION, WORKERS' RIGHTS, RELIGION,
       THE CHURCH (CHURCHES), POLITICAL PARTY, EUROPE, AMERICA,
       THE WORLD, THE EAST, THE WEST;

ii)   social concepts: HOME, FAMILY, NATION, HOMELAND, 'LITTLE
       HOMELAND' (HEIMAT), PATRIOTISM, NATIONALISM,
       CHAUVINISM, EQUALITY, HONOUR, TOLERANCE, HOSPITALITY,
       SOCIETY, HUMANKIND;

iii) moral values, especially 'civic virtues': JUSTICE, BROTHERHOOD,
       SOLIDARITY, INTEGRITY, VALOUR, COURAGE, HEROISM,
       RESPONSIBILITY; plus the relevant 'anti-virtues': TREASON, HATRED,
       VENGEANCE;

iv)   personal virtues: DIGNITY, FIDELITY;

v)   general concepts: HUMAN BEING, HUMAN DIGNITY, HUMAN
       RIGHTS, LOVE, FRIENDSHIP, EDUCATION, KNOWLEDGE, BEAUTY,
       PROGRESS, WORK, DILIGENCE, CAREER, CONSCIENCE, FAITH
       (RELIGION);

vi)   concepts of knowledge and cognition: TRUTH and FALSEHOOD; plus the
       anti-values: EVIL, LIE.[4]

The total number of these entries is in excess of seventy.

What remains is the problem of the methodology of comparative studies, which must be coherent and compatible for one to be able to juxtapose, interpret and synthesise results. None of the methods should disregard the cognitive aspect, very much present in the linguistic worldview conception. I am not in a position now to propose methods better than those used in *SSSL* (1996–1999), which, admittedly, can only be applied with some limitations. But even with that proviso in mind, such research can contribute to a better coexistence of nations.

Notes

1 Cf. Serebrennikov et al. (1988'), Bartmiński (1990a), Ożdżyński (1995), Pajdzińska and Krzyżanowski (1999), Arutyunova (1999), Dąbrowska and Anusiewicz (2000), Jedliński (2000), Nikitina and Kukushkina (2000), Kajfosz (2001), Vaňková (2001), Nowak (2002), Piekarczyk (2004).

2 *SSSL* (1996–1999, vol. 1–2: 254–265) contains the fullest survey of texts, comprising fifty stereotypical motifs with the lexeme *dunaj* in various genres of Polish folklore (proverbs, speeches, carols, wedding, courtship and love songs, lullabies and ballads).

3 Research confirms that the axiological canon of national culture is not very broad and only contains about sixty units, but there are disagreements as to what units these are. For example, according to Walery Pisarek (2002: 16–17), the set of slogans which a contemporary Pole would be ready to display on banners ('Long live *x!*' vs. 'Down with *y!*') consists of fifty-four concepts, including twenty-five antonymous pairs (Christian values vs. abortion, anarchy vs. dictatorship, beauty vs. ugliness, freedom vs. censorship, the good of others vs. one's own, equality vs. elitism, family vs. erotic conquests, homeland vs. Europe, patriotism vs. globalism, faith vs. clericalism, integrity vs. corruption, right vs. left wing, solidarity vs. luxury, tolerance vs. lustration, tradition vs. modernity, nation vs. foreign capital, work vs. privatisation, care vs. entrepreneurship, security vs. reforms of the state, success vs. advertising, self-government vs. state, capitalism vs. socialism, consensus vs. struggle, truth vs. hypocrisy, love vs. jealousy) and four items outside the oppositions (justice, health, education and dignity).

Michael Fleischer, who compared German, Russian and Polish 'collective symbols', first hypothesised that they number about two hundred (108 positive and 103 negative ones) (Fleischer, 1995: 58–60), but then reduced the estimation to 50 (Fleischer, 1998: 325–326) or even 39. For Polish, the positive symbols are, in that order: love, family, home, freedom, friendship, God, child, integrity, sun, truth, justice, fidelity, tolerance, culture, honour, Pope, patriotism, faith, homelessness, work, tradition, nation, money, democracy, state, Church, pluralism, ideology, police, right wing; the negative ones are: war, boorishness, totalitarianism, unemployment, intolerance, egoism, communism, politics, left wing (Fleischer, 2003: 117–118).

Ryszard Jedliński, who conducted research on the values of primary school graduates from 1994/1995, confirmed Fleischer's findings. In the light of his research, the values most readily accepted by young people include: family, love, God, health, friendship, life, work, integrity, justice, freedom, wisdom, frankness, responsibility, honour, truth, good, money, knowledge, tolerance and faith (Jedliński, 2000: 82).

4 The list of political and social concepts of the East and Central European countries presented by a group of scholars from Warsaw originally consisted of 101 elements and was later enlarged to 156 (Dubisz, Porayski-Pomsta and Sękowska, 2004).

Afterword

The approach to ethnolinguistics presented in this book amounts to what I hope can be considered an integral theory of language, with the human speaking subject (*homo loquens*) at the centre. Because the basic communicative function of language is strongly linked to its cognitive function, i.e. the perception and conceptualisation of reality along with an underlying system of values, the efficiency of communication largely depends on the compatibility of the values and worldviews that are entrenched in language and thus readily available to the speaker. This does not mean, however, that the speaker cannot overcome the pressure of language; indeed, through language we are able to actually *create* situations. But the relationship between language, the speaking subject and reality is a broader issue; in the present context, suffice it to say that certain obvious mental barriers exist in intercultural communication which result from the semantics of seemingly 'the same', international, transnational or pan-European concepts, such as *justice, equality, democracy* and their non-English 'equivalents'. But Eastern and Western Europe are very different (Davies, 2006). These differences infiltrate the consciousness of Central European nations, which lie 'between' East and West also in the mental sense and which seek new ways of coexistence and communication in the international community not only within the European Union but also in a wider, global context. Linguists face important tasks of describing these discrepancies and diagnosing the sources of misunderstandings, as well as identifying common denominators. Ethnolinguistics, especially in its cognitivist version with the conceptual apparatus discussed in the first part of this book, has much to offer in this respect.

Let me underline again at this point that all the crucial ideas discussed in this book – i.e. the linguistic worldview, stereotypes as colloquial images, the reconstruction of stereotypes by means of the cognitive definition, or the profiling of base images in discourse relative to a viewpoint and a system of values – relate to the subject as the prime experiencing, conceptualising and coding authority. Having been marginalised by structural linguistics, the subject – especially the individual but also the collective – is appreciated by cognitive ethnolinguistics. The individual subject is experienced empirically, the collective subject is a secondary conceptual construct, which is derived from the former, but which is also important for its role in establishing national identities. The analyses of selected concepts in the second part of this book (the sun, the mother, house/home, the political right and left, the varieties of fate or the national stereotype of a German) are illustrations of how theoretical assumptions can be applied in analytical practice. The last chapter discusses the perspectives of this type of research on a broader, comparative scale.

One can hope for a continuation of the ethnolinguistic endeavour in a formalised manner thanks to a number of events, some of which took place when the work on this book was in progress.

First, in the year 2000 research on linguistic worldviews was included into an international comparative research programme on Slavic languages, conducted partly under the supervision of Stanisław Gajda (University of Opole). After volumes on word formation, phonetics and phraseology, a similar publication is now planned on the worldviews of the Slavic peoples.

Second, research on the linguistic worldviews of Slavs and their neighbours has been undertaken by two ethnolinguistic teams: one within the Committee for Linguistics of the Polish Academy of Sciences, the other within the International Slavic Committee. This research includes the axiological aspect (the semantics of value terms), linguistic stereotypes (especially national self- and heterostereotypes) or the conceptualisation of space and time (cf. Niebrzegowska-Bartmińska, 2003, and Szadura, 2004, for reports).

Third, interest in comparative research on linguistic worldviews was openly voiced during the International Slavic Congress in Ohrid, Macedonia, September 10–16, 2008. Aleksandr Moldovan, head of the Institute of Slavic Studies within the Russian Academy of Sciences, said in his opening address that 'ethnolinguistics is a continuation of the former tradition of global approaches to Slavic languages, folk cultures and social and national life, with a view to reconstructing the relevant cultural content' (Moldovan, 2008: 9). It also responds to a wider need of developing a culture-oriented philology. Relating to the work of Nikita Tolstoy, Svetlana Tolstoy, Nina Arutyunova, Yuriy Apresjan or Yuriy Stepanov, he underscored the importance of research on 'cultural codes', of explicating 'cultural concepts', and of inquiring into the nature of words and texts from the perspective of the 'underlying categories of worldview and cognition, such as time, space, the human being, boundary/border, freedom, shortage, gender differences, eroticism, or the oppositions: centre–periphery, good–evil, us–them, sacred–profane, life–death' (Moldovan, 2008: 34–35). It is in this context that the speaker located the problem of the 'folk' or 'naive' linguistic worldview.

At the same event, the session 'Linguistic and cultural worldviews of Slavs in an ethnolinguistic perspective' featured a record number of participants, many of whom expressed their interest to participate in future joint projects. One of these projects, called EUROJOS ('European Linguistic Worldview(s)') will be coordinated by the Institute of Slavic Studies of the Polish Academy of Sciences in Warsaw. With sound and systematically applied methodology, its findings can shed extremely valuable light on how Europeans conceptualise and talk about the world.

References

Abramowicz, M. and Bartmiński, J. (1998) 'Peuple' et 'lud' – deux notions, deux paradigmes socio-cultureles. In D. Bartol-Jarosińska (ed.) *Langues et peuples d'Europe Centrale et Orientale dans la culture francaise*. 15–26. Paris: Institut d'études slaves.

Abramowicz, M. and Karolak, I. (1991) 'Wolność' i 'liberté' w języku polskim i francuskim. In. J. Puzynina and J. Anusiewicz (eds) *Język a kultura*, vol. 3. *Wartości w języku i tekście*. 51–59. Wrocław: Wiedza o kulturze.

Adamowski, J. (1999) *Kategoria przestrzeni w folklorze. Studium etnolingwistyczne.* Lublin: UMCS.

Adamowski, J. and Żuraw, G. (1979) Tradycyjne nazewnictwo gatunkowe folkloru wierszowanego. *Literatura ludowa* XXIII, 4–6: 25–33.

Ajdukiewicz, K. (1934/1985) Obraz świata i aparatura pojęciowa. In K. Ajdukiewicz, *Język i poznanie*, vol. 1. 175–195. Warszawa: PWN.

Ajdukiewicz, K. (1965) *Logika pragmatyczna.* Warszawa: PWN.

Anusiewicz, J. (1990) Problematyka językowego obrazu świata w poglądach niektórych językoznawców i filozofów niemieckich XX wieku. In J. Bartmiński (red.) *Językowy obraz świata.* 277–307. Lublin: UMCS.

Anusiewicz, J. (1995) *Lingwistyka kulturowa. Zarys problematyki.* Wrocław: Wydawnictwo Uniwersytetu Wrocławskiego.

Apresyan, Y. D. (1992) *Lexical Semantics. A Guide to Russian Vocabulary.* Ann Arbor: Karoma Publishers.

Apresyan, Y. D. (1994) Naiwny obraz świata. *Etnolingwistyka* 6: 5–12.

Apresyan, Y. D. (1995) *Izbrannye trudy. Vol 2: Intergral'noye opisaniye yazyka i sistemnaya leksikografiya.* Moskva: Yazyki russkoy kul'tury.

Arutyunova, N. D. (ed.) (1994) *Ponyatiye sud'by v kontekste raznykh kul'tur.* Moskva: Izdatel'stvo Nauka.

Arutyunova, N. D. (ed.) (1999) *Obraz cheloveka v kul'ture i yazyke.* Moskva: Indrik.

Austin, J. L. (1962) *How to Do Things with Words. The William James Lectures delivered at Harvard University in 1955.* Ed. J. O. Umson. Oxford: Clarendon.

Awdiejew, A. (2004) Kategoria obserwatora jako kategoria gramatyczna. In J. Bartmiński, S. Niebrzegowska-Bartmińska and R. Nycz (eds) *Punkt widzenia w języku i w kulturze.* 103–112. Lublin: UMCS.

Awdiejew, A. and Habrajska, G. 2004. *Wprowadzenie do gramatyki komunikacyjnej,* vols. 1–2. Łańsk: Oficyna Wydawnicza Leksem.

Bakhtin, M. (1979) Towards the Aesthetics of the Word. *Dispositio* 4 (11–12): 299–315.

Bakhtin, M. (1984) *Problems of Dostoyevsky's Poetics.* Trans. C. Emerson. Minneapolis: University of Minnesota Press.

Bakhtin, M. (1986) *Speech Genres and Other Late Essays.* Trans. V. W. McGee. Ed. C. Emerson and M. Holquist. Austin: University of Texas Press.

Bartmiński, J. (1973) *O języku folkloru.* Wrocław: Zakład Narodowy im. Ossolińskich.

Bartmiński, J. (ed.) (1980) *Słownik ludowych stereotypów językowych. Zeszyt próbny*. Wrocław: Wydawnictwo Uniwersytetu Wrocławskiego.

Bartmiński, J. (1981) Derywacja stylu. In J. Bartmiński (ed.) *Pojęcie derywacji w lingwistyce*. 31–54. Lublin: UMCS.

Bartmiński, J. (1984) Definicja leksykograficzna a opis języka. In K. Polański (ed.) *Słownictwo w opisie języka*. 9–19. Katowice: Uniwersytet Śląski.

Bartmiński, J. (1986) Czym zajmuje się etnolingwistyka? *Akcent* 26: 16–22.

Bartmiński, J. (1987) Ojczyzna. Projekt fragmentu hasła do słownika aksjologicznego. In A. Bogusławski, M. K. Byrski and Z. Lewicki (eds) *Co badania filologiczne mówią o wartości? Materiały z sesji naukowej 17–21 listopada 1986*. vol. 2. 133–182. Warszawa: Uniwersytet Warszawski.

Bartmiński, J. (1988a) Definicja kognitywna jako narzędzie opisu konotacji. In J. Bartmiński (ed.) *Konotacja* 169–183. Lublin: UMCS.

Bartmiński, J. (1988b) Kryteria ilościowe w badaniu stereotypów językowych. *BPTJ* XLI–2: 91–104.

Bartmiński, J. (1988c) Założenia teoretyczne słownika ludowych stereotypów językowych. *Etnolingwistyka* 1: 11–34.

Bartmiński, J. (1989a) Językowe sposoby porządkowania świata. Uwagi na marginesie biłgorajskich relacji o kosmosie. *Etnolingwistyka* 2: 49–58.

Bartmiński, J. (1989b) Kolekcja w strukturze tematycznej tekstu ustnego. La collection dans la structure thématique du texte oral. In M. Abramowicz and J. Bartmiński (eds) *Tekst ustny – texte oral. Materiały z międzynarodowej konferencji w UMCS w Lublinie, 15–17 września 1986*. 77–102. Wrocław: Wiedza o kulturze.

Bartmiński, J. (1989c) Projekt i założenia ogólne słownika aksjologicznego. In J. Puzynina and J. Bartmiński (eds) *Język a kultura*. Vol. 2. 293–312. Wrocław: Wiedza o kulturze.

Bartmiński, J. (ed.) (1990a) *Językowy obraz świata*. 109–127. 2nd ed. 1999, 3rd ed. 2004. Lublin: UMCS.

Bartmiński, J. (1990b) Ojczyzna w pieśniach i wierszach chłopskich. *Polska Sztuka Ludowa* 3: 9–13.

Bartmiński, J. (1990c) Punkt widzenia, perspektywa, językowy obraz świata. In J. Bartmiński (ed.) *Językowy obraz świata*. 109–127. Lublin: UMCS.

Bartmiński, J. (1991a) Miejsce hiperonimu w definicji leksykograficznej. In M. Grochowski and D. Weiss (eds) *Words Are Physicians for an Ailing Mind. Festschrift zu Ehren von Profesor Bogusławski*. 45–50. Sangers Slavistische Sammlung, 17. München.

Bartmiński, J. (1991b) Odmiany a style językowe. In S. Gajda (ed.) *Wariancja w języku. III Opolskie Spotkania Językoznawcze, Szczedrzyk 10–11. 10. 1989 r.* 11–16. Opole: WSP.

Bartmiński, J. (1991c) 'Prawica' – 'lewica'. Sposoby profilowania pojęć. *Poradnik Językowy* 5–6: 160–166.

Bartmiński, J. (1991d) Styl potoczny jako centrum systemu stylowego języka. In S. Gajda (ed.) *Synteza w stylistyce słowiańskiej* 33–48. Opole: WSP.

Bartmiński, J. (1993a) O profilowaniu pojęć w słowniku etnolingwistycznym. *Philologia Slavica K 70 letiyu akademika N. I. Tolstogo.* 12–17. Moskva: Nauka.

Bartmiński, J. (ed.) (1993b) *Pojęcie ojczyzny we współczesnych językach europejskich.* Lublin: Instytut Europy Środkowo–Wschodniej.

Bartmiński, J. (1994) Jak zmienia się stereotyp Niemca w Polsce. *Przegląd Humanistyczny* 5: 81–101.

Bartmiński, J. (1995) Nasi sąsiedzi w oczach studentów. In T. Walas (ed.) *Narody i stereotypy* 258–269. Kraków: MCK.

Bartmiński, J. (1997) Etnotsentrism stereotipa. Pol'skiye i nemetskiye studenty o svoikh sosedakh. *Slavyanovedeniye* 1: 12–24. Moskva.

Bartmiński, J. (2000) Izmeneniya yazykovoy kartiny mira polyakov. In: L. N. Zybatov (ed.) *Sprachwandel in der Slavia. Die slavischen Sprachen an der Schwelle zum 21. Jahrhundert. Ein internationales Handbuch.* Teil 1. 481–492. Frankfurt am Main: Peter Lang.

Bartmiński, J. (2001a) O językowym obrazie świata Polaków końca XX w. In. S Dubisz and S. Gajda (eds) *Polszczyzna końca XX w. Ewolucja i perspektywy rozwoju.* 27–53. Warszawa: Dom Wydawniczy „Elipsa".

Bartmiński, J. (ed.) (2001b) *Współczesny język polski.* 2nd ed. Lublin: UMCS.

Bartmiński, J. (ed.) (2003) *Język w kręgu wartości.* Lublin: UMCS.

Bartmiński, J. (2004a) Etnolingwistyka słowiańska – próba bilansu. *Etnolingwistyka* 16: 9–27.

Bartmiński, J. (2004b) Lublin ethnolinguistics. In I. Bajenowa (ed.) *Schools of Polish Language Studies in the 20th century.* 41–61. Warsaw: Wydawnictwa Uniwersytetu Warszawskiego.

Bartmiński, J. (ed.) (2006a) *Język – wartości – polityka. Zmiany rozumienia nazw wartości w okresie transformacji ustrojowej w Polsce. Raport z badań empirycznych.* Lublin: UMCS.

Bartmiński, J. (2006b) *Językowe podstawy obrazu świata.* Lublin: UMCS.

Bartmiński, J. (2007a) East–West: On the symmetry of senses and cultural differentiation of profiles. In W. Chłopicki, A. Pawelec and A. Pokojska (eds) *Cognition in Language: Volume in Honour of Professor Elżbieta Tabakowska.* Kraków: Tertium.

Bartmiński, J. (2007b) Opozycja *swój / obcy* a problem językowego obrazu świata. *Etnolingwistyka* 19: 35–59.

Bartmiński, J. (2007c) *Stereotypy mieszkają w języku.* Lublin: UMCS.

Bartmiński, J. and Mazurkiewicz-Brzozowska, M. (1993a) Lud. Profile pojęcia ich konteksty kulturowe. In J. Bartmiński and M. Mazurkiewicz-Brzozowska (eds) *Nazwy wartości. Studia leksykalno-semantyczne.* 213–230. Lublin: UMCS.

Bartmiński, J. and Mazurkiewicz-Brzozowska, M. (eds) (1993b) *Nazwy wartości. Studia leksykalno-semantyczne.* Lublin: UMCS.

Bartmiński, J. and Niebrzegowska, S. (1994) Stereotyp słońca w polszczyźnie ludowej. *Etnolingwistyka* 6: 95–145.

Bartmiński, J. and Niebrzegowska, S. (1998) Profile a podmiotowa interpretacja świata. In J. Bartmiński and R. Tokarski (eds) *Profilowanie w języku i w tekście.* 211–225. Lublin: UMCS.

Bartmiński, J., Niebrzegowska-Bartmińska, S. and Nycz, R. (eds) (2004a) *Punkt widzenia w języku i kulturze*. Lublin: UMCS.

Bartmiński, J., Niebrzegowska-Bartmińska, S. and Nycz, R. (eds) (2004b) *Punkt widzenia w tekście i w dyskursie*. Lublin: UMCS.

Bartmiński, J. and Pajdzińska, A. (2008) *Podmiot w języku i kulturze*. Lublin: UMCS.

Bartmiński J. and Tokarski, R. (1986) Językowy obraz świata a spójność tekstu. In Dobrzyńska, T. (ed.) *Teoria tekstu. Zbiór studiów*. 65–81. Wrocław: Zakład Narodowy im. Ossolińskich.

Bartmiński, J and Tokarski, R. (1993) Definicja semantyczna: czego i dla kogo? In J. Bartmiński and R. Tokarski (eds) *O definicjach i definiowaniu*. 47–61. Lublin: UMCS.

Bartmiński, J and Żuk, G. (2007) Polnisch *równość* 'Gleichheit' im semantischen Netz. Kognitive Definition der *równość* 'Gleichheit' im Polnischen. In B. Bock and R. Lühr (eds) *Normen- und Wertbegriffe in der Verständigung zwischen Ost- und Westeuropa*. 33–68. Frankfurt am Main: Peter Lang.

Bartoszyński, K. (1971) Zagadnienie komunikacji literackiej w utworach narracyjnych. In J. Sławiński (ed.) *Problemy socjologii literatury*. 127–148. Wrocław: Zakład Narodowy im. Ossolińskich.

Bayburin, A. (1983) *Zhylishche v obryadakh i predstavleniyakh vostochnykh slavyan*. Leningrad: Nauka.

Bednarek, A. (1996) Zdrada – ucieczką ze świata wartości. Rozważania semantyczne. In K. Kallas (ed.) *Polonistyka toruńska uniwersytetowi w 50. rocznicę utworzenia UMK*. 125–134. Toruń: Wydawnictwo UMK.

Benedyktowicz, Z. (1988) Stereotyp – obraz – symbol. O możliwościach nowego spojrzenia na stereotyp. *Zeszyty Naukowe UJ, Prace Etnograficzne* 24: 7–35.

Berting, J. and Villain-Gandossi, Ch. (1995) The role and significance of national stereotypes in international relations: An interdisciplinary approach. In: T. Walas (ed.) *Stereotypes and nations*. 13–27. Cracow: International Cultural Centre.

Bierwisch, M. (1969) Strukturelle Semantik. *Deutsch als Fremdsprache* 6–2: 66–71.

Bock, P. K. (2003) World view and language. In *International Encyclopedia of Linguistics*. Ed. W. J. Frawley. Oxford: Oxford University Press.

Bogucka, T. (1990) Przeciętny obywatel. *Gazeta Wyborcza* 127.

Bogusławski, A. (1988) Opinia o *Zeszycie próbnym Słownika ludowych stereotypów językowych, Wrocław 1980*. *Etnolingwistyka* 1: 14–15.

Bogusławski, A. (1994) Problem *tertium comparationis* w porównaniu lingwistycznym. In A. Bogusławski (ed.) *Sprawy słowa. Word Matters*. Warszawa: Veda. [first published in 1976, *Kwartalnik Neofilologiczny* XXIII–3: 295–303.]

Boryś, W. (2005) *Słownik etymologiczny języka polskiego*. Kraków: Wydawnictwo Literackie.

Buber, M. (1970) *I and Thou*. Translated by Walter Kaufmann. Edinburgh: T. & T. Clark. [Orig. (1923) *Ich und Du*. Leipzig: Insel-Verlag.]

Bühler, K. (1934) *Sprachtheorie. Die Darstellungsfunktion der Sprache*. Stuttgart: Verlagsgesellschaft.

Busse, D. (1992) *Textinterpretation. Sprachtheoretische Grundlagen einer explikativen Semantik*. Opladen: Westdeutscher Verlag.

Bußmann, H. (1990) *Lexicon der Sprachwissenschaft*. 2nd ed. Stuttgart: Alfred Kröner Verlag.

Być, M. (1993) Językowy stereotyp domu i rodziny w języku polskim. M.A. thesis, Maria Curie-Skłodowska University, Lublin, Poland.

Bystroń, J. S. (1924) *Megalomanja narodowa. Źródła, teorje, skutki*. Warszawa: Gebethner i Wolff.

Bystroń, J. S. (1980 [1924]) Niemcy w tradycji popularnej. In J. Bystroń *Tematy, które mi odradzano. Pisma etnograficzne rozproszone*. Ed. Ludwik Stomma. 335–354. Warszawa: LSW. [Orig. in *Megalomanja narodowa. Źródła, teorje, skutki*. Warszawa: Gebethner i Wolff.]

Canisius, P. (ed.) (1987) *Perspektivität in Sprache und Text*. Bochum: Brockmeyer-Verlag.

Chałasiński, J. (1935) *Antagonizm polsko-niemiecki w osadzie fabrycznej 'Kopalnia' na Górnym Śląsku. Studium socjologiczne*. Warszawa: Dom Książki Polskiej.

Charbonnier, G. (1961) *Entretiens avec Claude Lévi-Strauss*. Paris: Plon/Julliard.

Chlebda, W. (1993) Słownik a „dwuoczne' postrzeganie świata. In J. Bartmiński and R. Tokarski (eds) *O definicjach i definiowaniu*. 195–205. Lublin: UMCS.

Chlebda, W. (2000) Płaszczyzny oglądu językowego obrazu świata w opisie semantycznym języka. In: S. Gajda (ed.) *Komparacja systemów i funkcjonowania współczesnych języków słowiańskich*. 163–178. Opole: Wydawnictwo Uniwersytetu Opolskiego.

Chlebda, W. (2002) Polak przed mentalną mapą świata. *Etnolingwistyka* 14: 9–26.

Chlebda, W. (2005) *Szkice o skrzydlatych słowach. Interpretacje lingwistyczne*. Opole: Wydawnictwo Uniwersytetu Opolskiego.

Coşeriu, E. (1975) *Sprachtheorie und allgemeine Sprachwissenschaft*. München: W. Fink Verlag.

Coşeriu, E. (1988) *Einführung in die Allgemeine Sprachwissenschaft*. Tübingen: Francke Verlag.

Crystal, D. (1997) *The Cambridge Encyclopedia of Language*. Cambridge: Cambridge University Press.

Cywiński, B. (1986) Od redaktora. *Widnokrąg* 1.

Czarnocka, M. 1990. Stereotypy językowe Rosjanina, Francuza i Amerykanina w języku polskim. M.A. thesis. Department of Polish. Maria Curie-Skłodowska University, Lublin, Poland.

Czerny, A. I. (1981) *Teoria wyszukiwania informacji*. Warszawa: PWN. [Russian original published in 1975]

Danielewiczowa, M. (2004) Krzyżowanie się punktów widzenia jako kategoria organizująca znaczenie leksykalne (na przykładzie czasowników epistemicznych). In J. Bartmiński, S. Niebrzegowska-Bartmińska and R. Nycz (eds) *Punkt widzenia w języku i w kulturze*. 185–196. Lublin: UMCS.

Davies, N. (2006) *Europe East and West*. London: Jonathan Cape.

Dąbrowska, A. and Anusiewicz, J. (eds) (2000) *Językowy obraz świata i kultura. Język a Kultura* vol. 13. Wrocław: Wydawnictwo Uniwersytetu Wrocławskiego.

Dey, O. (1978) *Kompozytsiyni pryntsypy ta zasoby pismennosti skhidnykh i zakhidnykh slovyan*. Kyiv: Naukowa dumka.

Demidov, V. V. (1986) *How we see what we see*. Trans. from Russian by A. Repyev. Moscow: Mir Publishers.

Der Spiegel. 1991. *Furcht, Neid und Respekt. Umfrage in Polen und Deutschland über die Einstellung der beiden Völker zueinander,* 26. 48–57.

Doroszewski, W. (1982) *Język, myślenie, działanie: rozważania językoznawcy.* Warszawa: PWN.

Dubisz, S., Porayski-Pomsta, J., Sękowska, E. (red.) (2004) *Język – polityka – społeczeństwo. Słownik pojęć politycznych i społecznych krajów Europy Środkowej i Wschodniej.* Warszawa: Elipsa.

Dukova, U. (1992) Mitologiczna opozycja 'prawy' i 'lewy' w bułgarskich dialektach. *Etnolingwistyka* 5: 31–52.

Duszak, A., Pawlak, N. (eds) (2003) *Anatomia gniewu. Emocje negatywne w językach i kulturach świata.* Warszawa: Wydawnictwa Uniwersytetu Warszawskiego.

EJO (1999) *Encyklopedia językoznawstwa ogólnego.* Ed. K. Polański. Wrocław: Zakład Narodowy im. Ossolińskich.

EJP (1999) *Encyklopedia języka polskiego.* Ed. S. Urbańczyk and M. Kucała. 3rd ed. Wrocław: Zakład Narodowy im. Ossolińskich.

Elm, Th. (1997) O brakach historii i pożytkach z literatury. Ucieczka i wypędzenie jako problem przedstawienia. In H. Orłowski and A. Sakson (eds) *Utracona ojczyzna. Przymusowe wysiedlenia, deportacje i przesiedlenia jako wspólne doświadczenie.* 209–224. Poznań: Instytut Zachodni.

ESSD (1984) *Etnolingvisticheskiy slovar' slavyanskikh drevnostey.* Ed. N. I. Tolstoy. Moskva: Akademiya Nauk SSSR.

Evans, V, Bergen, B, Zinken, J. (2007) The cognitive linguistic enterprise: An overview. In: Evans, V, Bergen, B, Zinken, J. (eds) *The Cognitive Linguistics Reader.* 2–36. London and Oakville, CT: Equinox.

Filipiak, M. (1993) *Biblia jako tekst religijny i kulturowy.* Lublin: UMCS.

Fleischer, M. (1995) *Das System der polnischen Kollektivsymbolik (Eine empirische Untersuchung).* München: Verlag Otto Sagner.

Fleischer, M. (1998) Współczesna polska symbolika kolektywna (wyniki badań empirycznych). *Język a kultura* 12, 308–339.

Fleischer, M. (2002) *Teoria kultury i komunikacji.* Wrocław: Dolnośląska Szkoła Wyższa Edukacji Towarzystwa Wiedzy Powszechnej.

Fleischer, M. (2003) Stabilność polskiej symboliki kolektywnej. In: J. Bartmiński (ed.) *Język w kręgu wartości. Studia semantyczne.* 107–143. Lublin: UMCS.

Frank, R. M., Dirven, R., Ziemke, T., and Bernárdez, E. (eds) (2008) *Body, Language and Mind. Vol. 2: Sociocultural situatedness.* Berlin: Mouton de Gruyter.

Friedman, N. (1971) Punkt widzenia w powieści. *Przegląd Humanistyczny* 3: 109–130.

Gajda, S. (ed.) (2000) *Komparacja systemów i funkcjonowania współczesnych języków słowiańskich.* Opole: Wydawnictwo Uniwersytetu Opolskiego.

Gajda, S. (2001) Styl naukowy. In J. Bartmiński (ed.) *Współczesny język polski.* 2nd ed. 183–199. Lublin: UMCS.

Gasek, A. (1990) Stereotypy językowe Żyda, Niemca i Polaka w języku polskim. M.A. thesis. Department of Polish. Maria Curie-Skłodowska University, Lublin, Poland.

Genette, G. (1972) Discours du récit: essai de méthode. *Figures III.* 65–282. Paris: Seuil.

Głaz, A. (2004) Wielość punktów widzenia – następstwo czy równoczesność? In J. Bartmiński, S. Niebrzegowska-Bartmińska and R. Nycz (eds) *Punkt widzenia w tekście i w dyskursie.* 73–85. Lublin: UMCS.

Głowiński, M. (1986) Wartościowanie w badaniach literackich a język potoczny. In S. Sawicki, W. Panas (eds) *O wartościowaniu w badaniach literackich.* 179–195. Lublin: TN KUL.

Głowiński, M. (1990) Marcowe gadanie. *Tygodnik Powszechny* 33.

Goddard, C., Wierzbicka, A. (eds) (2002) *Meaning and Universal Grammar.* 2 vols. Amsterdam/Philadelphia: John Benajmins.

Godlewski, G., Mencwel, A and Sulima, R. (eds) (2003) *Antropologia słowa. Zagadnienia i wybór tekstów.* Warszawa: Wydawnictwo Uniwersytetu Warszawskiego.

Goodenough, W. (1964) Cultural anthropology and linguistics. In D. Hymes (ed.) *Language in Culture and Society.* New York: Harper & Row. 36–39.

Gostkowski, Z. (1959) Teoria stereotypu i poglądy na opinię publiczną Waltera Lippmanna. *Archiwum Historii Filozofii i Myśli Społecznej,* vol. V. 39–84.

Grochowski, M. (1993) *Konwencje semantyczne a definiowanie wyrażeń językowych.* Warszawa: Zakład Semiotyki Logicznej Uniwersytetu Warszawskiego.

Grochowski, M. (1995) *Słownik polskich przekleństw i wulgaryzmów.* Warszawa: PWN.

Gruszczyński, P. (1992) Szkolne wyobrażenia. *Res Publica* VI, 1–2: 11–17.

Grzegorczykowa, R. (1990) Pojęcie językowego obrazu świata. In J.Bartmiński (ed.) *Językowy obraz świata.* 41–49. Lublin: UMCS.

Grzegorczykowa, R. (2001) *Wprowadzenie do semantyki językoznawczej.* 3rd ed. Warszawa: PWN.

Grzegorczykowa, R. (2004) Punkt widzenia nadawcy w znaczeniach leksemów. In J. Bartmiński, S. Niebrzegowska-Bartmińska and R. Nycz (eds) *Punkt widzenia w języku i w kulturze.* 161–176. Lublin: UMCS.

Grzegorczykowa, R. and Szymanek, B. (2001) Kategorie słowotwórcze w perspektywie kognitywnej. In J. Bartmiński (ed.) *Współczesny język polski.* 469–467. Lublin: UMCS.

Grzegorczykowa, R. and Waszakowa, K. (eds) (2000–2003) *Studia z semantyki porównawczej. Nazwy barw, nazwy wymiarów, predykaty mentalne.* Vols. 1–3. Warszawa: Wydawnictwa Uniwersytetu Warszawskiego.

Gudavičius, A. (2000) *Etnolingvistika.* Šiauliai: Šiaulių universitetas.

Gusev, V. E. (1967) *Estetika fol'klora.* Leningrad: Nauka.

Habrajska, G. (2004) Kategoria obserwatora w komunikacyjnej analizie i interpretacji dyskursu. In J. Bartmiński, S. Niebrzegowska-Bartmińska and R. Nycz (eds) *Punkt widzenia w języku i w kulturze.* 113–128. Lublin: UMCS.

Halliday, M.A.K. (2004) *An Introduction to Functional Grammar*. 3rd ed. London: Edward Arnold.

Harris, R. (1990) The integrationist critique of orthodox linguistics. In M. P. Jordan (ed.) *The Sixteenth LACUS Forum 1989*. Lake Bluff, Ill.: LACUS.

Haugen, E. (1972) *The Ecology of Language. Essays by Einar Haugen, selected and introduced by Anwar S. Dil*. Stanford: Stanford University Press.

Helbig, G. (1986) *Entwicklung der Sprachwissenschaft seit 1970*. Leipzig: UMCS.

Herder. L. (1986) *The Herder Symbol Dictionary: Symbols from Art, Archeology, Mythology, Literature, and Religion*. Wilmette, IL: Chiron Publications.

Hernas, Cz. (1973) Ład życia w wierszach Rozalii i Wojciecha Grzegorczyków. *Literatura Ludowa* 1: 3–13.

Hjelmslev, L. 1943. *Prolegomena to a Theory of Language*. Madison: University of Wisconsin.

Humboldt, W. von. (1836) *Über die Verschiedenheit des menschlichen Sprachbaues und ihren Einfluß auf die geistige Entwickelung des Menschengeschlechts*. Berlin: F. Dümmler.

Hymes, D. (1968) The Ethnography of Speaking. In J. A. Fishman (ed.) *Readings in the Sociology of Language*. The Hague and Paris: Mouton. 99–138.

IEL (1992) *International Encyclopedia of Linguistics*. Ed. W. Bright. New York: Oxford University Press).

Iordanskaya, L. N. and Mel'chuk, I. A. (1980) Konnotatsiya v lingvisticheskoy semantike. Wiener Slavistischer Almanach, Bd. 6: 191–210.

ISJP (2000) *Inny słownik języka polskiego*. Ed. M. Bańko. Warszawa: PWN.

Ivanov, V. V. (1977) Rola semiotyki w cybernetycznym badaniu człowieka i społeczności. Transl. from Russian by O. Główko. In E. Janus and M. R. Mayenowa *Semiotyka kultury*. 75–90. Warszawa: PIW. [Orig. 1965. Rol' semiotiki v kiberneticheskom issledovanii cheloveka. In *Logicheskaya struktura nauchnogo poznaniya*. Moskva: Nauka.]

Ivanov, V. V. and Gamkrelidze, T. V. (1984) *Indoevropeyskiy yazyk i indoevropeytsy. Rekonstruktsiya i istoriko-tipologicheskiy analiz yazyka i protokul'tury*. Vol. 1–II. Tbilisi: : Izdatel'stvo Tbilisskogo Universiteta.

Ivanov, V. V. and Toporov, V. N. (1965) *Slavyanskiye yazykovye modeliruyushchiye semioticheskiye sistemy*. Moskva: Nauka.

Ivanov, V. V. and Toporov V. N. (1987) Dolya. In: Tokarev, S. A. (ed.) *Mify narodov mira. Entsiklopediya*. 391. Moskva: Sovetskaya entsiklopediya.

Jackendoff, R. (1983) *Semantics and Cognition*. Cambridge, Mass.: MIT Press.

Jacobs, N. J. (1958) *Naming-Day in Eden: The Creation and Recreation of Language*. New York: Macmillan.

Jakobson, R. (1966) *Selected Writings*. Vol. IV. The Hague: Mouton.

James, H. (1934) *The Art of the Novel. Critical Prefaces*. New York and London: Charles Scribner's Sons.

Jasińska-Kania, A. (1991) Transformacja ustrojowa a zmiany postawy Polaków wobec różnych narodów i państw. *Kultura i Społeczeństwo* XXXV, 4: 153–166.

Jay, M. (1996) Vision in context: Reflections and refractions. In T. Brennan and M. Jay (eds) *Vision in Context. Historical and Contemporary Perspectives on Sight.* 1–11. New York and London: Routledge.

Jażdżewski, B. (1992) *Wspomnienia kaszubskiego gbura.* Gdańsk: Instytut Kaszubski.

Jedliński, R. (2000) *Językowy obraz świata wartości w wypowiedziach uczniów kończących szkołę podstawową.* Kraków: Wydawnictwo Naukowe Akademii Pedagogicznej.

Jespersen, O. (1924) *The Philosophy of Grammar.* London: George Allen & Unwin.

Jodłowski, S. (1971) *Studia nad częściami mowy.* Warszawa: PWN.

Jodłowski, S. (2003) Kryteria klasyfikacji wyrazów na części mowy. In J. Bartmiński and M. Nowosad-Bakalarczyk (eds) *Współczesna polszczyzna – wybór opracowań.* Vol. 6. *Części mowy.* 9–34. Lublin: UMCS. [Originally published in Jodłowski, S. (1971) *Studia nad częściami mowy.* 7–49. Warszawa: PWN.]

Kajfosz, J. (2001). *Językowy obraz świata w etnokulturze Śląska Cieszyńskiego.* Czeski Cieszyn: Proprint.

Kamińska-Szmaj, I. (2001) *Słowa na wolności.* Wrocław: Wydawnictwo Europa.

Kapiszewski, A. (1978) *Stereotyp Amerykanów polskiego pochodzenia.* Warszawa: PWN.

Kardela, H. (1990) Ogdena i Richardsa trójkąt uzupełniony, czyli co bada gramatyka kognitywna. In. J. Bartmiński (ed.) *Językowy obraz świata.* 15–40. Lublin: UMCS.

Kardela, H. and Kardela, A. (2000) Subjectivity in Elizabeth Bowen's short stories. A cognitive linguistic approach. In S.-J. Spånberg, H. Kardela and G. Porter (eds) *The Evidence of Literature: Interrogating Texts in English Studies.* 331–348. Lublin: UMCS.

Karpiński, J. (1985) *Polska, komunizm, opozycja. Słownik.* London: Polonia.

KC (1975) *Księga cytatów z polskiej literatury pięknej ułożona przez Pawła Herza i Władysława Kopalińskiego.* Warszawa: PIW.

Keynes, J. N. (1906) *Studies and Exercises in Formal Logic.* London: Macmillan and Co.

Kiklevich, A. (2007) *Prityazheniye yazyka. Semantika. Lingvistika teksta. Kommunikativnaya lingvistika.* Olsztyn: Uniwersytet Warmińsko-Mazurski.

Kisielewski, S. (1983) *Bez cenzury.* Warszawa: CDN.

Kloskowska, A. (1993) „Kraj, do którego się wraca". Czym jest ojczyzna dla lubelskich studentów? In. J. Bartmiński (ed.) Pojęcie ojczyzny we współczesnych językach europejskich. 49–56. Lublin: Instytut Europy Środkowo–Wschodniej.

Kłoskowska, A. (1969) *Z historii i socjologii kultury.* Warszawa: PWN.

Kłoskowska, A. (1991) Kultura. In A. Kłoskowska (ed.) *Encyklopedia kultury polskiej XX wieku. Pojęcia i problemy wiedzy o kulturze.* 17–62. Wrocław: Wiedza o kulturze.

Knibiehler, Y. (1997) *La révolution maternelle: femmes, maternite, citoyennete depuis 1945.* Paris: Perrin.

Kołakowski, L. (1990) Z lewa, z prawa. *Gazeta Wyborcza* 174A.

Kołakowski, L. (2004) *Mini wykłady o maxi sprawach.* Kraków: Znak.

Komlev, N. G. (1976) *Components of the Content Structure of the Word.* The Hague: Mouton.

Korżyk, K. (1999) Język i gramatyka w perspektywie komunikatywizmu. In A. Awdiejew (ed.) *Gramatyka komunikacyjna*. 9–32. Kraków: PWN.

Kot, S. (1955) Nationum Proprietates. *Oxford Slavonic Papers*, vol. VI, 1–43.

Krzeszowski, T. P. (1994) Parametr aksjologiczny w w przedpojęciowych schematach wyobrażeniowych. *Etnolingwistyka* 6: 29–51.

Krzeszowski, T. P. (1997) *Angels and Devils in Hell. Elements of Axiology in Semantics*. Warszawa: Energeia.

Krzeszowski, T. P. (1999) *Aksjologiczne aspekty semantyki językowej*. Toruń: Wydawnictwo UMK.

Kudra, A. (2004) Językowe wyznaczniki obserwatora w tekście literackim (na przykładzie *Granicy* Zofii Nałkowskiej). In J. Bartmiński, S. Niebrzegowska-Bartmińska and R. Nycz (eds) *Punkt widzenia w języku i w kulturze*. 129–138. Lublin: UMCS.

Kuhn, T. S. (1979) *The Essential Tension: Selected Studies in Scientific Tradition and Change*. Chicago: University of Chicago Press.

Kurek, H. (2004) Punkt widzenia w językowym obrazie świata społeczności wiejskiej. In J. Bartmiński, S. Niebrzegowska-Bartmińska and R. Nycz (eds) *Punkt widzenia w języku i w kulturze*. 209–233. Lublin: UMCS.

Kurkowska, H. and Skorupka, S. (1959) *Stylistyka polska. Zarys*. Warszawa: PWN.

Kuroń, J. (1990) *Wiara i wina. Do i od komunizmu*. Warszawa: Niezależna Oficyna Wydawnicza.

Kwaśnica, R. (1991) Rzeczywistość jako byt sensu. Teza o językowym tworzeniu rzeczywistości. *Język a Kultura* 1: 31–60. Wrocław: Wiedza o kulturze.

Kwilecki, A. (1978) Z badań nad stereotypami Niemca w Polsce i Polaka w NRD i RFN. *Ruch Prawniczy, Ekonomiczny i Socjologiczny* 40, 3: 201–219.

Lakoff, G. (1987) *Women, Fire, and Dangerous Things. What Categories Reveal about the Mind*. Chicago: University of Chicago Press.

Lakoff, G. and Johnson, M. (1980) *Metaphors We Live By*. Chicago: University of Chicago Press.

Langacker, R. W. (1987) *Foundations of Cognitive Grammar*, vol. 1, *Theoretical Prerequisites*, Stanford: Stanford University Press.

Langacker, R. W. (1991a) *Concept, Image, and Symbol*. Berlin and New York: Mouton de Gruyter.

Langacker, R. W. (1991b) *Foundations of Cognitive Grammar. Vol. 2. Descriptive Application*. Stanford, CA: Stanford University Press.

Langacker, R. W. (2000) *Grammar and Conceptualization*. Berlin and New York: Mouton de Gruyter.

Langacker, R. W. (2001) Discourse in Cognitive Grammar. *Cognitive Linguistics* 12, 2: 143–188.

Laurenkienė, N. (2004) Tęcza. Nazwy i znaczenie w kontekście litewskiej narracji folklorystycznej. *Etnolingwistyka* 16: 215–239.

Léon-Dufour, X. (ed.) (1967) *Dictionary of Biblical Theology*. London: Geoffrey Chapman.

Levin, D.M. (1985) *The Body's Recollection of Being. Phenomenological Psychology and the Deconstruction of Nihilism*. London, Boston, Melbourne and Henley: Routledge & Kegan Paul.

Lewicki, A. M. (1976) *Wprowadzenie do frazeologii syntaktycznej*. Katowice: Uniwersytet Śląski.

Lewicki, A. M. (1993) Językoznawstwo polskie w XX wieku. In *Encyklopedia kultury polskiej XX wieku*, vol. 2, *Współczesny język polski*, ed. J. Bartmiński. 619–656. Lublin: UMCS.

Lippman, W. (1961 [1922]) *Public Opinion*. New York: The Macmillan Company.

Lipski, J. J. (1981) *Dwie ojczyzny, dwa patriotyzmy*. NOW-a.

Lipski, J. J. (1992) *Tunika Nessosa. Szkice o literaturze i nacjonalizmie*. Warszawa: Wydawnictwo PEN.

Lurker, M. (1990) *Dictionary of Biblical Terms and Symbols*. French and European Pubns.

Lück, K. 1938. Der Mythos des Deutschen in der polnischen Volksüberlieferung und Literatur. Posen: Verlag von S. Hirzel.

Lyons, J. (1977) *Semantics*, vol. 1. Cambridge: Cambridge University Press.

MacLaury, R. E. (1997) *Color and Cognition in Mesoamerica*. Austin: University of Texas Press.

Maćkiewicz, J. (1988) Świat widziany poprzez język. *Gdańskie Zeszyty Humanistyczne*, XXVI, 30: 131–150.

Majer–Baranowska, U. (1988) Z historii użycia terminu 'konotacja'. In J. Bartmiński (ed.) *Konotacja*. 185–2002. Lublin: UMCS.

Majer-Baranowska, U. (1993) 'Woda' – profile pojęcia w polszczyźnie ludowej. In J. Bartmiński and R. Tokarski (eds) *O definicjach i definiowaniu* 277–291. Lublin: UMCS.

Malinowski, B. (1965 [1935]) *Coral Gardens and their Magic. Volume II. The Language of Magic and Gardening*. London: George Allen and Unwin Ltd.

Markiewicz, H. and Romanowski, A. (1990) *Skrzydlate słowa*. Warszawa: PIW.

Martinet, A. (1967) Connotations, poesi et culture. In *To Honor R. Jakobson, Essays on the Occasion of his Seventieth Birthday*, vol.II. 1288–1294. The Hague: Mouton.

Mazurkiewicz, M. (1988) Etymologia a konotacja. In J. Bartmiński (ed.) *Konotacja*. 99–112. Lublin: UMCS.

Mazurkiewicz, M. (1989) Drogie kamienie w ludowym językowym obrazie świata. In *Język a kultura*, vol. 2. 165–183. Wrocław: Wiedza o kulturze.

Miłosz, Cz. (1985) *Zaczynając od moich ulic*. Paryż: Instytut Literacki.

Miłosz, Cz. (1999) *Road-side Dog*. New York: Farrar, Straus and Giroux.

Mitosek, Z. (1974) *Literatura i stereotypy*. Wrocław: Zakład Narodowy im. Ossolińskich.

Moldovan, A. (2008) *Puti slavistiki v sovremennom mire*. Moskva: Institut Slavyanovedeniya Rossiyskoy Akademii Nauk.

Monczka-Ciechomska, M. (1992) Mit kobiety w polskiej literaturze. In S. Walczewska (ed.) *Głos mają kobiety*. 95–101. Kraków: Convivium.

Monduzzi, G. (1991) *Manuale per difindersi della mamma*. A. Mondadori.

Moravcsik, J. M. E. (1981) How do words get their meaning? *The Journal of Philosophy* XXVIII-1: 5–24.

Muszyński, Z. (1982) Zależność znaczenia od koncepcji świata. Problem podmiotowej relatywizacji znaczenia. Ph.D. dissertation. Lublin: UMCS.

Muszyński, Z. (1988) Problem wiedzy pozajęzykowej w badaniach lingwistycznych. In J. Bartmiński (ed.) *Konotacja.* 129–153. Lublin: UMCS.

Nepop-Ajdaczyć, L. (2007) *Polska etnolingwistyka kognitywna. Pomoc dydaktyczna.* Kyiv: Centrum wydawniczo-poligraficzne 'Uniwersytet Kijowski'.

Niebrzegowska, S, (1986) Słońce się raduje – metafora czy mit? *Akcent* 26: 37–39.

Niebrzegowska, S. (1990) Gwiazdy w ludowym językowym obrazie świata. In J. Bartmiński (ed.) *Językowy obraz świata.* 147–166. Lublin: UMCS.

Niebrzegowska, S. (1996a) Gwiazdy. Entry in *SSSL* 1996–1999. Ed. J. Bartmiński. Vol. I-1. 203–221. Lublin: UMCS.

Niebrzegowska, S. (1996b) *Polski sennik ludowy.* Lublin: UMCS.

Niebrzegowska, S. (1996c) Świat wartości sennika ludowego. *Etnolingwistyka* 8: 99–112.

Niebrzegowska-Bartmińska, S. (2003) Komisja Etnolingwistyczna przy Międzynarodowym Komitecie Slawistów. *Etnolingwistyka* 15: 280–281.

Niebrzegowska-Bartmińska, S. (2007) *Wzorce tekstów ustnych w perspektywie etnolingwistycznej.* Lublin: UMCS.

Niewiara, A. (1992a) Das Stereotyp des Deutschen in der polnischen konspirativen Presse des Zweiten Weltkriegs. *Znakolog. An International Yearbook of Slavic Semiotics* 3: 181–200.

Niewiara, A. (1992b) Stereotype Assoziationen im Hinblick auf Bezeichnungen von Nationalitäten (Ergebnisse einer Umfrage). *Znakolog. An International Yearbook of Slavic Semiotics* 3. 201–207.

Niewiara, A. (forthcoming) Vantage theory, statistics and mental worldview. *Language Sciences.*

Nikitina, S. E. (1992) Metayazyki opisaniya fol'klornoy leksiki i nauchnoy terminologii. In S. Gajda (ed.) *Systematyzacja pojęć w stylistyce.* 63–68. Opole: WSP.

Nikitina, S. E., Kukushkina, E. J. (2000) *Dom v svadebnykh prichitaniyakh i dukhovnykh stikhakh. Opyt tezaurusnogo opisaniya.* Moskva: Institut Yazykoznaniya – Rossiyskaya Akademiya Nauk.

NKP (1978) *Nowa księga przysłów i wyrażeń przysłowiowych polskich.* Ed. S. Świrko, D. Świerczyńska and S. Świrko. Warszawa: PIW.

Nowak, P. (2002). *SWOI i OBCY w językowym obrazie świata.* Lublin: UMCS.

Nowakowska-Kempna, I. (1995) *Konceptualizacja uczuć w języku polskim. Prolegomena.* Warszawa: Wyższa Szkoła Pedagogiczna Towarzystwa Wiedzy Powszechnej.

Nowicka, E. (1991) Dystans wobec Niemców w społeczeństwie polskim. *Kultura i Społeczeństwo* XXXV, 4: 167–177.

Nowosad-Bakalarczyk, M. (2006) Rodzaj naturalny a rodzaj gramatyczny we współczesnej polszczyźnie. Ph.D. dissertation, Maria Curie-Skłodowska University, Lublin, Poland.

NSPP (1999) *Nowy słownik poprawnej polszczyzny PWN*. Ed. A. Markowski. Warszawa: PWN.

Obrębski, J. (1936) Problem etniczny Polesia. *Sprawy Narodowościowe* 10, 1–2: 1–21.

Obrębski, J. (1951) The Sociology of Rising Nations. *Unesco International Social Sciences Bulletin* 3, 2: 237–243.

Olechnowicz, E. (1990). Stereotypy językowe żeńskich członków rodziny w języku polskim. M.A. thesis. Department of Polish. Maria Curie-Skłodowska University, Lublin, Poland.

Osgood, C.E. (1980) The cognitive dynamic of synaesthesia and metaphor. In R.P. Honeck and R.R. Hoffman (eds) *Cognition and Figurative Language*. 203–238. Hillsdale, N.J.: Lawrence Erlbaum.

Ossowski, S. (1946) *Analiza socjologiczna pojęcia ojczyzny*. Łódź: Myśl Współczesna.

Ożdżyński, J. (ed.) (1995) *Językowy obraz świata dzieci i młodzieży*. Kraków: Wydawnictwo Naukowe WSP.

Pajdzińska, A. (1988) Udział konotacji leksykalnej w motywacji frazeologizmów. In J. Bartmiński (ed.) *Konotacja*. 67–82. Lublin: UMCS.

Pajdzińska, A. (1999) Jak mówimy o uczuciach? Poprzez analizę frazeologizmów do językowego obrazu świata. In J. Bartmiński (ed.) *Językowy obraz świata* 2nd ed. 83–101. Lublin: UMCS.

Pajdzińska, A., Krzyżanowski, P. (eds) (1999) *Przeszłość w językowym obrazie świata*. Lublin: UMCS.

Pajdzińska, A., Tokarski, R. (1996) Językowy obraz świata – konwencja i kreacja. *Pamiętnik Literacki* LXXVII, 4: 143–158.

Panasiuk, J. (1990) Wybrane stereotypy ludzi w środowisku studentów lubelskich. M.A. thesis. Department of Polish. Maria Curie-Skłodowska University, Lublin, Poland.

Pawlak, A. (1998) *A zmarli tak lubią podróże*. Kraków: Oficyna Literacka.

Pawłowski, T. (1978) Rodziny znaczeń i ich definiowanie. *Studia Filozoficzne* 2: 81–99.

Pawłowski, T. (1978) *Tworzenie pojęć i definiowanie w naukach humanistycznych*. Warszawa: PWN.

Permyakov, G. L. (1970) Ot pogovorki do skazki. Zametki po obshchey teorii klishe. Moskva: Nauka.

Permyakov, G. L. (1975) K voprosu o strukture paremiologicheskogo fonda. In *Tipologicheskiye issledovaniya po fol'kloru. Sbornik statey pamyati V. Ya. Proppa*. 247–274. Moskva: Izdatel'stvo Nauka.

Piekarczyk, D. (2004) *Kwiaty we współczesnym językowym obrazie świata*. Lublin: UMCS.

Piekot, T. (2004) Prywatny i publiczny punkt widzenia w dyskursie wiadomości dziennikarskich. In J. Bartmiński, S. Niebrzegowska-Bartmińska and R. Nycz (eds) *Punkt widzenia w tekście i w dyskursie*. 127–146. Lublin: UMCS.

Pisarek, W. (1975) Wyobrażenia o polskich stereotypach regionalnych. *Zeszyty Prasoznawcze* 1: 73–78.

Pisarek, W. (1999) Językowy obraz świata. In *Encyklopedia języka polskiego*. Ed. S. Urbańczyk and M. Kucała. 3rd ed. 168. Wrocław: Zakład Narodowy im. Ossolińskich.

Pisarek, W. (2002) *Polskie słowa sztandarowe i ich publiczność*. Kraków: Universitas.

Pisarkowa, K. (1976) Konotacja semantyczna nazw narodowości. *Zeszyty Prasoznawcze* 1: 5–26.

Plas, P. (2006) Slavic ethnolinguistics and Anglo–American linguistic anthropology: convergences and divergences in the study of the language–culture nexus. *Etnolingwistyka* 18: 135–143.

Płuciennik, J. (2004) Literackie i językowe punkty widzenia a empatyczne naśladowanie w tekście literackim. In J. Bartmiński, S. Niebrzegowska-Bartmińska and R. Nycz (eds) *Punkt widzenia w tekście i w dyskursie*. 203–218. Lublin: UMCS.

Pomorski, J. (2004) Punkt widzenia we współczesnej historiografii. In J. Bartmiński, S. Niebrzegowska-Bartmińska and R. Nycz (eds) *Punkt widzenia w języku i w kulturze*. 11–32. Lublin: UMCS.

Pope John Paul II. (2005) *Memory and Identity: Conversations at the Dawn of a Millennium*. New York: Rizzoli.

Popowska-Taborska, H. (1990) Językowe wykładniki opozycji swoi – obcy w procesie tworzenia etnicznej tożsamości. In Bartmiński, J. (ed.) *Językowy obraz świata*. 61–68. Lublin: UMCS.

Popper, K. R. (1979) *Objective Knowledge. An Evolutionary Approach*. Oxford and New York: Oxford University Press.

Prokop, J. (1992) Dom polski. In A. Siciński (ed.) Dom we współczesnej Polsce. 42–53. Wrocław: Wiedza o kulturze.

Propp, V. (1928) *Morfologiya skazki*. Leningrad: Akademiya. [English edition: 1958. *Morphology of the Folktale*. Transl. L. Scott. Bloomington: Research Center, Indiana University.]

Przybylska, R. (2002) *Polisemia przyimków polskich w świetle semantyki kognitywnej*. Kraków: Universitas.

Przybylska, R. (2003) On linkage among the different meanings of prepositions. In G. Hentschel and Th. Menzel (eds) *Präpositionen im Polnischen*. 299–315. BIS Oldenburg.

PSJP (1998) *Podręczny słownik języka polskiego*. Ed. E. Sobol. Warszawa: PWN.

PSWP (1994–1998) *Praktyczny słownik współczesnej polszczyzny*. Ed. H. Zgółkowa. Poznań: Kurpisz.

Putnam, H. (1975) *Mind, Language and Reality. Philosophical Papers*, Vol. 2. Cambridge: Cambridge University Press.

Puzynina, J. (1989) Jak pracować nad językiem wartości? In J. Puzynina and J. Bartmiński (eds) *Język a kultura*, vol. 2 . *Zagadnienia leksykalne i aksjologiczne*. 185–198. Wrocław: Wiedza o kulturze.

Puzynina, J. (1992) *Język wartości*. Warszawa: PWN.

Puzynina, J. (1992) Problematyka aksjologiczna w językoznawstwie. In S. Sawicki and A. Tyszczyk (eds) Problematyka aksjologicna w nauce o literaturze. 59–72. Lublin: RW KUL.

Puzynina, J. (1997) *Słowo – wartość – kultura*. Lublin: TN KUL.

Puzynina, J. (1998) Struktura semantyczna narodu a profilowanie. In J. Bartmiński, R. Tokarski (eds) *Profilowanie w języku i w tekście*. 259–276. Lublin: UMCS.

Quasthoff, U. (1973) *Soziales Vorurteil und Kommunikation. Eine sprachwissenschaftliche Analyse des Stereotyps*. Frankfurt a.M.: Athenäum Fischer Taschenbuch Verlag.

Quasthoff, U. (1989) Ethnozentrische Verarbeitung von Informationen: Zur Ambivalenz der Funktion von Stereotypen in der interkulturellen Kommunikation. In P. Mautsche (ed.) *Wie verstehen wir Fremdes? Aspekte zur Klärung von Verstehensprozessen. Dokumentation eines Werkstattgesprächs des Goethe-Instituts München vom 24–26 November 1988*. 37–62. München: Hrsg. von P. Matusche, Goethe-Institut.

Ranganathan, S. R. (1933) *Colon of Classification*. Madras: Madras Library Association.

Ranganathan, S. R. (1951) *Philosophy of Library Classification*. Copenhagen: Munksgaard.

REW (1950–1958) *Russisches Etymologisches Wörterbuch*. Ed. Max Vasmer. Heidelberg: Heidelberg University.

Romanowski, A. (1989) Prawica? *Tygodnik Powszechny* 51.

Rzepkowska, A. (2004) Punkt widzenia i punkt obserwatora jako środki perswazji. In J. Bartmiński, S. Niebrzegowska-Bartmińska and R. Nycz (eds) *Punkt widzenia w języku i w kulturze*. 139–148. Lublin: UMCS.

Sapir, E. (1957) Language. In *Culture, Language and Personality. Selected Essays*. Ed. D.G. Mandelbaum. 1–44. Berkeley and Los Angeles: University of California Press.

Sawicka, G. (ed.) (1997) *Dom w języku i kulturze*. Szczecin: Wydawnictwo JotA.

Schaff, A. (1978) Stereotyp: definicja i teoria. *Kultura i społeczeństwo* 3: 43–77.

Schaff, A. (1981) *Stereotypy a działanie ludzkie*. Warszawa: Książka i Wiedza.

Scheler, M. (1913–1916) *Der Formalismus in der Ethik und die materiale Wertethik*. [English translation: *Formalism in Ethics and Non-Formal Ethics of Values: A New Attempt Toward the Foundation of an Ethical Personalism*, trans. M. S. Frings and R. L. Funk, Evanston, Illinois: Northwestern University Press, 1973]

SD (1995–2004) Slavyanskiye drevnosti. Etnolingvisticheskiy slovar'. Ed. N.I. Tolstoy. Vols. 1–3. Moskva: Mezhdunarodnye Otnosheniya.

SEJP (1927) *Słownik etymologiczny języka polskiego*. Ed. A. Brückner. Kraków: Krakowska Spółka Wydawnicza.

SEJP (1952–1982) *Słownik etymologiczny języka polskiego*. Ed. F. Sławski. Kraków: Towarzystwo Miłośników Języka Polskiego.

SemD (1979). *Sémiotique. Dictionnaire raisonné de la théorie du langage, par A. J. Greimas et J. Courtés*. Paris: Hachettte/Université.

Senft, G. (1998) Ethnolinguistik. In *Ethnologie. Einführung und Überblick*. Ed. H. Fischer. 4th ed. Berlin: Reimer.

Serebrennikov, V. A., Kubryakova, E. S., Postovalova, V. I. et al. (eds) (1988) *Rol' chelovecheskogo faktora v yazyke: yazyk i kartina mira*. Moskva: Nauka.

SFPW (1990) Słownik frekwencyjny polszczyzny współczesnej. Ed. I. Kurcz, A. Lewicki, J. Sambor, K. Szafran, J. Woronczak. Kraków: Instytut Języka Polskiego PAN.

SGP (2004) *Słownik gwar polskich.* Kraków: PAN.

Simpson, P. (1993) *Language, Ideology and Point of View.* London and New York: Routledge.

SJP (1861) *Słownik języka polskiego.* Ed. A. Zdanowicz et al. Vilnius: M. Orgelbrand.

SJPDor (1962) *Słownik języka polskiego.* Ed. W. Doroszewski. Warszawa: PWN.

SJPLinde (1807–1814) *Słownik języka polskiego. By Samuel Bogumił Linde. Vols I–VI.* Warszawa: Drukarnia XX Pijarów.

SJPSzym (1994) *Słownik języka polskiego.* Ed. M. Szymczak. Warszawa: PWN.

Skwarczyńska, S. (1965) *Wstęp do nauki o literaturze.* vol. 3. Warszawa: PAX.

Smółkowa, T. (2001) Nowe słownictwo polskie. In J. Bartmiński (ed.) *Współczesny język polski.* 397–404. Lublin: UMCS.

SP (1984) Słownik prasłowiański. Vol. 5. Ed. F. Sławski. Wrocław: Zakład Narodowy im. Ossolińskich.

SPXVI (1966–1999) *Słownik polszczyzny XVI wieku.* Ed. S. Bąk, M. R. Mayenowa and F. Pepłowski, Wrocław: Zakład Narodowy im. Ossolińskich.

SS (1993) *Słownik synonimów.* Ed. A. Dąbrówka, E. Geller, R. Turczyn. Warszawa: Świat Książki.

SSGCP (1980–1992) Słownik syntaktyczno-generatywny czasowników polskich. Vol. 1–5. Ed. K. Polański. Warszawa–Wrocław: Zakład Narodowy im. Ossolińskich.

SSSL (1996–1999) *Słownik stereotypów i symboli ludowych.* Vols. 1–1 and 1–2. Ed. J. Bartmiński. Lublin: UMCS.

SStp (1953–2003) *Słownik staropolski.* Vols. I–XI. Ed. S. Urbańczyk et al. Kraków: Instytut Języka Polskiego PAN.

STIN (1979) *Słownik terminologiczny informacji naukowej.* Ed. M. Dembowska, K. Tittenbrun et al. Wrocław: Zakład Narodowy im. Ossolińskich.

Stomma. L. (2000) *Słownik polskich wyzwisk, inwektyw i określeń pejoratywnych.* Warszawa: Graf-Punkt.

Stróżewski, W. (1981) *Istnienie i wartość.* Kraków: Znak.

Styczeń, T. and Balawajder, E. (1986) *Jedynie prawda wyzwala. Rozmowy o Janie Pawle II.* Roma: Polski Instytut Kultury Chrześcijańskiej.

Suchecki, J. (1983) Status poznawczy wyrażeń metaforycznych. In I. Kurcz (ed.) *Studia z psycholingwistyki ogólnej i rozwojowej.* 83–110. Warszawa–Wrocław: Zakład Narodowy im. Ossolińskich.

Sułek, A. and Kublik, A. (2002) Żydzi? Wiadomo! *Gazeta Wyborcza* 25 July, 2002.

SWB (1971) *Słownik wyrazów bliskoznacznych.* Ed. S. Skorupka. 5th ed. Warszawa: Wiedza Powszechna.

SWJP. 1996. *Słownik współczesnego języka polskiego.* Ed. Bogusław Dunaj. Warszawa: Wilga.

SWO (1980) *Słownik wyrazów obcych.* Ed. J. Tokarski. Warszawa: PWN.

Symotiuk, S. (1996) Język losu. *Etnolingwistyka* 8: 314–316.

Szadura, J. (1996) Ogień. Entry in *SSSL.* Ed. J. Bartmiński. 264–285. Lublin: UMCS.

Szadura, J. (2004) Inauguracyjne posiedzenie Komisji Etnolingwistycznej Komitetu Językoznawstwa PAN. *Etnolingwistyka* 16: 267–269.

Szarota, T. (1978) Niemcy w oczach Polaków podczas drugiej wojny światowej. *Dzieje Najnowsze* X, 2: 143–172.

Szpyra, J. (1996) Dlaczego „za i przeciw", a nie „przeciw i za' – czyli o językowym obrazie świata Polaków, Anglików i Węgrów. *Etnolingwistyka* 8: 57–88.

Szpyra-Kozłowska, J. and Karwatowska, M. (2005) *Lingwistyka płci. Ona i on w języku polskim.* Lublin: UMCS.

Szymański, M. S. (1993) Nahe Fremde. Über das Bild von den Deutschen bei polnischen Schülern. (Vortrag am 8. Dezember 1993 an der Ruhr-Universität Bochum).

Szymborska, W. (1995) *View with a Grain of Sand. Selected Poems.* Trans. from the Polish by Stanisław Barańczak and Clare Cavangh. San Diego, New York, London: A Harvest Original, Harcourt Brace and Company.

Święch, J. (1977) *Okupacja i stereotypy: studium z dziejów poezji konspiracyjnej 1939–1945.* Lublin: UMCS.

Tabakowska, E. (1993) *Cognitive Linguistics and Poetics of Translation.* Tübingen: Gunter Narr Verlag.

Tabakowska, E. (1995) *Gramatyka i obrazowanie. Wprowadzenie do językoznawstwa kognitywnego.* Kraków: PAN.

Tabakowska, E. (2004a) O językowych wyznacznikach punktu widzenia. In J. Bartmiński, S. Niebrzegowska-Bartmińska and R. Nycz (eds) *Punkt widzenia w języku i w kulturze.* 47–64. Lublin: UMCS.

Tabakowska, E. (2004b) Point of view in the theory of literature and in linguistics: Grammar or 'a logic of reading'. In Lewandowska-Tomaszczyk, B. and Kwiatkowska, A. (eds) *Imagery in Language.* 693–710. Frankfurt am Main: Peter Lang.

Taylor, J. R. (1989) *Linguistic Categorization. Prototypes in Linguistic Theory.* Oxford: Oxford University Press. (3rd ed. 2004)

Tischner, J. (1998) *Przestrzeń jako projekt wolności.* In A. Dylus (ed.) *Europa. Fundamenty jedności.* 229. Warszawa: Fundacja ATK.

Tokarski, R. (1990) Językowy obraz świata w metaforach potocznych. In J. Bartmiński (ed.) *Językowy obraz świata.* 69–86. Lublin: UMCS.

Tokarski, R. (1991) Człowiek w definicji znaczeniowej słowa. *Przegląd Humanistyczny* 3–4: 131–140.

Tokarski, R. (1998) Językowy obraz świata a niektóre założenia kognitywizmu. *Etnolingwistyka* 9/10: 7–24.

Tolstaya, S. M. (1993) Etnolingvistika v Lubline. *Slavyanovedeniye* 3: 47–59.

Tolstaya, S. M. (2004) Znaczenie symboliczne a punkt widzenia: motywacja znaczeń symbolicznych (kulturowych). In J. Bartmiński, S. Niebrzegowska-Bartmińska and R. Nycz (eds) *Punkt widzenia w języku i w kulturze.* 177–184. Lublin: UMCS.

Tolstaya, S. M. (2006) Postulaty moskovskoy etnolingvistiki. *Etnolingwistyka* 18: 7–27.

Tolstoy, N. I. (1990) Yazyk i kul'tura. Nekotorye problemy slavyanskoy etnolingvistiki. *Zeitschrift für Slavische Philologie* L-2: 238–253.

Tolstoy, N. I. (1995) *Yazyk i narodnaya kul'tura. Ocherki po slavyanskoy mifologii i etnolingvistike.* Moskva: Indrik.

Tolstoy, N. I. (1997) *Izbrannye trudy. Vol 1: Slavyanskaya leksikologiya i semasiologiya.* Moskva: Yazyki russkoy kul'tury.

Tolstye, S. M. and N. I. (1984) Printsypy sostavleniya etnolingvisticheskogo slovarya slavyanskikh drevnostey. In *Etnolingvisticheskiy slovar' slavyanskikh drevnostey. Proekt slovnika. Predvaritel'nye materialy.* Moskva. 6–22.

Trzebiński, J. (1981) *Twórczość a struktura pojęć.* Warszawa: PWN.

Tyler, S. (1978) *The Said and the Unsaid.* New York: Academic Press.

Urban, J. (1993) Wybrane stereotypy narodowościowe we współczesnym języku polskim. M.A. thesis. Department of Polish, Maria Curie-Skłodowska University, Lublin, Poland.

Urry, J. (2000) Sociology of time and space. In B. S. Turner (ed.) *The Blackwell Companion to Social Theory.* 416–443. Oxford: Blackwell.

USJP (2003) *Uniwersalny słownik języka polskiego.* Ed. Stanisław Dubisz. Warszawa: PWN.

Uspensky, B. (1973) *A Poetics of Composition. The Structure of the Artistic Text and Typology of a Compositional Form.* Los Angeles, London, Berkeley: University of California Press.

Van Dijk, T.A. (1972). *Some aspects of text grammars. A study in theoretical linguistics and poetics.* The Hague: Mouton.

Van Dijk, T.A. (1998) *Ideology: A Multidisciplinary Approach.* London: Sage Publications Ltd.

Van Dijk, T.A. (2002) Political Discourse and Ideology. In C. Lorda, M. Ribas (eds) *Análisi del discurs polític.* 15–34. Universitat Pompeu Fabra.

Vaňková, I. (ed.) (2001) *Obraz světa v jazyce.* Praha: Univerzita Karlova.

Vinogradova, L. N., Góra, A. W., Kabakova, G. I., Ternovskaya, O. A., Tolstaya, S. M. and Usacheva, V. V. (1989) *Skhiema opisaniya mifologicheskikh personazhey.* In *Materialy k VI mezhdunarodnomu kongressu po izucheniyu stran yugo-vostochnoy Evropy, Sofiya, 30 VIII 89 – 6 IX 89.* 78–85. Moskva: Institut slavyanovedeniya i balkanistiki AN SSSR.

VOLA (1965) *Voprosnik obshcheslavyanskogo lingvisticheskogo atlasa.* Moskva: Izdatel'stvo Nauka.

Vygotsky, L. S. (1971) *The Psychology of Art.* Cambridge, Mass.: MIT Press. [Orig.: 1925. *Psykhologiya iskusstva.* Moskva: Iskusstvo.]

Wandruszka, M. (1990) *Die eurcpäische Sprachengemeinschaft. Deutsch – Französisch – Englisch – Italienisch – Spanisch im Vergleich.* Tübingen: Francke Verlag.

WE PWN (2000–2006) *Wielka Encyklopedia PWN.* Warszawa: PWN.

Weljand, A. (1989) Stereotyp grupy zawodowej. Analiza odpowiedzi na pytania otwarte o jej typowego przedstawiciela. In Z. Gostkowski (ed.) *Analiza i próby technik badawczych w socjologii*, vol. 7, *Społeczne obrazy i stereotypy chłopa, urzędnika i robotnika. Studia eksploracyjne.* 62–116. Wrocław: Zakład Narodowy im. Ossolińskich.

Wejland, A. (1991) *Obrazy grup społecznych. Studium metodologiczne.* Warszawa: IFiS PAN.

Wierzbicka, A. (1978) Wstęp. [Introduction] In Sapir, E. *Kultura, język, osobowość: wybrane eseje.* 5–31. Warszawa: PIW.
Wierzbicka, A. (1983) Genry mowy. In T. Dobrzyńska, E. Janus (eds) *Tekst i zdanie. Zbiór studiów.* 125–137. Wrocław: Zakład Narodowy im. Ossolińskich.
Wierzbicka, A. (1984) Apples are not a kind of fruit: The semantics of human categorization. *American Ethnologist* 11–2: 313–328.
Wierzbicka, A. (1985) *Lexicography and Conceptual Analysis.* Ann Arbor, MI: Karoma Publishers.
Wierzbicka, A. (1988) *The Semantics of Grammar.* Amsterdam/Philadelphia: John Benjamins.
Wierzbicka, A. (1991) *Cross-cultural Pragmatics. The Semantics of Human Interaction.* Berlin and New York: Mouton de Gruyter.
Wierzbicka, A. (1992) *Semantics, Culture and Cognition: Universal Human Concepts in Culture-Specific Configurations.* Oxford and New York: Oxford University Press.
Wierzbicka, A. (1993) Nazwy zwierząt. In J. Bartmiński and R. Tokarski (eds) *O definicjach i definiowaniu.* 251–267. Lublin: UMCS.
Wierzbicka, A. (1994) Emotion, language, and 'cultural scripts'. In S. Kitayama and H. Markus (eds) *Emotion and Culture: Empirical Studies of Mutual Influence.* 133–196. Washington: American Psychological Association Press.
Wierzbicka, A. (1996) *Semantics. Primes and Universals.* Oxford: Oxford University Press.
Wierzbicka, A. (1997) *Understanding Cultures Through Their Key-Words. English, Russian, Polish, German, Japanese.* Oxford and New York: Oxford University Press.
Wierzbicka, A. (1999) *Emotions across Languages and Cultures. Diversity and Universals.* Cambridge: Cambridge University Press.
Wierzbicka, A. (2006) *English. Meaning and Culture.* New York: Oxford University Press.
Wierzbicki, P. (1985) *Myśli staroświeckiego Polaka.* London: Puls.
Wilska-Duszyńska, B. (1992) 'Swoi' i 'inni' – postawy studentów wobec etnicznie innych. *Kultura i Społeczeństwo* XXXVI, 3: 99–106.
Wojtak, M. (2001) Styl urzędowy. In J. Bartmiński (ed.) *Współczesny język polski.* 2nd ed. 155–171. Lublin: UMCS.
Wrzesiński, W. (1992) *Sąsiad czy wróg? Ze studiów nad kształtowaniem obrazu Niemca w Polsce w latach 1795–1935.* Wrocław: Wydawnictwo Uniwersytetu Wrocławskiego.
Wunderlich, D. (1970) Die Rolle der Pragmatik in der Linguistik. *Der Deutschunterricht* XXII, 4: 5–41.
WVB (1979) *Wörterbuch der vergleichenden Bezeichnungslehre. Onomasiologie.* Begründet und herausgegeben von Johannes Schröpfer. Band I, Heidelberg: Carl Winter Universitätsverlag.
Yudin, A. (1998) Etnolingvistika. In *Kul'turologiya. XX vek. Entsiklopediya.* Ed. S. J. Levit. Vol. 2. 408–409. Sankt-Petersburg: Universitetskaya kniga.

Yudin, A. (2004a) *Yordan* i *Dunay* v vostochnoslavyanskom magicheskom fol'klore. *Voprosy onomastiki* 1: 55–74.

Yudin, A. (2004b) Rozumienie terminu *obraz świata* i *model świata* w semantyce i lingwistyce rosyjskiej. *Etnolingwistyka* 16: 315–323.

Zaron, Z. (1985) *Wybrane pojęcia etyczne w analizie semantycznej (Kochaj bliźniego swego)*. Wrocław: Zakład Narodowy im. Ossolińskich.

Zawisławska, M. (2004). *Czasowniki oznaczające percepcję wzrokową we współczesnej polszczyźnie. Ujęcie kognitywne*. Warszawa: Wydział Polonistyki UW.

Zieniukowa, J. (1998) Z problemów etnolingwistyki. In E. Jędrzejko (ed.) *Nowe czasy, nowe języki, nowe (i stare) problemy*. 233–241. Katowice: Wydawnictwo Uniwersytetu Śląskiego.

Zinken, J. (2002) Imagination im Diskurs. Zur Modelierung metaphorischer Kommunikation und Kognition. Ph.D. dissertation, Bielefeld.

Zinken, J. (2004a) Metaphors, stereotypes, and the linguistic picture of the world: Impulses from the Ethnolinguistic School of Lublin. *metaphorik.de* 7: 115–136.

Zinken, J. (2004b) Punkt widzenia jako kategoria w porównawczym badaniu dyskursów publicznych. In J. Bartmiński, S. Niebrzegowska-Bartmińska and R. Nycz (eds) *Punkt widzenia w języku i w kulturze*. 65–78. Lublin: UMCS.

Ziółkowski, M. (1987) Etnolingwistyka. In *Słownik etnologiczny. Terminy ogólne*. Ed. Z. Staszczak. 94–97. Warszawa–Poznań: PWN.

Znaniecki, F. (1930) Studia nad antagonizmem do obcych. *Przegląd Socjologiczny* 1: 158–209.

Żuk, G. (2004) Językowy obraz Europy w polskim dyskursie publicznym w przededniu integracji. Ph.D. dissertation. Maria Curie-Skłodowska University, Lublin, Poland.

Żywicka, B. (2007) *Miejsca i wartości. Zmiany w językowym obrazie świata przestrzeni we współczesnej polszczyźnie*. Lublin: Polihymnia.

CPSIA information can be obtained at www.ICGtesting.com
Printed in the USA
BVOW051453141211

278079BV00007B/1/P